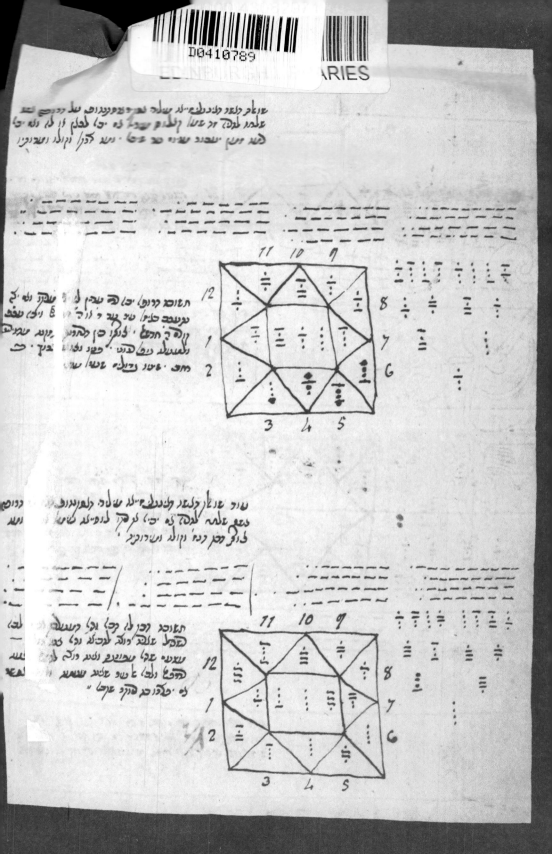

*Star of the Morning*

*Star of the*

*of the*

*Morning*

The Extraordinary Life of
LADY HESTER STANHOPE

# KIRSTEN ELLIS

Harper
Press

Harper*Press*
An imprint of HarperCollins*Publishers*
77–85 Fulham Palace Road
Hammersmith, London W6 8JB
www.harpercollins.co.uk

Visit our authors' blog: www.fifthestate.co.uk

First published in Great Britain by Harper*Press* in 2008

A catalogue record for this book
is available from the British Library

ISBN 978-0-00-717030-2

Typeset in Minion by Palimpsest Book Production Limited,
Grangemouth, Stirlingshire

Printed and bound in Great Britain by Clays Ltd, St Ives plc

*For Michael and Nathaniel*
*and*
*the Stephan sisters, Rania and Wafà*

Dayr, the Lion of the Desert, to Hester, the Star of the Morning, sends greeting, with love and service. Those who obey the sabre of Dayr, hold the Great Desert in the hollow of their hand, even as the ring encircles the finger. Warriors without number, horses, camels, powder and shot, what is required . . . all is ready. You need only to send your orders.

Your true friend, Dayr

DAYR AL FADIL, Bedouin Sheikh of the Anazeh, To Lady Hester Stanhope

If you were a man, Hester, I would send you on the Continent with 60,000 men, and give you carte blanche and I am sure that not one of my plans would fail.

WILLIAM PITT THE YOUNGER, Prime Minister of England

The Arabs have never looked upon me in the light either of man or woman, but *un être à part*.

HESTER LUCY STANHOPE

# Contents

# List of Illustrations

**Colour Plate Section**

Chevening © Author's collection.

Chevening's entrance hall © Chevening Trust.

Lucy Pitt, Hester's great-grandmother, by Michael Dahl (undated, probably *c*. 1713) © Chevening Trust.

William Pitt the Elder by Richard Brompton (undated) © Chevening Trust.

Hester, Countess of Chatham, by Thomas Hudson (1780) © Photography by Matthew Hollow/Chevening Trust.

Lady Grizel Stanhope by Allan Ramsay (*c*. 1764) © Chevening Trust.

Charles, 3rd Earl Stanhope, Hester's father, by John Opie © Kent County Council.

Hester Pitt, Lady Mahon, Hester's mother, artist unconfirmed (undated) © Chevening Trust.

Self-portrait of Charles, Viscount Mahon © Chevening Trust.

'Patriotic Regeneration – viz. – Parliament Reform'd, a la François, – that is – Honest Men (ie – Opposition) in the Seat of Justice' by James Gillray (1795) © The National Portrait Gallery, London.

'Democratic Leveling; – Alliance a la Françoise; – or – The Union of the Coronet & Clyster-pipe' by James Gillray (1796) © The National Portrait Gallery, London.

Hester Stanhope (unconfirmed), Continental school (possibly 1810) © Chevening Trust.
'Lady Stanhope as Hebe' by Richard Cosway (1808) © The National Portrait Gallery, London.

Philip Henry Mahon, 4th Earl Stanhope, by William Owen (undated) © Chevening Trust.
James Hamilton Stanhope by Edward Scriven, after Samuel John Stump (early 19th century) © The National Portrait Gallery, London.

Bust of William Pitt the Younger by Joseph Nollekens (1808) © The National Portrait Gallery, London.
Walmer Castle © Author's collection.

'Death of Lord Camelford' by unknown engraver (undated) © The National Portrait Gallery, London.
Sir William Sidney Smith by William Say after Robert Ker Porter (c. 1802) © The National Portrait Gallery, London.
'Portrait of George Granville Leveson-Gower and his Family' (oil on canvas) by Thomas Phillips (1770–1845). Private Collection, Photo © Bonhams, London, UK / The Bridgeman Art Library.

### Black and White Plate Section

William Noel Hill, 3rd Lord Berwick, by Richard Cosway (c. 1800) © Attingham Park, The National Trust/Courtauld Institute of Art.
Sir John Moore by Sir Thomas Lawrence (c. 1800–4) © The National Portrait Gallery, London.
'Miranda en La Carraca' by Arturo Michelena (1896) © Colección Fundación Museos Nacionales – Galería de Arte Nacional, Caracas, Venezuela.

Charles Lewis Meryon by Arminius Mayer © Royal College of Physicians.
'Michael Bruce During His Trial in Paris 1816' by Augustin Neveu, in Ian Bruce, *Lavallette Bruce* (Hamish Hamilton, London, 1953).
Howe Peter Brown, 2nd Marquess of Sligo, by William Beechy (1809) by

kind permission of the Marquess of Sligo, Lord Altamont, and Lady Altamont, Westport House.

View of Therapia, engraving by W. H. Bartlett, in William Henry Bartlett and Julia Pardee, *The Beauty of the Bosphorus* (1835).

Illustration of Turkish Women by Hester Stanhope (*c.* 1811) © The Bodleian Library, Oxford University, MSS Eng c. 5759 fols. 173–174.

'Interview With Mehemet Ali In His Palace' by David Roberts (1839) © Mansell Collection/Time & Life Pictures/Getty Images.

'Arab caravan in the desert', engraving (1860) © Mansell Collection/Time & Life Pictures/Getty Images.

John Lewis Burckhardt by Angelica Clarke, after Mr Slater, etching (published 1819) © The National Portrait Gallery, London.

James Silk Buckingham, 'Three sketched heads in Arab dress' by Henry William Pickersgill © V&A Images, Victoria and Albert Museum.

Self-portrait in Comte Waclav Seweryn Rzewuski, *Impression d'Orient et d'Arabie* (Librairie José Corti/Muséum National d'Histoire Naturelle, Paris, 2002).

Count Rzewuski's sketch of Hester's residence of Mar Elias at Abra in Comte Waclav Seweryn Rzewuski, *Impression d'Orient et d'Arabie* (Librairie José Corti/Muséum National d'Histoire Naturelle, Paris, 2002).

'View of Djoun' by W. H. Bartlett © Courtauld Institute of Art/Searight Collection, Victoria and Albert Museum.

A letter to Meryon in Hester's handwriting (1818) © Kent County Council.

Meryon in old age, Blythe House portraits (undated) © The British Museum.

Lucy Meryon © Courtesy of Rusty Arran Smith.

Hester Stanhope in old age © Reproduced with kind permission of Guy Abela.

*Integrated*

Insignia, copied from an original design by Lady Hester Stanhope, based on the name given her by the Bedouin: Al-Uzza (Venus) or 'Star of the Morning'. Copied by Count Rzewuski and reproduced in Comte Waclav Seweryn Rzewuski, *Impression d'Orient et d'Arabie* (Librairie José Corti/Muséum National d'Histoire Naturelle, Paris, 2002).

*Endpapers*

Facsimile of a letter from Lady Hester Stanhope, esoterica, found in Lady Hester Stanhope's papers © Kent County Council.

While every effort has been made to trace the owners of copyright material reproduced herein, the publishers would like to apologise for any omissions and would be pleased to incorporate missing acknowledgements in any future editions.

# Lady Hester Stanhope's Family Tree

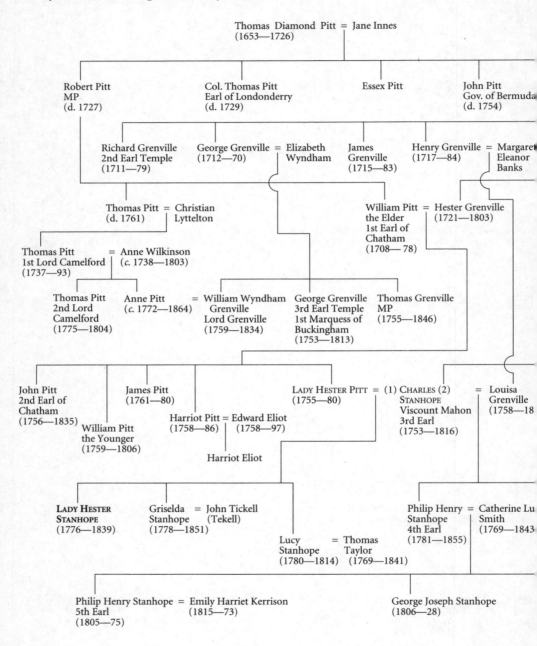

Thomas Diamond Pitt = Jane Innes
(1653—1726)

Robert Pitt
MP
(d. 1727)

Col. Thomas Pitt
Earl of Londonderry
(d. 1729)

Essex Pitt

John Pitt
Gov. of Bermuda
(d. 1754)

Richard Grenville
2nd Earl Temple
(1711—79)

George Grenville = Elizabeth
(1712—70)       Wyndham

James
Grenville
(1715—83)

Henry Grenville = Margaret
(1717—84)        Eleanor
                 Banks

Thomas Pitt = Christian
(d. 1761)     Lyttelton

William Pitt = Hester Grenville
the Elder     (1721—1803)
1st Earl of
Chatham
(1708— 78)

Thomas Pitt
1st Lord Camelford
(1737—93)

= Anne Wilkinson
  (c. 1738—1803)

Thomas Pitt
2nd Lord
Camelford
(1775—1804)

Anne Pitt    = William Wyndham
(c. 1772—1864)  Grenville
                Lord Grenville
                (1759—1834)

George Grenville
3rd Earl Temple
1st Marquess of
Buckingham
(1753—1813)

Thomas Grenville
MP
(1755—1846)

John Pitt
2nd Earl of
Chatham
(1756—1835)

James Pitt
(1761—80)

William Pitt
the Younger
(1759—1806)

Harriot Pitt = Edward Eliot
(1758—86)   (1758—97)

Harriot Eliot

LADY HESTER PITT = (1) CHARLES (2) = Louisa
(1755—80)            STANHOPE      Grenville
                     Viscount Mahon (1758—18
                     3rd Earl
                     (1753—1816)

LADY HESTER
STANHOPE
(1776—1839)

Griselda    = John Tickell
Stanhope     (Tekell)
(1778—1851)

Lucy        = Thomas
Stanhope      Taylor
(1780—1814) (1769—1841)

Philip Henry = Catherine Lu
Stanhope       Smith
4th Earl       (1769—1843
(1781—1855)

Philip Henry Stanhope = Emily Harriet Kerrison
5th Earl                (1815—73)
(1805—75)

George Joseph Stanhope
(1806—28)

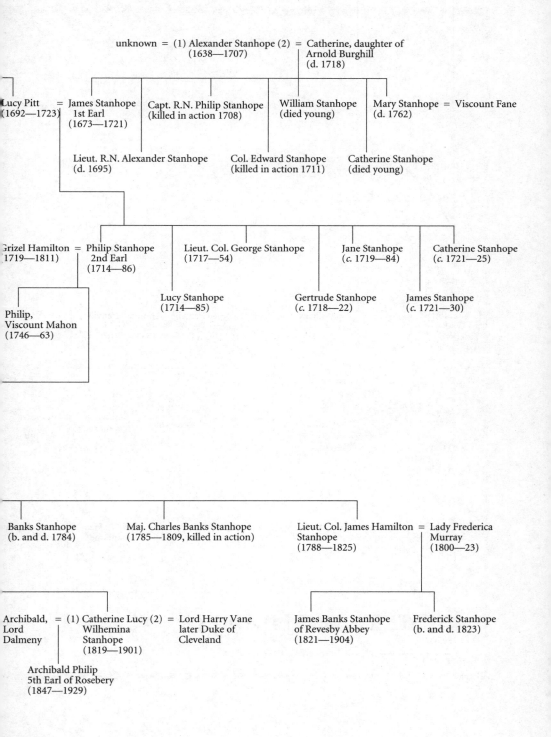

unknown = (1) Alexander Stanhope (2) = Catherine, daughter of
                     (1638—1707)                    Arnold Burghill
                                                     (d. 1718)

Lucy Pitt = James Stanhope    Capt. R.N. Philip Stanhope    William Stanhope    Mary Stanhope = Viscount Fane
(1692—1723)  1st Earl          (killed in action 1708)       (died young)        (d. 1762)
             (1673—1721)

        Lieut. R.N. Alexander Stanhope    Col. Edward Stanhope         Catherine Stanhope
        (d. 1695)                          (killed in action 1711)      (died young)

Grizel Hamilton = Philip Stanhope    Lieut. Col. George Stanhope    Jane Stanhope      Catherine Stanhope
(1719—1811)      2nd Earl             (1717—54)                      (c. 1719—84)       (c. 1721—25)
                 (1714—86)

                        Lucy Stanhope                    Gertrude Stanhope    James Stanhope
                        (1714—85)                        (c. 1718—22)         (c. 1721—30)

Philip,
Viscount Mahon
(1746—63)

Banks Stanhope        Maj. Charles Banks Stanhope         Lieut. Col. James Hamilton = Lady Frederica
(b. and d. 1784)      (1785—1809, killed in action)       Stanhope                     Murray
                                                          (1788—1825)                  (1800—23)

Archibald, = (1) Catherine Lucy (2) = Lord Harry Vane    James Banks Stanhope    Frederick Stanhope
Lord             Wilhemina            later Duke of       of Revesby Abbey        (b. and d. 1823)
Dalmeny          Stanhope             Cleveland           (1821—1904)
                 (1819—1901)

        Archibald Philip
        5th Earl of Rosebery
        (1847—1929)

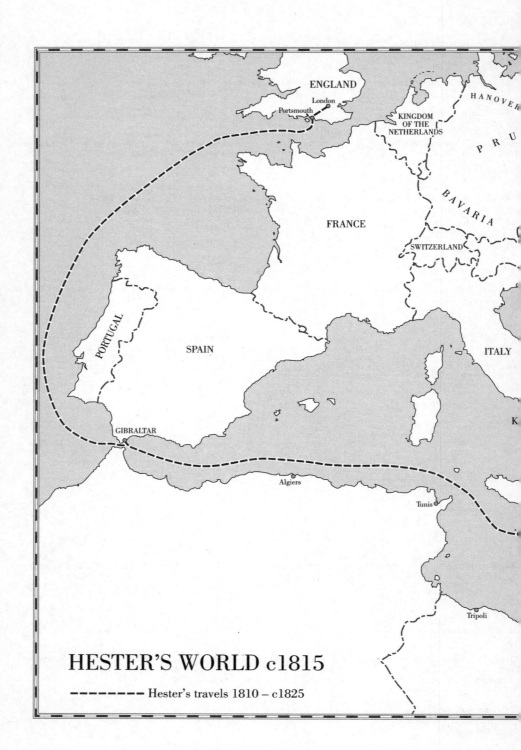

# HESTER'S WORLD c1815

------- Hester's travels 1810 – c1825

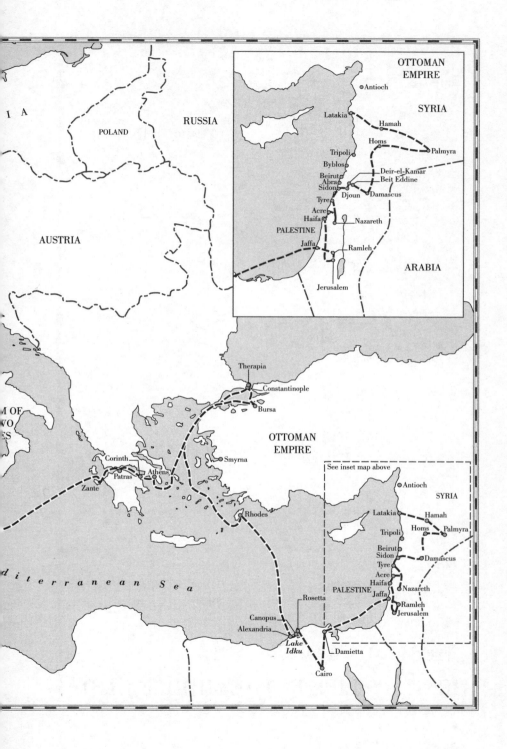

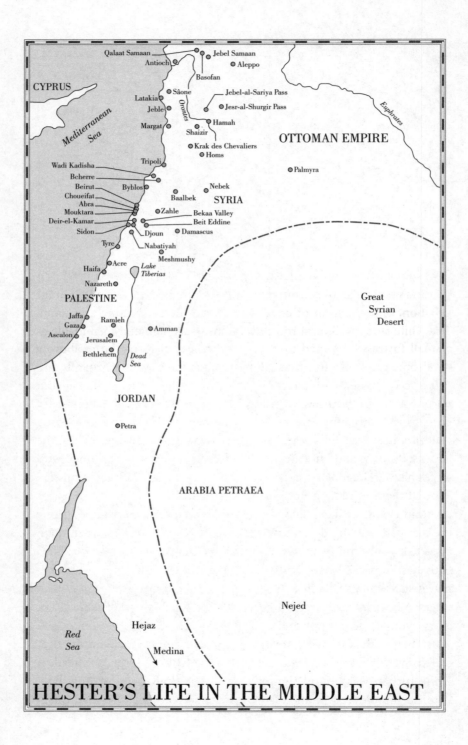

# HESTER'S LIFE IN THE MIDDLE EAST

*Prologue*

It was four o'clock on Sunday, 23 June 1839, the second year of Queen Victoria's reign. Far away from England, on a hill in the shadow of Mount Lebanon, only the hum of cicadas stirred in the suffocating afternoon. The white stone walls and roofs of a house – as high and formidable as a small fortress – seemed to hover in the heat-distorted haze, above a handsome grove of olive trees. Round about there were other hills and ridges, crisscrossed with terraced fields, and gashes of that same chalky, porous stone. In the distance, bells pealed from the tower of a monastery; perhaps the only hint of what a European might recognize as kindred civilization. These hills were renowned as ancient cemeteries for the Greeks, Romans and Phoenicians, their warrens of tombs crammed with sarcophagi and hidden treasures invisible to the eye; superstition had allowed them to remain undisturbed for centuries.

Amid clouds of dust, half a dozen household servants scurried along the dirt path leading down to the village of Djoun, bringing with them a skittish collection of mares, donkeys and goats, the sturdiest saddled with hastily-packed bags and whatever furniture could be lashed into place, such things of value they hoped would compensate for unpaid wages. A boy clutched a red leather-bound book filled with strange divinatory symbols he did not understand.

In her bedroom with its stone-cut windows, the woman they called Syt Mylady was dead. Her open eyes stared straight ahead. A white turban was bound tightly around her skull-cropped grey hair. Incense smouldered in an earthenware saucer and candles had burnt to waxy stubs. She had died in the house which she had first glimpsed more than a quarter of a century earlier, not realizing then that it would become the one true object of her ambitions. How the light had glittered and danced about her then! Light, which she craved as a young woman, light that was exhilarating and alive under a cobalt-blue sky.

For the last seven years she had remained within her fortress walls, leaving her private quarters only to walk in her garden whenever it pleased her, at any hour of night or day. She would visit her mares, rest her hand on their warm flanks as they slept, or lie under her bitter orange trees, scrutinizing the constellations.

Now her body lay on coarse Barbary blankets, on a low-slung bed that was nothing but five planks nailed together, tilted slightly to incline her head. She was dressed in her customary night-dress – a chemise of cotton and silk, a white, quilted *abaya* and with a striped pale red and yellow *keffiyeh* tied under her chin, the way she had learned from the Bedouin. Her fingers still gripped a crooked staff with a naïve carving at the top shaped to resemble a ram's head.

In death, her features – which were those of an old woman, for she died in her sixty-third year – seemed to soften. Her face was very pale and gaunt, making what some had affectionately called her famous Chatham nose look even more pronounced. This was the same unmistakable nose that had perched defiantly on the faces of four generations of Pitts before her, including not only two of England's most outstanding and powerful Prime Ministers, father and son – both wartime leaders – but also 'Diamond' Pitt, her great-great-grandfather, curmudgeon of the first order and maker of the family fortune. It was his ability to thrive in an alien country, and by a combination of boldness and tenacity to rise from the rank of humble merchant, firstly, by founding a trading concern which grew formidable enough to rival even the East India Company, and later, to be Governor of Madras. She often used to say it was the blood of this Pitt that 'flowed like lava' through her veins.

Yet of all her relatives, aside from her mother, it was her grandfather, Pitt the Elder, she resembled most as she grew older. Indeed, by the age of fifty, she could have been his female incarnation: the same large, almond-shaped blue-grey eyes, with their direct, contemplative gaze; the refined oval face and high forehead.

These last few nights she had dreamed such living dreams. Herself, strong again, with all of her youth and boldness restored. Visions, half-dreams, half-memories from a time long distant, came to her. Footsteps echoed down familiar passageways, but this time she recognized them as the impatient, joyful steps of her younger self. Voices called to her, chided her in the old, loving ways. In sing-song French and Arabic: '*Ne verse pas des larmes, ma chère et belle marquise . . .*' and in English.

There she was again at Walmer, standing on the drawbridge in the sunlight near the shore, laughing after her straw hat as it blew away, her long dark chestnut hair like an aureole, and her blue dress billowing, a vision so unrestrained that the red-coated soldiers turned to stare. She had the ears and the heart of the Prime Minister. 'Oh, *Hester*,' he would say, with the tender exasperation he reserved especially for her. Not the love between father and daughter, or brother and sister, but something possessive all the same. Their secret language when in company, much of it conveyed implicitly by the eyebrows and in sideways glances, gave no clue to the paroxysms of laughter they shared later in private. What could she not have achieved, had she set her mind to it? Before, when every expectation and anticipation she held of life had not been disappointed.

On Friday, she wavered from her appointment with death, and sent one of her men down the hill with orders to bring back the first European doctor he could find. She seethed, knowing that an Italian doctor – 'that *useless* Lunardi' – was at that very moment hurrying on his way to return to her service, no doubt hopeful that the fee for this voyage, as well as the large sum owing on his earlier ministrations, would be reimbursed upon his arrival. Unable to eat, and barely sipping water, her coughing became worse, and with each attack, blood poured from her mouth. She acknowledged defeat, too weak even to pull at the hemp rope within her reach, attached by an apparatus of pulleys to a large brass bell. She ordered only that the candles be kept constantly lit in the whitewashed alcove at her bedside, so she could watch the flames. That night the moon and stars were clear, and she could smell the breath of jackals as they prowled beneath her window. Did she fear death then? Many believed her fear-less. She believed in the divine, in the transmigration of souls – that she herself was marked for greatness. She had looked death in the face many times, and fancied she could see it written in the faces of men, and so could judge their fate.

Now Lady Hester Stanhope lay dead, and all that she had been was gone. Her garden would be left to run wild – the arbours of yellow jasmine, fountain pavilions and her favourite archways of periwinkle with its bright blue flowers – and her splendid house would be left to rot and crumble, the bricks themselves to melt back into the earth. Her hill would become no more than a place you might climb for a better view of the sea, as it was when she came.

It was not until ten o'clock the next night that two strangers could be seen making their way up the hillside to the house, their torches bobbing like fireflies, their horses stumbling at the steep incline. A guide from the village walked alongside, fearful in the darkness of snakes, wild boar, jackals, wolves and even panthers. The journey had taken the two men more than ten hours of hard riding. It had fallen to the British consul in Beirut, Niven Moore, to investigate the death of Lady Stanhope. She was, after all, granddaughter of the Great Commoner himself and the niece of William Pitt, even if she had placed herself beyond the reach of reasonable society in such curious and remote circumstances. He had asked an American missionary, the Reverend William McClure Thomson, a man well liked by the British community in Beirut, to accompany him and conduct whatever funeral service they could manage.[1]

Moore was already well acquainted with the affairs of 'Her Ladyship'. He was in glum possession of a dispatch box of documents bristling with notarized seals thrust upon him by her numerous creditors. It was said that not only had Lady Hester Stanhope descended from bankruptcy to penury – patronizing moneylenders all the way up the coast from Sidon to Tripoli, with escalating debts in half a dozen currencies – but was now quite mad. Gossip about her was as commonplace in the Beirut souk as in a Bath tearoom. Of all the young Victoria's subjects in this part of the world, he mused, she was surely one of the most problematic. Or at the very least, notorious.

Nothing had deterred her, not travelling at sea during the Napoleonic wars, not riding through deserts of warring Bedouin, nor the threat of assassination during civil war in Syria, a semi-barbarous country at the best of times. Who could resist speculating about the lovers she had entertained in her fairytale fortress, about the way she presided like a chieftain over her raggle-taggle band of servants, about what fate befell those whose throats she had threatened to have cut, in her make-believe kingdom, with its dungeons and secret passages. Many times she had sheltered refugees: Arabs, Jews, Armenians and Albanians who fled to her after the siege of Acre, and scores of panicked Europeans after the Battle of Navarino. It was true that for a time she was more like a warlord than a woman, and she had hired her own army of Albanian soldiers. Had not the wily Mehemet Ali, ruler of Egypt and her erstwhile friend, grumbled: 'The Englishwoman has caused me more trouble than all the insurgent people of Syria or Palestine.'

It was said she was like Scheherazade and could transport her listeners to other worlds. To all those of a certain age who heard her talk, it was impossible not to think of her grandfather, the greatest orator that England had ever produced. Was she so notoriously vain that she met her guests only at dusk and by candlelight, and in some cases, let them see only her hands in the gloom?

When Moore first arrived in Beirut, he had anticipated a cordial summons to the Chouf mountains. He was even disposed to do what he could to assist her with the horrible state of her financial affairs. Indeed, he opened the first letter from her with something approaching elation. Instead, he was stung by her reply, for she treated him like a peon. Her pension – granted by the King himself for her services to the country – was to be confiscated in order to pay her debts, a move that would render her worse than penniless.

Her defiant letters – one to Lord Palmerston, another to the Duke of Wellington, and the last to Queen Victoria herself – were published in *The Times*. The latter was generally held to be, as one wag observed, 'the letter to a Queen from a Queen'.

But the Queen had other matters on her mind, including her own coronation. War appeared inevitable, with campaigns in both Afghanistan and China, and then there was the looming Eastern Question. She had no wish to indulge an old relic who had been a favourite of her grandfather's and certainly not one who had made the mistake of addressing her with such familiarity.

Many in England were sympathetic, especially those who had come to think rather fondly of Lady Hester as something of an institution, but mostly because her well-publicized exploits and grandiose foibles had never failed to provide amusement over the decades. Mothers would warn their daughters they must not be too headstrong or they too might end up as unfortunate a creature as Lady Hester Stanhope. She hardly set a proper example, even for young women wishing to broaden their horizons through travel. She was altogether an exotic from the Romantic era, which to current taste was overblown, dissolute and even vulgar. Simply put, for the Victorians, she was out of fashion.

As they approached, Moore and Thomson were taken aback by the imposing appearance of the house. Two gateways with heavy wooden doors were flanked by high walls which encircled a residence of seemingly indeterminate size. There seemed no way to make their presence known, aside from hammering their fists first against one door, then the other. 'No one met them: a profound silence was all over the place; they lighted their own lamps in the outer court.'[2] It seemed to the men that passages branched off in all directions. They had the sense of becoming trapped in a maze. As they went on there were glimpses of other inner courts and pavilions linked by vaulted arcades, as well as those along the route they took. One seemed particularly grand, sheltering a *liwan*, a hall open to the sky, lofty and gracious with rows of cushioned divans and a trellis of climbing roses and jasmine. Although this house was not as grand as the grandest Damascus mansion, it was something else entirely: whoever had created it had the soul of a magician. They also began to be aware of large numbers of restless cats beneath their feet, curling around their ankles and clinging to their boots. A young African woman appeared in the passageway, and made a gesture towards a thick red door.

In a room with green walls, stripped of all furnishings, they found the body of Lady Hester.

Moore was slight and handsome with a moustache and sidewhiskers which he kept neatly clipped, but which nonetheless he worried at constantly with his fingers when under strain, as he did now. For this event, he had been careful to wear a black armband and dress in sombre colours with a high stiff collar. 'It was an intensely hot Sabbath,' Thomson would record. The idea of a woman's corpse lying here for over a day in such unbearable warmth made him nauseous. Sweat dripped from his temples and soaked his jacket. He did not wish to investigate further.

Behind the men, a small tribe of servants had assembled. Decisive action was required. There had been thirty-seven servants in the fortress in the morning. They had watched 'every motion of her eye' until she died. Most had taken what they could and fled. Now, some ten or so remained. Moore noticed that many of the servants seemed to be wearing what he surmised to be cast-off robes and hats from the wardrobe of their mistress. As his eyes adjusted to the gloom, he saw that their ragged clothes were incongruously matched with brilliant velvet and brocade cloaks, red turbans, silk stockings and carpet slippers.

By midnight the men had ascertained several facts. Although she had left no written instructions, it was clear that Lady Hester had managed to convey how she wished to be buried. At least five of her servants professed to be expert on the subject, and one in particular had apparently been entrusted with duties he had sworn on his life to carry out. This was her most trusted servant, Almaz – her dragoman – who combined the roles of translator, secretary, gardener and general factotum.

They decided to do as she had apparently asked. Lady Hester was to be buried in a grave at a specified place in her garden, which already contained a vault, along with the bones of a Frenchman by the name of Loustaunau, who had been buried there before. 'The vault in the garden was hastily opened and the bones of General Loustaneau [*sic*], or of his son, I forget which – a Frenchman who died here . . . were taken out' and readied for burial.[3] How he had died and why Her Ladyship commanded this posthumous mingling, which Moore regarded as immoral, it was difficult to say. Such an indelicate request on the part of this spinster might be best left out of his report.[4] He would have to decide whether or not it would be necessary to mention this detail when he informed the ladyship's younger brother. A more chaste companion had been intended for the burial ceremony: the jaunty square of the

Union Jack flag which he had brought for the purpose, folded away in his saddlebag. A roll of white muslin would do as a shroud. The vault would be opened and its contents were to be arranged according to Lady Hester's instructions. Reverend Thomson would perform the Church of England service.[5]

Despite the heat and disrepair, the garden impressed the men. Thomson would later describe it as 'a wilderness of shady avenues, and a paradise of sweet flowers . . . I have rarely seen a more beautiful place'. They left the dragoman to open the vault and arrange its contents according to the instructions Lady Hester had given him and returned to supervise the removal of the body into its waiting shroud, and its placement into the plain wooden coffin they had brought with them from Djoun. The carved staff was clasped between her hands. After draping the Union Jack over the open coffin, they followed the procession of her servants bearing her aloft, threading their way through the passageways and out to the garden. Thomson wrote of the macabre sight awaiting them: 'When at length I enterered the arbour, the first thing I saw were the bones of the general, in a ghastly heap, with the head on top, having a lighted taper stuck in either eye-socket – a hideous, grinning spectacle.'[6] The servants were clearly no less taken aback. They stood aside, respectfully, as though this arrangement had a dignity of its own. Moore stared in shock at the open vault for some moments. There was nothing to be done except to conduct the funeral as rapidly as possible.

The next morning, after a rough night, overhearing shouting between the squabbling servants, who were anxious about their unpaid wages, the men went around the premises to make an inventory of Lady Hester's assets. They had not been the first to inspect her Djoun fortress, for as soon as news of her death had reached Sidon, the British consul there, a wealthy Maltese Jew by the name of Joseph Abela, had immediately hurried up in order to prevent her house from being ransacked. Abela had ordered the more valuable-looking furniture and possessions to be piled up together in rooms which he had sealed up.

They counted thirty-five rooms, not including the cellars or the stables. Thick curtains were draped across the windows, but the light was just bright enough to see tables, chairs and chests, all inlaid with mother of pearl; cushions in Aleppo silk and bright woven carpets; bolts of calico, brocade and linen; large brass lanterns, damascene glass and brassware; and carved, painted wooden doors off their hinges, rich in geometric star patterns. There were stained-glass windows, blue and white Mameluke jars, and large circular pewter trays. One room contained countless letters, some filed, some heaped at random, and papers of esoterica scrawled with strange diagrams and notes in a language Moore surmised to be Hebraic, as well as boxes of books. Another was filled with more than forty oil jars, but they were all empty, and spiders nested between them; in still another, there were enough Arab saddles for a small army. Two more were crammed with medicines – a madwoman's pharmacopoeia of phials, pills and powders, with medical almanacs and instruments of all descriptions. A store-room contained shelves of stacked boxes, some of whose contents were emptied out: cases of Promethean matches, silver snuff boxes, a few prized canisters of tea and jam from Jermyn Street, candles, Epsom salts, watercolours of English soldiers on horseback, a portrait of the Duke of York, green umbrellas and English gunpowder. There were a great many *narguileh* and *tchiboque* pipes. They speculated as to how many of the ladyship's most valuable possessions had been stolen the previous day.

When Moore opened the closet in what he assumed to be Lady Hester's dressing room, out spilled models cut in paper of rooms with arches, vaults and pavilions and buildings, and fountains, all scrawled with her comments in the margins. Gradients, plans for borders and paths and notes for unusual trees and shrubs. He found himself admiring the determination of this singular woman, cutting out shapes with her scissors, studying books – designing, building and furnishing her mansion of dreams – so far from home.

# 1

## *Beginnings*

She came into the world with a shock of chestnut hair and bright, greyish-blue eyes, blinking at the watery sunshine that came slanting in through frosted windowpanes. It was Tuesday, 12 March 1776, a clear, chill day in London. That morning, Handel's *Messiah* was being rehearsed at the Theatre Royal in Covent Garden; a short distance away in Hanover Square, J. C. Bach was preparing for his performance the following evening.

It had been one of the coldest winters on record; the Thames had frozen over, and the city was blanketed by great drifts of snow. At the first hint of the child's arrival, Lord Mahon, Charles Stanhope (the future third Earl Stanhope), sent urgently for a trusted doctor. By the standards of the day it was considered an easy delivery.

Instructed to remain completely supine for at least a week before attempting to sit up and not to leave their Marylebone townhouse on Queen Anne Street for another month (a ruling she would soon ignore) the new mother contemplated her daughter, now bathed and dressed in a flannel gown and cap. She was a healthy size, with an equally healthy pair of lungs. She was to be called Hester, after her mother.

Hester Pitt, the new Lady Mahon, was twenty and had been married for just over a year. She herself had been named after her mother, the redoubtable Lady Chatham, formerly Lady Hester Grenville. The Pitts were fond of the name, thinking it unusual and unconventional. The choice of her daughter's middle name – Lucy – for her great-grandmother, also leaned towards her mother's side of the family.

Within hours, news of Hester's arrival was sent to Lord Mahon's parents at Chevening, as well as to the Chathams and the Pitts. Charles's mother, Lady Grizel Stanhope, immediately left for London so she could make herself useful, no doubt leaving her husband, Philip, the second Earl Stanhope, buried in his library. If ever a woman could be described as a dominant matriarch, it was shrewd Scottish-born Grizel, who supervised the day-to-day running of the family estate with a precision and fortitude that marked her out as an exceptionally well-organized woman. She would have been a comforting presence for the anxious new mother.[1]

Grizel was delighted to note the tenderness evident in her son. She thought his comment, on seeing his naked daughter being dressed, that he hoped 'no other gentleman will ever see her in' such 'attitudes', amusing enough to pass on.[2]

Hester Pitt, then nineteen, optimistic, pretty and popular by all accounts, had married her cousin, Charles, two years her senior, tall, lanky and angular-featured, at the end of 1774. The family connection was dismissed as relatively unimportant, a commonplace amongst aristocratic families. Their grandparents, Lucy Pitt and James, first Earl Stanhope, had married in 1713, producing six children, including Charles's father, Philip. Therefore, when both sides of the family were peering into the crib to look upon the newly-born Hester, it was entirely debatable whether the Pitt and the Stanhope noses were merely variations of the same.

Had it not been for a stone found on the northern banks of the Krishna river near the medieval city of Hyderabad three-quarters of a century before, Hester Stanhope's parents might never have met. It was no ordinary stone, but a diamond that weighed 410 carats, the largest of all Indian diamonds in its rough form. It was this discovery, and the tremendous fortune it bestowed upon its owner, Hester's great-great-grandfather – the supremely wilful and enterprising Thomas Pitt – that made the family fortune. Without it, perhaps the histories of the Pitts and the Stanhopes would not have collided the way that they did, setting the seal on the earlier marriage between the two families and bringing Hester Pitt and Charles Stanhope into each other's orbits.

Thomas Pitt, then Governor of Madras, acquired the stone that would be known as the Pitt diamond from an Indian trader for 48,000 Indian *pagodas* which was some £20,400 at the time. Pitt was already a shrewd investor in substantial quantities of gems and gold as a means of easily transporting his accumulated wealth back to England. He knew this stone had been smuggled out from the arid, boulder-strewn Deccan plateau, from one of a cluster of the Golconda mines, but he could not have foreseen that the stone would make his name; that ever after he would always be known as 'Diamond Pitt'.

By the time it sat like a bulbous paperweight on his teak desk at Fort St George in the East India Company's garrisoned White Town, the diamond had a whiff of scandal attached to it. The story went that it had been smuggled out of the Mughal Emperor's lands by a slave who had slashed open his thigh and concealed it in the wound. At least one man had been murdered for it. The slanderous chatter about how Pitt came by his impressive rock would follow him to the grave, and even find its way into his funeral oration.[3]

When Thomas Pitt finally saw his stone after it had been cut with great skill over two years by Messrs. R.H. Long & Steele in London at a cost of £6,000, he was ecstatic. It was a 136-and-a-half-carat cushion brilliant, reflecting the light in lozenge-shaped and triangular facets, with only one very small imperfection. By any estimation it was the most beautiful blue-tinged stone, the colour of a dawn sky and the size of a large cherry. Valued at £125,000, it was acknowledged as the finest and largest of all Indian brilliants.

Sold to Philippe, the Duke of Orleans, Prince Regent of France, for the sum of £135,000, it became known as the Regent diamond, and was placed as the centrepiece of the crown worn for the coronation of King Louis XV in 1723. Two generations later, Marie Antoinette adored it at first sight, and wore it frequently, sewn into her large black velvet hat. Once it was in Napoleon's possession, he had it placed in his sword, which he wore for his coronation in December 1804. When his second wife, the Austrian Archduchess Marie-Louise, was forced to leave Paris with her family as fugitives in 1813, she took the diamond with her; it was later returned to France by her father, the Austrian Emperor Francis I. It was placed back into the French crown for the coronation of Charles X in 1825, and was taken out again so that the Empress Eugenie, wife of Napoleon III, could wear it as a diadem in her hair.

During World War II, as the Nazis reached the outskirts of Paris, it was smuggled to the Château du Chambord in the Loire, where it was hidden behind a stone panel for the duration of war. Today, Pitt's priceless diamond – sometimes called the Millionaire Diamond – can be seen in the Apollon Gallery at the Louvre.

In many ways, the diamond that had shaped the fortunes of Hester's family, and its trajectory through the changing fortunes of France's rulers, would become a potent symbol of the power and glory – abroad – that she herself would spend her entire life seeking.

There can be no mistaking the fact that Hester Stanhope came from a family of passionate egotists. She lived with the perpetual awareness that not only was she descended from a line of exceptional achievers, but also that the traits they had in common represented her best characteristics: the ability to think and act for themselves, often in a highly unconventional way, and sometimes in the face of considerable public scorn. Added to this was a family propensity towards imperiousness, extravagant behaviour and quixotic ambition, which sometimes tilted towards an unbalanced and volatile temperament. At least one Pitt had been shut away in a mental asylum. It had been observed that there was 'a great degree of madness in the family'.

Yet nothing out of the ordinary seemed to distinguish the earlier Pitt clan. They knew themselves to be descended from the Pitts in Hampshire and Dorset, mostly gentry, with several eminent local magnates among them. It was the family fortune-maker, Thomas 'Diamond' Pitt, who set the trend for greatness. In 1673, when Thomas Pitt had just turned twenty, much to the disquiet of his mother he announced he was taking off for India, joining the East India Company as a lowly clerk. His beginnings were humble: a trading practice on the salty banks of Balasore, a fetid but profitable British cantonment in Orissa. But not content with slaving for the Company, he absconded and began to buy goods from Indian merchants, shipping them back to England on his own account. He also made the first of many trips to Persia, primarily on the lookout for well-bred horses. There was nothing that so riled the East India Company as a turncoat agent like Pitt. But he showed himself to be a skilled negotiator, capable of passionate, even brutal fits of ranting, but expressed with such force and persuasion that he quickly established a kind of rogue authority. Even his rivals admired his energy, his belief that the future of England's success in the world depended on opportunistic profit-seekers like him. In the end the East India Company decided they had better have him on their side. Pitt was able to buy respectability along with the medieval borough of Old Sarum in Wiltshire, for which he later successfully ran as Member of Parliament.[4] In 1698, following a parliamentary ruling that relaxed restrictions on trade in India, allowing interlopers to follow Pitt's example and deal freely, the Company decided to appoint none other than their notorious old adversary as Governor of Madras. For eleven years, the Madras Residency echoed with his blustering rages. Family legends about Diamond Pitt's bombastic personality were picked over for generations.

It was Thomas Pitt's second daughter, Lucy, a great beauty of her day, who first brought together the Pitts and the Stanhopes. Lucy Pitt could have had her pick of any number of suitors, but it was the dashing, hard-drinking and impetuous James Stanhope, a man twice her age, a hero in the War of the Spanish Succession, who took her fancy. The Stanhopes were a clan of diplomats and warriors. James was the son of Alexander Stanhope, the grandson of Philip Stanhope, whom Charles I had in 1628 created Earl of Chesterfield. Despite his inherent dislike of foreigners, Alexander himself had been distinguished as a diplomat in the time of Oliver Cromwell and was William III's ambassador at Madrid and afterwards at The Hague. In 1708, as commander of the British forces in Spain, James led his men in the capture of Minorca and the nearby naval base of Fort Mahon.

Shortly after the couple's marriage, George I made James Stanhope successively Secretary of State and Leader of the House of Commons. From their house in Whitehall, they became a formidable, glamorous political couple. By 1717, James had become one of George I's most trusted confidants, and he was rewarded with the sinecure of Chief Minister, and raised to the peerage as Viscount Mahon, thus earning the Stanhope title. It soon became necessary to find a family mansion. Because of its relative proximity to London, Chevening, tucked away in the chalky hills of the North Downs in Kent, surrounded by enchanting countryside, was thought suitable.[5]

Lucy Pitt put her own strong mark on Chevening, the family estate where her great-granddaughter would grow up. The original house, built in 1620 and attributed to Inigo Jones, and the 3,500-acre estate were bought in 1717 for £28,000, some £10,000 of which was paid with Lucy's dowry. While her husband was continuously busy in high office, Lucy preoccupied herself between her frequent pregnancies with supervising extensive alterations to their new house. A thermometer-shaped canal was created in front of the house – where black swans, geese and wild birds still flock – and extensive gardens were laid out in a formal pattern of box hedges, yew trees and intersecting pathways fashionable at the time; meanwhile the original doll's-house design of the house was extended with pavilions and the forecourt enclosed with elegant wrought-iron gates, with the Stanhope crest triumphantly on top.

A new road was created to make a stately loop along the high ridge on Star Hill, where pheasants still whir through woods of silver beech on the one side, allowing the contemplation of far-reaching vistas across Chevening and the surrounding countryside on the other. Anyone passing would marvel at one particular spot along the road – a sudden and unexpected vista through a towering arcade of trees in which the prospect of Chevening is perfectly framed. This view especially pleased Lucy, who designed it, planting the row of trees and coaxing them to form an arch, nicknamed the Keyhole.

It was this landscape that the young Hester Stanhope would grow up to love, more than the house itself. It was on these wide undulating hills that she would first learn to ride. The view through the Keyhole took on a magical significance for her. It was the portal through which four generations of her family had passed, and an unchanging link to the women of her family, her namesakes.

Diamond Pitt's grandson, William Pitt, the Earl of Chatham, came to be regarded as the greatest politician of his time. Known to a generation as 'the Great Commoner', he was revered as the man who had led the country through the Seven Years War, presiding over a series of victories, wresting the provinces of Quebec and Montreal from French settlers, thereby bringing much of the eastern seaboard of North America under British control, and reinforcing British supremacy in India. His granddaughter would be raised on accounts of his thunderous orations and grandiloquent gestures in the House of Commons.

Chatham's firstborn child, Hester Pitt, now Lady Mahon, always had every expectation that her lot in life should include both the grand lifestyle and intellectual stimulation that had always surrounded her. Yet her father, despite his brilliance, had also been profligate, almost maniacally so, and was too debt-ridden to offer any suitor she might have an enticing dowry. Much of the family money had been plunged into renovating and beautifying Chatham's house and garden at Hayes, near the village of Bromley in Kent. It was left to her mother's relatives, the Grenvilles, one of the most powerful Whig aristocratic families, to provide the bare minimum that might be expected for a 'polite' marriage: jewellery and the endowment of a thousand pounds to the young couple.

There were five in the Pitt brood – John, Harriot, William and James as well as Hester – all born within five years of one another. Unlike most girls at the time, Hester Pitt benefited from a careful education, being tutored at home along with her brothers, one of whom, William, would follow in the family political tradition and earn the distinction of becoming Britain's youngest Prime Minister at the age of twenty-four. By the time William left to study at Cambridge university, where he would be admitted as an undergraduate to Pembroke Hall at the age of fourteen – an achievement which was as exceptional then as today – brother and sister were proficient in the classical languages, able to translate ancient Greek at sight with impressive fluency, and apt to quote long passages from Thucydides and Polybius.[6]

In all ways, as she entered the first year of her marriage, Lady Mahon – a slender, self-possessed girl with wide, expressive dark eyes – was an advanced young woman at the height of her powers. She was described by a family friend as 'one of the most accomplished persons of the age'.[7] It would have been impossible for her not to have a political consciousness: not only her father, but her great-grandfather, grandfather and uncle had all been Members of Parliament.

Shortly before he married Hester Pitt, Charles had returned to England after more than ten years away in Europe. His family had moved to Geneva in 1763 when Charles was ten, in the hope that the better climate would improve the health of their ailing elder son Philip, who nonetheless died of consumption six months later at the age of seventeen. Philip was the son on whom all hopes were pinned, while Charles had been so obstinate as a child his parents called him 'the little Devil'. The Stanhopes had stayed on so that Charles might continue his education. Geneva was then the centre of extreme radical thought, where the theories of the city's famous residents Jean-Jacques Rousseau and Voltaire were respected. At a young age, Charles was fired with enthusiasm for social reform, and his intense idealism was infectious.

Charles Stanhope was not obviously handsome at first glance; he was lithe and gaunt, and bore a strong resemblance to his mother with his smooth high forehead, aquiline, almost beaky nose and clear dark-blue eyes. But his face was that of a thinker and he had a proud, confident manner. Hester Pitt was used to successful, clever men, mostly politicians, many of them dissident Whigs as well as leaders of the Opposition in her father's circle, and was also accustomed to her father's adept command over them. The fact that her father warmed to Charles and clearly enjoyed talking to him, when he was hopeless at disguising his impatience with intellectual inferiors, would not have been missed by her.

Considered a genius by his tutors, Charles had created a stir with his original thinking and aptitude for taking unfamiliar, difficult theoretical problems in his stride. His first love was science, and he was perpetually at work on idiosyncratic experiments and inventions. At seventeen he had invented a mathematical device, an early prototype of the calculator, the ingenuity of which amazed those who saw it. He also won a prize offered by the Swedish Academy for the best essay on the construction of the pendulum; drawings and doodles of clocks and pendulums cover his school-books from the time. The Royal Society invited him to be their youngest Fellow. Just as his mind seemed constantly to be ticking, he was always in motion – with an erratic, hurrying gait that made him frequently clumsy, although his hands were extraordinarily nimble. He and his daughter were to resemble each other more than she would later care to admit.

It was not surprising that Charles's intended plan was to go into politics. His closest male friendship was with his cousin, Hester Pitt's brother, William. Although Charles was six years older than William, they marvelled at how alike they were. At that time, both young men held similar idealistic views, reading Adam Smith and Thomas Paine, brooding critically about society, the rights of the common man, and the need for parliamentary reform. Yet where Charles was frequently impetuous, even zealous, William tended towards caution and reserve.

In October 1774, several months after his return from Geneva, and just weeks before his marriage, Charles, as Lord Mahon, unsuccessfully contested the seat for the City of Westminster. His candidature as a radical had been warmly endorsed by the Lord Mayor elect, John Wilkes, the popularist radical. But his defeat did not appear to put any damper on the couple's wedding on 19 December that same year. The Reverend Francis Fawke presided, a great friend to both Dr Johnson and Lord Chatham, and he read aloud a little composition of his own:

> When gentle hearts in faithful union join
> And mix the Hero with the Patriot's line
> With every charm uniting every grace
> And all the virtues of the Temple race
> The happy omen we with joy admit
> And bless the match of Stanhope and of Pitt.

Hester, or Hetty as she was often called, was handed over to the servants in her first month of life. Chevening was Hester's first playground, set amid a swathe of parkland and carefully cultivated pleasure grounds, requiring a small army of servants, farmers, foresters and seasonal hop-pickers. It would been difficult for an impressionable young mind not to be struck by the sweeping entrance hall with its great wooden staircase, which was a hymn to weaponry, bristling with rifles, bayonets and daggers, crosshatched into geometric decorations across the walls, the pièce de résistance a whorl of tightly packed rifles from which a giant lantern hung suspended from the ceiling.

Hester grew accustomed to the excitement of frequent guests and the constant presence of servants. It was obvious to her, even when she was very small, that her family name was something to be proud of. In the kitchen, linen-capped servants scurried about under a giant iron-worked 'S' – for Stanhope – set in a coronet in a pentagram on the wall, under a ceiling as high as a church.

Although they did not realize it, Hester's parents would never be happier.

Since his marriage, Lord Mahon had been content to let his charming, pretty wife take charge of their social life. From their new Harley Street house, which they moved to shortly after Hester's birth (then a smart residential address before the doctors invaded around the turn of the nineteenth century), the young couple enjoyed an enviable town life, with their own carriage and a household staff. As a member of the Royal Society, Mahon frequently haunted the Society's club, and held regular meetings and scientific demonstrations. He was well known to the Society's members, eminent scientists and philosophers such as William Watson, Joseph Priestley, and Dr Richard Price. The brilliant naturalist Sir Joseph Banks, shortly to be elected the Royal Society's president, became his particularly close friend.*

Hester was raised in a household busy with scientific discussions and political debate, talk of playhouses and the season, fashionable masquerades and dinner parties. The Mahons thrived on concert-going: Mozart, J. C. Bach and Haydn were all then working in London. The house at Harley Street was often a second home for the Pitts; Harriot came to live with them there, and William visited when he could from Cambridge.

Throughout Lady Mahon's second pregnancy, the young family spent more time at Chevening, where Charles was engrossed in his latest experiments. One quest was to strike upon the best method of fire-proofing, and he hit upon a technique that involved the suctioning-out of air, based on the principle that when a quantity of oxygen is removed, there can be no fire. A grand demonstration took place in the grounds at Chevening, attended by some of London's greats, including the Royal Society president Sir John Pringle. With his parents looking on, Charles invited his guests to sit on a row of chairs he had placed on the second floor of the small wooden building he had constructed in the estate grounds. With a show of theatrical display he set torches to the lower room, the floors of which he had strewn with a highly combustible mixture of wood shavings and dried faggots mixed with chips of coal. As he described it himself, when the fire took hold, 'the heat was so intense that the glass of the windows was melted like so much common sealing wax and ran down

---

* There was a family connection to the Banks through Lady Mahon, for one of her uncles, Henry Grenville, had married Banks's aunt, Eleanor Margaret. Their young daughter, Louisa, one of Banks's cousins, was also cousin to the Pitt sisters, and was a great friend of Lady Mahon's sister Harriot, who was then nineteen.

in drops; yet the flooring boards of that very room were not burnt through; nor was one of the side-timbers, flooring-joints or ceiling-joists damaged in the smallest degree'. It was deemed a brilliant success.

When she was not shuttling back and forth to London, Lady Mahon was hard at work assisting her husband. William Pitt gossiped to his mother that he hoped to see his sister 'as soon as she can find a leisure moment. Her great business is that of secretary to Lord Mahon, whose "Electricity" is nearly ready for the press and will rank him, I suppose, with Dr Franklin.' Charles had by now thrown himself into one of the most dominating preoccupations of the second half of the late eighteenth century, and with his new friend Benjamin Franklin's encouragement, was writing an ambitious treatise, *Principles of Electricity*. He embarked on a series of perilous experiments devoted to explaining the phenomenon with a great deal of his research based on the close observation of lightning strikes. At the slightest hint of a thunderstorm, he would stride up to Star Hill where he would try and induce lightning strikes using all sorts of imaginative devices, attaching lightning conductors to an ever-changing variety of connective materials, including in one instance a cow.

Chatham's health had been declining to the point where he now spent most of his time in seclusion, suffering not only from the physical ailment that tormented him – described by his own doctors as 'diffused gout' – but also from terrible fits of depression. Lady Chatham shielded his friends and to a large extent his family from the truth of how ill he really was, and how much she worried about their finances.*

In the spring of 1778, Hester's dying grandfather provided one of the great dramatic moments in the history of the House of Lords. Chatham's conscience had been once more roused by what he considered to be the greatest of all threats against Britain: a French invasion. That February, the conflict in America escalated when France announced it would fight for the American cause, so that now, once again, the two countries were at war. On 7 April, to the horror of his doctor, a cadaverous Chatham appeared before the assembled members to make what would prove to

* Perhaps it was her extreme discretion and tact that led the banker, Thomas Coutts, to declare Lady Chatham 'the cleverest man of her time, in politics or business'. The Pitt women, especially in their maturity, seem to have been altogether formidable.

be his final speech. Stumbling on his wooden sticks, pale and emaciated, he had dressed grandly for the occasion in black velvet, with a large wig wobbling on his domed forehead, his head shrunk with illness. His legs were an unsightly mess of bedsores; blood seeped through his flannel bandages. As he staggered, raising his hand in a wispy salute to his old friends and foes, he reminded his onlookers of a ghostly seer. The real enemy, he warned them, was not America but France.

> Shall a people that fifteen years ago were the terror of the world now stoop, so low as to tell its ancient inveterate enemy . . . You cannot conquer the Americans. You talk of your powerful forces to disperse their army, but I might as well talk of driving them before me with this crutch.

With these words he faltered, falling back as though in a death trance, and as his son William and Charles rushed to catch him, he managed one last prayer: 'Let us at least make an effort; and if we must fall, fall like men.' Gasping for breath, he was borne back to the Prince's Chamber and the debate was adjourned.*

Chatham died on 11 May 1778 in his seventieth year and was buried in Westminster Abbey on 9 June. 'The concourse of people assembled', it was reported the next day, 'was beyond belief; the windows of all the houses, and even the tops of some were crowded; as were the streets, though the spectators had been not only exposed to the rain for several hours, but to stand in dirt and wet nearly to the ankles.' The previous day, around a hundred thousand people had filed past his body in the black-draped Painted Chamber of Westminster Palace. The Commons had agreed to pay off Chatham's debts, which amounted to some £20,000, the equivalent to some £2 million today.

Hester grew into a sturdy child with dark hair and long limbs; she was an early and voluble talker, who struck her family as having definite

---

* The heroic image of the dying statesman collapsing in Parliament, surrounded by more than fifty noblemen, would be committed to legend by an expatriate Bostonian, painter John Singleton Copley, in his painting *The Death of Chatham*. It took Copley two years to complete, painstakingly recording each detail of dress and interior, with most of the portraits made from life, and was regarded by many as the greatest historical painting ever done in England.

opinions. When she was two and a half, her mother gave birth to her sister, Griselda. To the Mahons' anguish, an earlier pregnancy had resulted in the birth of a son who died shortly afterwards. After being invited to inspect Griselda, William Pitt wrote to his mother, clearly showing his preference. 'I am told my little niece is a perfect beauty, though I own I am hardly persuaded of it, and have extremely offended the nurse by not preferring her to Hester.'[8]

No matter what sweetness little Griselda exhibited, her grandmother could not help showing favouritism. Writing to her friend Lady Chatham, betraying a grim pride at their wilful granddaughter, Grizel wrote: 'Hester is quite wild. I am forced to send assistance from here to keep her within bounds'.[9] In an earlier letter, Lady Chatham too had noted with delight that 'My namesake is so merry, she not only laughs all day, but also all night, to the no small disturbance of those who during the latter would choose to sleep'.[10] The following year, while her daughter-in-law, pregnant for a third time, was in London, Grizel wrote: 'I am grown quite a fool about Hester. What a wonderful and amiable child . . . I have hopes her sister will be such another. Hester said – the next must be a boy, for two girls are enough for anybody. If like her, a dozen would be welcome to me, so I am quite calm and feel no impatience on that score.'

In February 1780, a month before Hester's fourth birthday, Lady Mahon gave birth in London to a third daughter, Lucy, a frail and pretty newborn, but her recovery was complicated by the onset of puerperal fever. At twenty-five, Lady Mahon was exhausted by her succession of pregnancies. She seemed at first to improve, and rallied slightly in spring. Her sister Harriot wrote from Harley Street that she is looking after the 'Invalid' in April, telling her mother hopefully that 'she gains strength visibly every day'.[11] By May she reported that her sister 'bore a drive in the hottest day imaginable without suffering from it in the least', and how they went shopping for lute strings and chintzes.[12] The 'Invalid' was apparently well enough to attend a ball at Gloucestershire House, and Charles was so convinced of her good progress that he went on a tour of Buckinghamshire, where he planned to run for Parliament.

Before the summer was out, however, Lady Mahon's condition suddenly worsened, possibly due to a weakened heart. She died at Chevening on 18 July 1780 and was buried in the family chapel. Three weeks later Grizel wrote to her friend Lady Chatham, deep in mourning for her daughter's death. 'Poor Charles has passed a melancholy day. I keep him amused as much as I can, and nothing but hindering him to think is service. Alas! when he does – but I will not dwell upon a subject that must be heart-breaking to us all. The sweet children are perfectly well and thrive amazingly in the good air. I see poor Charles grow thoughtful when they are present, though he takes great notice of them when they are present, more I think, than he used to. Time alone can do good to us all.' In reality, she despaired. Her eldest grandchild asked her constant, confused questions about death to which she had no answer, while her son retreated into silence, barely eating, his skin suddenly ashen, his eyes red-rimmed. When Charles returned to London to throw himself into politics, the girls stayed behind at Chevening.

Within months of becoming a widower, Charles's eye fell on Louisa Grenville, his late wife's cousin. It was another politically advantageous marriage: Louisa's father Henry Grenville had already served as Governor of Barbados and ambassador at Constantinople. Writing from Bath, Charles's former sister-in-law, Harriot, described a day she spent with his bride-to-be over the summer of 1780: 'Poor Louisa is a little of a Coward, and has not rode often enough to be a very good Horsewoman, but her Figure is remarkably pretty in a riding dress, and she looks vastly well upon her Horse.' Louisa, apparently susceptible to Charles's forceful personality, believed he was marked for a brilliant future.

Charles could see Louisa lacked the intellect and the wit of his first wife, but he craved the reassurance and the routine of marriage. At twenty-three, with her ash-blonde hair and blue eyes, Louisa was in all ways a contrast to the former Lady Mahon. Her background of privilege and carefully managed wealth was a different cut from the brilliant, volatile and impulsively spendthrift Pitts. Within months of being widowed, Charles remarried; within the year, the new Lady Mahon gave birth to their first son, Philip Henry, the future heir.

For both Charles and his former brother-in-law William Pitt, this was a time of rapid political advancement. Charles was elected for Chipping Wycombe (later known as High Wycombe) in Buckinghamshire, not as a radical, as he had first wished. Instead, his candidature had been endorsed by the Earl of Shelburne, most prominent among a small group of Whig parliamentarians still loyal to the ideals of Chatham. Like William Pitt, Charles passionately favoured the American rebels and parliamentary reform. Shortly afterwards, Pitt followed Charles into the House of Commons as an MP, aged just twenty-one. The two young men shared a common purpose, each determined that his voice would soon provide a rationale for a vision of a better England. At the time, it was greatly in vogue, especially among the Whigs, to appear to flirt with reform, but both Charles Stanhope and Pitt went further than most. It soon became obvious that of the two, it was Pitt who was born for a career in politics. Not only was he the more effective speaker and a naturally charismatic politician, he was unshakeably ambitious and ultimately a pragmatist. He always knew when to draw back. Charles, on the other hand, refused to climb down on any issue once he had taken a stand; he would prove both mercurial and unpopular.

Pitt's ascent was spectacular. By the age of twenty-three, he found himself in the new Cabinet as Chancellor of the Exchequer. Shelburne, who preferred to stay in his comfortable house on Berkeley Square, offered Pitt the Downing Street house that had been given by King George II in the 1730s as official residence for the First Lord of the Treasury. (It was one of a row of townhouses; when Pitt moved in, it had only recently been renamed as No. 10.) Around this time Pitt wrote to Charles saying he hoped to visit him at Chevening. 'I trust you will be in town in a very few days, for there are several things in which I am quite at a loss without you.'[13] Whatever Pitt might have wanted to discuss, he evidently relied on Charles's judgement.

On 19 December 1783, the twenty-four-year-old Pitt kissed the King's hand as First Lord of the Treasury and Chancellor of the Exchequer, the youngest Prime Minister in history. Hester, who was then seven, was well aware of the significance of this achievement and the importance of her uncle's position. Pitt moved back to Downing Street, and saw a good deal of the Mahons, who often stayed with him. It was from the Prime Minister's residence, at half past three in the morning on 3 June 1785, that a thrilled Charles wrote to his friend Joseph Banks, informing him that Louisa had just given birth to another boy, and that he would be 'extremely flattered' if he would be the child's godfather.[14] This was Hester's second half-brother, Charles.[15]

To their doting Uncle William, Hester was the tomboy he called 'the Jockey Girl', Griselda was 'the little Book-devourer', Lucy, 'the Beauty'.

It seems that early on, Hester had acquired both her rebellious streak and her ability to present a stalwart face to the world. When she was eight, on a family outing to the beach at Hastings on the Kentish coast, she slipped away unnoticed, clambered aboard a boat and rowed herself out to sea, utterly confident that she would be able to navigate her way to France. The fast current swept her away from the pebbly shore, but she later claimed she had not been frightened, merely amused by the look of pure terror on her governess's face. In her memory, she was always that precocious, self-aware girl, only happy when acting of her own volition.

On his father's death in 1786 Charles became the third Earl Stanhope. As the new Earl his presence in Parliament took on an immediate edge when he disagreed publicly with Pitt over the latter's establishment of a Consolidated Fund to reduce the national debt, arguing with him vociferously and publishing a pamphlet against the scheme, much to the Prime Minister's embarrassment.[16] To his family, it seemed as though almost overnight they were dealing with a different man, one prepared to be openly hostile to his former close friend and ally. There were other changes. He began to criticize his wife's taste in clothes, in the theatre, in friends. He was a hard man to live with, often going into what his family called one of his 'republican fits'. Chastised for the things that gave her pleasure, Louisa quickly lost her bloom, although James, the third and last son, was born in 1788.

Hester recalled once going to find her father at the impeachment trial of Warren Hastings, former Governor of Bengal and Governor-General of India, after he took it upon himself to become an independent observer of the judicial system. (He attended every session religiously; and since proceedings began in February 1788 and lasted until Hastings' acquittal in 1795, this was no small undertaking.) She would recall:

I can recollect, when I was ten or twelve years old, going off to Hastings' trial. My garter somehow came off, and was picked up by Lord Grey, then a young man. At this hour, as if it were before me in a picture, I can see before me his handsome, but very pale face, his broad forehead; his *corbeau* coat, with cut-steel buttons; his white satin waistcoat and breeches; and the buckles in his shoes. He saw from whom the garter fell; but in observing my confusion, did not wish to increase it, and with infinite delicacy gave the garter to the person who sat there to serve tea and coffee.[17]

Hester was on the brink of adolescence already; aware of the power of simply being a young woman. Her father took measures to repress his daughter's budding sexuality, such that Louisa feared that in society the girls would get a reputation as drabs. 'My father,' remembered Hester years later, 'always checked any propensity to finery in dress. If any of us happened to look better than usual in a particular hat or frock, he was sure to have it put away the next day, and to have something coarse substituted in its place.'

Even so, by the time she was twelve, Hester was used to a rather sophisticated life, split between London and the country, along with young Philip, who was known by all now simply as 'Mahon', a name which stuck. She appears to have been her father's favourite 'when he bothered to notice any of them'. Earl Stanhope imposed upon his children a type of education that from today's perspective seems almost guaranteed to create intellectual frustration for an intelligent child. He was determined that his children should, as Rousseau propounded in *Émile*, 'learn nothing from books that experience can teach them', a regime he prescribed until each child was about twelve. He restricted their exposure to books of all sorts, including the Bible and any prayer books, until such time when he judged that 'nature's lessons' had been thoroughly learned. Considering the fact that he was a voracious reader himself, and the possessor of an impressive, highly eclectic library, this was extraordinary.

Any impression that Stanhope ignored his children's education altogether would be false. He made sure they mastered the basics of reading, writing and arithmetic, as well as French, and developed complicated games of logic for them, frequently setting them philosophical problems. Hester seems to be the only one amongst them who responded to this regime; her name for her father was tellingly sarcastic: 'The Logician'. She was painfully aware that not all fathers apprenticed their sons to the local blacksmith in order to teach them humility and the fundamentals of mechanics. Unlike her own mother, who read and wrote Greek, Latin and French by the time she was twelve, Hester – whose intelligence was never in question – unconsciously absorbed the Rousseauian ethos. Hester recalled the rare occasions when she was summoned to her father's study.

> He would turn to me and say, 'Now we must talk a little philosophy,' and then with his two legs stuck up on the sides of the grate, he would begin. 'Well, well,' he would say, after I had talked a little, 'that is not bad reasoning but the basis is bad'. My father, with all his mathematical knowledge, said I was the best logician he ever saw – I could split a hair. 'Talk to the point' was his cry; and I could bring truth to a point as sharp as a needle. The last time he saw me he repeated the same words, and said I had but one fault, which was being too fond of royalty.

From a very early age, she nourished the sense that she was quicker and cleverer than others; physically she was impatient, confident and advanced beyond her years. She did not respond well to petty punishments. She recalled one governess 'had our backs pinched in by boards, that were drawn tight with all the force the maid could use; and as for me, they would have squeezed me to the size of a puny miss – a thing impossible!' Another attempted to reshape her feet, trying to flatten her high instep.

She spent much time bolting about the countryside on horseback and dominating her siblings in a quasi-maternal role. She played pranks on staid Griselda, the most conventional of the girls; taunting her into violent fights, knocking over furniture and leaving them both scratched and bruised. Guitar and voice lessons were acceptable to the young Hester. 'The first amuses her and the latter I hope will be of use to me in softening her voice,' Grizel commented. Perhaps because of her father's restrictions, Hester rebelled by being ever alert to the latest fashions.* 'She has a very good taste for dress; but one of her jokes is to overdo the

---

* Writing in 1793 of what he termed 'the era of Jacobinism', Sir Nathaniel Wraxall noted 'it was then that pantaloons, cropt hair, and shoestrings as well as the total abolition of buckles and ruffles, together with the disuse of hair powder, characterised men, while the ladies, having cut off those tresses which had done so much execution, exhibited heads rounded *à la victime et à la guillotine*, as if ready for the stroke of the axe'.

fashion in something or other when she comes to me, to amuse me or make me laugh,' Grizel wrote to Lady Chatham.[18] As she entered adolescence, it seems Hester liked to charm and shock in equal measure.

When the Bastille was stormed on 14 July 1789, Earl Stanhope was jubilant. Many admired the way in which the French people had revolted in the name of liberty. Stanhope's idealistic fervour for the principles of the Revolution intensified; he was instrumental in forming the Revolution Society, and was a natural choice as chairman. He determined to divest himself of his peerage and signed all his correspondence as 'Citizen Stanhope'. He ordered that the armorial bearings be taken down from Chevening's gates, much to the disgust of the servants. His speeches in support of the revolutionaries, and his *Letter to Burke*, his refutation to the man the French regarded as the Englishman most antagonistic to their Revolution, quickly translated and distributed, carried his name into the remotest corners of France. The teenage Hester must have been aware that for many French people, her renegade aristocratic father's name meant more even than Pitt's or Chatham's.

Fear that London mobs might follow the example from across the Channel began to grow. At first, Pitt's attitude was measured; although he evinced some sympathy for its early reforms, events swiftly moved to harden his heart: the mounting radicalism of the Jacobins, and news of the grisly butchering of priests and prisoners in France, caused him and many others who had previously been supportive to feel revulsion for the *sans-culottes*. Despite this, Earl Stanhope believed France would remain true to the virtues of liberty and equality. From that autumn, he and his former brother-in-law would regard one another as little better than enemies.

## 2

### The Minority of One

As the French Revolution raged, everyone in London knew about 'Citizen Stanhope'. He was mercilessly lampooned in satirizing cartoons by Gillray, who enjoyed depicting him as an emaciated, wine-drinking sozzle-head rallying cockade-wearing mobs, usually with an equally emaciated, vexed-looking Pitt lurking about in the background.

As far as the Stanhope children were concerned, their father the freedom-lover was a domestic tyrant. Hester began to mimic him; demanding that her siblings never enter a room unless they first sent a servant to ask whether they could be admitted. She disapproved of her father's many 'republican' measures, such as doing away with the carriage and horses his wife had relied upon to ferry her about. Louisa reacted with predictable exasperation. By then the relationship between them was becoming irretrievable. Hester went to elaborate lengths to keep the peace. In her own words:

Poor Lady Stanhope was quite unhappy about it: but when the whole family was looking glum and sulky, I thought of a way to set it all right again. I got myself a pair of stilts, and out I stumped along a dirty lane, where my father, who was always spying about through his glass, could see me.

So when I came home he said to me:

'Why little girl, what have you been about? Where was it I saw you going upon a pair of – the devil knows what? – eh, girl?'

'Oh! Papa, I thought, as you had laid down your horses, I would take

30

a walk through the mud on stilts, for you know Papa, I don't mind mud or anything – 'tis poor Lady Stanhope who minds these things, for she has always been very accustomed to her carriage, and her health is not very good.'

'What's that you say, little girl,' said my father, turning his eyes away from me, and after a pause, 'Well little girl, what say you if I brought a carriage again for Lady Stanhope?'

'Why papa, I would say it was very kind of you.'

'Well, well,' he observed, 'we will see; but damm it! No armorial bearings.'

So, some time afterwards, down came a new carriage and new horses from London, and thus by a little innocent frolic I made all parties happy again.[1]

Hester makes her father sound quite acceptably human, not at all a monster, and goodhearted beneath his somewhat autocratic exterior. Despite her claim, her ruse did not alter the growing coolness between her father and Louisa, whom all the children called 'Mama'. Hester was old enough to observe cracks in the marriage and noted that 'we children saw neither one nor the other'. It was usually Grizel who watched over the girls as they dressed for local balls and dances. 'The Three Graces', as she called them, were often up 'all night, at least until five . . . dancing their hearts out'. But Grizel noted that Stanhope regularly took his daughters 'some sixteen miles over the heavy Kent roads, waits patiently . . . and return[s] at seven in the morning'.[2] He did this several times a week over the winter 'season', for at least three years. It is hardly the picture of an unloving father.

Acutely aware of her father's embarrassing behaviour, Hester's letters are primarily concerned with finding creative ways around his restrictions on her movements. Unlike most daughters of her generation, Stanhope was doing his best to discourage her from having anything to do with families he thought too 'aristocratical' or 'too bourgeois society'. To her closest friend from this time, Evelyn St Clare, Hester complained about his guests. He spent much of his time with Varley, his great ally and friend, and the blacksmith to whom he apprenticed his sons. 'Oh defend me from Citizens and Philosophers if this is the life they lead.' But she was also proud of her father's brilliance.

Hester came of age in the 1790s, a time of revolutionary enthusiasm and political agitation that created a generation of thinkers, poets and artists. But it also ushered in a new wave of repression in Britain, for which her uncle Pitt was directly responsible. He feared civil strife, whether it stemmed from revolutionaries, anarchists or reactionary 'Church and King' mobs. Pitt regarded societies like the Revolution Society, and the Corresponding Societies, which by now had acquired hundreds of members, especially in the industrial centres of the north and in Scotland, as a particular threat.

Unconcerned, Earl Stanhope forged strong ties with many of the Revolution's loftier theorists, notably the Marquis de Condorcet, the mathematician and Revolutionary martyr, whom Stanhope felt to be his true brother-in-arms, and the Duc de La Rochefoucauld.* Stanhope's pacifist views were well known to these Frenchmen, as was his desire to see France and England 'united by indissoluble bonds'.†

Hester was almost seventeen when Louis XVI was guillotined. Although reluctantly drawn into war, Pitt was of the widely-held opinion that this could only be a limited conflict. In fact, the conflict between the tradi-tional foes would ultimately last, short intervals aside, for twenty-two years. Even Pitt's great rival Charles James Fox, who had condemned the 'madness' of the war, conceded that the French regime had taken on a criminal nature. Under Robespierre and the Jacobins, political prisoners of all backgrounds – out-of-favour Girondins and generals as well as

* Condorcet would go on to inspire one of the most enduring achievements of the Revolutionary period, the founding of the scientific Institut de France, which replaced the Old Regime's Académie des Sciences and prestigious Académie Française, which would not be revived until 1815. His friendship with Earl Stanhope was indeed close; he asked the Englishman to become a guardian to his child in the event of his arrest and execution.
† When, in February 1792, Talleyrand – who would go on to become Napoleon's Foreign Minister – came to London seeking support for the cause, he went directly to the famous Earl, hoping he might act as a mediator with Pitt. It was no good: Pitt curtly ignored them both. Despite this, for the duration of his stay, Talleyrand was the toast of London's leading revolutionary sympa-thizers and Dissenters. Stanhope made sure Hester accompanied him to a dinner held in Talleyrand's honour in Hackney. No doubt he thought she could benefit by observing that not all revolution-aries were unwashed rabble.

Marie Antoinette – had been sent to the ever-clattering guillotine. Walpole wrote that its 'horrors make one abhor Lord Stanhope and his priestly firebrands' and derided his pronouncements as the 'ravings of a lunatic, imagining he could set the world on fire with phosphorus'.

Over the next few years, the 'White Terror' unleashed by Pitt would suspend constitutional freedoms, such as habeas corpus, and introduce the Treason and Sedition Act, the Unlawful Oaths Act and the Corresponding Societies Act. Determined to prevent any incitement to revolution, he instituted gagging measures such as the banning of public meetings, and employed indeterminate numbers of spies and informers. Hundreds of those deemed seditious would be arrested; many houses of Dissenters and Unitarians attacked and burnt.[3] Stanhope was among those whose letters and communiqués were routinely intercepted and read. Although Pitt's popularity sank – he was despised and pilloried in the radical press – he succeeded in consolidating power among the splintered Whigs. Indeed, his grip on Parliament during those repressive times would never be stronger.

By 1794 it would have been impossible for Hester to ignore the fact that her father was rapidly becoming a political pariah. Many on both sides in the House shunned his zealous views. But he was not merely a contrarian. A fierce champion of democracy, a pacifist and a republican, he saw himself as one of the few men in Parliament motivated by his conscience alone. For that reason, he adopted with particular pride the title 'The Minority of One', and even had a medal struck in his own honour.* Around this time, Coleridge wrote a poem, *To Earl Stanhope*.

But where Stanhope saw encroaching darkness, many of his fellow peers looked at him and saw precisely what Pitt warned them against, one of an emerging breed, a viperous 'British Jacobin'. Stanhope's exhortations not to interfere in the internal affairs of France appeared distinctly unpatriotic.

Pitt decided that his tolerance had been stretched far enough. He made a string of arrests. One of them was the Reverend Jeremiah Joyce, employed by Stanhope as his secretary and tutor for his two elder boys. Joyce was

---

* In January 1795, Lord Stanhope's vote was recorded as being 'in the minority of one', after the House was divided 61–1 against his second protest at the interference in the internal affairs of France; the one being himself.

seized at Chevening, in front of the gawping Stanhope children.* That same night Stanhope was woken by a large crowd outside his house at 20 Mansfield Street, who at first shouted insults, then began breaking windows and throwing torches. Hester remembered her father telling them how he was forced to make his escape over the roof while the mob jeered. Stanhope was convinced the crowd had been paid to incite violence against him – even to cause his death. But this served to increase his radical activities.

Hester was torn between childhood pride in her father, whom she had always more or less sought to please, and the gnawing sense that ominous repercussions were about to fall on all their heads because of him. She enjoyed the notoriety of knowing clever radicals like the clergyman Horne Tooke. 'I am an aristocrat,' she told an amused Tooke, 'and I make a boast of it'. When she told Tooke, 'I hate a pack of dirty Jacobins that only want to get people out of a good place to get into it themselves,' he roared with laughter, and had to admit she had a point.

But now Horne Tooke, like Jeremiah Joyce, was imprisoned in the Tower.† Stanhope did his utmost to lobby on behalf of his imprisoned friends – Joyce, Hardy and Tooke among them – all of whom faced certain death if found guilty of high treason. Hester worried that if her father were arrested the same fate would await him.

Disgusted with political life, Stanhope would resign from the House of Lords by the end of the year. Two days before Christmas, to celebrate Joyce's acquittal, in which he played no small role, Stanhope staged a grand ball at Chevening, inviting more than four hundred guests for dancing and feasting. He hoped to please Hester by making this her unofficial coming-out party. She was, her grandmother commented, 'looking incomparably well'. How pleased she was to dance with the bumpkinish sons of local squires around a centrepiece display of life-size mannequins meant to depict prisoners being unchained, under a large banner emblazoned with 'The Rights of Juries', was not recorded.

---

* Jeremiah Joyce had been amongst a band of English and American expatriates drawn to Paris in the winter of 1792, hopeful that the tide would soon turn, and that revolution would come to England. He was a member of both the Society for Constitutional Information and the LCS.
† Horne Tooke was one of the most celebrated radicals to be arrested; his memoirs were a best-seller.

Hester would look back upon this as a happy period. She was closer to Louisa now that she was of age, and theoretically in search of a husband, while her stepmother was grateful for any excuse to escape hers. There were visits to Bath and to Louisa's Grenville relatives in London. 'Every amusement that riding, visiting &c. can produce, they have had without interruption, and which the uncommon strength of Hester bears most amazingly, for none can keep up with her,' wrote Grizel, apparently missing the irony that while her son would sooner see the monarchy dispatched, her granddaughter insisted it was her duty to attend a ball celebrating the Prince of Wales's birthday.

In 1795, Hester heard that another notorious prisoner at Newgate, the self-declared millennial prophet Richard Brothers, had asked to see her. It would have been easy to dismiss Brothers as a raving lunatic; he was, after all, about to be transferred to Bedlam. Although arrested on charges of sedition, he had been found criminally insane. He had declared himself to be a prophet, the 'nephew of the Almighty, descendant of David and ruler of the world'. Brothers informed her that she was among a select group of people he believed would play a profound role in the 'future Kingdom'. He himself would be the future King, he told her, and she was a chosen one, destined to be the 'Queen of the Jews'. One day, he informed her, she would 'go to Jerusalem and lead back the chosen people; that, on her arrival in the Holy Land, mighty changes would take place in the world and that she would pass seven years in the desert' before her destiny revealed itself to her.

Hester mentioned her visit to Brothers in somewhat scathing terms to Horne Tooke. He teased her that he and his colleagues intended to establish 'a new hospital for the diseases of the mind' and that she was to be placed in charge of it, 'for nobody knows so well as you how to cure them'. It was true that, at nineteen, Hester had every reason to congratulate herself on being the possessor of a formidably shrewd, even intimidating intellect, able to spar with many of the sharpest wits of the period.

She cannot have failed to be impressed by her father's unusually fertile mind. He was fascinated more than anything by clever mechanics and by the power that might be harnessed through the invention of ships that could be self-propelled. The design of docks, canals and bridges obsessed him to an equal degree; he saw a future driven by steam.

Throughout Hester's childhood, Earl Stanhope worked on his great dream, to create a workable steamship; he designed several modest prototypes which he tested out on Chevening's small lake, and on the Thames. As soon as Watt's steam engine appeared, Stanhope tried to apply the new technology, experimenting for a decade with various ingenious but cumbersome designs. Soon he had a flotilla of boats, including his pride and joy, the 111-foot *Kent*, the 'Stanhope Ambi-Navigator', which weighed over 200 tons even before it was fitted out with its heavy steam engines and boilers.*

In the end, the *Kent* would neither win Stanhope his elusive dream, nor bring his family the satisfaction of seeing him publicly honoured. The sailing trials were delayed, first by the Navy Board, and then by the Admiralty itself. John Leard, the Admiralty-appointed commander of the *Kent*, was the first to alert Stanhope somewhat apologetically that there were those who would prefer that he did not succeed. 'I have two charges,' he wrote, 'to shew their unwillingness to attend to anything belonging to the *Kent*. But it was all leveled at your Lordship. They are afraid of you.'[4]

Stanhope must have known that conservatism and hostility towards innovations at the Navy Board were hardly new. To many of the Admiralty Lords, new technology, no matter how exciting, could be a potential threat to comfortable financial arrangements and contracts.† Orders were given to remove the ship's steam engine. Stanhope was incensed.

It was Pitt's revenge, or so it must have seemed. The Admiralty removed

---

* The Admiralty, whom Earl Stanhope had sufficiently intrigued to part-finance the *Kent* (on which he had already spent £8,000 of his own money), were waiting to see whether the ship could live up to the claims of its inventor, although they had pronounced steam navigation 'a wild scheme'. Still, the newly-formed Society for the Improvement of Naval Architecture was so impressed by the *Kent* they made Stanhope one of their vice-presidents.

† Scientific shipbuilding in Britain was then practically non-existent. When the *Kent* finally sailed from Deptford on 22 February 1797, reaching Chatham on 1 March, the crew had been placed under instructions not to use the boilers; only Stanhope's 'vibrators' or oars were tested and they were hand-operated and employed only to ferry the ship downstream from Deptford. The official report on the *Kent*'s performance seems to have been a thinly-veiled stitch-up; ostensibly praising the ship for its speed and weatherability, but evaluating it as though it were an ordinary vessel. By finding one elaborate reason after another not to witness it performing under steam, they would not be in a position to comment on it. The Kafkaesque farce that ensued lasted until the end of the decade. Nor could Stanhope take his invention elsewhere; the deal he had signed with the Admiralty meant they owned the ship's bond, while he remained responsible for many of its expenses. Finally he was curtly informed that 'an invention of this kind could never be applied to any advantageous purpose in His Majesty's Navy'.

the unused boilers and refitted her as a gun-vessel, but soon the Navy Board had their way, and had her broken up.* To Stanhope, it was as though all his early promise and his scientific genius had been betrayed: it was perhaps the most crushing of all blows.†

Early in January 1796, Hester's sixteen-year-old sister Lucy eloped; it seems she was already pregnant. The man in question, Tom Taylor, was a pleasant-looking twenty-seven-year-old apothecary who had been living quietly in Sevenoaks, until catching sight of Lucy. Before she fled, Lucy left a note for Hester, the only person she believed she could trust, counting on her not to raise the alarm, and hopefully to delay telling their father. Hester turned to Pitt, who was only too aware of the lasting shame the elopement could bring upon the family, and after his intervention, Lucy returned with her suitor and meekly asked for her father's permission to marry.

Whatever Stanhope gave Lucy as dowry, it was not enough to stop Taylor from accepting a highly prestigious position offered to him by Pitt, that of Comptroller General in the Customs Service. He had few qualifications for the job but Pitt assessed that he had an excellent brain, and would thrive quickly, which seems to have been the case. This sinecure in a government he loathed greatly angered Stanhope. Lucy, with a measure of her sister's defiance, refused to bow to his pressure that Taylor should not take the job. An angry estrangement ensued. It was to become a familiar Stanhope pattern.

---

* Stanhope's next invention was the Stanhope *Weatherer*, which he believed would be the 'perfect' frigate, but the Commissioners were as disparaging as before. Yet in 1816, the year Stanhope died, a Captain Tuckey would sail out on a mission to explore the Congo in a new vessel built for the purpose by the shipbuilder Seppings. Called the *Congo*, it was acknowledged officially as being almost identical in design to the *Weatherer*. Not long afterwards, the design for the *Congo* won the government stamp of approval; and Seppings's ship became almost universally adopted by the merchant service. And so, the ghost of Stanhope's *Weatherer* found its way into countless ports in far-off lands after all.
† Stanhope was perhaps too inventive for his own good. Still, several enduring inventions bear his name. The Stanhope printing press, for which he pioneered a process of stereotyping designed to reduce costs, was later acquired by the Clarendon Press at Oxford, along with his system of logotypes. The Stanhope lens, a small but powerful microscopic lens, was the only invention of his that achieved widespread commercial success during his lifetime. Many of Stanhope's designs – from his calculating machines ('The Stanhope Demonstrator, an Instrument for performing Logical Operations') to his steam-powered vessels, as well as his innovations for canal construction – using a system of inclined planks and improved locks – would ultimately be perfected by others.

Later that year, Hester caused her own sensation, appearing alone at Lord Romney's military review. It was the most spectacular event held in Kent in 1796, staged to celebrate Pitt's government's successful raising of volunteers – six thousand in that county alone – who would parade and perform splendid feats dressed in their brand-new regimentals; fencing; charging across the field to swipe the heads off turnips with their swords; and marching before a crowd of landowning families; a grand feast would be held in a tented encampment. As well as Pitt, the King and Queen were there; and their sons, the Duke of York, then commander of the British army, the Duke of Sussex, the Duke of Clarence and the future Duke of Kent.

To Hester, who adored pomp, horses and dancing, and the sight of soldiers, the lure was obvious. Her father was equally determined that neither she nor the rest of the family should go; one corrupted daughter was quite enough.* The matter of getting there would prove more difficult than Lucy's elopement; not least because Hester had to borrow both a carriage and something suitably elegant to wear. She found her first taste of freedom glorious. The fact that she was un-chaperoned was held to be highly improper. By the time Pitt arrived, she was something of a celebrity.

According to Hester, the King teased out of her stories of her father's eccentricities. He took it into his head that she must be rescued, and carried back to Windsor to be made part of the Court.† Hester might have been willing, but Queen Charlotte did not seem enthusiastic. Nonetheless this marked the beginning of Hester's firm friendship with the princes, of whom she would later say: 'I loved all the princes, all, except George the Fourth – they were all so lively, so good-natured; people who would laugh at a straw.'

---

* Stanhope's distaste for the royal family was by then shared by large numbers of British citizens. The previous year, at the height of his unpopularity, on his way to the House of Lords in October 1795, the King's coach was pelted with stones amid cries of 'Down with George!'
† King George III habitually appointed women he liked or admired to the Court, a sinecure viewed as a form of social advancement for women of the middle classes. Between 1786 and 1791, the writer Fanny Burney was employed as Second Keeper of the Robes to Queen Charlotte; for which she was given an apartment at Windsor, a maid and footman to attend her and £200 a year. Her only duties were to help the Queen select her outer garments and to make witty conversation, but she found the position socially humiliating and stifling.

She was certainly ready to be noticed. When she was much older, she had an acute sense of what her beauty had once been:

At twenty, my complexion was like alabaster; and at five paces distance the sharpest eye could not discover my pearl necklace from my skin; my lips were of such a beautiful carnation, that without vanity, I assure you very few women had the like. A dark blue under the eyes, and the blue veins that were observable through the transparent skin, heightened the brilliancy of my features. Nor were the roses wanting in my cheeks; and to all this was added a permanency to my looks that no fatigue could impair.[5]

Until the sudden scandal with Lucy, Pitt had become quite remote from her; now the ice was broken. She made him laugh with a quip about his dog, who had made it into the gossip pages of *The Morning Post and Fashionable World*.* In contrast to her unorthodox father, he must have seemed the model of decisiveness and stability. 'I thought it was better to be where I should have Mr Pitt at my side to help me, should he get into great difficulty.' It would not be long before her uncle would come to be her touchstone for all important matters.

'She had on a costume, which had nothing feminine about it, but the mask. She seemed very tall, very thin, very decided, very independent.'[6] This is how the Duchesse de Gontant, a fashionable refugee from Paris, described Hester, meeting her at a masked ball in London around this time. These were rare qualities for a woman of twenty. Hester now made it her mission to get away from Chevening as much as possible. Her father relented under the barrage of her willpower and energy. Her grandmothers were anxious; the matter of whom she might marry was a pressing one. From them, the nod was given to Pitt to see that she was chaperoned when she was in London. This would be a thankless task, as society hostesses Mrs Pole and Lady Clarendon found out. 'Don't bother

---

* Pitt had, that year, vexed squires across the land by the introduction of his tax on both dogs and hair-powder; although the fashion for the latter waned virtually overnight, the Englishman's attachment to his dog remained. Hester is said to have joked that Pitt's great hound at Holwood was so fat it should be taxed twice.

yourself about me; I am quite independent,' she smiled at them, shocking them with her announcement that she was capable of making her own introductions. The Comtesse de Boigne, who met her *en passant*, observed she was 'well-made' and 'fond of society, of dancing, and of any public function. She was something of a flirt . . . with ideas of striking originality', although she noted dryly, 'for a Stanhope, she was prudence itself'.[7]

Hester's risk-taking instinct came to the fore. As far as she could see, in the wealthiest and most privileged circles, it was never enough to have merely good breeding and a title. Wit was what was prized above all, and she did her best to flaunt her own. With Pitt taking her part, Hester felt secure enough to be cleverly irreverent. She thought the Duchess of Rutland's parties were a 'heavy, dull business . . . all high breeding and *bon ton*'. As for the Duchess of Devonshire's, 'there they were, all that set, all yawning and wanting the evening to be spent, that they might be getting to the business they were after'.[8] But Pitt did not wish Hester to be overly exposed to the 'business' she glibly refers to – bed-hopping; heavy drinking, whoring, juggling lines of credit and gambling away vast amounts late into the night. In the end, he took on the role of chaperone himself. He 'remained with infinite kindness until four or five o'clock in the morning at balls which wearied him to distraction', wrote the Comtesse de Boigne of Hester's introduction to London society that year. 'I have often seen him sitting in a corner, waiting with exemplary patience until Lady Hester should be pleased to end his sufferings.'[9]

By softening to the Stanhope tribe, Pitt may well have wondered what he had taken on. Griselda also turned to him, announcing her intention to marry John Tickell, an army officer from Hampshire. Earl Stanhope likened himself to King Lear; deserted by his daughters. But Hester, still semi-loyal to her father as well as her brothers, continued to return home, and when in London, to stay at Mansfield Street. There was in any case a well-established overlap between Pitt's world and Stanhope's, the fashionable world mingling with the radical elite. But Pitt, to a modest extent, had begun to subsidize Hester's adventures.

By the time she was twenty-three, Hester had danced at ball after ball and dined on champagne and turtle all over town. Toasts were proposed to her beauty, much was made of her 'magnificent and majestic figure' and the way 'roses and lilies were blended in [her] face', and the way she 'diffused happiness around [her]'.[10] She had many admirers. Two men in particular, however, stood out.

George Bryan ('Beau') Brummell was the most fashionable man in London. Society hostesses sent him fawning invitations; even though he habitually ignored them for the most part, talked only to his friends and refused to dance. Here, finally, was someone Hester could share the latest intrigue with and count on to draw her away from any tedium. Hester laughed at his jokes, discussed horses with him (he named his favourite Stiletto) and adored his outrageous behaviour.* She affected some of his rebellious style, and paid ever greater attention to her dress. It is fairly certain Hester never seriously considered Brummell as a romantic prospect, nor vice versa. Nonetheless, a strong chemistry between them was noticed, and there was speculation she was in love, at least a little. He came up to her at a dinner and coolly took out her earrings in front of everyone, telling her they could not match the beauty of her skin, and spoiled the delicate line of her face. Brummell's anarchic charm came as a heady relief to a fun-starved Hester.

It was the other man who appeared in Hester's life who seemed to promise the possibility of a serious attachment. Thomas Pitt, Lord Camelford, Baron of Boconnoc, was her cousin, a year older than her. When she met him at a family dinner shortly before Christmas 1799, she had not seen him since they were both infants. His looks were fierce and wild; he was six foot two inches tall, powerfully muscled and dark. He was the sole heir to the Camelford fortune, and the owner of vast estates in Cornwall and Dorset, as well as a palatial London mansion, with an income of more than £20,000 a year (roughly £1 million in today's money).†

From the start, it looked as though history might repeat itself; the Pitts and the Stanhopes destined to find their way to one another once

---

* 'Brummell would commit . . . freaks at the house of parvenus, or people who were not exactly of *haut ton*, where, sometimes at dinner, he would all of a sudden make horrible ludicrous grimaces, as if he had found a hair in his soup, or would abruptly ask for some strange Palmyrene sauce, or any out of the way name that nobody ever heard of, and then pretend he could not eat his soup without it,' Hester remembered of his outrageous behaviour. Palmyra was evidently a topic of conversation even then.
† Camelford House, fronting Oxford Street, near Park Lane, which had been built for the 1st Baron of Camelford, was demolished in 1913 to make way for a 'cinematograph palace'.

again. She would say she 'admired Lord C's character, and in some things, imitated him'. He was, she said, 'a true Pitt, and like me, his blood fired at a fraud or a bad action'. Camelford was notorious. He was known for having shot a fellow Royal Navy officer, apparently in cold blood, and his life was a tangle of duels and skirmishes. He had a sailor's taste for prize-fighting, and was often seen at the ring. He was a connoisseur of pistols and swords. If anyone introduced Hester to her later love of weaponry and to the art of the duel, it was him. She certainly took up both passions at this time with an unusual relish. Not many men would have been willing to show a young woman how to fight, but Camelford was.

It was obvious that Camelford was hell-bent on doing something extraordinary. He was already the veteran of remarkable travels, notching up exploits as far away as Chile, Malacca and Ceylon, and having landed at Madras, had sailed to the Red Sea and crossed the desert from Suez to Alexandria. He felt a rivalry with their mutual cousin, Captain Sidney Smith, who months before had defeated Napoleon at Acre. They both knew what the Emperor had famously fumed about Smith: 'That man made me miss my destiny.' Smith was a hard act to follow, but Camelford had every expectation that he would find a way to out-do him.

At the beginning of 1799, Camelford had been arrested on a shingle beach in Deal for trying to cross the Channel on a smuggling boat, then a prosecutable offence. He had on him nothing but some money, a pair of pistols, a short, two-edged dagger, and a letter of introduction in French to Paul Barras, considered by the Pitt administration to be the most shrewd and unscrupulous of Napoleon's advisers. A discreet royal pardon was given, on condition he resign his captaincy in the navy, a terrible humiliation. Speculation remained rife that Camelford, who spoke flawless French, intended to infiltrate himself into France and offer himself as a turncoat intelligence agent, a role that he hoped might bring him close to Barras – or Napoleon himself. The *London Chronicle* reported that he had 'been prompted by a too ardent desire to perform some feat of desperation, by which, he thought, the cause of Europe might be served' – in other words, a political assassination.

Hester appears to have been struck with admiration for her danger-seeking, intrigue-loving cousin. The attraction was mutual. She is widely credited as being the only woman he loved, aside from his beautiful sister, Anne. Soon after meeting her, he moved into a bachelor apartment, first on Baker Street, near Pitt's house, then to New Bond Street.

Another clue that reveals Camelford's feelings for Hester was his sudden appearance at the House of Lords, alongside the equally conspicuous Earl Stanhope, returned after a five-year absence. The House was debating Pitt's and Lord Grenville's rejection of Napoleon's Christmas Day offer to negotiate peace. On 28 January 1800, Earl Stanhope, along with a small group in the Opposition, cast his vote to express disapproval, while Lord Grenville reiterated the administration's position. The vote, 92 to 6, was unsurprising. What baffled everyone there was the fact that Camelford voted with the Opposition, for despite his erratic attendance in the House, Camelford had always voted reliably for Pitt and Grenville. The following day, after Stanhope made a speech to the Lords 'on his knees' to reconsider, the House divided once more. This time, Stanhope found only one other peer willing to take sides with him: Camelford. Hester's father was not pleased to find himself supported: minority of two had no triumph to it. 'Why!' he harrumphed to Camelford afterwards, 'you spoiled that division!'[11] If Camelford had wanted some measure of Hester's father's approval, he certainly did not get it.

The following month Camelford challenged one of his closest friends to a duel over Hester. Camelford was charged with grievous assault, but before it could go to the courts, which would have meant the explicit revelation of the details of the slight, the matter was quietly disposed of by a cash settlement.[12]

Pitt put his foot down. Hester was ordered back to Chevening. Whatever liberty her father might have allowed her in the past, he now curtailed. They were now all locked in at night. Hester alternately raged and moped, protesting at her own lack of freedom and at her father's treatment of her brothers. Mahon was then eighteen, his movements far more circumscribed than Hester's had ever been. He bitterly resented that he had not been sent to school nor prepared for university. As for Hester's middle brother Charles, she was shocked to see he 'could hardly write legibly' and 'cannot spell three words'.[13] None of them was remotely equipped to 'shift for themselves'.

Earl Stanhope was determined to dissolve his hereditary privileges, but this could only be achieved if Mahon agreed to break his entailment once he had reached his majority, in other words to sign away his inheritance. Stanhope, whose expenditure on his various experiments now amounted to many tens of thousands of pounds, was growing short of funds. He wanted eventually to sell Chevening, and was prepared to barter with his eldest son over a suitable lump sum if he complied.

On her return to Chevening early in the spring of 1800, Hester wrote to her older married friend Evelyn. 'I want to ask advice about an unfortunate woman who was my playfellow and whose faults and misfortunes have given me great concern . . . I am too inexperienced to know how to act.'[14] Might she possibly have been asking for advice for herself, and needing to conceal her own difficulties? It is not clear.

Hester later claimed that Ann Fry, a young chambermaid at Chevening, came to her in tears. She was pregnant. A house where the girl could spend her confinement was quietly arranged. The fact that her child would be baptized at the village church later that year despite her stubborn silence about who had fathered the child is intriguing, for the church rarely gave charity to unmarried mothers and their illegitimate children; a chaplain's first task was always to establish the identity of the father, who might contribute to the child's keep.[15] In light of Hester's later remarks and her own material support for the girl, the possibility that her father, or one of her brothers, may have been responsible cannot be overlooked.

Whatever the cause, around this time, some kind of violent confrontation occurred between Hester and her father. He lost his temper and pinned her to the wall, threatening her with a dagger. 'The Logician often has said that from the hour I was born I have been a stranger to fear. I certainly felt no fear when he held a knife to my throat – only pity for the arm that held it; but this was a feeling I should rather not again experience . . .'[16] She fled as soon as she could, taking little with her, and promising her brothers she would do what she could to help them. Camelford pressed her to stay with their uncle and aunt, Lord and Lady Chatham, at their St James's home; Pitt was drawn into the debate about who should take care of the runaway. His initial reaction is revealing; he worried that Hester might be untameable, and might bring scandal with her. 'Under no circumstances could I offer her a home in my own house,' he wrote at the time. Recovering from raw shock, Hester wrote to her grandmother, the Dowager Chatham:

> It had hitherto been my fate to lead the strangest, as well as the most unforgettable life . . . I shall therefore gladly profit by this occasion to improve my mind, terribly neglected, and recover that flow of spirits natural to me but which a constant state of anxiety has rendered very unequal . . . It would be my wish when brought into society to *appear* as happy as I naturally might feel from the kindness of my uncles, but the heartfelt gratitude I feel towards them would at this moment rather serve to give me a contrary appearance for I should unavoidably be led to draw comparisons between their conduct and that which I have been used to, painful reflections must of course follow, but this will shortly wear off when the treatment I have been in the habit of receiving is less pressed in my mind.[17]

It is not clear whether Hester believed herself to be in love with Camelford, but she certainly saw a good deal of him that year. Despite his brush with the law, Camelford was regarded as a great catch. It was around this time, at a society gathering, that Hester met Lady Henrietta (Harriet) Bessborough, and she noted what the older woman made of her cousin, how he had 'such delightful manners, such fascinating conversation, how charming, irresistible and well-bred' he was. Hester and Camelford were sighted openly together a great deal – at plays, the opera, riding in St James's Park, but more often on long excursions alone together to the countryside in his carriage, apparently making it a particular game to keep everyone in suspense, especially the Chathams. 'How frightened Lady Chatham was for fear he should marry me!' Hester recalled. Later, she described her behaviour around this time as 'wild and reckless'. Their association was intense for at least eight months, and her wanderings with him took her as far as his estate at Boconnoc in Cornwall, where, if they wished it, they might have become lovers.[18]

Camelford suddenly transformed himself from being rather scruffy into something of a dandy. He looked like a man who had taken a sweetheart's comment that he smarten himself up to mean that he should buy himself a new set of clothes from every fashionable tailor on Jermyn Street. But he kept his old brown coat, which he always wore with the collar turned up to his ears, and a slouch hat for one of his habits, apparently known only to Hester and his lawyer: do-gooding around the fleshpots and slums of Seven Dials, Southwark and Wapping. He would sometimes prowl these areas in disguise and press large sums of cash into the hands of those whose stories particularly affected him. He put £5,000 aside each year for his lawyer to distribute among the poor.

Hester appears to have influenced him to do things he would otherwise not have done. At her urging, Camelford approached Horne Tooke, with the suggestion that he put him forward as candidate for Old Sarum, Diamond Pitt's famous 'rotten borough', located on land in Wiltshire he now owned. It was a move calculated to unnerve Earl Stanhope, who would be forced to concede that by bringing Tooke to Westminster, his daughter's would-be suitor pulled off the coup of drawing attention to the very man whose cause he once championed, while at the same time showing up the scandalous loophole in the unreformed parliamentary system.[19] There were dinners with Sir Francis Burdett, a rich radical politician friend of her father's, who sympathized with Hester's determination to ensure that her half-brother Mahon would not be strong-armed into surrendering his inheritance.

It was then that Hester devised a careful escape plan for Mahon, for which she secured Pitt's approval. With the pledge of money from Burdett and another of her father's former friends, William Lowther, the second Earl of Lonsdale, and the help of an urbane young diplomat, Francis James Jackson, Hester obtained a passport and letters of credit for Mahon, and recommendations that would ensure his acceptance for study at Erlangen University. She contrived a waiting carriage, and advised the time-honoured trick of using tied-together, twisted sheets to descend from a high bedroom window. Mahon's successful escape early in 1801 caused a lifelong rift, not just with her father but also her grandmother Grizel, who bitterly blamed Hester for fomenting and publicizing family tensions.

Hester was perturbed only by the thought that her father might take his fury out on the 'remaining captives', Charles and James, whom she feared might be 'flogged to death to make them confess what they are really ignorant [of]'. She would hear that Louisa too had reached breaking point, and would soon demand a separation.

For much of 1801, Hester came and went to London freely, while staying at the Pitt family home at Burton Pynsent in Somerset, where her grandmother left her free to do much as she liked, riding 'at least twenty miles a day, and often forty'. She would be remembered from this time 'as the intrepid girl who used to break in her friend's vicious horses for them'.[20]

By now Hester was the same age as her mother when she died. Although mindful of the freedom her unmarried state gave her, she was certainly aware that everyone close to her was anxious she make a good match. But she seems to have been reluctant.

She had suitors, including a wealthy landowner's son, 'Mr Methuen of Corsham', with whom she danced repeatedly at the Assembly Rooms during the 1801 season in Bath, but turned them down. Something of her defiance for the institution – any institution – of courtship and marriage is revealed by a remark she made around this time to Jackson. 'I have been going to be married fifty times in my life; said to have been married half as often, and run away with once. But provided I have my own way, the world may have theirs and welcome.'

On 5 February 1801 Pitt formally resigned over the King's refusal to grant Catholic emancipation, after a term as Prime Minister that had lasted for seventeen years. Overnight, Pitt was no longer the invulnerable creature Hester had grown accustomed to. He was £45,000 in debt and faced bankruptcy; he was 'very unwell . . . gouty and nervous'. He declined the King's offer to pay his debts, but he would accept a personal loan put up by a circle of his friends, including Wilberforce. Hester's chance to repay her uncle's kindness would come later that year.

She appears to have been as astonished as everyone else when Camelford disappeared at the end of October 1801, shortly after the announcement that war with France was at an end, although she suspected where he might have gone. She would soon write to her friend Jackson, now British Minister in Paris, asking if he knew anything. 'If I may ask a question of you, how is Lord Camelford? I

47

like him better than people do in general, and am anxious about him, after the strange reports I have heard, but do not answer if you do not like it.'[21]

Almost immediately, she began to prepare her own plans for departure, something that was unthinkable without being accompanied. She hoped to meet with Mahon – and perhaps Camelford. Whom she petitioned for funds is not known – she had no money of her own. She chose a stolid, elderly and well-connected couple, the Egertons, who planned to leave, although not until the following spring. 'You may wonder why I have not fixed upon more dashing persons for companions . . .' she wrote to Jackson. 'I shall have perfect liberty to act in all respects as is most pleasing to myself . . . they want a companion, and I want a *nominal* chaperone.'[22]

In the meantime, in early 1802, she went to Weymouth to be one of her cousin Sir Sidney Smith's party. She did not miss the fact that Princess Caroline, the estranged wife of the Prince of Wales, cast lascivious looks at her thirty-seven-year-old cousin. Indeed, Hester's presence was requested so often by Princess Caroline as a ruse so that she could also have Smith along that many assumed she was the Princess's new lady in waiting. Hester enjoyed renewing her friendship with the royal family, and the rapport she formed with the Duke of York allowed her to make him a proposition concerning her brothers, Charles and James, now sixteen and thirteen. She secured a commission for Charles in the 25th Foot, based in Gibraltar; while James was to go into the navy as a midshipman. With this in place, all that was required was for another escape plan to be laid. Once again it was successful, and the boys took up their new lives.

By the end of April 1802 Hester learned exactly what Camelford had been up to. It was splashed over the newspapers. What was not reported was that the French authorities considered him a serious threat as soon as news of his disappearance reached them: Napoleon's Minister of Police, Joseph Fouché, lost no time in putting out an alert that he be apprehended. But Camelford managed to baffle everyone (including a spy sent to Paris at his brother-in-law Lord Grenville's expense to make discreet enquiries about the peer's whereabouts). He slipped in and out of France undetected, spending several months lying low in Geneva and Italy. By the end of March 1802 Camelford had entered Paris, having adopted an American alias, with French travel papers issued in the name of 'John Rushworth'.

Camelford intended to be in Paris on 5 April, the day he knew Napoleon planned to attend a review at the Tuileries, where English visitors might present themselves to him at the Salle des Ambassadeurs, but two days beforehand, Fouché had him arrested after he was sighted at the Palais-Royal. Camelford had with him a small, specially designed magazine pistol, able to fire nine shots in succession without reloading, the perfect weapon for close-range assassination. If any doubted his target was Napoleon, the French police report was unequivocal:

> Lord Camelford, first cousin of Mr Pitt, brother-in-law of Lord Grenville and near-relative of Sidney Smith, gives much money to the émigré Chouans living in London, particularly to Limoëlan, whom he sees often. His close relationship with these scoundrels gave him the idea that he himself should assassinate the First Consul.[23]

Yet Camelford was able to save himself by his gift of the gab. When interrogated by Fouché, he presented a passionate case for being an admirer of France, citing his close association with Earl Stanhope and Horne Tooke. Aside from the offending weapon, nothing could be found to support Fouché's suspicions. Camelford was escorted to Boulogne, warned never to return and put on a ship to England.

Undoubtedly Hester must have seen Camelford. One way or another, her travel plans were put on hold. Whatever occurred at this juncture between them remains a mystery. There had undeniably been an infatuation and most likely a physical affair. But if she had toyed with him as a marriage partner she knew that, despite his wealth, he was full of darkness and rough edges. He drank, fought and was used to bedding the women he came across in ports and brothels. Perhaps the truth can be found in a comment she made many years later, that 'the violence of my character [is] something like Lord Camelford's'. Together, they were too volatile and headstrong to last.

\* \* \*

On her way to join the Egertons at Dover, Hester stopped at Pitt's residence at Walmer Castle, with the intention of staying no more than a few days before setting sail. The visit proved to be longer than expected. Pitt had been suffering periodic fits of stomach pains, cramps and vomiting, usually exacerbated by overwork, but this relapse was particularly extreme. She stayed long enough to supervise his recovery, and to demonstrate that 'I have talents as a nurse'. Pitt was reluctant to see her go.

That October, the Egertons and Hester travelled first to Lyon, where they were met by a very grown-up Mahon. There had been so much anticipation on both sides that the meeting was almost anti-climactic. Hester was anxious to see Mahon's transformation into a cultured gentleman, but her first impression was somewhat critical. He 'converses not pleasantly, like a Frenchman out of humour', she noted, although she was impressed at the extent of knowledge he had acquired, and noticed he studied 'from morning to night'. At Hester's urging, they crossed Mount Cenis in the French Alps by mule, undoubtedly a tortuous enterprise for the Egertons.

Brother and sister parted angrily in Florence after an explosive argument. It appears that she had trusted him with a confidence and that he took a vehemently moral stance against her; certainly his subsequent treatment of her suggests he viewed her as a 'fallen woman'. 'In truth, his conduct disgusted me extremely,' she wrote. From this moment on, Mahon's treatment of his sister was very frosty, even vindictive.

A larger drama was now the backdrop to their travels. War was declared against France in May 1803; the Treaty of Amiens had lasted less than fourteen months. After a winter spent in Naples and Venice, Hester's patience with the Egertons had frayed too. Mrs Egerton, she noted scathingly, was 'a fidget married to a fool'. In Germany the Egertons dithered about their itinerary, not wanting to budge from the communities of English expatriates, infuriating Hester by deciding in the end not to go to Vienna or Berlin – or Paris, while the chance still remained. By now Camelford had returned to France, only to be apprehended once again, and incarcerated for a time in the infamous Temple prison, before his release was engineered, no doubt through Pitt's and Grenville's efforts.

Hester was away for almost nine months. When she returned to

England again in July 1803, Pitt gently informed her that his mother – her grandmother – had died that April. Burton Pynsent had passed to the Chathams. She was not, of course, on speaking terms with her remaining grandmother, Grizel. She was homeless.

## 3

## The Company of Men

Pitt offered Hester a life with him, on the condition that she avoid Camelford, 'whom', as Hester put it, 'he liked personally as much as [I] did, but considerations of propriety obliged him to keep him at a distance'. He knew her too well to tell her what she must do, but he certainly knew how to ask her to respect his terms.

Pitt remained Lord Warden of the Cinque Ports, and had made his home at Walmer Castle. He had already done much to improve the speckled-stone castle with its bulbous bastions, one of a line of coastal forts built by Henry VIII as protection against the invasion the Tudor monarch feared would come from the combined forces of France and Spain. For Pitt, this was where he hoped to recover his health, repair the appalling state of his personal finances and spend more time reading and gardening. Hester was quickly caught up by day-to-day distractions at Walmer. She informed Jackson:

> Here, then I am happy to a degree; exactly in the sort of society I most like. There are generally three or four men staying in the house, and we dine eight or ten almost every other day. Military and naval characters are constantly *welcome* here; women are not, I *suppose*, because they do not form any part of our society. You may guess, then, what a pretty fuss they make over me.[1]

That Hester felt most at ease in the company of men we have already seen; she knew what to expect from them and, as a rule, was far more stimulated by their interests, their talk of war and politics, horses and journeys, and tended to be amused rather than offended by their dirtier jokes. She gave the impression of knowing more about worldly matters than she would have others believe. Something of this quality was sensed by her uncle, who told her he did not know if she were 'a devil or an angel'.

Many of Pitt's friends and colleagues were also not sure what to make of Hester in her decidedly public new role. She was a talented mimic; her timing was perfect and often cleverly nasty. She could be sharp and scintillating; she also made flippant off-colour jokes, commenting on the shape of a man's bottom, for instance, '*He* would not do for a hussar' and laughing at one of Pitt's visitors, who made a sweepingly low bow with his hat and a stoop in front of her: 'One would think he was looking under the bed for the *great business*.' Pitt did reprimand her: 'You are too *bad*, Hester,' he would say, adding weakly, 'You should not be so personal.' But he seems to have enjoyed her witticisms, and being teased out of his usual intimidating aloofness. Above all, she felt close to him. Hester would remember that 'He used sometimes to say to me when talking away after my fashion, "You put me so in mind of my Father!"'

An observer of her at the time, the nineteen-year-old William Napier, the future general, wrote: 'Lady Hester . . . was very attractive, so rapid and decided was her conversation, so full of humour and keen observation, and withal so friendly and instructive, that it was quite impossible not to fall at once into her direction and become her slave.'[2]

What became clear was that after the successive deaths of two sisters and his mother, Pitt warmed to having her loving and vivacious presence in his life. She was exuberant and irreverent, a player of innocent pranks. Although he continued to watch over her sisters Lucy and Griselda, it was Hester who became the privileged keeper of many of his past and future confidences, and his châtelaine at Walmer.* She was a sympathetic ear and could be surprisingly non-judgemental. Of his campaigns to

---

* Pitt's bachelor status puzzled the nation. It seemed that he somehow lacked the nerve for marriage. In the twenty-first century it is easy to speculate that he may have had homosexual tendencies but there seems to be no evidence for this. What Hester thought about this state of affairs is difficult to decipher. That she would later tell Meryon that she believed Eleanor Eden was 'the only women Pitt had ever loved' might be misleading. She, like many close to Pitt, concluded that his life was absolutely wedded to politics.

eradicate sedition, which so enraged her father, she would later say that '[he] used to say that Tom Paine was quite in the right, but then he would add, "What [was] I to do?"' She found that she had a unique influence; a position that must surely have been gratifying.

One of the first things that strikes a visitor to Walmer today is how – for a castle – altogether intimate and informal it feels. It is easy to imagine Hester feeling content and self-important here. From the dining room, with the doors open, they could watch the spray over the Goodwin Sands and the great panorama of the Channel. She could choose her hours; she was free to stay for after-dinner discussions, and frequently to add her opinion. War stratagems and news from Westminster were constantly mulled over. Although he was courted by the Opposition, Pitt wished to maintain his mandate within the existing government; his return to power was germinating.

Hester's room was directly beneath Pitt's chambers, and she often heard his footsteps pacing on the ceiling above her; she could even hear the clink of decanter against glass. From her room she could wander freely up the stone stairs to the bastion to spy on the night patrol or into the garden, no matter what the hour. Her windows overlooked the moat and the garden; a view which encompassed a magnificent magnolia tree. The scent of its opening flowers she would always afterwards associate with heightened expectation, a feeling that something marvellous was yet in wait for her.

Two pursuits she took up at Walmer became lifelong obsessions: stargazing and gardening. She made use of the tomes on astronomy from Pitt's library, and often looked through the Herschel reflecting telescope, a gift from William Herschel, the Astronomer Royal, to Pitt so he could use it to watch for the invading fleet.

After overhearing Pitt tell a friend that Walmer was not as beautiful as it might be due to a lack of trees, Hester took action. As soon as her uncle was next called away to London, the transformation of the garden in his absence became Hester's most ambitious project to date. She commissioned samples and seeds of plants from all over the country and managed to convince all the regiments quartered at Dover to help 'in levelling, fetching turf, transplanting shrubs, flowers . . .' for no extra pay, while she kept a close eye on them, commenting that by deploying some of her feminine charm, 'with a few civil words, and occasionally, a present,' the work was quickly done. She redesigned the main lawn, planted flower borders along Walmer's distinctive thick yew hedges, and managed to import and plant some fully-grown horse chestnut trees, adding to the formal groves of yew and lime trees already planted by Pitt. On his return, she was thrilled with his reaction:

> When Mr Pitt came down, he dismounted from his horse, and ascending the staircase, saw through a window, which commanded a view of the grounds, the improvements that had been made. 'Dear me, Hester, why this is a miracle! I declare it is quite admirable; I could not have done it half so well myself.'[3]

By the autumn of 1803, the entire nation was braced for an invasion across the Channel. Walmer, and the entire south coast between the Cinque Ports, were the frontline. Pitt was disgusted with his successor, Addington, whom he thought devoid of all military vision. In his role as Lord Warden he announced he would step in, taking on a voluntary but highly symbolic military role as Colonel Commandant of the Cinque Port Volunteers, a corps of 'gentlemen volunteers'. In his two-corned cocked hat, his buttoned red jacket, grey breeches and with his ceremonial sword, Pitt looked almost boyish that autumn, riding out, very often with Hester, to inspect the training of all battalions. War created the perfect climate for a fightback, and Pitt now lived as he meant to go on, mobilizing all his strengths, his health much improved.

The new mood also gave Hester a sense of mission. She felt both needed and useful. There was an exciting tension in her world, and few rules. A great deal about her strength of character is revealed by how she handled a group of would-be rapists one evening in Ramsgate.

> Five of the Blues, half-drunk, not knowing who I was, walked after me and pursued me to my door. They had the impertinence to follow me up-stairs and one of them took hold of my gown. The maid came out, frightened out of her senses, but just at the moment, with my arm I gave the foremost of them such a push, that I sent him rolling the others down the stairs, with their swords rattling against the balusters. Next

day, he appeared with a black patch as big as a saucer over his face, and when I went out there were the glasses looking at me and the footmen pointing me out – quite a sensation.[4]

It is easy to see why the troops nicknamed her the 'Amazon'. She wore a jaunty riding habit, styled in bright red wool with military braid, buttoned up against the sea wind like a man's greatcoat, and knee-high nankin boots. She loved to watch duelling soldiers, following all the moves closely, and rating them. She wrote to Jackson that Pitt 'promoted' her as nominal commander of her own 'army', 'the first and last' of the Berkshire Militia.

Adding to her contentment was the presence of her younger half-brothers. All the Stanhope boys were close by. James had decided to leave the navy to join the Guards, and was living close to Dover Castle. Charles had returned from Gibraltar, and for a time stayed at Walmer. He was soon promoted to the 57th Regiment, at Ashford. 'Charles is by nature my favourite,' she had confided to a friend several years earlier, 'he has the least ability of the three, but a degree of openness and good nature which wins every heart, and an air of nobility his quizzical education can never destroy.'

About Mahon she was even cooler than before, however. The previous autumn, on his return from Europe, Pitt had appointed him Lieutenant-Governor of Dover Castle and made him colonel of one of his battalions. Mahon was about to be married. His choice of wife was Catherine Lucy Smith, one of Lord Robert Carrington's four daughters. The wedding would be held that November at Deal Castle. Mahon found Hester's presence very disquieting, for reasons that beg some interpretation. He wrote to his father-in-law:

> I hope that Catherine does not see Hester much alone; this intimacy can be productive of no good consequences, but probably of much mischief. I have endeavoured this week to prevent it by painting with truth and sincerity and I trust with candour and impartiality what Hester's character was and the evils that too great an intimacy might occasion.[5]

Almost certainly, Mahon's account concerned Hester's association with Camelford, who now filled newspapers with his brawls and duels, and continued to be tailed by Fouché's spies.* Whatever the cause, there was something Mahon did not want Catherine to know and did not trust Hester to be discreet about, or he truly believed that his wife would be compromised in some way by associating with her. Either way, his letter shows that as far as he was concerned, his sister's reputation had already been sacrificed.

By early 1804, the political winds were blowing in Pitt's favour. Lord Grenville, his cousin and ally, had been repeatedly urging him to lead the Opposition factions against Addington; surely, he reasoned, together, they would form an unbeatable alliance. But Pitt was not prepared to capitulate to the Whigs. Frustrated, Grenville took the hitherto unthinkable course of aligning himself with the one man who had been their mutual arch-rival for two decades: Charles James Fox.

In February the King, now sixty-five, once more had an attack of the symptoms that afflicted him earlier, the second time in three years. His mental health was hotly debated. As soon as his father showed signs that could be construed as lunacy, the Prince of Wales began making plans for a new government, hosting numerous dinner parties for Pitt's opponents. One of the Prince of Wales's most valuable assistants in once more galvanizing the Whigs and forming the Fox–Grenville coalition had been the formidable Whig hostess, Georgiana, Duchess of Devonshire. She proved to be a particularly effective go-between in the setting-up of meetings between her close friend Fox and Grenville, and was instrumental in trying to persuade George Canning – regarded as the cleverest of Pitt's trusted Ministers of Parliament – that he should

---

* But there was something else, about which it seems the entire family closed ranks: the birth of an illegitimate child in Europe that was certainly Camelford's. The mother's identity was never revealed. Shortly after the time Hester had travelled with Mahon in Italy, Lord Grenville had written to Camelford on 10 February 1803, just before his ill-fated arrest in France, with news 'of a very painful communication which I have to make to you and which it is of the utmost importance for you to know'. More tantalizingly, Grenville had been informed that Camelford had fathered a child, a daughter, about whom the young peer had apparently known nothing. The child had been discreetly adopted immediately after birth. By August 1810, the mother would be vaguely described as being now 'principally abroad'. No money was ever requested. In my opinion, the possibility that Hester might in fact have been the mother and gone abroad to have the child cannot be ruled out, and would certainly explain her eldest brother's reaction to her in Florence.

find a way to convince Pitt that his decision not to join them was political suicide.

In February, in a series of rousing parliamentary speeches, Pitt made a devastating assault on Addington, accusing him of almost criminal negligence in his inability to sufficiently protect the nation from invasion. Few failed to be moved. The writing was on the wall. Addington would have to go.

It was at one of Pitt's gatherings that February that Hester met Lord Granville Leveson Gower.* Pitt thought highly of him, going so far as to observe, as though he were a connoisseur of male beauty, that he had the looks of 'Hadrian's Antinous'. Granville had been elected as Member of Parliament for Staffordshire at twenty-two, and before he was thirty had already served as a middle-ranking diplomat in Paris and Lille. In 1800, Pitt had made him a Lord of the Treasury, a position he was forced to give up when Pitt resigned a year later.

When Hester met him, Granville was thirty, a charmer, groomed for success by his wealthy, well-connected parents. An aristocratic bachelor, he was moneyed and refined, conversational and amusing. In country houses across England, he was being referred to as one of the best-looking men of his generation. His expensive tastes in travel, wine, gambling and women were indulged by his loving parents.

Hester was instantly besotted. Granville was politically ambitious, and clearly destined for success in the world of high diplomacy. Marriage to him would bring her exactly the sort of life she wanted: it would place her in the salons of Paris and St Petersburg, close to the corridors of power. She immediately began a campaign to make him fall in love with her, acquiring his sprightly mother, Lady Stafford, as her 'leading female acquaintance'. She would have been acutely aware that the Staffords would have preferred their son to marry into a family able to confer the assurance of wealth, and she could offer no such enticement. All the same, she must have felt confident that with Pitt once more in the ascendant, her proximity to power might act in her favour. For the first time, she

---

* Lord Granville Leveson Gower, who would become 1st Earl Granville in 1833, is variously referred to here as Leveson Gower and Granville, the name used by his intimates.

worried about what might be said about her in society and appears to have been almost relieved when she heard, two days before her twenty-eighth birthday, that Camelford had been fatally shot in a duel. She confided cryptically to her friend the diplomat Jackson: 'Lord Camelford has been shot in a duel, and there is no chance of him recovering. You know my opinion of him, I believe, therefore can judge if I am not likely to lament his untimely end. He had vices, but also great virtues, but they were not known to the world at large.'*

Hester became a regular guest at Lady Stafford's house in Whitehall, opposite the Horse Guards, and Granville in turn visited Pitt and saw her frequently at York Place. As intent as she was on her own crusade for his affections, she did not allow any details of Pitt's battle for power to escape her, some of which likely provided more erotic leverage than she would have wanted her uncle to know. Politically, Hester had become a behind-the-scenes dynamo. That the brilliant and shrewd Canning consistently sought her opinion demonstrates the degree to which it was valued.

At first she was convinced her passion for Granville was returned. He would come to call on her; she was not always there or was delayed; he would wait for her, not wanting to miss the chance of seeing her. Having spent long months away at Walmer, if not in near solitude, then at least deprived of the many temptations of London, Hester was in a mood to be diverted. As part of Pitt's inner corps of two, she was invited to a dizzying number of events. Her life was a Cruikshank caricature come to life; a never-ending round of dinners, parties and dances at which she came to know all the leading personalities of the day.

When Pitt and Hester returned to Walmer in April, Granville was invited. It seems that shortly after this, Hester and Granville became lovers. Physically, she thought Granville 'perfection'. She certainly does not appear to have behaved like a shy virgin. Instead, she seems to have launched herself fearlessly into her new affair. If Granville's record was anything to go by, he preferred sexually experienced – or married – women. He was also an enthusiastic collector of what he called 'dirty Books', preferably French, and when 'infected with a Bibliomanie' would

---

* Camelford's fateful duel had taken place in the early hours of the morning in the meadows outside Holland House in Kensington; he died on 10 March 1804, aged twenty-nine. He was buried in the crypt of St Anne's Church in Dean Street, Soho.

hunt the bookshops for hours 'in the hope of finding something curious'.

He met Hester for rides in St James's Park. If they felt in need of more privacy, they would take the carriage out beyond the bucolic meadows surrounding Primrose Hill to Hampstead, warming themselves up with a drink in the village before wandering upwards onto the Heath, walking along its pathways around the ponds and through meadows, where the grass was no longer wet from the rain.

It would be misleading to think that the late Georgian era was not in some ways as rambunctiously sexual as our own. Although English society was hardly permissive, there was certainly a frank acknowledgement of sexual pleasure and desire, much more so in the Georgian and Regency periods than in the Victorian era.

The sort of erotic engravings that titillated Granville were all the rage. In Britain, probably best known at that time were those by the celebrated satirical illustrator Thomas Rowlandson; for instance, *Meditation among the Tombs*, a raunchy depiction of a couple making love against a church wall as a funeral takes place in the background, and *The Willing Fair*, which shows a couple in hasty coitus at their lunch table, the young woman's mountainous buttocks visible, but her dress otherwise unruffled, from her perfectly coiffed hair and pearl-drop earring to the shoes still firmly on her feet. The implication of these prints being that in the Georgian era, when it might have been difficult for amorous couples to find privacy in their own homes, the fully-dressed 'quickie' was perhaps by no means uncommon.

In the first flush of her love affair with Granville, Hester did everything she could to look her best. She became guiltily familiar with *Ackerman's Repository*, the bible of well-dressed women. Pitt had generously suggested she put all her purchases of new clothes on his account, but even he raised his eyebrows at the extravagance of her hasty pilgrimages to London's best seamstresses, shoemakers, hatters, hosiers and glovers.

Although inclined to be critical of her looks, Hester was in fact quite vain. Men certainly found her extremely attractive. She said about herself later: 'I was never what you call handsome, but brilliant. My teeth were brilliant, my complexion brilliant, my language – ah! – there it was – something striking and original that caught everyone's attention.'

Other suitors idled in the wings, plenty of them handsome and eligible, but none apparently able to deflect Hester's attention from her new-found object. Among them was William Noel Hill, the second son of Lord Berwick, already the Tory Member of Parliament for Shrewsbury and a clever diplomat a few years younger than her, who had been stead-fastly pursuing her since her return to London.* Although he lacked Granville's impossible good looks, he was a sympathetic, amusingly self-deprecating character, and Hester was fond of him. She enjoyed his flirtations, which seem to have been frank. He asked Hester to marry him. Hill was aware of his rival, but clearly had Hester in his sights for when – inevitably – that attraction waned. This was a possibility Hester considered so absurd she laughed about it with Granville, making a joke of the hapless Hill.

By the end of April 1804 Pitt had pulled off an impressive coup. At the King's invitation, he was welcomed back into power with the approval of the former government, and in alliance with a significant faction of the Opposition. It was his intention to form a strong government that could withstand Napoleon. Even the threat of Fox's powerful supporters could not moderate his optimism.

On 18 May 1804 Pitt, now almost forty-five, once again received from the King the seals of office as First Lord of the Treasury and Chancellor of the Exchequer. Once more, Downing Street beckoned. Ten days later, on 28 May, across the Channel, at Saint-Cloud, the Senate proclaimed the thirty-five-year-old Napoleon to be 'Emperor of the French Republic'. The coronation was to take place later that year. Pitt's dance with Napoleon was beginning again.

Shortly after Pitt returned as Prime Minister, Hester was conducted around Downing Street, as liveried servants jumped to attention. She was in a triumphant mood; overnight, Pitt – and she – was now at the centre of the universe. She saw no noticeable elation on his part; but the old power had returned; his playfulness, which she had seen so much of,

---

* While William Noel Hill's elder brother Lord Berwick was wealthy, with a stately pile in Shropshire, Hill was less so. Famously, the two brothers stood against one another in the Shrewsbury elections of 1796, each spending what others would have regarded as fortunes several times over to secure votes in a spectacularly corrupt campaign. Hill won, and kept his seat as a Tory MP until 1812.

could dissolve in an instant. He went back to his old work habits, with the dogged persistence of a horse tethered to its plough.

By the end of May, she noticed that dark circles hollowed his eyes, and worried that all the good work of Walmer was already undone. His only concession to moderation was to substitute his preferred vintages with the occasional bottle of redcurrant wine; otherwise the standing order from Berry's Wine Merchants continued as before. She would later remember how he would always drive himself hard. 'People little knew what he had to do. Up at eight in the morning, with people enough to see for a week, obliged to talk all the time while he was at breakfast, and receiving first one, then another, until four o'clock; then eating a mutton chop, hurrying off to the House, and there badgered and compelled to speak and waste his lungs until two or three in the morning! – who could stand it?'

Her mocking wit was not reined in. Soon after being made Foreign Secretary, Lord Mulgrave came to stay, and when at breakfast he complained to Hester that he had been given a defective spoon, her response was typically quick. 'Have you not yet discovered that Mr Pitt sometimes uses very slight and weak instruments to effect his ends?'

Despite high expectations and rousing support for Pitt, especially in the House of Commons, the new Prime Minister was forced to admit that his planned administration was not going to be as strong and inclusive as he had hoped. Pitt's position was now entirely dependent on the King's ministry and he faced a strengthened Opposition, making it impossible for him to hold a majority in the Commons. The last time he had taken office during the crisis of 1783, more than twenty years before, he had faced overwhelming odds and outright hostility. This time, he could not count either on the King's longevity or his sanity; nor were his opponents likely to be swayed by threat of a general election, which had given him such critical leverage the first time around. In any case, clearly the war had to be his first concern. He would have to provide leadership, even if he met resistance at every step. When Pitt's new Cabinet was hurriedly assembled, the Prime Minister himself assumed so much responsibility that many members joked it was 'the new Administration of William and Pitt'.

While Pitt was preoccupied with consolidating his position, Hester was concerned with what appeared to be a slackening of interest on

Granville's part. In July, after Pitt appointed him a member of his Privy Council, Granville's attentions waned. Letters that she sent him (signed with a big looped 'H'), which once might have been replied to within a matter of hours, now took a day or more to summon a response. Once, he did not arrive for one of their pre-arranged walks; she found herself having to idle along a row of chestnut trees in Marylebone Fields 'like any common strumpet'.

Had Hester known the truth behind Granville's absences, it might have come as a shock. Granville was a serial romancer, not always a very faithful one, of a number of women. He had fathered two children with the married Lady Bessborough – Henrietta, always known as Harriet – sister of Lady Georgiana Spencer, a secret which they had managed to successfully conceal from everyone except Georgiana, whom they could trust. Nor did Hester realize that Harriet continued to exert a strong sexual and emotional power over Granville. (Their affair had begun in 1794, when Harriet was thirty-three, and he was twenty. She was by then already the mother of four children with her husband, among them, Caroline, who would grow up to become Lady Caroline Lamb.)

Harriet was well-known to Hester. Although Harriet was loyal to Georgiana's fervently Whig ménage, like most of London society, both sisters had now thrown their parlour doors open to welcome Pitt's niece, calling her 'Hetty'. Of the two, Hester preferred Harriet, thinking her 'ten times cleverer' than her sister. It seemed to Hester that Georgiana's 'reputation was in great part, the effect of her position; for fine horses, fine carriages, and the *éclat* that attends a great personage wherever she goes, made up the greatest part of it'. Throughout that summer, as Hester agonized over her affair with Granville, Harriet frequently invited her to her residence at Cavendish House for a *tête-à-tête* or a small gathering. Hester noticed on one such visit that Granville had left Harriet a miniature statue of Antinous in the vestibule, identical to one he had given her. A fraught Hester was encouraged by the older woman, who was well practised in the art of eliciting confidential information, to pour out her worries.* Soon Harriet chided Granville:

---

* Hester was aware that Harriet devoured French novels; she might not have known that one of her favourites was *Les Liaisons dangereuses*, and that she had teased Granville for being a little like Valmont.

Is it quite honourable, dear G, to encourage a passion you do not mean seriously to return? And which if you do not, must make the owner of it miserable? And how can you be certain of what lengths you or she may be drawn into? We know she has strong passions and indulges them with great latitude: may you not both of you be hurried further than you intend? If Mr Pitt knew even what had passed already, do you think he would like it?

In the same letter, Harriet pleads with Granville to spend the night at her house, rather than 'sleeping at Mr Pitt's'.[6] Meanwhile, Hester's quick scrawls to him are full of reminders about how welcome he is at Downing Street, telling he could always spend the night 'if you prefer staying to driving back at night'.[7]

By early August 1804 Granville had neither broken off his affair with Hester nor entirely resumed it. He kept raising her hopes with some throwaway half-hearted comment or suggestion. Hester began hinting to her closest friends, as well as to Pitt himself, that she expected marriage. Suspecting this was not Granville's intention and worried that the attachment was unhinging her, Pitt called Granville to Downing Street for a private talk. Granville, who was expecting a reprimand, was instead offered the highly prestigious post of Ambassador to St Petersburg, effective immediately. Pitt was anxious to prevent the embarrassing spectacle of his niece being publicly jilted. But he also needed Granville's charm on his side. St Petersburg, the court of Tsar Alexander, could not have been a more critical posting: Pitt was endeavouring to form an alliance with Russia against Napoleon, and hoped to convince Austria, Prussia and Sweden to join, a move that would pave the way for the creation of the Third Coalition.

Granville, not brave enough to inform Hester in person, sent her this news by letter. He obviously dreaded the prospect of her making an embarrassing scene with Pitt. Granville's departure was meant to be swift but owing to various delays, he was forced to linger in London for another two months, a highly awkward situation that was not helped by the disconcerting announcement of their engagement in one of the newspapers that September. (Granville assumed Hester had placed it herself, a charge she indignantly denied.) Harriet was greatly rattled, saying that 'everyone is talking of it' and adding, 'I dread this subject coming on the *tapis* between you . . .'[8] Perhaps Harriet feared that faced with an ultimatum, this time Granville might indeed decide to marry, a possibility that filled her with dread. (During his final preparations to leave, the physical affair between Harriet and Granville resumed.)

Right up to the last moment, Hester still teetered on the possibility of a change of plan, half-expecting Granville to turn up suddenly and ask her to go with him. A few days before he left on 11 October 1804, she wrote him a letter that has not survived, but apparently contained the warning words: 'You shall see what I shall do'. Granville sealed up Hester's letter and sent it, along with one of his own, to Harriet; he also showed it to Canning, along with a necklace he meant to give her, but Canning advised total silence. Harriet's reply gives some indication of its content:

How strange Hetty's note is. It admits but of two interpretations, neither of which I like to give it. The first (her meaning to destroy herself) is too horrible, and the second raises my indignation, and I don't like believing that, finding there was no hope of your returning her passion enough to marry her, she resolv'd to indulge the inclination – which we know she possesses but too strongly – to the utmost, trusting to your honour for secrecy and to your absence for putting an end to what could not continue without danger. Hetty is so kind to me, it seems ungenerous in me to say this, and perhaps I am mistaken, but it is very odd. I shall always be kind to her, from a strange reason – she belongs in some manner to you.[9]

Hester's anguish, when she discovered that Granville intended to abandon her, was so great that she did indeed try to kill herself.[10] She did not say whether she did this at Downing Street, York Place or Putney, but she was undoubtedly in London. It must have been on 7 or 8 October. She posted her letter to Granville first. Hester's body proved to be stronger than she supposed, as she would later confide. She was violently sick, enough to expel the fatal dose, although she managed to severely poison herself, causing damage to her liver, kidneys and lungs. Hester's suicide attempt was a grave shock to Pitt. He did not call his own doctor, Sir Walter Farquhar (who also tended the gossipy Spencer sisters), but summoned another eminent physician, Dr Henry Cline. Hester was to say that she intended to kill herself, although laudanum was also commonly used to induce abortion. Both the doctor and the servants who attended her would have been sworn to secrecy.

In the immediate aftermath of the overdose, she was in such discomfort from her injured organs that she could not sleep for twelve days, nor could she keep any solid food down. She was in misery not just at the failure at her attempt but because of her physical pain. As she would tell her doctor many years later, she put a lancet under her pillow, hinting that she might once more attempt suicide. She also recalled that even when she was out of danger, for some weeks she remained an alarming scarlet colour, and her forehead was continually prickled with sweat. One of her visitors was her suitor William Noel Hill, who made her smile weakly, comparing her appearance to that of Christ's on the cross: 'You will set a crown of thorns on your head – you will sweat blood presently'.[11]

Hester was convinced that Harriet – with the help of the Devonshire House circle – had conspired against her, and had encouraged Granville to believe she was less than he deserved. From Hester's perspective, Harriet did not want Granville to escape her clutches. (This turned out to be an accurate prediction. Five years later, Granville would marry Lady Harriet Cavendish, Georgiana's daughter, his former lover's niece. As soon as it was decently possible, Harriet, or Harryo as she was called, adopted both children from her husband's former liaison with her aunt. Harryo was apparently prepared to extend her affections to the children, but retained a lifelong jealousy of Harriet, whose influence over Granville remained undiminished.)

Hester compounded her humiliation by pursuing Granville with a torrent of letters, which soon afterwards she would look back upon with mortification. He did not burn them as she asked; they are by turns plaintive, self-recriminatory and confessional. She wanted him to know how she suffered:

You know that I loved you! Yes, to idolatry; still I wd by no means have you to understand that I offer this as a vindication for the folly of my

conduct, on the contrary . . . the natural *levity* of my disposition offers
no excuse, as from the first moment I discovered that every thought was
devoted to you, which was too early in our acquaintance . . .[12]

She reminded him of the 'sacred seal of confidence' agreed between
them; and tried to undo the damage of the 'miserable scrap' written to
him as 'the dread hour approached' on the eve of his departure, which
was 'like the hour of death to me'. Pitt, she told him, urged her to put
him out of her thoughts: 'God, what a dunce!' She wanted to apologize
for her behaviour, but claimed she could not control it. 'I have often told
you I was born a *tyrant*; it is therefore in vain for me to deceive myself'
– and to exonerate him. She blamed herself for being so passionate. 'As
a man, how could you have acted otherwise, persecuted by the affections
of a woman whose only object was to gain you, at any price, & who felt
but too conscious you never shared the passion you inspired. Oh strange
fatality!'[13] One of her sentences trails off pitifully, 'My heart is at this
moment breaking . . .'

Although he had done everything possible for Hester, Pitt was horrified.
Every day, the newspapers reported suicides, of sad and varied circumstances and methods, described in graphic detail. The official verdict on
any suicide was always the same: 'lunacy'. 'Self-murder' was considered
deeply shameful. Pitt's many biographers have never examined the impact
that his niece's suicide attempt might have had on his ability to function,
on his own inner sense of confidence, perhaps because he kept it so well
hidden. But it is possible that Hester's crisis was a blow that precipitated
his own descent into ill-health. He felt responsible; he may also have felt
guilty, not only for concocting the plan to take Granville away from her,
but perhaps even for drawing her attention to him in the first place.
There are consistent reports of Pitt's distraction at the end of August that
corroborate Hester's account of her own growing unhappiness and instability. One official noted on 31 August 1804 that he had seen Pitt 'completely
under the influence of anxiety and depression', and another observer saw
him walking alone early in the morning in St James's Park, 'looking like
death with his eyes staring out of his head'.

As soon as she was able, in early November, Hester fled to Walmer.

Pitt had extracted from her the promise that she would never again harm herself and that she would try to forget Granville.[14] While she recovered, Hester consoled herself with the fact that she continued 'to please Mr Pitt more than ever, if I may judge by his kindness, which if possible, augments'. Still she brooded, refusing to believe that Granville never loved her or intended to marry her.

Although secluded away – first on the Kentish coast and later in Putney – Hester was by no means forgotten, either in London or in St Petersburg. Harriet and Granville exchanged a series of semi-cryptic letters discussing her. Hester's whereabouts, and the reason for the lengthy amount of time she had remained away from London, apparently remained topics of great interest in society. On 5 March Harriet wrote to Granville:

> Hetty is still at Walmer, where she has been very ill and confin'd to her room for some time. I wonder whether my fears were justified . . . She publishes everywhere your having completely jilted her. I always fear'd this.'[15]

Harriet also told him she saw Hester's would-be suitor, William Noel Hill, and discussed 'Hetty', and gathered that at one time there had been 'great *tendresses* between them' until Granville had come along 'and had driven all the others out'. Harriet had a firm suspicion Hester was pregnant. She wrote to Granville:

> My Sis and all her family returned home from a ball last night full of Hetty and the story of the *accouchement* which they insist upon which she *affichés* – that is, she goes out without rouge, much fairer than she was, and so languid and faint that she did faint at Mad. Dupre's. I wonder what all this means. I should not have any doubt after the letter I saw, only you say nothing of it. From my soul I pity her.[16]

On 28 June, Harriet wrote again that she had talked with Pitt's close colleague George Rose about her suspicions about Hester being pregnant. She refers to this as:

* There are conflicting reports of Hester's whereabouts and condition throughout this time: in a letter to her son on 7 March 1805, Lady Stafford mentions going to the King's ball at Windsor the previous Monday, where she says 'Ly S was there' and that 'Ly B' was not.

... that *other* circumstance so much believ'd in London. I told him I was certain, what-ever passed between them before his departure, he never gave her the least reason to imagine he had any thoughts of her as a wife; that I believed all the stories were false, but if true, that my opinion of [Granville] was such I was sure it must have been her fault as much as his. He agreed with me in this, but Heaven knows how it is to end.[17]

The fact that Harriet went to great lengths to relay these conversations in such detail in her correspondence suggests that Granville refused to give her a straight answer.

The possibility that Hester was indeed pregnant is intriguing. She deliberately made sure Harriet did not see her for months. Even so, she was glimpsed at least once by her sister. Georgiana's assessing eyes would have been familiar with every sign. Apparently, she was convinced. Still, it would have certainly suited all those who would have preferred to see Fox in place of Pitt if indeed it became widely known that Hester had fallen from grace in such a way. Hester did make at least one and possibly several brief visits to London during this otherwise unusually reclusive time; she had also been sighted in February by Lady Stafford, Lord Granville's mother, who wrote to her son:

I was sadly disappointed the other day when I saw Ly. Hester Stanhope with Susan. I had figured her to myself as very pretty, in Place of which she look'd like a middle-aged married woman with a dingey Complexion, no Rouge, a broad Face and an unbecoming fur cap.[18]

That certainly was a vision calculated to cure any romantic nostalgia.

At Walmer that winter Hester was often alone. Expecting Pitt to return at Easter, she had been busily distracting herself with a surprise for him. At the very edge of Walmer's grounds, she had often walked by a deep chalk quarry, which had been left as a bleak ravine. She sent the resident gardener, Burfield, to Maidstone to bring back 'creepers, furze and broom', which she used to soften the overall effect, having landscaped fully-grown trees and shrubs in amongst the ferns and mossy hollows. It became her own secret garden, a place that somehow represented for her the transformative powers she knew she possessed. But Pitt, prevented by work and ill-health, was never again to return to Walmer.

She and Pitt agreed that it was better for her to live separately for a time. Pitt wanted to avoid any kind of scandal or emotional turbulence. The months between March 1805 and January 1806 are unaccounted for, nor do any letters seem to have been preserved from this time. Where was she living? Harriet, it seems, rarely lost an opportunity to track down her erstwhile friend, especially when she sensed a tantalizing secret. In August 1805 she noted: 'Hetty is living by herself in London, with Mr Hill there from Morning till Night. Mr Pitt is displeased with her for something.'[19] By December she commented that Hester had been seeing a great deal of her cousin, and possibly living under the same roof: 'I saw Sir Sydney [*sic*] Smith yesterday, he has been living with Hetty. I wonder whether acting the part of a *consolateur*!'[20]

Hester developed a particular disdain for women like Harriet and Georgiana, so apparently decorous, artful and 'modern', yet bankrolled and ultimately controlled by their rich husbands, whose censure they feared beyond any passion they felt for their lovers. She had grown up in the era in which Mary Wollstonecraft had stated in print that society made a fatal mistake by allowing women only the role of domestic slave or 'alluring mistress' without recourse to any financial freedom, and by encouraging women to think only of their looks and charms. This was a viewpoint that Hester instinctively held and she expressed it by her actions. But she was no radical polemicist – her father had cured her of that. Hester would have thought feeble-minded Wollstonecraft's urgings that society divest itself of the monarchy, the military and the church, and she certainly did not believe in the social equality that Wollstonecraft maintained was as necessary to happiness between a man and a woman. If anything, she was an aristocratic individualist, with more than a touch about her of Lord Stanhope's Minority of One.

Hester was not the only one who felt her reputation was under attack. The winter of 1805 was particularly fraught for Pitt, who was coming under increasing fire from the Opposition. Despite his intensified efforts to create a broader-based administration, he was unable to lure the Fox and Grenville factions into the government, a rapprochement that could only be successful if an agreement could be reached between the King and the Prince of Wales. As long as their estrangement continued, so did their respective vetoes on Fox and Grenville. Pitt was forced to fall back on his last resort – to patch up his friendship with Addington, and the sixty MPs who took their lead from him, whose support he now desperately needed.

A window on these proceedings is provided in a letter written to 'Dearest Lady H' from an extremely agitated Canning, dated 1 January 1805, in which he expresses his shock at Pitt's decision. He is replying to a letter Hester had sent him the day before in which she had obviously 'leaked' the information to him that Addington was to be made a Minister, and that he himself was not; the inference being that Canning had obviously expected to be made Foreign Secretary, and had now found that the position will be going to Pitt's old loyalist, Lord Mulgrave. He wrote to her early that morning, after 'as much sleep as I could get after such a letter' and told her '. . . I am nothing, I cannot help it; I cannot face the House of Commons or walk the streets in the state of things as I am'.[21] It is a lengthy, detailed and personal letter, in which he agonizes about his colleagues, written in the kind of shorthand that suggests he had long since let her into the inner workings of his mind. He asks her to intercede with 'Mr P' on his behalf:

> Through you I come to him with more confidence in not being misunderstood . . . *You* stood instead of pages of preface and apology and are a vouchee for us to each other that we mean each other kindly and fairly.[22]

Canning clearly expected her to still be privy to the sort of confidences from Pitt that kept him writhing in anticipation. Many of Pitt's ministers had pointedly suggested to Pitt that her influence on state matters would not be tolerated. Pitt laughed this off as an absurdity. Hester would later say:

There might be some apparent levity, both as regarded affairs of the Cabinet and my own, but I always knew what I was doing. When Mr Pitt was reproached for allowing me such unreserved liberty of action in State matters, and in affairs where his friends advised him to question me on the motives of my conduct, he always answered: I let her do as she pleases, for if she were resolved to cheat the devil, she could do it.

The mood towards Pitt had soured. The fact that Britain was at war – engaged on two fronts now, having committed the country to the Spanish conflict – enraged his countrymen further. Pitt's popularity sank lower when, in February 1805, he presented his budget to the Commons requesting a loan of £20 million and further tax rises on salt, postal services, horses, property and legacies.

Meanwhile the Opposition was seeking out damning evidence wherever it could. Finally a chink in Pitt's armour came in the form of the Tenth Report of the Commission of Naval Inquiry, which had been set up as a watchdog over the navy's management practices. It was the perfect opportunity to point the finger of financial indiscretion at the otherwise incorruptible Pitt. The matter became one of grave moral laxity, on which the very integrity of the administration rested. Even Pitt's dearest friends, such as Wilberforce, were moved to vote against him.

When the vote took place on 9 April 1805, the numbers were equal, so that the Speaker, whose face 'turned white as ashes', was forced to cast the deciding ballot. After a pause of ten minutes, the visibly uneasy Speaker announced his vote against the government. Pitt was seen leaning in his chair, pushing his little cocked hat down to obscure his face, so that only those near to him could see that tears coursed down his cheeks.

Hester knew him well enough to let him be, knowing that after the humiliation of such a defeat, and having so many among his former followers vote against him, he needed comfort more than righteous indignation. From that point on, she felt contempt for a great many of those men she had formerly entertained on Pitt's behalf. The stirrings by those loyal to Pitt but now anxious for the formation of a new administration were increasing, but they did not dare to act while he was still in power.

Early in January 1806, the devastating news of Napoleon's triumph at Austerlitz and the collapse of the Third Coalition proved to be Pitt's death-blow. Hester rushed to his side and was deeply shocked to see his altered appearance when he was brought to Putney Heath. As he was helped out of his carriage, she knew he would not survive long. 'I said to myself, "It is all over with him." He was supported by the arms of two people, and had a stick, or two sticks, in his hands, and as he came up, panting for breath.'

Traditional dinners were held at Downing Street without Pitt. On 18 January, Pitt ordered Hester to attend the official celebration of Queen Charlotte's birthday, insisting he did not want her social life to be curtailed. An issue of the *Lady's Magazine* for the following month describes her appearance at the event:

> Lady Hester Stanhope, was, as usual, dressed with much style and elegance, in black and green velvet ornamented with embossed gold, and studded with rubies, which had a most brilliant effect. Headdress: feathers and diamonds.[23]

Parliament opened on 21 January 1806. The mood was subdued; the Opposition agreed to defer their action to bring down the administration for a week, as they waited to see how long Pitt might last. On the morning of 23 January, Pitt agreed to pray, saying that he had 'neglected prayer too much to allow him to hope that it could be very efficacious now'. He then asked to rewrite his will. Had he not managed this last act, Hester's future might have been quite different. Pitt knew he had only debts to leave behind him, but he also knew that his request for specific bequests would receive serious consideration by the Crown and by Parliament.

James would recall that Hester was infuriated that Pitt's doctor, Farquhar, would not let her in to see Pitt for a final farewell. But when the doctor had slipped out for dinner, she went into his room.

> Though even then wandering a little, he immediately recollected her, and with his usual angelic mildness wished her future happiness, and

gave her a most solemn blessing and affectionate farewell. On her leaving the room I entered it; and for some time afterwards Mr Pitt continued to speak of her, and several times repeated, 'Dear soul! I know she loves me. Where is Hester? Is Hester gone?'[24]

Pitt died later that day, and Hester cut a lock of his grey hair before his body was removed. She would keep it all her days in a little pearl locket, as one of her most precious possessions.

Within a week of Pitt's death, the House of Commons voted to put £40,000 towards Pitt's personal debts – the present-day equivalent would be more than £2 million. In addition, the King personally granted Pitt's dying wish to leave Hester and her sisters with pensions. Hester would be given £1,200 a year – around £60,000 today. It was an extraordinary sum for one who had never held any political office. (By comparison, her cousin, Sir Sidney Smith, the hero of Acre, had been awarded a pension of £1,000.) Grizel and Lucy were also provided for, and received £600 each. The King understood Pitt's request to be somewhat unusual, but he granted it in the knowledge that Pitt wished it. Besides, he had always liked Hester's spirit.

Pitt's funeral on Saturday, 22 February 1806, was a solemn and grand event. Preceded by fifes, drums and trumpets, the cortège passed from Westminster Hall to the Abbey, and was attended by a black-suited multitude of all the Members of Parliament and the peerage, as well as three royal dukes. Pitt's elder brother Chatham, along with the Stanhope brothers, walked beside the coffin, following the same route as the procession in 1778 for Lord Chatham; once again the Abbey's cavernous halls echoed the name of William Pitt, Prime Minister. For two days, Pitt's body had lain in state in the Painted Chamber of the Palace of Westminster, hung with banners of the Chatham arms. Tens of thousands of mourners paid their respects. Many were visibly affected during the ceremony: Wilberforce was seen crying openly, Mulgrave was 'scarcely . . . able to support himself', and Canning described 'a feeling of loneliness & dismay which I have never felt half so strongly before'. Even Fox was heard to say that it was 'as if there was something missing in the world – a chasm, a blank that cannot be supplied'. Amongst them, dressed in black, a stricken, dry-eyed Hester watched as Pitt's body was lowered into the Chatham family vault.

# 4

## A Summoning of Strength

Today, a passer-by stopping at the corner of Montagu Square (which Hester always pronounced '*Mount*ague') might peer curiously at No. 4, a plain, three-storeyed, brown-brick building in a row of elegant Georgian townhouses. It overlooks a long, rectangular garden, planted with plane trees and orderly flower beds, which like most of London's private gardens can only be entered with a resident's key. Hester might well have enjoyed the irony that had she lived several generations later, she might not have needed to go to the Middle East: by then, the Middle East would have come to her. Hardly more than a hundred metres away is Edgware Road, which although a greyer, less vibrant version of Beirut's Hamra, is nonetheless a mecca for London's Arab community, bustling with news-stands touting the latest copies of *L'Orient Le Jour* and men in cafés puffing away at *narguileh* pipes. Black-robed women flit by; supermar-kets sell *mahmoul* cakes, orange-blossom water and *zahtar* along with other staples for anyone homesick for the sight of Mount Lebanon.

When Hester came to live here in 1806, Edgware Road was known as Watling Street, part of the old Roman road to St Albans. No. 4 would be her home for just over three years. It was close to Marylebone Fields (now Regent's Park), and just a short hackney ride from some of her haunts: Jermyn Street for cheese at Paxton & Whitfield; Hatchards book-shop and the Royal Academy on Piccadilly; Hookham's Circulating Library and Burlington Arcade and her equestrian outfitter, Mr S. Clark of Golden Square. Her local shops were on New Quebec Street, which had a butcher, dairyman, cheesemonger, tea dealer and grocer. In the mews was a livery stable where horses could be hired; Hester would go to ride with what she termed the 'swinish multitude' in Hyde Park whenever she could on Sundays, not just at the fashionable hour of five o'clock, when 'the Ring' was so full of elegant coaches the air was thick with ochre dust.

After Pitt's death, Hester found herself in a limbo on all fronts. Although a royal pension had been granted her, it would not commence until 30 June, and the various formalities attached to it would all take time. After legal fees and other costs, it would be reduced to less than £1,000 per annum. If she was cautious, and especially if she lived away from London, she ought to have been able to manage comfortably on such an amount.

Fox, in a mood of beneficence, made Hester an offer that may in fact have come from the King himself, and must have imagined she could not refuse it. She was given a choice of residences. One was apparently 'as good as ten thousand pounds a year'. As Hester recalled, 'He was to make me ranger of some park, with a house; and then I was to have a house in town, and the rest was to be done the way they shuffle those things through the public offices.' The alternative was for her to live in a grace-and-favour royal apartment, possibly at Windsor Castle, although this was conditional on her becoming a courtier. Hester rejected both offers: 'I rather chose to live independent'. When Fox's emissary Mr Ward told her she would live to repent her refusal, she told him that it was not

> ... from a personal disregard from Mr Fox that she refused; because when I asked Mr Pitt, upon one occasion, who was the cleverest man in England, he answered, 'Mr Fox'; but as the world only knew Mr Pitt and Mr Fox as opposed [*sic*] to each other, I should be considered as receiving benefits from Mr Pitt's enemy.

As for Mahon, she loathed him more than ever before. He reneged on the promise he had made Pitt, to shoulder the expenses accumulated by his brothers for their military uniforms and provisions, and refused to vouch for their debts. He told her that as far as he was concerned his promise to Pitt was now void. Horrified, Hester had replied: 'Good God, would you have your brothers arrested?' to which he answered, 'It would not be the first time that a Captain of a regiment had gone to gaol.' Pitt's friend, William Lowther, the second Earl of Lonsdale, came to the rescue, giving James a draft for two thousand pounds, a loan that Hester, in time, repaid.

Meanwhile, there was not a great deal of respect between Mahon and his father. Pitt's connections had gained Mahon a sinecure; and with his father-in-law's help, he had embarked on a political career, that year becoming Tory MP for Windsor and later successfully running for Hull. He had tried, and ultimately failed, to take legal action against his father, accusing him of squandering the family estate.

Hester took the house in Montagu Square as a home not just for herself, but for her brothers, Charles and James, when they were on leave, aware that they needed to make a good impression to move up in the world. When 'the boys' were in town, she always had breakfast on the table from nine to twelve, 'with tea and coffee and chicken, and tongue, and cold meat, and all that'. It was the first time she had ever had a house of her own; for the next month or so, she set about furnishing it in her own style 'with everything customary in fashion-able life'. Some of the furniture she had brought over from Downing Street, where she had decided it had been of 'no use', including some of the stiff, formal leather-backed sofas and chairs Pitt had used for his bad back and camp beds for her brothers' officer friends whenever they stayed the night.

Her ménage included the twenty-year-old Elizabeth Williams, formerly a servant in Pitt's household. Elizabeth and her sister Louisa were the daughters of Pitt's trusted equerry, Edward Williams; they came with him from Holwood to Walmer and Putney Heath, and for a time they were educated at his expense. Bright, gentle and pretty, Elizabeth had been Pitt's particular favourite, and had been in his service at York Place. As well as Miss Williams, Hester employed a housekeeper, a doorman and a small number of servants, among them Ann Fry, the girl who had become pregnant at Chevening. Calling herself 'Mrs' Fry now, Ann told Hester that she had managed to spend nine years at a respectable insti-tution in London – Mrs Davis's Boarding School for Girls – 'without anyone guessing she was a mother'.[1] Now she had come to Hester to beg employment and to be given shelter. In the years to come, both Elizabeth

Williams and Ann Fry were to find their lives inextricably bound up with the path their mistress was to take.

If Hester needed any reminder of the descent that even an aristocratic lady like herself could face if her fortunes turned entirely, she did not have to look far. On nearby Paddington Street, just off Baker Street, there was a large workhouse, whose inmates included the old and infirm, lunatics, orphans, foundling children and vagrants. Among them could be found formerly beautiful, once-fêted mistresses of wealthy men, now discarded, destitute and shunned.

She was well aware of how thin was the line between having a lover and becoming a kept mistress. Nearby Gloucester Place was full of wealthy mistresses and courtesans, some discreet, some ostentatious. One of them was Harriette Wilson. Another was Mary Ann Clarke, the blonde mistress of the King's son, the Duke of York, then Commander-in-Chief of the army. Mary Ann, who was sometimes glimpsed walking along Bond Street with a retinue of African servants, would be undone by too flagrantly using her influence to sell army commissions; the Duke would desert her in 1809. But for the moment, she held amusing soirées full of uniformed men, and if the Duke was there, Hester and her brothers would often drop in. Although not overly impressed with Mary Ann, she loved to poke fun at the Duchess, whom she described as 'a painted wife, with half a dozen fine gentlemen about her, shaking the hair-powder on her face' and ordering the windows open 'at dinner time, in a cold November day, to let out the smells of a parcel of dogs'. It was quite natural, she thought, with such an 'uncomfortable home' that the Duke thought himself 'at liberty to take a little pleasure elsewhere'. Although she could be blind to her own lapses of romantic judgement, Hester was a shrewd observer of those of others. Hester mimicked women like Mary Ann, rolling her eyes, sucking in her cheeks, smirking and assuming her mock-lascivious look. She may have been damning, and she tried to ensure that her brothers were never prey to such women – 'the rascally set' she called them. But as she was well aware, being a woman in Georgian London could be a precarious business.

Hester was now thirty. Having discovered the freedom of independence, she was loath to give it up. Some of that independence meant that she was free to establish friendships with men of her choosing, and if it was considered slightly scandalous that she was an unmarried woman in a house that was often full of men this was how she preferred it. One of her most persistent callers was William Noel Hill, fresh from a diplomatic posting in Austria, evidently still holding out hopes that Hester might settle down with him.* That October, once again, Harriet Bessborough set the rumour mill in motion:

> Ly. Hol [Lady Holland] told me yesterday as *certain* that Hetty's marriage with Mr Hill is *declared* and is to take place immediately: can this be so? If it is, *il est bien bon*. God bless you. I wish it may be true, for I sincerely wish poor Hetty to be well and comfortably settled.[2]

The engagement never materialized. Feeling himself rejected, the disgruntled Hill commented around this time that he thought Hester 'must have some strong occupation' or outlet for her talents. Sardonically, Hester began to refer to him as 'Christ Jesus', resenting his preachings. Some months later, Canning's visits had also become noticeably frequent. In March 1807 he accepted the position of Foreign Secretary, and the degree to which he continued to seek out Hester's company indicates how useful he found her political insights.

In July 1807 a familiar face from her Walmer days came back into her orbit. She had met Sir John Moore when he was in command at nearby Shorncliffe Camp, and immediately liked him, finding the Scottish-born-and-bred soldier refreshingly scornful of politicians. Then – as again now – he was a particularly handsome man; tall, with his greying locks close-cropped and his military greatcoat and necktie always slightly askew. Now he came to see her, to pay his respects and talk about Pitt. He found her changed, perhaps less impetuous. Her political understanding, her mental quickness and her familiarity with the preoccupations he faced, impressed him. It may not have taken long for Hester and Moore to realize they wished to spend more time in each other's company.

---

* William Noel Hill would go on to a distinguished diplomatic career, first in Austria, then Turin, returning for a time to be an MP for Marlborough, then taking up duties again as a diplomat in Naples.

Judging by the trust and respect, and sheer frequency, of the letters that followed, Moore, who had managed to remain a bachelor all these years, may well have felt that he had finally met his match. Pitt's old offer to make her one of his generals was a standing joke between them. Moore was forty-seven, and was in many ways a far more realistic choice for Hester than Granville. It would not have been his nature to mislead her, and he also had an air of sophistication unusual for a soldier, spoke several European languages and had already distinguished himself in America in the War of Independence and among other posts, in Corsica, the West Indies and Egypt. A complicity grew between them, much more than mere friendship. Moore seems to have been good for Hester; the influence of his methodical but passionate nature allowed her to regulate her otherwise erratic moods.

On his return to London Moore had been informed that his services would be welcome in Spain, but not as Commander of the Peninsular Campaign as had been widely predicted. It was a humiliating blow. Moore did not mix well with authority; his superiors and the current administration generally frustrated and exasperated him. In October 1807, a peace treaty was signed with Portugal, followed by another with Spain in January. Both Canning and Castlereagh, the Secretary of War, were impatient to make a real strike at the French. A decision was made to send the British army already in Portugal, reinforced with an expeditionary force from Britain, to support the Spanish.

With Hester, Moore felt free to pick over every conceivable angle of his position, to fulminate about what he thought of Castlereagh's military plans ('plausible verbose nonsense and a sort of gibberish', he complained to her) instead of having to censor himself. She was indignant on his behalf, perhaps – and this would have been something entirely novel for both of them – recognizing the pleasure of being two against the world.

It is fair to guess that Moore might not have been her choice when she was younger, nor she his, but now they were no longer so young. In March 1808 she was thirty-two, and she must have recognized that Moore was not the kind of man to make her suffer deliberately. As often happens when people know they are about to be separated, emotions surfaced at the last minute. By the time of Moore's departure, they both realized the extent of their attachment. What precisely had been agreed between them is not clear. Everything about his letters to her from the frontline suggests that he felt very tenderly towards her, greatly respected her opinions and actively missed her. He trusted her with highly confidential information about his superiors. She meanwhile appeared to be full of the sort of optimistic energy and quiet purpose that only a woman confident in a new love can be.

Her brothers would be leaving for Spain too. The hope that they might be near Moore at least gave her greater confidence that she would see them all safe again.

In the autumn of 1808 British forces marched into Spain and Portugal, in the sanguine belief that the patriots would soon loosen the French grip on the country, and expecting to be greeted with open arms by the inhabitants. Immense amounts of financial aid and military provisions had been shipped to the insurgents. Yet the British were in for a shock. The Spanish and Portuguese armies were disorganized and poorly commanded; as well as shortages of food, clothing and equipment, there was a complete lack of cavalry and artillery.

After his arrival, first in Portugal and then in Spain, Moore wrote to Hester every few days, letters of great length and unwavering fondness. It is clear that hers are just as urgent and detailed, and that she is all the time worrying about him in the field, and about his reputation, which is under fire from ministers at home; she sends him every useful tidbit she can. 'I believe they will make no attack on me until they see how I extricate myself here,' he tells her, adding that he intends to let the public judge him by releasing his letters, 'which contain a plain narrative'. He hopes she can look at them all before he publishes them, he tells her, 'if ever I have the pleasure of seeing you again'. He reassures her that although he has not yet seen Charles with the 50th, he has 'at last contrived an arrangement . . . with Sir Henry, who is the most liberal of men, to take the 50th with me' so that Charles should be with him as aide-de-camp soon. He tells Hester: 'I wish you were here with us. The climate now is charming; and we should give you riding enough, and in your red habit *à la Amazone*, you would animate and do us much good.'[3]

A month later, on 20 November, from Salamanca, Moore reassures her again after she has written to him asking him to receive James too. 'I can refuse you nothing,' he tells her. He advises her to notify James that he must obtain leave to come to Spain and join him, but warns her: 'He will, however come too late; I shall be already beaten. I am within four marches of the French, with only a third of my force, and as the Spaniards have been dispatched in all quarters, my junction with the other two-thirds is very precarious. When we do join, we shall be very inferior to the enemy, we have been completely deceived . . . and now the discovery comes a little too late.'[4]

Moore disagreed with his government's military tactics in Spain from the outset. Left in command in the Peninsula, he was faced with overwhelming odds. Moore's troops left Salamanca for Old Castile on 11 December, hoping to distract the French away from Madrid. Very soon afterwards, however, he heard that not only had Madrid fallen, but that Napoleon, having only now realized the British were there, was unleashing the full force of his army against them – some 80,000 men. Knowing there was no glory in a vanquished army, Moore immediately realized his only objective was to save his forces from annihilation, and marched them north in the hope they would be smoothly evacuated by the Royal Navy.

For more than two weeks after the fall of Madrid, things seemed to be going well. By the end of December, though, a combination of poor logistics and horrendous weather caused chaos on both sides. By 27 December, Moore had managed to reach what appeared to be reasonable safety, and the next day began what would become known as the 'retreat to Corunna'. His forces were then joined by some 6,000 Spanish soldiers, many barely able to stand, malnourished and a great number succumbing to infectious diseases such as dysentery, typhus and cholera. Soon the mood of desperation spread to the redcoats, and discipline began to break down. Moore would have been horrified at the trail of theft, rape and murder left behind by his fine battalions. By the time his depleted army reached Corunna, it was in a disastrous state. The ships had been held up, while the French were pressing hard, and before the British could be evacuated they were subjected to heavy bombardment.

At Corunna on 16 January 1809 Moore made a last-ditch stand against intensified assault by Marshal Soult. Late that afternoon, while directing his reserves, Moore was cut down by a cannonball volley that seemed to onlookers to strike from nowhere. It shattered his vital organs and bones; it was clear to those who ran to help him that he was beyond help, although he was not, it seems, disfigured. Moore's long-time companion and closest friend Colonel Paul Anderson was with him. When two surgeons came hurrying up to him, he told them they would do better to attend injured soldiers; he knew he was dying. As he lay on his camp bed, the anxious faces of his men pressed around; he tried to give Anderson instructions for his mother and sister, and asked about other officers who had been wounded. At that moment, young James Stanhope rushed up in time to catch the General's last words: 'Stanhope, remember me to your sister.'

It was a memorably graceful death; he was buried on the ramparts of Corunna the following day. By 17 January most of the British troops had managed to board the waiting HMS *Victory* – later known to the world as Nelson's ship at the Battle of Trafalgar – and the following day, the entire fleet sailed for home. They would not receive a hero's welcome when they arrived on 23 January. Instead, a bewildered British public would watch aghast as Moore's headless army returned, having lost some 2,000 men, with one-fifth of their number missing, presumed dead, and several thousand more wounded and sick.

Hester heard the news about Moore within hours of the *Victory*'s arrival. She was devastated. Everything she had begun to hope for – a new life – had been taken away from her at a stroke. In the first days after Moore's death, Hester behaved like a war widow.

What she did not learn immediately was that her brother – 'dearest, delightful amusing Charles' – died the same afternoon as Moore. A bullet ripped through his heart as he turned to congratulate his men in the 50th Regiment, which Moore had put him in charge of. 'Moore received his death-blow shortly after, and my poor brother fell nearly at the same time. Thank heaven the latter did not suffer one instant . . . the gallant General lived for three hours, but the agony he was in never deranged his senses; he was perfectly collected . . .' It was Colonel Anderson who brought her the news, and who stayed while she broke down. Continuing her letter to an unidentified friend, she confides:

You may wonder why I tell you all this; but grief has its peculiarities, and thinking of nothing else but those I have lost, I like to talk of them, and the only one I have devoted my time to since is Colonel Anderson, knowing the nature of my feelings, the instant he arrived in town he came to me and told me everything in detail.[5]

She went on to say it was a miracle that James survived; his cloak had been shot through, he was hit and wounded; four men standing close to him were mown down by a cannonball. 'I feel as though I have just waked from a horrid dream . . .'[6]

Grief left a powerful mark on Hester. Within the space of three years, she had lost her favourite brother, and two dearly loved men, one of whom might have become her husband. To those whom she felt had engineered the circumstances that had led to the débâcle at Corunna, and who now came to offer her sympathy, like Canning and her uncle Chatham, she was cold. She felt deeply aggrieved for Moore, aware that in the souring of the public opinion about the Peninsular War, the general had played a part. She especially blamed Castlereagh for his readiness in the House of Commons to inculpate Moore; on that subject she felt 'my indignation is so great that I should have torn out his black heart'.[7] She immediately wrote to the Prime Minister, her cousin Lord Grenville, in a tone brimming with accusation, fearing that he would somehow deny Moore 'the honours he is so well entitled to from his country'. She wanted him to know of the 'unlimited confidence' that Pitt had 'placed in Sir John Moore's judgement and exertions', adding that 'no man could have been more ill-treated than the General'.* Hester was clearly worried that his reputation would be tarnished – 'I have great apprehensions that they will even persecute him beyond the grave, by blackening his memory . . .'.

---

* Pitt had intended Moore to fight Napoleon's armies in France, making a bold landing, and with a spectacular showdown, partnered by an army to be led by Sir Sidney Smith. 'He promised General Moore the command of 30,000 men; indeed of all the disposable force of the country, if he thought such a force necessary.' (The plan was not adopted; Moore did not think it was tactically prudent, as he made plain in his *Narrative of the Campaign of the British Army in Spain*, published posthumously that same year.)

So, for Hester, 1809 began as a year of terrible sorrow. It was hard for her to see much point to her life in London. Her one concern was James, who although he had recovered physically from his ordeal, showed every sign of what today would be called post-traumatic stress disorder. On 27 April, at Montagu Square, Hester rewrote her will, which she had witnessed by Colonel Anderson. With Charles dead, she made James the heir to all her belongings, as well as her share in their dead mother's estate, which they would be entitled to only if their uncle Lord Chatham died without issue.

She and James had decided to go abroad together for a while. Sicily was to be their destination. The balmy island climate had long been considered the best place for convalescence, but getting there was not an altogether easy proposition. All but the most determined travellers deferred their journey to Europe around this time; Hester and James would have to find passage on a naval frigate. With the French chafing at the blockade, private vessels, although tolerated in the main, were generally thought too dangerous. Still, Hester had friends in high places; arrangements would be made.

In the meantime, Hester set about packing up Montagu Square. She took a small set of rooms at 14 Green Street, just off Oxford Street, and cast about for somewhere to rent cheaply for the summer. Soon after Moore's departure the previous year, she had gone to Bath for several weeks, and on one of her lengthier jaunts had discovered the beautiful scenery of the Wye Valley in Wales.

She returned to Builth Wells, an otherwise unprepossessing, rather closed-faced town that sat on some of the most bucolic landscape she had ever seen. On her last visit she had stayed at the Royal Oak (now the Lion Hotel) for several weeks. This time her past happiness was a painful reminder of what she had lost: she stayed no more than a night in May 1809, before making her way further up the valley.

On that first visit, Hester had befriended the town's best-known residents, the Reverend Price and his son Thomas, both fiery Welsh nationalists she had taken a great liking to. For the time being, father and son offered Hester kindly, lively company, though if she had come to Wales to find quiet, she would hardly have found it in the Prices' dining room, which was invariably full of impressionable, ideal-istic young men, shouting and speaking in Welsh, then apologizing and translating for the English-speakers. Although remote, it was not as removed from the war as one might suppose. The Black Mountains had several camps where French prisoners of war were being held; Thomas Price spent part of his time teaching them Welsh.

It was to Reverend Price that Hester had written to ask if she could rent a property on the banks of the Irfon, three miles from town, that she remembered seeing the previous year. 'Glan Irfon' was a simple, dark-slate-walled gabled farmhouse, sheltered by a ridge, with a pleasant view overlooking meadows. By late spring the landscape would have been soft and green, with hill-slopes full of lazing cattle and forest-like thickets; wildflowers everywhere and wild roses tumbling over the hedgerows. The farmhouse was never meant to sleep more than four or so people; there was only one other guest bedroom. During the time Hester was there, with James and other visitors, as well as Elizabeth Williams, it was packed to the rafters.

By the time Hester arrived in the Wye Valley, she had made a new acquaintance. The friendship she would form with the flamboyant Venezuelan revolutionary General Francisco de Miranda would do much to help her recover her enthusiasm for life, and galvanize her ambitions. He was fifty-nine to her thirty-three, well-built and olive-skinned with piercing hazel eyes, his greying hair tied back in a ponytail which gave him a piratical look.

On 29 April 1809 Miranda scrawled his first impressions of Hester on the back of a dinner invitation from James, who declared his sister was 'very anxious' to make his acquaintance:

> I have dined with Lady Hester Stanhope who enchanted me with her amiability, erudition, and liberal conversation. At one time she talked about Rome and Italy, which she had visited; at another time she talked about Greece, which she wished to visit and which she was not able to see when she was in Naples. She also talked about Venezuela whose independence she wished to see established upon a basis of rational liberty. In this connection she said to me that her uncle Mr Pitt had upon various occasions talked to her with interest and warmth about this affair, and had particularly lauded my patriotic ideas. Ever since Lady Hester had wished to become acquainted with me, and had also wished to visit my

interesting country. She said further that if I needed a recruit of her species, she was ready to follow me there though it should be to do nothing else than to manage schools and hospitals. All this she descanted upon with greatest jocularity and grace until midnight when I retired most highly impressed with her conversation, good judgement . . . and interesting person. She is one of the most delightful women I have ever known – and if her behaviour accords with my first impressions – she is certainly a rarity among her sex.[8]

Pitt had first encountered Miranda in 1790, and initially encouraged his idea of a British-sponsored expedition to South America. But he may have deliberately made sure the dashing, much-travelled, multi-lingual ladykiller did not meet his niece. By 1809 Miranda's life history was a complicated one that had encompassed manifold allegiances. In the name of fighting for liberty, his many adventures had already included stints as a Spanish military officer, a colonel in the Russian army, and a commander of French Revolutionary forces in the Netherlands. Whichever country he was in, he was invariably accused of being an enemy spy. Around London, Miranda was celebrated for his spell-binding tirades at the tables of Charles Fox, Joseph Priestley, Jeremy Bentham and William Wilberforce.

Shortly after their first meeting, Hester dined with Miranda again, and this time Bentham – Miranda's neighbour on Grafton Street – was present.* Within two weeks Miranda was calling Hester 'Querida' and told his friends that she was 'the most delicious woman I have yet encountered'.[9] This, from a man whose nickname was 'the Casanova of the New World', was indeed a high compliment.

In Wales, Hester lost no time in writing to Miranda. She knew that he was anxious for definite action to bring about Venezuelan independence, his 'Great Cause' he called it, in pursuit of which he had already accumulated considerable debts. Just as she had been with Moore, she was sympathetic to Miranda's misadventures in his attempts to interest

---

* Bentham observed Hester's interest in going out to South America, and they had discussed the idea of establishing Quaker schools in Venezuela based on the so-called Lancaster method. Joseph Lancaster (1778–1838) was an English educationist who had developed a system of schooling based on non-denominational, monitorial principles.

Canning and Castlereagh in funding his proposed expedition. She shared admiration for his zeal with Bentham and Wilberforce – the former was already drafting legislation for the new Venezuelan Republic, while the latter, who found Miranda 'very entertaining and instructive', hoped he would be of some influence in abolishing slavery in his own country.[10] Miranda promised to come out to see her in August. She replied in a slightly teasing letter dated 31 July 1809:

> I cannot wait until I receive your letter to express how much I am delighted with the prospect of seeing you in this part of the world; I wish I could flatter myself with the idea that I could contribute to your amusement while here . . . and that you will spend as much *more* of yr time as you can spare from yr *books*, a certain number of which I suppose travel with you . . .'[11]

The farmhouse, she told him with some circumspection, would be too small and cramped for him to find comfortable, and she suggested he stay at the Royal Oak. All the same, he seems to have dined with her every night, bringing with him his two flutes – ebony and silver – on which he played melancholy tunes. Miranda remained long enough to ride with Hester through the Brecon mountains to Abergavenny and other beauty spots, staying at small inns along the route.

The question of whether Hester had an affair with Miranda has been raised many times. Almost all of Miranda's biographers boldly assert this was the case. The stronger possibility, given the age difference, is that she did not. Yet there was undoubtedly something of an erotic charge between them, and a passionate enthusiasm to their meetings. Hester did not seem to care what others thought of their travelling together or the fact that they were often alone together. Both were flamboyant extroverts who craved public acclaim, and in Hester, Miranda clearly recognized a kindred spirit. But although he was regularly unfaithful to the mother of his two sons, Sarah Andrews, he was not seeking a permanent replacement. What is certain is that within a short time, they had achieved the kind of intimacy only very close friends can manage.

He called her 'the divine Irenide', a teasing reference to the woman she might become in 'his' South America. Miranda may have been a daredevil and a dreamer, but his dreams had real substance. He inspired Hester to think that life could be different and better. Miranda's belief that men and women should be equal in society, and that women should be admitted to higher education and free to direct their talents where they saw fit, was probably for Hester a revolutionary idea (and to her far sweeter on Miranda's lips than the same notions already expressed by Mary Wollstonecraft). In his new South America, there would be no limit to human achievement; the new Venezuela would be the most enticing of all future meritocracies, set against marvels of natural beauty and without the weight of the old, exhausted, and over-refined cultures of England and Europe. Certainly, he caused Hester to rethink much of what she believed about a great many things; and once Miranda had begun opening doors in her mind, it was hard for her to shut them.

As summer drew to an end, Hester packed up once more. Like anyone who moves around a great deal, she seems to have felt a certain fatigue towards her belongings. She left behind two of her prized possessions, large paintings of Pitt and the Duke of York.[12] She also planted an orange blossom tree – the ancient symbol of marriage and fertility – at the foot of the farmhouse garden.[13] Perhaps this was a gesture towards what she felt had been taken away from her, or an expression of hope that her chances were not all over – or perhaps there was something that had been precious to her that she wanted to bury underneath it.

When Charles Meryon stepped through the door of Hester's temporary lodgings at Green Street, he was surprised to be met not by a footman or maid, but by a foreign-looking gentleman who introduced himself as General Miranda.[14] Meryon, who was still only partially qualified, was completing his medical studies at St Thomas's. Nonetheless, 'Dr Meryon' was ushered directly into the dining room to sit at a table, which was scattered with maps and books.

The man whose future would for ever be entangled with Hester's was tall and slender, with pleasant, somewhat deferential features, and a mouth that had a tendency to curve upwards into a smile no matter what his mood. His chestnut hair was fashionably close-cropped, and he often blinked his long sand-coloured lashes. He had pink-rimmed eyes. Unknown to Hester, his eyes were raw from crying. Four days earlier, a nineteen-year-old girl with whom he had been conducting an affair had died as she gave birth to their daughter. By cruel coincidence the day of her funeral – Tuesday, 9 January 1810 – was the same day he had received a note from Hester summoning him. One of Meryon's friends was the son of Dr Cline, under whom he studied, and his name had been put forward.

By the time Meryon left that night, he had accepted all Hester's terms. They were to spend a year or more in Sicily. He had to be ready to leave immediately. She asked him about his family at Rye, and about his travels to France. He was startled when she suddenly changed the subject and told him that she hoped she could rely on his discretion. She related an anecdote about a certain doctor employed by someone she knew, and whose name was also familiar to Meryon, who lost his practice after saying of a patient after her death that she 'was one of the most beautiful corpses he had ever seen, and that he had stood contemplating her for a quarter of an hour'. This woman had been 'a person of rank', like herself, Hester warned, and that doctor's 'comment, made in an unguarded moment to a friend, ruined him'.

Certainly, as he mulled over the meeting that night, Meryon must have wondered at what an extraordinary turn his life had just taken.

Around three in the morning on 13 January 1810 Hester closed the door of 14 Green Street for the last time. James and his army friend Nassau Sutton were already in Portsmouth, as was Meryon; she had also sent her servants Elizabeth Williams and Ann Fry ahead of her. There were no witnesses to her sudden mood of agitation. By the time she reached Portsmouth late that evening, a steady icy rain assaulted the carriage windows. Instead of feeling tired, when she settled into her room at the George Inn on the High Street, Hester's mind was racing.[15]

Indecision plagued her. The previous week, she had sent a flurry of letters to Miranda; she had requested immediate replies, indeed she called for a *verbal* answer. Miranda dined with her twice that week. Something was discussed between them, something so important to Hester that it could not be written down. When her emotions were engaged, Hester often acted precipitously. That week, it seems that without too much discretion, Hester put out her own feelers on Miranda's behalf. She approached Lord Mulgrave, an old Pitt loyalist, to see whether the Admiralty might offer Miranda passage at least part of the way to Caracas.

Perhaps she misunderstood one of Miranda's throwaway comments: that he would go away with her if he could, if they were on their way to South America. Judging by her actions in the week before her departure, whatever he said was strong enough for her to consider changing her own plans. He seems to have told her to await word from him, while he toyed with the possibility that he might join her in Portsmouth, either to bid her farewell, or even – and he may not have expected her to truly believe this – to board a frigate together.

On 15 January, having not heard from him but expecting him to materialize at any moment, Hester could bear the uncertainty no longer. That afternoon, around four o'clock, she wrote a long letter – insistent and urgent – to Miranda:

> As I cannot guess what you have done, I can only advise in case you have done nothing adverse to what I propose. The wind is foul & has every chance of remaining so. I should at all events leave town on Wednesday morning & go with Seymour, with his present convoy, if we cannot manage what I now recommend. There are 3 convoys here, one for the West Indies, which runs for the South, one for the Straits & one for Lisbon, the latter of which the Manilla [*sic*] belongs to. There are no less than 12 frigates exclusive of Line of Battle attached to these convoys & certainly the Manilla [*sic*] might well be spared – Seymour has no objection whatever (& he mentioned even solicited) to take you all the way though he fears you will be uncomfortable . . . I should at any rate go with Seymour if you can leave town Wednesday & Doctor Maryan [*sic*] on Thursday night by mail or Thursday morning in a chaise, we shall be able to embark this Friday . . . The town is quite full but I will get you lodgings in time for you if you write tomorrow night – I am quite well . . . I entreat you, come off on Wednesday, if the wind is the same. Do not be deceived about it – there is a fine weather cock on Chesterfield House. If the wind remains from the South, to West & North West, they cannot sail. God bless you . . .[16]

The letter details preparations Captain Seymour is ready to make on his behalf:

Seymour has a fire, is putting up bulkheads, will accommodate your maids on sophas [*sic*] in your own cabin & will manage the baggage as well as he can – and insists that once they have set off he will be duty-bound to carry his passengers all the way – They cannot refuse you his ship to go on with from Lisbon.[17]

She apologizes for sending the express so that the letter would reach him by one o'clock that night, a service which cost a shilling per mile. In order to receive the letter, Miranda would have had to pay almost £4, an astronomical sum.[18]

Miranda clearly considered leaving on the same ship as Hester, but he was weighing up his options. He was aware of the latest reports from Spain, which was now almost entirely subjugated by Napoleon's armies, and he was convinced that soon the British government would find it impossible to disregard the Spanish-American cause, and would become as favourable to his plans as it had hitherto been 'vacillating and contra-dictory'. Replying to Hester six days later, it is clear that he had probably made up his mind by the time she reached Portsmouth. It is a gentle letter to his 'dear and amiable Lady Hester' apologizing for not replying earlier – 'What series of disappointments, and vexation follows you now? But your superior mind is above them I hope' – and telling her that he envies James the 'pleasing task' of taking 'peculiar care of his inestimable Sister'. He told her she was 'irreplaceable', that she was 'dear and beloved' and wished she 'was near to copmunicate [*sic*] & to give advice' and ends:

And do not forget that if a Profile of devine [*sic*] *Irenide* was ever to be taken (and I think it ought), you promised me a Copy

Farewell – better in Greek
Ever & sincerely yours
M[19]

Hester replied in a similar graceful tone, with none of her earlier urgency. But she was hurt. The winds, which had been perfect, changed. Despite all the hurry for departure, they had no choice but to wait. In the end, they would stay in Portsmouth almost an entire frustrating month. She let Miranda think she was already on her way.[20] Calling each other lifelong friends, they would never see one another again.

She took disconsolate walks along the harbour, which was crowded with captured French warships used as prison hulks, their masts removed and decks refitted with odd-looking huts for the guards. She gazed at HMS *Victory*. Having returned from the blockade of the Russian fleet, its gigantic frame had been hauled up on to land in the Royal Dockyards to be refitted. In the winter of 1808, the *Victory* had been sent out as a troop ship with the remaining forces of General Sir John Moore's army; her dear Charles had been on board. Within three months, the ship had returned with Moore's defeated army, the wounded James among them. James had brought with him two small parcels of possessions, one that had belonged to Charles, the other to Moore; correspondence and notes that were now bloodstained, as well as her own letters to both men. Colonel Anderson had given her a lock of Moore's hair and his bloodstained glove. These had been too precious for her to leave behind; she had them with her now. The sight of the *Victory* broke her heart.

On 9 February, knowing finally she would leave the next day, Hester wrote a last farewell letter, late at night, feeling wretched and alone. She knew the sight of her handwriting made him blanch but she could not help it. It was to Granville, who she knew had recently married. It is undated, a wild, ungainly sprawl:

> The wind is fair, the ship soon in sight, we embark tomorrow morning . . .
> I hope you will respect my absence a little . . . Think sometimes of me
> when I am far, far off which now will soon be the case. May every blessing
> attend you & when we meet again I hope it will be with equal joy on
> both sides, once more. God bless you . . . I fear I shall scarce be able to
> send this.[21]

Early the next morning, they left from King's Quay in the Royal Dockyards, boarding the war-bound Royal Navy vessel *Jason*, a regular fifth-rate frigate carrying dispatches for Lisbon, accompanied by the *Jamaica*, a larger third-rater, for transporting the 4th and 28th Regiments under convoy, to be sent off to the frontline in Spain from Gibraltar. With one last look, Hester turned to watch England drift away. As she described it to herself, the coming weeks and year would 'decide her fate'.

## 5

## *Love and Escape*

Gibraltar was not the 'abroad' Hester had in mind when she left England. The island, although bathed in strong sunshine, struck her as squalid and small-minded. In some ways, it seemed merely a rougher version of the regimental life she had left behind at Walmer. The knowledge that both Charles and Sir John Moore had passed this way so recently depressed her. She could see no joy in the faces of the Spanish refugees who thronged the cramped, cobbled alleys. She was, however, warmly welcomed by the Governor, Colonel Colin Campbell, a doughty Scotsman, who invited Hester and James to stay with him in the official residence, known by all as the Convent, an austere former Franciscan monastery.

In the meantime Meryon was becoming familiar with what was required of him in his new role. He wrote to his family that his employer was 'on the whole, much better than when we left England. She rises at midday, breakfasts in her chamber, and at one or two, makes her appearance. At this time I converse with her about her health, if occasion require, or walk with her for half an hour in the Convent garden. I then ride, read, or amuse myself as I please, for the rest of the day until dinnertime.' Warming to his theme, he added, 'Her disposition is the most obliging you can possibly conceive, and the familiar and kind manner in which she treats me has the best effect on persons around me, from all of whom, through her, I experience the politest civilities.'[1]

To brighten the mood, the Colonel staged a series of dinner parties – the first for Hester's birthday on 12 March – inviting any high-placed acquaintances he could find. Within barely a fortnight of one another, two Englishmen – Michael Bruce and the Marquess of Sligo, Howe Peter Browne – had arrived in Gibraltar. Both men were curious to meet Hester.

At twenty-three, Michael Bruce, the son of Patrick Crauford Bruce, a rich nabob, was undeniably good-looking, tall and slim, with fine tanned skin, fledgling sideburns on his downy cheeks, grave blue eyes and long lashes. When he smiled, he revealed beautiful, even white teeth. The night Hester met him, Campbell staged his dinner party in the ballroom, which had been fashioned from the nave of an adjacent chapel. Hester found herself looking into Bruce's eyes, studying the exact colour; as well as each button and the fabric of his jacket; the delicate indentations in his wrists, and watching his handsome head and neck as he turned to refill a glass. Afterwards the party had wandered into the courtyard garden, stuck about with dragon trees. Hester and Bruce stayed talking there for a while, sitting by a small fountain.

Bruce came from enterprising, rather exotic Scottish stock. In the late eighteenth century, one of his forebears, the explorer James Bruce, made epic voyages through Syria, Egypt, Arabia and Abyssinia (Ethiopia), where he had been the first European to reach the confluence of the Blue Nile and the White Nile.* Hester learned that Bruce had been born in Bombay and that his mother had been a great beauty, painted by Romney. His father, an East India Company man, had founded a highly successful importing business. It was a delightful life for a beloved first son in a household full of servants who doted on him, to whom pet monkeys and caparisoned elephants were commonplace. He and his mother and siblings had returned to England when he was five. He had gone to Eton and St John's College, Cambridge. He admitted to being a good rower, and told her that his father, having become a banker, had embarked on another career as a Member of Parliament, buying various seats, including one in Rye, one of the Cinque Ports.

Bruce had been away from England for almost three years – his father

---

* James Bruce had made a copy of the apocryphal *Book of Enoch*, in Ethiopic, or Ge'ez, to the marvel of scholars who believed it had vanished. On his return to London, the extraordinary account of his travels was considered so outlandish and unbelievable that he was mocked as 'Liar Bruce'. Not until after his death did his five volumes, *Travels to Discover the Source of the Nile in the Years 1763–73*, become bestsellers. They were reprinted in 1804, and Pitt had them in his bookcase at Walmer. Hester had read them there, prompting her to ask to see some of Bruce's drawings of Gondar, presented to the King at Windsor Castle.

hoped he might become a diplomat. In Scandinavia he had met all the princes and nobles, and had instructions from his father to continue onwards to mingle with rarefied society in St Petersburg and Moscow. But he never got there, although he was in Copenhagen in 1807 when Canning gave the order for the British fleet to launch a hasty, unprovoked pre-emptive attack on the city. Outraged, Bruce took the Danish side, and had been the first British civilian to return to the city and give an eyewitness account of the destruction.*

It would emerge that Hester and Bruce were linked, in a roundabout way, through the misdeeds and deeds of men with whom she had been on intimate terms. Her second cousin, Lord Grenville, had been a neighbour and friend of Bruce's father, and in 1807 had bartered a seat in Ireland to be accepted by Crauford Bruce if he would agree to pay off the present incumbent with the exact amount of the debt (some £2,500) he was owed by a certain Lord Camelford, Grenville's brother-in-law, who had recently died. That this same Camelford had been Hester's first lover, Bruce was, of course, unaware.

There were other coincidental crossings of paths. When Bruce's father saw him off on his travels, bound for the royal courts of St Petersburg and Moscow, he had every expectation that his son would be warmly received by Ambassador Lord Granville Leveson Gower in St Petersburg, to whom he had a letter of introduction.

But the last association could not have failed to make Hester sad. Instead of going to Russia, Bruce had gone to Spain. Towards the end of 1808 he went to the Peninsula, to tour the battlefronts, hoping to present himself as a 'free lance' to Sir John Moore, a particular hero of his. Moore had been 'very civil and kind' to him at Salamanca, and with the general's consent, he had made his way to Madrid – alone – just as the French were massing around the city, with the apparent aim of bringing back news of the enemy's movements. It was obvious nothing could be done

---

* Bruce's account of returning to Copenhagen, written to his father on 8 July 1807, gives a revealing portrait of the man Hester fell in love with: 'As I had a great curiosity to see with my own eyes the ravages which had been done by our own shells and canons, I formed the resolution of entering, either by fair or foul means. It required some ingenuity and some boldness to carry my project into execution. If the Danes knew we were in Copenhagen, such was the state of their irritations, and so exasperated were they against the English, that they would not have hesitated to put us to Death.'

to prevent the capital from falling. Just before the attack, in the dead of night, Bruce had walked his way out, covering a distance of twenty-eight miles on foot to reach the safety of Aranjuez. He then retreated alongside Moore's army to Corunna, an experience that made him deeply bitter. He held Wellesley – soon to be the Duke of Wellington – personally responsible.

Three days before Moore and Charles Stanhope were killed, Bruce had still been at Corunna. Was he present at the battle, or had he managed to avoid it? Had he also met Hester's brothers? Neither he nor James ever mention this detail; it is safe to assume he stayed out of danger's way. If he despised Wellesley, he reserved an even greater hatred for 'Bony'.

It is easy to see that Bruce, with his strong political opinions, would have been immediately disarmed by Hester's equally confrontational attitudes. Her forthrightness in discussion about the war and military tactics impressed him. Meryon noted that at this time she 'often mention[ed] Mr Pitt's opinion of her fitness for military command. Had she been a man and a soldier, she would have been what the French call a *sabreur*; for never was anyone so fond of wielding weapons and of boasting of her capability of using them as she was.' Hester boasted to the young man that she liked daggers, but 'her favourite weapon was the mace'.[2] Wilful and independent, with her impressive connections, she immediately signalled a challenge. Her more sophisticated, ironic utterances caused Bruce to question his own, somewhat more woodenly expressed views.

The other dinner guest at the Colonel's table was Howe Peter Browne, the second Marquess of Sligo. Having only recently succeeded to his father's title, he was now impulsively in command of a considerable fortune and impressive estates in Ireland. He was embarked on a tour of the Mediterranean, and planned to join Lord Byron, who was, like Bruce, a Cambridge contemporary and friend. The chance meeting with Bruce seemed fortuitous; there was much back-slapping and laughter.

Certainly Hester liked Sligo. At twenty-four, a year older than Bruce, Sligo affected something of the look that would soon become known as Byronic: he had grown his hair so it hung in tendrils. He was fond of quoting lengths of poetry, often in Greek, and forever making allusions to classical literature, but always in a way that seemed wittily *louche*.

There was something very boyish about his soft plumpness and his gleeful humour, despite his evident attempts at corruption, and Bruce's teasing hints at his promiscuity. He was immediately deferential to Hester, and always aware of her, leaning in close when they sat together. Bruce noticed this from the first, and became more reckless with Hester himself that same evening, teasing her, becoming more animated. When he left that night, he pressed her hand to his lips and looked at her face, touching her cheek gently as he did so.

At what point did the sexual hesitancy of the woman who had begun to believe herself past her prime give way to the passion that she so craved? It came as a pleasant shock to her to discover that she still had power over such a man, especially so deliciously unformed a creature as Bruce.

At thirty-four, Hester looked, in this new climate, younger than when she had set off from Portsmouth. Bruce put her age at no more than twenty-eight. She had cut her hair to shoulder-length, and the 'cropt' look suited her; she held the curls back from her face with woven strips of cloth. Her face struck many as enigmatic: she had learned to put on an inscrutable look, a habit, she would say, she got from Pitt. Unless she would have it otherwise, 'nobody can ever observe in me changes in my countenance; or I will venture, what was in me,' she said. She was vain enough to know that her looks might not outlast the attraction; she wasn't deluded about her chances with Bruce.

Still, Hester was falling passionately in love. Powerful restless emotions were brought to the surface. Despair and tragedy had forced her vibrant and impetuous nature underground. But now, the physical attraction gave her an oddly gratifying sensation of danger. Once again, she was on a high wire, hostage to an unpredictable outcome. She was captivated by Bruce's half-cocked, enquiring smile, the weight of his hand lightly touching her shoulder, the way he turned for a last backward glance as he disappeared out into the night. She did not want to let him go.

Within days of meeting Hester, perhaps trying to out-do Bruce, Sligo committed the extravagance of hiring an armed brig, the *Pylades*, for six months, and set about outfitting it, hiring some twenty or thirty hands. In his rush to assemble a working crew he chose to ignore the fact that his ablest men were in fact bound to the navy, a key detail he would later come to regret. Both Sligo and Bruce announced independently that they had changed their plans. They agreed that they would travel on together to Palermo: she could consider them her advance guard, for they would send her word on the situation there, as there were rumours that Napoleon's armies threatened to invade Sicily.

Now James too suddenly changed his plans. It is obvious from later letters that Bruce confessed the 'connection' and 'unguarded affection for his sister' almost immediately. Although disapproving, James had seemed to accept the liaison, but he had no intention of being around to witness it. Privately, he urged Hester 'to be prudent, and to lay herself as little as possible to the observation of the world'. On 2 April James received an official letter, which he chose to view as a summons, informing him that the battalion of Guards to which he belonged had arrived at Cadiz and were now readying themselves for the campaign. Although he had been granted permission for six months' absence and had promised Hester he would accompany her to Sicily, he decided to leave immediately. Nassau Sutton, who was to have been of their party, would go with him.

When it came to saying goodbye to James, Hester could not bear to be the one left behind. When the Colonel informed her that a suitable frigate, the *Cerebus*, would be sailing for Malta, from which the onward journey to Sicily could be made, she asked him to arrange for passage to be prepared three days ahead of her brother's departure. On 7 April 1810, stiffly refusing to cry, brother and sister embraced each other on the docks, and parted ways.

Hester sailed into Valletta harbour on 21 April, in time for Easter celebrations. The Governor, Major-General Sir Hildebrand Oakes, sent one of his men to meet her, bearing traditional almond-paste *figolli* along with an unexpected invitation to stay at the official residence.

But Hester had already made arrangements to stay with Malta's Deputy Commissariat General, Alexander Fernandes, and his wife Sarah, who were close friends of John David and Louisa Jane, the elder sister of Elizabeth Williams. The Davids had by now been living as a married couple in Valletta for three years. Both men had been offered administrative posts in Malta through their connections with Pitt; David had risen in the ranks of the commissariat and was now in charge of the

King's bakery; Fernandes was his direct superior. The Williams sisters were overjoyed to see one another again; Louisa Jane was bursting with pride over her first child, Hester Louisa, who was now two years old. Hester was both namesake and godmother. The Fernandeses lived close to the harbour, having made their home in what used to be a lodge for the Knights of St John of Jerusalem. Hester liked Sarah, an unusually resourceful woman who was mulling over a speculative venture to manage a farm on the island of Lampedusa; she was to go on ahead with their son, a remarkably brave thing to be contemplating, while her husband remained in Malta.[3]

Meanwhile, the news from Sicily was confusing, and their plans hung in the balance. After a week with the Fernandeses, Meryon was aware of a rising tension between all parties. He observed that his employer, who had been all sweetness at the commencement of their stay, was demonstrating her unpredictable temper. She had, he noted:

> . . . contrived to affront almost all the women in the place. She has the most thorough contempt for her sex, at least that part of it who converse on nothing but visits, caps and bonnets and such frivolous subjects. Hence it is that the moment she discovers one to be of that class, and her knowledge of mankind very soon puts her in possession of a person's character, she seldom fails to manifest her disgust and to give rise to as much disgust as she feels. She accepts no invitations except from General Oakes, and therefore cuts me off, who necessarily go only where she does, from many pleasant parties.

With no word from Bruce, Hester was fretting. However, to her delight, within ten days, instead of a letter Bruce turned up. With him came Sligo, and Hester's cousin, Lord Ebrington, whom they had brought along with them from Palermo.* Hester, Meryon noted, suddenly glowed, and was good-humoured again. Not bothering to conceal his annoyance, Meryon

---

* Lord Ebrington, a connoisseur of the arts and a great admirer of Napoleon, was 'the handsomest, most sensible and distinguished looking young nobleman in Europe . . . whose manners were as gentle, shy and graceful, almost as those of Lord Ponsonby himself. Few women could have disliked a *tête à tête* with Lord Ebrington'. So opined Harriette Wilson, the reigning courtesan of the day, who later succeeded in seducing him.

reported to his parents that 'Bruce is handsome enough to move any lady's heart that is not too much a valetudinarian to find a moment for love ... I don't like Mr Bruce. He seems desirous of excluding me from the Governor's parties, with whom he is intimate, and of inducing Lady Hester not to bring me forward so much as her accustomed goodness prompts her to do.' No word was spoken of Bruce's departure, and Meryon was forced to conclude: 'However, as he will always be with us, we shall find it to our mutual interest to be as agreeable to each other as possible.' He resented Bruce, envying his easy arrogance, his 'allowance of £2000 a year, and bills of unlimited credit besides'.

Hester – with Bruce, Sligo and Ebrington in tow – now found herself dining with exactly the sort of people she thought that she had left behind in London and being subjected to the same kind of scrutiny. Bruce explained to all of them that as a friend of James, he had taken his place as Hester's escort, a display of chivalry that struck some as a little forced. Sligo, rather jealous, abruptly announced his departure for Greece.

Knowing she was being gossiped about infuriated Hester. When she met another of Bruce's Cambridge friends, John Cam Hobhouse, he was taken aback at her vehemence. 'I met Mr Bruce and Lady Hester Stanhope, a masculine woman, who says she would as soon live with packhorses as with women. I met her again the next day at dinner. She seemed to me a violent, peremptory person.' As an afterthought, however, Hobhouse added mildly, 'We went together to the Opera.'

Malta's Governor, General Oakes, became one of Hester's great admirers. They quickly recognized one another as kindred minds; indulgent and humorous, he became something of a father-figure. At the great event of the Maltese season that summer, he gave Hester place of honour. For the celebration ball for King George III's birthday on 4 June, there were races and at night the grand palace ballroom was lit with candles, and a small orchestra assembled to play.

Oakes insisted that Hester and her party should take advantage of his palace, built for the summer heat, five miles out of town. It was at the Palacio de St Antonio, with cool breezes and views across the sea from their bedroom, that the lovers found some much-wanted privacy. Meryon was banished to a room in a separate wing. He made no comment on the couple, whose whisperings and low laughter he often heard gaily echoing up from the garden, other than to mention that she was suffering from a complaint that meant she was 'confined to her bedchamber for ten days'. Hester and Bruce made use of the General's boat to explore the nearby coastline, and find secluded bays where they could enjoy lazy picnics.

Two months earlier, Meryon had written glowingly of his new employer: 'She is the best lady that ever breathed and makes me grateful for the kind treatment I have received from her.' Now, on 15 June, he conceded of Bruce that 'although his age, his person, his known gallantry would be enough to make the tongue of scandal wag against any other woman who, unmarried and in her prime, should trust herself with a single man in a large house, and in the country, yet Lady Hester contrives to do anything that others could not, without incurring the same blame that they would. Besides, she is mended in her health considerably of late, and really begins to look rather winning.'

The relationship began with a strong physical attraction. Neither of them wanted to resist it, nor saw any reason to. There was no way around the age difference. Hester seems to have been willing to live for the happiness of the moment, for as long as it might last. She was conventional enough to find the thought of claiming him in any permanent way – through marriage – somewhat shocking. If she considered it, the thought of becoming his wife repelled rather than excited her. Very early on she believed their eventual separation was inevitable, a sense Bruce may have been too inexperienced to have developed.

On the morning of 27 June the lovers embarked upon a course of action. No doubt this was determined by Hester. She decided that she would write privately and directly to Bruce's father and make her intentions clear. It was a highly unusual thing to do, the sort of action only a worldly-wise woman – and someone scrupulous about honour – would take. She informed Crauford Bruce – paying the most flowery tributes to his son's 'elevated and Statesmanlike mind, his brilliant talents to say nothing of his beautiful person' – that 'to know him is to love & admire him, & *and I do both!*'

Should you hear of this in any irregular way, it might give you uneasiness & you might not only mistake the nature of the sentiments I feel towards him, but my *views* altogether, & imagine that he had fallen into the hands of an artful woman who wd. take him in, as far as lay in her power. Sir, you need not be under any of these apprehensions, the affection I feel for him wd. only prompt me the more to consider his advantage in every point of view, & at this moment (while loving him to distraction) I look forward to the period when I must resign him to some thrice happy woman really worthy of him. While seeking knowledge & calculating plans of future ambition, few people are perhaps better calculated for his companion than I am, but when he has once taken his line & become a public character, I shall like a dethroned Empress, resign to virtue the possession of that perfection which she alone has a right to . . . Sir, if you knew me, I flatter myself that it wd. be unnecessary to give you any further assurance of the sincerity of my intentions, but as you do not, there is *no promise however solemn* I am not willing to make upon this subject. After what I have said I trust that no feeling of anxiety will remain as far as relates to your Son's welfare. It wd. be a satisfaction for me to learn (tho' I do not wish you to write to me) that this candid confession of my sentiments, has not displeased you; do not however Sir, mistake the tone of humility I have adopted thro' this letter, which proceeds from my being one of the proudest women in the world, so proud, as to despise the opinion of the world altogether, as far as it relates to myself, but when I am addressing the parent of a man I tenderly love; (& for whom he has so great an affection) a sacred sort of reverence steals upon my mind, which I hope has communicated itself to my expression, as I have intended they should convey the confidence and respect with which Sir I have the honour to remain . . .[4]

It was an extraordinary appeal, striking a tone that managed to be earnest and high-minded, but never beseeching, and not admitting any vulgarity. Hester had raised her flag. Bruce might not have felt he was really in danger of risking his father's displeasure; but he knew him well enough to expect the news would come as a shock. Added to that, there was the uncomfortable matter of his allowance. His whereabouts and his expenditure would now be under scrutiny. Only with his father's approval could he continue his travels with Hester.

\*    \*    \*

As the French army massed in Calabria readying to invade Sicily, refugees in passage boats had been quitting the island in droves, many of them making their way to Malta. Palermo, which Bruce had, on his brief stay, pronounced 'one mass of Moral and Political corruption', seemed an unwise choice, if they were not to end up as prisoners-of-war, or at the very least, have their vessel stolen out from underneath them as they attempted the crossing. Meanwhile, the peaceful neutrality that had existed between England and Turkey now appeared to be faltering in the wake of Napoleon's powerful new alliance. The thought that Constantinople too might now be snatched from their reach suddenly made the city appear irresistible to Hester.

In early August the plan to go directly to the Turkish capital was complicated by a new factor in the unstable political climate: the Turks feared repercussions if they appeared to favour the English, and ruled that no more than one English vessel that could conceivably be considered a ship of war could be admitted to the capital at any one time. Since the frigate *Salsette* was already there, the travellers would head for the Adriatic islands, then travel along the Greek coastline in stages, with the aim of reaching the Turkish capital before the end of summer.

Elizabeth Williams intended to remain in Valletta with her sister and brother-in-law. She had acquired an admirer and hoped he would marry her. It is possible that the arrangement suited Hester, who was becoming jealously possessive over Bruce. The thought of having Elizabeth – who was, after all, a very pretty young woman – so much in their company might have irked her. They parted with some awkwardness. The Davids wanted to see Hester happy, but were alarmed at her affair with Bruce. Ann Fry would henceforth assume Elizabeth's responsibilities.

In preparation for crossing the Greek mainland, they had all scaled down their luggage. 'My baggage will amount to a dozen shirts, my cot and my saddle; Lady Hester's and Mr Bruce's on the same scale. All useless luggage is to be left behind,' wrote Meryon.[5] Hester planned to return to Malta eventually, having deposited much of her luggage with the Davids, taking with her only her most precious possessions and what could be easily carried by a packhorse.

\* \* \*

Hester was joyful and exuberant. Her enthusiasm now extended to a quixotic plan which had been apparently been percolating in her mind since early June, giving new cloak-and-dagger impetus to the Constantinople venture, and for which she had enlisted as her co-conspirators both Bruce and Meryon. Unable to contain the secret more than a night after hearing it, Meryon confided to his diary:

> She intends at Constantinople, to make friends with the French ambassador, and through his means to obtain a passport to travel through France. Protected by this, she will set off from Turkey, proceed through Hungary, Germany, and arrive at Paris. When there she intends to get into Buonoparte's good graces, study his character, and then set sail for England to plot schemes for the subversion of his plans. Her wonderful mind is equal to the accomplishment of all this, if she can but overcome the first difficulty of entering a hostile country. What she, Lady Hester, will do, time will show, but if Heaven give her health I do not despair the rest.[6]

If we take Meryon's comment at face value, Hester intended to become some kind of double-agent. Such a plan has more than a hint of her dead cousin Camelford's impulsiveness about it. Napoleon, she was sure, would be intrigued to meet her, a blood-relative of Pitt, his former adversary, who had been his close confidant. She knew that despite his designs on Britain, he was a great admirer of British institutions, especially the constitutional monarchy. In her imaginary audience with Napoleon, conversation would simply evolve. Whatever Hester proposed, it seems to have been well thought out. It may have involved offering herself as a 'mole' into British plans, which, with her impressive connections, was no small enticement. Bruce, whom she trusted with more details, was deeply impressed. Meryon's unguarded account is the first hint we have of Hester's ambitions and her willingness to go to great lengths to charm and intrigue in the name of war – and politics. After one of their dinners, Meryon wrote home:

> I hardly know to whom to liken her. In person and sentiments she is not unaptly represented by an Elvira, a Portia or a Semiramis. She is not

beautiful like Aspasia, but she would guide a state as well. For talent there is nobody equal to her but Buonaparte himself.[7]

With this wind in their sails, the travellers left Malta, heading for the rocky Ionian island of Zante, now garrisoned by British troops. They rested ashore for a fortnight, admiring the elegant *palazzi* and country houses. Everything was going well with Bruce, and Hester was allowing herself to be deferential towards him, even a little dependent. For him, the pleasure of feeling himself in charge, of having tamed such a decisive and strong-willed woman, was considerable; there would be nothing transitory, it seemed, about his affections. They seemed to create good luck and laughter wherever they went. The further they drifted away from St Antonio, the less they worried about Crauford Bruce. The lovers enjoyed feeling they were offending no one; Bruce's long life and Hester's beauty were toasted wherever they went. They ate their meals in modest taverns; they took siestas and walked in the late afternoon when it was cooler. The glow of Zante stayed with them long after they had left the island.

The next stage in their planned journey was Patras, on the northern tip of the Peloponnese, which they reached on 23 August. Sligo had hurried back from Athens on the *Pylades* to see them. He had been in Greece all summer, and had embarked upon an ambitious programme of excavations at many ancient sites on the mainland, including Mycenae and Sparta, as well as some of the islands and the Morea.* The last guest on the *Pylades* had been Byron, who toured the Morea with Sligo, bringing along his own entourage, including a Greek boy who shared his bed below deck.

The friends agreed that Sligo should accompany Hester and Bruce and her party along the coast to Vostizza, on the south side of the Gulf of Corinth, where she could then board an open boat for Corinth city, while Sligo and his contingent would take the horses overland, 'and get a house ready for her before she came'.

Meanwhile, Meryon was finding the role of a travelling English

---

* That summer, Sligo would ship back to his family home, Westport, in County Mayo, Ireland, two columns from the doorway of the Treasury of Atreus at Mycenae. In 1906 the sixth Marquess presented them to the British Museum, where they can be seen today.

gentleman remarkably easy to adapt to. He paints an evocative group portrait as they boarded Sligo's boat at Corinth:

First goes the guide, next Lord Sligo's two Albanians, dressed in magnificent clothes in the fashion of their country, with each a brace of silver-stocked pistols and a silver-hilted dagger at his girdle. Then comes the dragoman . . . Mr Bruce and Lady Hester's two Turkish servants, our cook, who is a Persian, two Greeks, who serve to point out the curiosities, and Lord Sligo's cook, a Turk. Each of these has a sabre and a brace of pistols. Lord Sligo, Lady Hester, Mr Bruce and Lord Sligo's painter (to take views of the country, of antiquities etc) form the centre of the procession, and last of all Lord Sligo's three servants in livery, armed with blunderbusses and sabres, with Mr Bruce's and Lady Hester's valets following, and the whole is closed with the baggage.

Sligo was more delighted to see Hester than Bruce. He confided to his mother that it was 'really quite a delightful thing travelling with such a woman' and 'besides which she is so clever that no moment hangs heavy on our hands in her presence'. That he felt in no small degree competitive with Bruce is clear. 'I suppose finding me to be useful to her, for Bruce is so little a man of business and *I* am so *completely* one, that I would do everything for her: I hire servants for her, I act the part of interpreter, in short without me she would be cheated abominable [*sic*]. Bruce, whom you may recollect seeing one day in Grafton Street, is accompanying her, and what I may be induced to do I don't know.'[8] But Sligo's next remark about Hester was prickly, suggesting that Bruce and Hester had finally admitted to being lovers. By then Sligo was starting to resent the fact that his brig was turning into a well-used stage-set for the amorous adventures of others.

As they sailed into Piraeus on 12 September 1810, just after nine in the evening, Sligo caught sight of Byron first, near-naked, his familiar dark curls plastered to his head. He was about to dive from the pierhead at Cape Colonna. A young boy was with him. Excitedly, Bruce and Sligo bellowed that he must come and join them that evening for dinner.

As far as Hester was concerned, their first night in Athens was not auspicious. She had taken an instant dislike to the accommodation chosen for them by Sligo; two private houses side by side, close to Byron's old lodgings in Monasteráki, near the Ottoman mosque. The premises had recently been vacated by a party of English travellers, who had left behind only tables and chairs, and a few beds. Hester (who, as Meryon put it, could 'contrive to metamorphose a barn into a palace') despaired. According to Meryon 'it was as much like the loft over the stable where the riding horses stand at home as any place you can imagine'.

Dinner was not a great success. They lacked the proper utensils for cooking and had to make do with local wine and fruit and whatever else they could find, a hastily-laid table, and not enough chairs. Byron appeared, with a lad, Nicolo, a long-lashed French boy who had grown up in Greece, whom Bruce recalled as a 'miserable looking creature'. Hester, who immediately deduced the nature of the relationship between them, was not impressed.

Conversation flickered, spluttered and ranged. Meryon remembered that Byron spent half the night wheeling about theatrically from chair to chair, trying to disguise his limp. They would have talked of the sights of Athens and what Byron would have them see. Under the Turks many of the city's ancient buildings and magnificent sculptures were left to crumble; most melancholy of all, the Parthenon now stood ruined and roofless. Talk at some point would have turned to Lord Elgin's entourage, engaged in what Byron called 'the robbery of ruins from Athens'.

Now that their affair was an open secret, there were tensions between Hester and Bruce. Hobhouse had already gossiped to Byron, relaying Bruce's description of her to him as 'the most superior woman in all the world'. Byron, who later described one of his lovers as 'autumnal' (this was Lady Oxford, who was then not yet forty), almost certainly commented on their difference in age. Hester, who was never gracious on the defensive, would have been sensitive to this. She also knew that she was not a conventional beauty; and she was aware of Byron's critical gaze. She was no 'sylph' of twenty – or fourteen for that matter. With bad wine on empty stomachs, the young men were riotous. She was not.

She and Byron sparred over the relative equality of men and women, but he, whose banter was tinged with self-mockery, had no desire to pursue the subject and would not argue, which enraged Hester. She would not stand down. Although she often professed to despise her own sex, and would criticize the female tendency to weakness and manipulation, she sensed an underlying cruelty beneath Byron's supposed romanticism; moreover, while they were speaking, she felt some of his barbs about women were aimed directly at her.

Three days after that first dinner Byron abruptly left again for the Morea. Perhaps the prospect of the forthright Lady Hester making herself comfortable in 'his' Athens was not to his taste. Meryon, who was so frequently to misinterpret the motives of others, noted that he thought she was 'much pleased with' him, 'which is saying not a little in his praise, since there are few of the present young nobility [to] whom she will allow herself to be tolerable; the man she dislikes may as well go hang himself, for nothing is so damning as her disapprobation'.⁹ Bruce's comment was more ambiguous: 'Byron had no chance with her, but took gentlemanlike assent and silence.'

The travellers spent a month in Athens, and most of that time, Byron was notable for his absence. Several others had joined their party at this stage, including John Fazakerley, the Whig MP for Lincoln, Henry Gally Knight, and two jovial Scotsmen, one of whom was John Galt, to add to the 'whole herd of English' then in Athens, including Lord Plymouth and Stratford Canning, cousin of the statesman so well known to Hester, who was visiting from Constantinople. They also frequently saw Thomas Gordon, the campaigner for Greek freedom.

Before the end of September, Sligo and Bruce took themselves off on a short tour of Delphi, Thebes, Livadia and the Temple of Apollo at Castri. By this stage, Byron had chosen to make his reappearance. Around this time, the travellers made plans to hire a vessel to take them all to Constantinople and invited Byron to join them. He declined.

It seems that Bruce made some kind of overture to Byron after dinner on his last night in Athens, shortly before he and Hester were due to board ship at Piraeus on 16 October. Byron described it in a letter to Hobhouse after the event. Apparently, whatever Bruce said or did came as a surprise to Byron, and he claimed not to have encouraged it. 'Seriously, I can't think for the soul of me, what possessed Bruce,' he wrote, 'but the truth is, he is a little chivalrous & romantic, and is smitten with unimaginable fantasies ever since his connection with Lady H. Stanhope.'¹⁰ Quite what Byron meant, and to what degree this was an aberration in Bruce's behaviour, it is interesting to speculate.* After observing him in Malta, Hobhouse had made a piquant comment about Bruce to Byron. Quoting Horace, he said Bruce, like Byron, 'is much upon the "nil admirari" plan: in other words, "wonder at nothing"; he is not quite the "Nissus" he was formerly, but still, in my mind, very handsome'. Perhaps Bruce's college friends all knew something about him that Hester did not.

Whatever the truth, the poet's verdict on Hester was swiftly filed to Hobhouse:

> I saw the Lady Hesther Stanhope at Athens, and do not admire 'that dangerous thing a female wit'. She told me (take her own words) that she had given you a good set-down at Malta, in some disputation about the Navy; from this, of course, I readily inferred the contrary, or in the words of an *acquaintance* of ours, that 'you had the best of it'. She evinced a similar disposition to *argufy* with me, which I avoided by either laughing or yielding. I despise the sex too much to squabble with them, and I rather wonder you should allow a woman to draw you into a contest, in which, however, I am sure you had the advantage, she abuses you so bitterly. I have seen too little of the Lady to form any decisive opinion, but I have discovered nothing different from other she-things, except a great disregard of received notions in her conversation as well as conduct. I don't know whether this will recommend her to our sex, but I am sure it won't to her own.

In Athens Byron employed Meryon in some discreet moonlighting. He was worried about his young lover Nicolo, who did not seem to be recovering from what seemed to be at first a mild fever; the boy had wasted away, with his teeth chattering, he could barely drink, let alone eat. Meryon found that the boy was suffering from internal injuries and early symptoms of septicaemia as a result of an anal rupture. Whatever conversation passed between them as a result, he did not say, and seems

---

* Byron's biographer, Fiona MacCarthy, felt this indicated Bruce had made a pass at Byron. But even if the poet had rebuffed such advances, it seems unlikely he would have found them 'unimaginable fantasies'. It seems much more likely that in Byron's view, Bruce's fantasies involved Hester. Was Bruce trying to enlist him in her Napoleon plan?

to have kept the matter to himself. No doubt it would have remained a secret, had not Vassily, Byron's Albanian servant, spread gossip about Nicolo's ailment and the visits of the English doctor. That Meryon kept utterly silent about this matter is both important and revealing. Discretion counted for everything in his position with Hester.

# 6

## A Bolt-hole on the Bosphorus

Hester's first sight of Constantinople was on a cold wintry night, around midnight on 11 November 1810. Aboard the *caïque* – which Meryon described as 'as clean, trim, and as richly gilded as a nobleman's barge on the Thames' – they anchored near the Tophane, a brick and stone foundry close to the Kiliç Ali Paşa Mosque, having drifted past the sleeping city with its mosques, tall white minarets and cypresses. Thousands of small boats – *caïques*, specially designed for manoeuvring on the fast currents of the Bosphorus, as well as small gondola-like vessels for scurrying around the water's edge – bobbed almost soundlessly by the waterfront. From the Tophane fountain, they picked their way along the warren of narrow alleys ascending steeply to Pera, the European quarter, lined with brick and stone houses, and as they climbed higher, they passed increasingly elaborate stone mansions and veritable palaces that were the European embassies, complete with stable courtyard and vineyards.

Hester was carried in a sedan chair; the others walked behind her, their way lit by a huge lantern, menaced by the mongrel hounds that roamed the city's streets. Their lodgings were halfway up the hill, on one of the streets looping beneath the pointed Galata Tower. Hester and Bruce took their own rooms. On the subject of settling in Constantinople they were divided; they had still not heard from Bruce's father, and their luggage had been sent ahead by mistake to Smyrna (now Izmir), then the commercial capital of the Ottoman Empire.

Hester found Constantinople magnificent but oppressive, and like Sligo, was worried about spending too much: in Pera they had no choice but to stay at over-priced lodgings where they were charged by the day and had to have exorbitantly expensive meals and spring water ferried up to them morning and night. It was cold, and worse, Sligo claimed, than any cold in England. He mused that 'were it not that Lady Hester is here I should not stop a week, but I dine there every day and that makes the evening pass pleasantly'.[1] He complained of the distracting state of anxiety induced by lusting after Ottoman objects of desire: carpets, ceramics, textiles, silverware, lanterns and, especially, costly fur-lined pelisses, the modish dress coats worn by both sexes. Due to his weakness for honeyed pastries and sugared coffees, it was also about this time that Hester began to refer to him, rather unkindly, as 'Whale'.

Hester had no intention of leaving quickly, despite the fact that life in Constantinople was proving more expensive than in London. She wanted to see the city at its best, its gardens in bloom; the glorious, dagger-shaped tulips over which the Turks went into raptures; the magnificent costumes; the secrets waiting to be divulged in its harems and inner courts of its palaces. It was then winter; people hid their finery away under shapeless, plain-coloured robes. So far they had met no real Turks, nor seen a single tulip.

The lovers finally received the long-awaited response from Bruce's father. A bundle of letters had arrived, addressed to them separately. The first to Hester had been complimentary to her, even fawning.[2] Although concerned that there should be no scandal attached to her liaison with his son, Crauford seemed anxious that she know he thought her influence – having walked in the corridors of power and seen something of the business of politics – might well be fortuitous:

In you my Son has placed himself under the direction of a Lady who has from Ancestry a Hereditary claim to the most superlative Talents, and in the very point of character for which I wish him to distinguish himself as an enlightened Statesman – permit me therefore Madam, by the Names of your Grandfather the truly Great Lord Chatham, and from the affection and reverence you must ever bear to the Memory of the ever to be lamented Mr Pitt your Uncle, by whom I have understood you was [sic] selected and distinguished by his peculiar affection . . . I entreat you to impress on the Mind of my Son all the inventive particles you possess of their genius.[3]

To Bruce he was stern. While acknowledging the power of the 'fascinating attraction' that bound him to Hester, he cautioned that she was 'giving to the Winds what seemingly are to her minor considerations, the taunts and censures of the World'.[4] But he seemed to give his blessing to the liaison, making the suggestion that he and his wife bring out Bruce's convalescent sister Jane for a reunion in the Mediterranean. He was worried enough to want to see this object of his son's affections for himself; on the other hand, he did not consider her to be so morally reprehensible that he would hesitate to expose his daughter to her influence.

But as soon as Hester read the first few lines of the next letter, written two weeks later, her heart sank. Something had happened to radically alter his view, for now Crauford announced that no matter how 'superior may be the mind and abilities' of Lady Hester, he feared the inevitable scandal. He begged Bruce not to be swept away by 'a short moment of delicious enjoyment' and consider the matter of his own respectability and future.[5] He made a damning comment about Hester: 'However illustrious her descent and connections, however superior her own powers . . . there must be something fallacious in the mind when a woman can depart from the circumspect proprieties of her sex and yield her reputation in society for the temporary gratification of any passion.'[6] He gave no hint that he intended to cut Bruce off from his allowance, but he urged him to break off the connection.

Between writing the first and second letters, Crauford had received an anonymous note, describing Hester as 'an artful woman'. It warned: 'She means to make him marry her; he knew her first criminally in Malta. For God's sake do not neglect this caution but send for him without a moment's delay or it will be too late.'[7] It is unlikely that this in itself changed his mind. But it is possible that, having enquired more particularly about Hester's past, he had not liked what he heard.

But the woman who had Napoleon in her sights was hardly about to let Crauford Bruce win this round. She immediately drafted her reply, and the tone moved up into high opera. She told Crauford that she was prepared to return alone to England, where she would throw herself at his feet to beg his forgiveness, and 'if I had outlived the misery I had brought on myself, given you full power to banish me to what part of the globe you thought fit with a promise never to see him again'.[8] Knowing he had no desire for such a spectacle, Hester then launched into an impassioned plea for mistresses: 'a man in no age has ever suffered in the public opinion by his intimacy with a woman who had his real interests at heart, did Mr Fox's attachment to Mrs Armstead, or that of Bonaparte's to the late Empress . . . make them *less* great men'. She continued:

> I believe it has never yet been expected that a man sd. be a saint, at least till he is married, & and if I *most solemnly* declare that I *never had* or ever *will have further claims* on your son, than any women he might have picked up in the streets, how can he shock the world? At a time when I held up my own head very high in society, I always blamed & lamented those women who had erred from sheer vice, or from some unfortunate attachment, being placed upon the same footing as virtuous women, & thrust into society; if my judgement was a severe one, at least it extends to myself, & so far from wishing to be received into society, I shall most scrupulously avoid ever setting eyes on a modest woman; besides I am too proud not to dread humiliation & putting the virtuous part of my sex out of the question, I will never give an opportunity to those fair ladies who have married for a title, a house, & fine diamonds, having previously made up their minds to be faithless wives, to sneer at me, inferior as I may be to one of these class of women, I consider myself to be far superior to the other.[9]

In the room where she wrote this letter, Hester could crane her neck to see the city's bewitching and beautiful skyline, with its domes and needle-like minarets. She could look in the direction of the waters of Seraglio Point, said to be restless with the spirits of drowned concubines, sent to meet their fate in sacks loaded with stones. It had not escaped her notice that in the expatriate circles at Pera, most other women of her own age were already mothers of adolescents. She wanted to have her happiness while she could.

\*   \*   \*

That December another unmarried woman in her thirties, barely four months older than Hester, was quietly engaged in contemplation on the subject of how far society would allow a woman to express her emotions freely, especially when it came to love. The extent to which an individual should conceal and censure her own behaviour, and even her own thoughts, lies at the heart of the novel *Sense and Sensibility*. At the very moment that Hester was still waking in the arms of her wealthy young lover, Jane Austen was in all probability quietly correcting her proofs at her tiny desk at Chawton in Hampshire.

What might Jane Austen have made of Hester's unvirginal predicament? That she had read and heard reports about Pitt's outspoken niece was certain: by the standards of the day Hester was a public figure and Jane was a great consumer of news of the fashionable world. Hester's exotic, aristocratic background with its roots in India; her sister's elopement which made its way into the popular press; her own reluctance to marry – these reasons alone would have made Hester interesting to Jane Austen. The author was fascinated by the lure of sex and its powerfully unhinging effect on the lives of women; she was a self-confessed observer of the small signs that often betrayed hidden passions between those married to other people.* It is unlikely she would have judged Hester as morally reprehensible for having taken a younger lover, nor indeed for her earlier love affairs. Jane Austen rarely punished her characters who strayed when it could be said their motives were pure. Indeed, she may well have fantasized about the life she herself would have embarked upon had a dying uncle left her an independent income of £1,200 a year. Would she have dared choose the kind of life more appropriately matched to her rather more lurid juvenilia, with its sexually impulsive young lovers, who run off with one another, forsaking spouses and children, and travelling to distant locations? In one of her early writings, *Sir William Mountague*, her anti-hero plots adultery with a Miss Wentworth barely a fortnight after his marriage to a Miss Stanhope.[10] What Jane Austen makes plain in her mature fiction, however, was the way in which society rarely tolerated open admissions of either premarital or adulterous sex. The stakes – usually financial – were generally too high.

---

* 'I am proud to say that I have a very good eye at an Adultress,' Jane Austen wrote to her sister Cassandra in 1801.

'Miss Stanhope'. Was this name of one of Jane Austen's early protagonists entirely coincidental? She is known to have visited Hester's
childhood home at Chevening, and certainly gazed at it from the ridge
along Lord Chatham's Ride. She visited the area twice, once in 1788 and
again in 1796; on the first occasion she spent the summer with her great-
uncle Francis Austen, a lawyer who had settled in nearby Sevenoaks, and
whose shrewd investments and two advantageous marriages made him
a very rich landowner. He was introduced to Hester's grandparents, and
is thought to have taken his grand-niece along to tea or dinner. Jane
Austen may have glimpsed or even met the rambunctious Stanhope
brood, who were unlikely to have regarded her with any interest whatsoever. Chevening itself is widely thought to be a model for Rosings Park
in *Pride and Prejudice*, which Jane Austen described thus:

> But of all the views . . . which the country, or the kingdom could boast,
> none were to be compared with the prospect of Rosings, afforded by an
> opening in the trees that bordered the park . . .[11]

The Dowager Grizel Stanhope is also thought to be a model for the Lady
Catherine de Bourgh.[12] As for the young Hester, if she resembles any of
Jane Austen's creations, it is Marianne in *Sense and Sensibility*:

> She was sensible and clever; but eager in every thing; her sorrows, her
> joys, could have no moderation. She was generous, amiable, interesting:
> she was every thing but prudent.

As Meryon recorded, Hester once told him of an incident that occurred
at Chevening, when she was about the same age as the fictional Marianne.
She had been out riding when suddenly there was a 'pelting shower of
rain' and a certain Colonel Shadwell materialized. Chivalrous and
concerned, he also eyed her with interest. But unlike Jane Austen's
Marianne and Colonel Brandon, Hester and her admiring Colonel did
not go on to make a neat match. That Hester could in fact easily outride
her Colonel would have made her altogether too unfeminine to popu-
late the Jane Austen landscape.

By no means all women in 1810 would have considered themselves to be ruled by Jane Austen's set of conventions. The Georgian era was about to give way to the Regency period, and although a subtle repressive shift had begun in the sexual politics of the burgeoning middle classes, for the upper classes, sexual dalliances were the popular pastime they had always been. Only those aristocratic women who failed to keep their affairs secret were punished; even notorious rakes did not find themselves excluded from society. It was hard to escape the topic of sexual impropriety in what would be dubbed the Age of Scandal, when so many famous men were widely known to have mistresses and illegitimate children, and when at aristocratic parties, especially masked balls, it was not uncommon for couples to pair off in search of available bedrooms. The penalties for any flagrant indiscretion, however, could be crushing.

It would take a particularly brazen young woman to really shock society, and that woman was Lady Caroline Lamb, Hester's former friend Harriet's – Countess Bessborough's – daughter. The following year, in 1811, all those in Hester's circle would have heard the vicious gossip circulating about Lady Caroline Lamb when she failed to observe what her mother-in-law Lady Melbourne called 'the decencies' over an affair she began shortly after her marriage. Lady Melbourne, who was a member of what Byron called London's 'gynocracy', warned her: 'When one braves the opinion of the World, sooner or later . . . [one] will feel the consequences of it . . .'[13] Caroline, who was soon to seduce Byron, made no attempt to conceal either infatuation from her husband. Her name became synonymous with scandal and social ostracism.*

In any case, by making her extraordinary, unsolicited pact with Crauford Bruce, Hester felt pulled back by strong, invisible threads to the world she had left behind. She disliked any form of hypocrisy, and seems to have held the rather modern view that acknowledging a deeply-held passion went a great way towards mitigating any guilt that might be attached to it.

---

* It is interesting to note that Lady Caroline Lamb, when she met Hester, who was nine years older, worshipped her. Caroline had informed Hester that she 'doats' upon all her qualities, her 'talent, common-sense, good nature & superiority, conversation & silence, good humour & genius . . . an extreme love of music besides beauty' and had sent her constant invitations to musical soirées and masquerades. Hester, however, thought Caroline somewhat feeble-minded; she pitied her and did not take up her overture to friendship with any great enthusiasm.

In her reply to Crauford she acknowledged that if the price of having his son in the here and now meant the loss of her reputation in the eyes of English society, she was prepared to pay it, as long as Bruce's reputation did not suffer. Were she ever to be considered to be 'the unfortunate cause of his ruin,' she would, 'by breaking my own heart, atone in some degree for the sin of being too sensible of that perfection, which I am so removed from'.[14]

Bruce himself made a passionate appeal, listing the reasons why Hester should remain his lover, at least for the time being. 'My fate is in your hands,' he wrote, 'and I throw myself upon your indulgence, your liberality and your generosity.' In trying to placate his father and therefore, in good conscience, draw upon the necessary parental funds with which to set up a Turkish ménage, a priggish tone crept into his words. He earnestly recounts Hester's merits, and says he believes 'it will be her study' to promote his 'happiness and welfare'. But it is clear that he was fighting for his right to keep her. He was even prepared to risk puncturing her vanity. His love was, he said, not 'an attachment rising from the charms of beauty, but for the generosity of her character and superiority of her talents'. He told his father: 'She has not only a perfect insight into the history of the times, but likewise in the characters of the leading men of the present day . . . I have gained more knowledge within these six months with Lady Hester than I have acquired for the last ten years of my life . . . thus you will see that this connexion [sic] is far from being a disadvantage, will prove of the greatest advantage to me . . .' He added, perhaps not realizing what his father might deduce from it: 'My Lord Sligo is almost as fond of her as I am'.[15] Once the letters had been sent off, Hester took a six-month lease on a house, paying 500 piastres a month. She intended it to be a home for Bruce too. By making a show of mastering her sorrow that she would one day lose him – making a virtue of her own pain – she was also able to suppress any irritation she had begun to feel about him. Bruce, being so much younger than her, had begun to exasperate her in countless small ways. Yet with an operatic ending in sight, the anxiety that they might be separated led to renewed ardour, and love was restored to its former intensity.

The charming fishing village of Therapia, or Tarabya, as it is now called, was about seven miles up the Bosphorus from Pera towards the mouth of the Black Sea, and the principal summer residence for the foreign embassies. The English, French, Germans, Italians and Austrians all had elaborate wooden mansions close to the shore, the land having been given to them by Sultan Selim II as a gift. The village was the site of an ancient hot spring that had existed since the Byzantine era, only to be destroyed by an earthquake; nonetheless curative properties were still attributed to its waters.

Hester rented a three-storey house perched in the curve of the bay. She was delighted with it, even though there were no fireplaces, or a stove, and it was obvious the cavernous rooms would be hard to heat. But many of its rooms and ceilings were painted with landscape scenes: there were velveteen sofas, harem quarters, and a bedroom with a small marble fountain. There were no good roads, but taking the *caïque* was easy enough in good weather.

As soon as they arrived at Therapia, Hester found herself the object of curiosity. A Turkish noblewoman, hearing about her, wanted to pay her a visit, on the condition, as was the usual custom, that all the men in the house remove themselves while she was there.

> Bruce & Ld. Sligo complained bitterly of this, & wickedly contrived to make peep holes in the ceiling, the Lady & a train of females arrived who took off veil upon veil, & robe upon robe, & having fastened and unfastened various parts of their dress, & displayed magnificent bracelets . . . the fair Turkish Lady expressed great surprise at my eyes not being blackened & produced a little gold machine out of her pocket requesting she might black them. I agreed, & they all began to assist at the operation and appeared so overjoyed when it was done & *laughed so loud* that it became infectious, & out burst Lord Sligo. The horror that a man's voice created is not to be described . . .[16]

The 'Turkish Lady' was worldly enough to shrug off the incident. Hester, however, vowed that she 'would never trust Lord S. again for he might have got us all into a fine scrape'.[17]

Much to the envy of the men, Hester had been able to visit the secretive world of the women's quarters of the Turkish baths. Constantinople contained the most beautiful, elaborate *hamams* in existence. Early in her stay, Hester had to make do with the public Cagaloglu Hamam, not far from the Hagia Sophia, rather than the far more impressive imperial *hamam* used by the Sultan's wives and concubines closer to the Topkapi. She describes her regular visits:

> I go into a vast chamber filled with steam and lay down on the marble floor, they threw basins of water over me, soap me all over with a whisk like a horse's tail, then immerse me in a large bath, roll me up in cloths and lay me on a bed where I fall asleep and wake hungry and refreshed . . . the women make a parade of bathing; their *patterns* are set with pearls, the cloths they are wrapped in are worked with gold and coloured silks. A bath full of Turkish women is a magnificent sight; they are like so many statues in graceful drapery and some without any . . .[18]

She was given the usual treatment, unchanged for centuries, and it would become a familiar ritual. A female attendant would gesture for her to lie face down on the slab, then, manipulating her arms and legs, scrub, pummel and massage. In other rooms, women had hair removed from their arms, legs and private parts, using a warm waxen paste made of lime and arsenic water; afterwards bathers companionably drank sweet mint tea and coffee. As Hester quickly discovered, Turks were fastidious about the removal of all superfluous hair, and she almost certainly submitted to the process herself; later she mentions that she thought Bruce was overdoing it a little, having the hair between his eyebrows waxed.

Hester arrived in Turkey two years after the new Sultan, Mahmud II, then twenty-three years old, came to power over the mutilated corpse of his predecessor and cousin, Sultan Selim. He broke with tradition, and spent most of his time away from the Topkapi, spending his time up the Bosphorus between his winter and summer palaces outside the city. Although he shied away from westernizing Turkey, he believed the strength of the Ottoman Empire required a new breed of 'modern Muslim', able to assimilate new technology and science into traditional thinking.

The travellers saw the Sultan's magnificent procession passing out of the Topkapi gates on his *Selamlik* or public visit to a mosque for midday

Friday. The Sultan passed in a flash of diamonds and gold, and they could barely catch a glimpse. On this expedition, as on all of her jaunts around the city, Hester rode her horse, unveiled. For a Turkish woman to behave in such a way would have been unimaginable, and even in Pera, European women tended not to linger long in public view. She was noticed, and was soon being discussed in Turkish circles as a glamorous curiosity.

That December, the travellers spent Christmas at Therapia, dining in their mirrored rooms and peering out at the star-speckled sky from their seaward terrace. It was too cold to be entirely comfortable and it was a complicated time between the lovers.

Earlier that month Bruce had asked Hester to marry him. She was then thirty-four; he was twenty-three. A line in one of her later letters to General Oakes hints that she had been for a time distraught, and subsequent remarks by both James and Sligo strongly hint at the possibility of a pregnancy.[19] Even Crauford, in one of his letters around this time, seemed to be fishing for information, wanting to know if it were true Hester 'had taken a solitary house on the Bosphorus and is engaged in Solitary Work'.[20] If she were pregnant, it is possible that if she did not suffer a miscarriage, she took a more extreme measure. (Judging from the careful way she – and others – allude to this as a particularly difficult, even shameful period, such a possibility has to be considered.)

Whatever happened, it was an overwhelmingly painful time for the lovers. Hester knew that if she accepted Bruce's offer, she would make a mockery of her earlier promise. Even if they did marry, their age difference would mean they were permanently seen as mismatched in society's eyes. It would not be the powerful political – or military – alliance she had once hoped for. Her doubts outweighed her courage; gently she refused.

A few days before Christmas Bruce had received a furious letter from James, attacking him for having ruined his sister in the eyes of society. He lectured Bruce 'on the misery attending those who are not born in wedlock' and ended his letter by challenging Bruce to a duel. James's attack of moral indignation had been festering for months, coinciding with the happy, detail-laden letters sent to him by both his sister and

Bruce. To Hester he wrote a threatening letter, 'saying that one or the other of you must fall'.[21]

Bruce's reply betrays controlled anger. Could James not guess, he asked, that he had already asked Hester but been refused? He pointed out that James had known of the relationship for some time yet in past letters, had embraced them both. Bruce asked him, 'What has led to this revolution in your feelings?'

> Have you heard that I have ill-treated your sister? that I have deserted her, that I have left her to her fate in a foreign city without funds and without support, that I have been dead to all . . . great and generous feelings . . . that I have made myself a monster? Why not state it manfully?[22]

As for a duel, Bruce told him: 'I am ready to stand the responsibility of my own conduct and give you the satisfaction you require and in the hour of trial you will find me a man of honour, courage and spirit.'[23]

The truth was that some uncomfortable gossip had reached James in Cadiz and seriously unsettled him. It was not only that Hester might be pregnant, which was shocking enough. Could rumours about Bruce's past – with at least one presumed homosexual attachment – somehow have reached him?

A clue may be found in whatever Bruce had written earlier that autumn to his old Cambridge friend, William Bankes. Bankes talked of wanting to come out to Constantinople, but said he feared 'the risk of losing you'. No sooner might Bruce set himself up in a house on the Bosphorus, he predicted, than 'you will instantly take your flight, and then I shall be half-mad. Remember the [words obscured] on taking leave of you on board the *Woolwich*?'[24] This hint of a painful, erotic shipboard parting recalls Byron's recollection of Bruce's behaviour in Athens. Bankes is widely credited with introducing Byron to what Byron's biographer Fiona MacCarthy has called 'the thriving subculture of sodomy, with its own rituals and codes' at Cambridge. That Bankes considered Bruce an object of adoration appears certain. If nothing else, Bruce was at least familiar with the subculture in question. Like several important relationships around Hester, the one with Bruce, it would seem, was destined to frame itself in a series of sharply-angled triangles.

Hurt by Hester's rejection, Bruce now decided to accompany Sligo for a few weeks on his expedition to Persia, and talked of afterwards pushing onwards.

While she was preparing to adjust to winter life on the Bosphorus, Bruce and Sligo spent barely more than a week there. Hester waved them goodbye as they sailed away on 26 December. Expecting to be left alone for months, she must have been astonished when Sligo turned up a day or two later, with half his entourage and no Bruce. Sligo appeared on the point of collapse: Meryon diagnosed 'an attack of rheumatism in the muscles of the abdomen'. While Bruce had headed on towards Smyrna, Sligo had returned, somewhat bashfully, to be nursed by Hester. As Sligo wrote to his mother, she was 'so kind to me that you can have no idea of it'.[25] On Meryon's advice, he was to try long sweating sessions in the *hamam*. By the end of January, he was ready to set off again, promising to bring her back beautiful Persian horses.

February was bitter. 'A series of blizzards of snowstorms and tempests exceeding what I had ever witnessed elsewhere,' wrote Meryon. Hester was soon battling an attack of pleurisy. She acquired a small Turkish dog to keep her company, a cheerful mongrel puppy. She was also training Georgaki ('Giorgio') Dallegio, a Syrian boy from a Greek Orthodox family, to be her dragoman. Handsome and bright, he had offered himself to Bruce when they first arrived in Constantinople. Hester swiftly commandeered him. She had plenty of time for reflection, and to try to reconcile her conflicting feelings, which she had freely confided to Sligo. That she would have to let Bruce go, she already knew. She was too proud to imagine how she might feel when inevitably he fell in love with someone else. There must have been one small part of her that simply did not want to face the truth; by openly becoming Bruce's lover she had already made her own bargain by turning her back on convention. But she knew this was her bargain; not Bruce's. She knew how painful it would be for her if she were to return to England with him, only to separate; and how she would be shunned. There are many hints that Hester was overwrought. She asked Meryon to bleed her more than he felt was safe, something she always resorted to when feeling distraught and bleak.

As she recovered, Hester cultivated friendships with those who could be useful to her. Stratford Canning visited her for dinners, passing on selective intelligence so she could follow any news of James, and sent her cases of wine. She liked Canning, but thought him far too inexperienced for his position. It was to Canning that she hinted where she might go next; mentioning a plan to exchange the 'banks of the Bosphorus' for the 'banks of the Orinoco'.[26] It seems she was tempted by the thought of Venezuela and General Miranda's revolution. Even if she must lose her lover, she was not ready to give up her hopes of a life elsewhere.

But Crauford's heart had apparently softened: their combined appeal had worked. In Bruce's absence, Hester received a letter from his father that instantly lifted her mood. He was unwilling to risk a bitter confrontation with his son, and was prepared to strike a bargain. Letters now began to fly between father and mistress. Hester's trump card was her offer to groom Bruce for a successful life in politics. Meanwhile, he could continue to do as his father wished, to broaden his mind on his travels – with her. She informed Crauford that she thought Bruce had 'all the essentials to form the most distinguished public character the country can at present boast of'. Crauford admitted to her that he thought his son could gain much from time spent with 'an accomplished well-informed Woman of superior mind'.

They struck a bargain which Crauford urged must remain very discreet. If she took charge of Bruce's education, with a view to pressing him 'forward in the line of honorable fame and ambition', to 'arrange and declaim' in her presence and learn 'Elegant postures of the body', he was quite willing for them to continue their life together for the moment. He was keen for Bruce to 'get acquainted with' Russia, Hungary and Austria, which he felt would give him 'a decided superiority' when he got into the House of Commons; and he did not forbid her to go with him. As long as Hester herself stayed well away from the sort of expatriate society that would broadcast the affair, he was willing to turn a blind eye.

Relieved, Hester immediately wrote to reassure him once again that her claim on his son was loving but not permanent. She told him that in fact she imagined Bruce was at that moment 'deeply wounding some fair Turkish woman' with his 'fine eyes', a crime for which, she added airily, 'he might be in danger of having his head cut off'. She knew Crauford was a hardline Whig, who had admired Pitt for his tenacity rather than his politics, and made it plain that as much as she 'adored Mr Pitt', it was her grandfather who was her 'political oracle' and that what was needed was 'a man like him . . . for these times'.

She was glad Crauford agreed that there are 'faults in Bruce which like specks in the Sun do exist'. In case he had forgotten them, she reminded him that he could be 'very irritable'; had some 'foolish ideas' and his tendency to 'pull faces' would not do in a statesman.

Crauford was a pragmatist. He expected Bruce's feelings for her would shift in time. For this reason, he may have felt a little sorry for her. He kept their correspondence away from his wife, knowing she would think her beautiful son had fallen into the clutches of a Circe. But he was explicit with Hester about when he thought Bruce should return home. To 'get into Parliament' he reckoned Bruce 'should be no more than twenty-five'. By this calculation, Hester could have Bruce for just under a year.

In the meantime, Meryon was adapting to life in Turkey. He began to lead a semi-independent existence, supplementing his income, and going to Constantinople a good deal. He was now sought after by the families of many of the Turkish elite, as well as wealthy Armenians, willing to pay him well for his services. For the first time since he embarked on his travels he felt respected in his own right; independently of Hester and Bruce, he now was invited to the grandest homes. He was in a buoyant frame of mind. His extra income allowed him to send money home, and he had taken up a hobby: shooting pelicans from a small boat on the Bosphorus with his new Albanian pistol.

It was Meryon who engineered Hester's first invitations to Turkish households – and harems. Her initial impression was favourable; the women she met she thought 'the best-natured people in the world'. She made drawings of them, fascinated by their mystique, the way they wore their voluminous *ferigé* so closely that their eyes could barely be seen.[27] She enjoyed her initiation into the ritual offerings of the *chubuk* and *narguileh* pipes, with their mixture of tobacco, opium and rose-scented water.

By contrast, the open sexuality of the harem shocked her. On one visit, her hostess ordered some of the slave girls to dance for her as their guest. She found their gestures and movements grotesquely lewd, especially as some of the girls were below puberty. The older girls cupped their breasts and swayed in front of her. She reported back to Crauford: 'Their dancing by far the most disgusting thing I ever saw . . . I have no idea of passions being excited except by that which God created for the purpose, a *man*.'

The man Hester called 'the handsomest Turk here', Hafiz Aly, the Kapitan Pasha, became an unexpected friend during this time.[28] Few men were as influential in the Ottoman Empire: Aly was the supreme commander of the Turkish fleet and the governor of the Greek archipelago. His wife was deathly ill with consumption, and he had appealed to Meryon to cure her. Like the Sultan, Aly lived at Beshiktash on the Bosphorus during the winter months in order to be close to his Black Sea fleet. Aly met Hester when he brought Meryon back on his ship after one of his visits, and while Bruce was away, Aly regularly sent his vessel laden with exotic Turkish dishes, hoping to please her.

To Crauford she boasted that 'one of the greatest men here likewise is to show me his Harem *himself* when he comes back from Bagdad [*sic*] where he has been cutting off heads'.[29] This was, of course, the Kapitan Pasha. When the weather improved, on one of her visits to Hafiz Aly, Hester saw one of these severed heads for herself; 'the poor head was handed about on a silver dish as if it had been a Pine Apple', the brain, eyes and other soft tissue extracted and replaced with perfumed cotton.[30]

Hester hosted a dinner for Aly at Therapia, receiving her guests with her hair tied up in cloth and an Albanian dagger tucked into a silk sash around her waist. The evening was a great success. She later boasted to Canning: 'When did four Turks, and one the brother of the Captain Pacha, visit and dine with a Christian woman? I wore my sword with such an air that it has made a conquest of them all, and they begin to find their women rather stupid (at least they say so, but men fib sadly).'[31] These were men who, she pointed out, deliberately ignored all foreign women in public, 'looking at them all as if they were sheep in a field'.[32] She, of course, was the exception.

Appearances were deceptive. Soon afterwards, Aly would ask Meryon to induce an abortion in one of his concubines, a young blonde Circassian whose 'beauty was considerable'. Evidently, he assumed Meryon would not hesitate: the doctor noted that plenty of Turkish doctors had 'no scruple of resorting to a variety of methods for attaining that end'.* In his book, published many years later, Meryon's version of this seems too carefully worded to be quite believable. 'I told him plainly that by the laws of my country, I should be considered a criminal, if I were, in any shape whatever, to consent to such a deal.'[33] Somehow you feel that this might be an indirect attempt to put the gossip-mongers to rest, for there were those in England who would speculate that Hester herself was bound to have fallen pregnant.

Bruce and Sligo returned to Therapia towards the end of March, accompanied by half a dozen magnificent Persian horses. Still drunk on their adventures, their beards long, the men recounted their exploits to Hester until late into the night. Sligo had caught up with Bruce at Scutari; together they had visited Gebesha in the Gulf of Nicomedia, Magnesia and the plains of Gallipoli; they tried in vain to find Troy, consulting Bruce's battered copy of *The Odyssey*.

The delirious happiness of the lovers quickly made Sligo feel excluded. He was anxious to get to Malta, where he had been informed that General Oakes was to invest him with the Order of St Patrick. His dreams of being a gentleman explorer in the East had begun to pall, and even he was appalled at how much money he had run through – '£7,000 or £8,000' in two years. Laden with letters and presents, he bade the lovers an emotional farewell. Sligo promised Hester he would return through Cadiz to see her brother James, so that he could talk him out of his anger. He was also trusted to tell both General Oakes and Crauford Bruce the exact nature of their relationship, a matter far too delicate to express in a letter.

At Bruce's urging, the lovers now made for Brusa (now Bursa), sprawled across the northern foothills of Turkey's Mount Olympus (Mount Uludağ). All the almond and cherry trees were in flower. Brusa was the first capital of the Ottoman Empire, and remained a great provincial

---

* From his contacts with Turkish doctors, Meryon knew that abortion was often resorted to as a means of birth control, and that women commonly made contraceptive pessaries using soap and a half-lemon.

city. Its covered bazaar delighted Hester, but having explored the city once or twice, Bruce and Hester stayed away. Brusa's residents were far less tolerant of infidels than those of Constantinople. For the first time, they were hissed at. Here, wrote Meryon, 'a Turk would as soon receive a viper into his house as an infidel into his house'. They were horrified at the sight of beggars with oozing sores, and saw several hundred wretched Bulgarian refugees, whose villages had been razed to the ground by Russians and Turks; they saw soldiers herd them out of the city with long staffs.

They stayed near Cekirige – 'Realm of the Cicadas' – very close to the famous hot springs, and rode across the valleys and slopes of Olympus, setting out while they could still taste the dew of the night air, to gallop unhampered across open stretches, returning at dusk with their faces flushed. Bruce was mesmerized by Hester's skills as a rider. She, meanwhile, marvelled at the baths. She wrote teasingly to General Oakes:

> If you leave Malta, you must not come here, for you would fall in love if you did. How beautiful are these Asiatic women! They go to the bath from fifty to five hundred together . . . they bathe with all their ornaments on – trinkets, I mean . . .[34]

The summer passed quickly. Looking for a winter residence, they settled on Bebec, a more populous Bosphorus town, closer to Constantinople. They rented a tawny-red wooden *yali*, the residence of Baron Sturmer, an Austrian diplomat, which had harem quarters, a beautiful marble bath and a well-stocked garden.

Hester had not forgotten her Napoleon plan. In Bruce's absence, she had sought out Stratford Canning's opposite number, the French *chargé d'affaires*, Latour Maubourg. The British law forbidding contact between English and French citizens remained strict, even when they were in neutral countries. Nevertheless, in a series of surreptitious meetings, Hester told Latour Maubourg of her wish to spend the coming winter in the South of France and then visit Paris. Latour Maubourg led her to believe the French republic would readily admit her: Earl Stanhope's daughter certainly qualified as a friend of France.

Although she hoped that Bruce would come with her, she seems to have been prepared to travel to France alone. Soon after his return to Hester, Bruce had made a reference to her plans in a letter to his father.

I am afraid of entering into particulars at the present moment, for fear of Committing the persons concerned. Lord Sligo is already acquainted with all the circumstances. The letter is already sent and we may expect an answer in two months. My name is not to appear and thus in case of consent or refusal I shall be perfectly uncommitted. Women are privileged to do many thing [sic] which would be unbecoming the dignity of Man. Be assured that there is no person living who is more zealous of the honour of the name which he bears or the Country to which he belongs.[35]

He would also, he added ominously, 'if necessary, sacrifice everything for [Hester]'. While they were at Bebec, the meetings with Latour Maubourg started up again, and this time the Frenchman had apparently been instructed to ask her a series of penetrating questions about Napoleon. What was her personal opinion of him? To what degree did she consider him hated in England? Who were his supporters? What sort of treatment would he receive at the hands of the English? After submitting detailed answers (which, alas, do not appear to have survived), which were to be sent to Talleyrand, Hester was confident they would have their French passports soon.

Around this time, Hafiz Aly, who eyed Bruce with less delight than Hester, nonetheless invited the two of them to tour the pride of the Turkish navy, his 124-gun battleship *Sultan Selim*, manned by '1200 sailors & 200 of the Pacha attendants'. He sent a deputy to fetch them and show them around, asking only that Hester observe Turkish etiquette in her dress, which Hester took to mean she should not be 'a real fine lady in her shift and gown and half-naked besides!' Whatever Aly might have expected, it was probably not Hester dressed in 'men's clothes, a pair of over-alls, a military overcoat and cocked hat'. After Hester and Bruce had admired Aly's magnificent cabin, which outshone 'the finest English drawing room', with all of its gilt, satin and velvet 'in the best taste' and all of his nautical instruments, the latest models from England and France, they returned to their host's house, where he 'was low but very civil . . . he was delighted with my dress & has talked of nothing else since'.

That same night, Aly's sick wife died, and she was buried at dawn the next morning. Hester noted: 'The house was deserted for one day, the next he returned and said God's will be done, put on a smiling face and talked and laughed as usual'. Meryon noted in his journal that Aly sounded him out some weeks later, asking his frank opinion about whether Hester might consider marrying him. Bruce found the proposition highly entertaining. He told his father: 'You will not be a little amused when I tell you that the Pasha had serious thoughts of making proposals of marriage to Lady Hester. He expressed a great admiration for her talents and said she would produce a noble race of *djerid* players.'[36]*

Before any word reached her from Paris, Hester had to face Stratford Canning. Incandescent, he had stormed over to Bebec to confront her in person. One of his spies had seen her with Latour Maubourg. What in the devil's name was she doing? Why was she fraternizing with the enemy? He questioned her for half an hour. She ridiculed him for creating a diplomatic scandal out of nothing and told him he was jealous because the Turks now thought so highly of her while they treated him as a mere minion; he accused her of having suspicious motives and a lack of patriotism. Canning left, shouting that the English Palace, as the consulate was called, would from now on be closed to them all, and that none of them would be given any mercy should they get into any trouble while in Turkey. As a parting shot, he announced he would be writing to Marquess Wellesley, to see that the Foreign Office was warned about her.

Hester, as ever, was determined to get the upper hand. If Canning was going to write to Wellesley, then she would do the same. The result was an extraordinarily personal and self-righteous three-page letter detailing the Latour Maubourg affair, mocking Canning for putting himself 'into greater convulsions than the Dervishes at the mention of Buonoparte's name'. But if she hoped for an apology from Wellesley, that would not be forthcoming.†

---

* The *djerid* was a ceremonial weapon, similar to a javelin or lance, used to great effect by the Turkish cavalry.
† Wellesley wrote across the top of Hester's letter: 'Received: 18th October. Answer: None required'.

# 7

## Indecision

By October, there was still no word from France. There was, however, word from General Oakes, who had seen Sligo, and who now knew about the 'secret' affair. His letter to Hester is carefully worded; it is clear he felt protectively towards her. But Oakes was deeply perturbed to hear that she had refused Bruce's offer of marriage, a decision, he thought, that could only bring 'much trouble and distress' to both of them, and he wondered at her willingness to throw away her chance of ever being accepted in English society, regardless of the age difference. He informed her that James was still as angry with them as ever, and warned that Sligo did not know how to be discreet. He wished '[Sligo] was a little older, and had a greater knowledge of mankind and the world'.

The fact was that no sooner had Sligo returned home than the affair between Hester and Bruce, and her intention to make Bruce 'one of the finest characters in the Kingdom', became a much-repeated piece of gossip. Crauford Bruce received more malicious anonymous letters attacking Hester. 'My old enemies, I suppose are still at work, lamenting that all their former wicked intrigue to ruin my happiness has not, as they hoped it would, ended by sending me into the next world,' she wrote. Her already strong sense of betrayal and exclusion from society intensified, while her gratitude deepened towards those friends who had shown themselves to be loyal and kind, such as the Duke of York and General Oakes. As for James, she wrote:

Thank God, upon his own account he has not my death to reproach himself with, nor would I wish him to know not only all the misery but sufferings his imprudence has caused me . . . if he chooses to act as a brother towards me in private, it is all very well; if not, I shall never cease to pray for his welfare but I shall never see him again, nor will I allow him to torment me by letter: he might know me well enough to be aware that when my mind is made up upon any subject it is unchangeable.[1]

Winter was fast approaching. Around this time, Hester's cousin, Henry William Wynne, Lord Grenville's nephew, arrived in Constantinople, and was made welcome at Bebec. She fussed over Wynne, but also swatted him like a playful lioness. 'The day I first saw her, I had not been in the room ten minutes before she opened her batteries, abusing or laughing at every individual in the family . . . I gave as good as she brought and we were therefore excellent friends,' he wrote to his mother, adding, 'I must however, say that at the time when she is abusing everything which is most dear to me, she does it in a manner that it is impossible to be angry with her, and I believe it proceeds more from a love of ridiculing than from the heart.'[2]

Wynne was taken aback when she told him late into the evening after they had drunk several bottles of wine, 'half-joking and half in earnest', that she meant to go to Palestine to see whether Brothers might have got it right, for perhaps she really was destined to preside over a new Jerusalem. 'She says she will not go there till she knows I have left it, for fear that any branch of the Grenvilles will come under that denomination,' he wrote, still smirking at the joke.[3]

Not wanting to give up on France, however, Hester and Bruce reviewed their plans. One of Bruce's friends, Henry ('Harry') Pearce, offered to join them, and there was talk of going to Armenia, or even Abyssinia. In the end they decided to head to Egypt and Syria for a few months to indulge Hester's desire to see Jerusalem. Little realizing what he had triggered, Wynne had planted a competitive seed in Hester with his blithe announcement that he intended to go to Palmyra. The horses were sold; local servants – excepting Giorgio – dismissed, and trunks of books and possessions sent back to England.

They left Constantinople on a Greek *caïque* on 23 October 1811. By the time they reached Chios, a storm had set in, and they anchored there until it had completely cleared. Bruce was touched to find this was the island of Homer's birth. 'We unmoored from Chios and were carried without any accident to Rhodes, where we stopped but a few hours to take in water and fresh bread,' Meryon would write to his sister, 'little imagining how soon we should return.' Hester wanted to stay for a week and see Rhodes, but was overruled by the captain, who was anxious to press on.

They were halfway to Alexandria when the skies darkened and the heavens opened; they found themselves facing into gale-force winds, against swelling waves. Hester cursed herself, wished they had not spared the expense and had taken a larger boat with a British captain. There was little they could do except turn back towards Rhodes.

Five days later, on 27 November, water gushed through a sizeable hole in the ship's hold. The leak was impossible to staunch, so all available men set to work bailing out as fast as they could while remaining under sail, barely able to hear each other's voices as the storm raged. Hester would later recall how she made sure everyone drank some wine to numb their rising terror, feeling unnaturally calm herself. To their joy, they saw the distant outline of Rhodes, and did their best to steer towards an outcrop of rocks about a mile from land where they might anchor, but by now the *caïque* was so flooded, they were forced to let down the long-boat and with only moments to spare, all twenty-seven people managed to cram aboard. There was no time even to bring water or food. Everyone now knew their chance of survival was slim; some of the servants had begun shrieking and whimpering. Hester did her best to stop them panicking. 'Could the fashionables I once associated with believe that I could have sufficient composure of mind to have given orders as distinctly and positively as if I had been sitting in the midst of them,' she would later say, 'so away I went, putting my faith in God who has never quite forsaken me in all my various misfortunes.' But she wept as her little dog, who refused to jump from the ship, was swallowed by the sea. Rowing desperately, they managed to steer the longboat into a small gash-like inlet on the rocky outpost, and collapsed, their limbs bleeding and their clothes half torn away.

By around three in the morning, there was a lull in the storm. The captain insisted this was the time to row ashore with some of the crew to get help; it would be faster and safer with fewer of them in the boat in such bad weather. Hester had caught a chill and was feverish; she remembered little discomfort. The crew returned, some thirty hours later when the storm had abated somewhat, bringing 'bread, water, honey and a few fowls', buoyed by drink, and a second landing was attempted. After four hours of fighting the surging sea, a wave upturned them all violently on a stony beach. It took them another day to reach the nearest village.

They had lost everything: all their provisions and weapons. Meryon had lost his diary, copious notes and drawings, his precious new fur pelisse and pistols, as well as his medicine chest and supplies; Mrs Fry had nothing but her torn petticoats and a lock of her daughter's hair; Bruce had only a little money tied about his waist. Hester managed to grab only two pelisses, a dressing box and a small tin in which she had put General Moore's bloodstained glove, Charles's last letter to her, and a lock of his and Pitt's hair, as well as a Persian snuff box Sligo had given her. Hester's new Turkish silks, daggers and her cherished possessions, including jewels and a necklace that had belonged to her mother, and her extensive wardrobe of European clothes, all went to the deep.

Hester felt oddly purified by the shipwreck. She was prepared to believe that a greater, unseen force had saved them, and for a reason, and chose to see this as her break with the past. 'I am never low, but when I think of England and the monsters it contains – when I put them out of my mind I am happy, for I have great reason to be so; but who do I owe my comforts to? – to strangers!'

She shaved her hair, and suggested that all of her party do the same. It seems a powerful, penitent gesture, and certainly seems symbolic of a new beginning, but it was probably for the more prosaic reason that after accepting the villagers' hospitality in houses 'only fit for poultry', they had all become infested with lice. The resurrection of their lives began with getting hold of funds; they had only £30 between them, a loan grudgingly given by the Bey at Rhodes.

Next came the question of what to wear. Hester rejected the idea of European clothes. They were not available, and there was no point baffling local tailors with requests for them. To dress as a Greek – at a time when Greece was under the thumb of Ottoman domination – was unthinkable for Hester. 'To dress as a Turkish woman would not do, because I must not be seen to speak to a man; therefore I have nothing left for it but to dress as a Turk.'[4]

She wore mannish layers of silk and cotton shirts, a waistcoat and long breeches, tucking a pistol and a knife into her sash, as well as a 'turban of several colours, put on in a particular way, with a large bunch of natural flowers on one side'. At times she was mistaken for a boy. Delighted with her appearance, she told Oakes, 'I can assure you that if I ever looked well in anything it is in the Asiatic dress'.[5] In their borrowed Turkish clothes, with their assorted high-waisted embroidered jackets, kidskin boots, turbans and swords, they perplexed the villagers, who could not establish any rank between them.

In Triandra, a seaside village not far from Rhodes town, a Turk had offered them his house, which had its own small *hamam* in the middle of an orange orchard. They used what money they had for food and wine, and to send Meryon off to Smyrna a few days before Christmas. He was welcomed by the accommodating British consul, and was soon in possession of £500 in Turkish currency, drawn on Hester's account with Coutts, with which he was to restock medicines (at five times their cost in England), riding equipment and essential goods. Hester had ordered him to buy Turkish travelling clothes for the entire group, and hire a messenger to go to Constantinople to re-apply for their precious lost *firmans*, granting them permission to travel throughout the Ottoman territories. In Smyrna, Meryon heard of the grim fate of the *Pomane*, the ship which had left Constantinople laden with their possessions. It too had been wrecked. Gifts and bank drafts from Meryon for his family, Hester's peace offering to Crauford Bruce, an extravagant Turkish pelisse that had cost them £200, as well as trunks of books and Bruce's exotica from his travels were all lost. There was one piece of good news: Captain Henry Hope of the *Salsette* had heard of their misfortune and would offer them passage to Alexandria.

Hester's new identity was more than just a superficial transformation. Her strong personality, which often got her into trouble in England, made her a fascinating curiosity here. 'The Turks also estimate a person by their riding well or ill . . . they argue that I must be very extraordinary indeed.' Bruce teased that she made 'conquests of the Turks everywhere'. He seems not to have minded her shaven head; as her hair grew back he claimed to like her gamine look. He reported to his father that he had never felt better: 'Shipwrecks, storms and campaigns seem to agree with my constitution,' he wrote, exuberantly; Crauford no doubt wondered what campaigns he was talking about.

If anything, Hester was emboldened. She had set her sights on going to Palmyra herself, determined to see the ruins of Queen Zenobia's city among the date palms in the Syrian desert, no matter that everyone warned that the journey through Bedouin territory was regarded as immensely dangerous. She persuaded Bruce that such an achievement – in the footsteps of his own relative James Bruce – would do his career no harm. Bruce, who had lingered over his forebear's rapturous descriptions and drawings of Palmyra, was inclined to indulge her.

On Valentine's Day 1812 they sailed into Alexandria's harbour. Watery sunshine made the handsome stone houses along the wide bay look like a buttery mass. They were expected by Colonel Edward Misset, the British Resident, a cultivated and elegant Irishman, an ex-officer of the Inniskillen Dragoons, who suffered from a crippling degenerative disease, and had to be carried everywhere in a palanquin.

Misset arranged for his energetic secretary to welcome them at the docks, and had secured accommodation for them in several houses in the French quarter, close to the sea walls. They were whisked around Alexandria's sights, including a den of lions, the bazaars and the sixty-foot-high obelisk we know as Cleopatra's Needle. Misset's unusually sophisticated grasp of Middle Eastern politics and customs endeared him to Hester. His house parties were stylish affairs, with the best 'caviare' and champagne in town. That night, he assembled an impromptu welcoming party.

Misset ignored the diplomatic rule of segregation between the English and the French, and among other guests was Vincent-Yves Boutin, a dark-haired, athletic-looking, deeply-tanned Frenchman. He had trained as an engineer, he told them, and had once served in the military. But now, at forty, he described himself as 'a poor archaeologist', driven by his fascination to uncover the secrets of the ancients. He had already sailed up the Nile to Aswan with the French Consul-General and entrepreneurial treasure-hunter Bernadino Drovetti, and crossed the Sahara to the Red

Sea. Now he was headed for Egypt's Western Desert, to the remote-sounding oasis of Siwa. He had the look of a loner; guarded, unwilling – or perhaps unable – to be too friendly. In his dispatches, Misset explicitly suggested that he suspected intelligence-gathering was Boutin's real speciality. The night she met him, Hester reached the same conclusion. 'Are you not a spy for Bonaparte?' she asked him outright, keeping her eyes fixed on him, and her gaze neutral. Boutin flinched, but concealed his anger.

For Hester, this was the moment when her interest began. Bruce was not the only one who observed that confrontation was often Hester's way of flirting. Boutin melted into the night, leaving her wanting to talk to him again. A day or two later, they heard he had left for Marsa Matruh – said to be where Antony and Cleopatra once trysted – and the sand-seas of Siwa.

The meeting, however brief, was significant. Hester never hid her enthusiasm for men she found worth admiring. Later she told Bruce that she thought 'Le Boutonné' (buttoned-up), as she nicknamed him, one of the most impressive men she had ever met, 'as delightful, as talented and [with] a singular well-organized mind' and 'finest' sense of 'public principle' as she could imagine.[6] Bruce was irritable and jealous, feeling for the first time that his position as her lover was by no means stable. They both knew they were only delaying their eventual separation. Although quick to flout convention in other respects, Hester seems to have placed a high value on fidelity. But for the first time since she had met Bruce, she had come across a man she felt she might console herself with when he was gone.

Perhaps these thoughts gave her the sensation that she was losing her grip on her emotions; uncharacteristically, her nerves and temper frayed around Bruce. She felt divided, overtaken by a new restlessness. The niggling thought that she would soon be what she called a 'free agent' had been brought to the fore. She provoked a stormy exchange by bringing up the subject that they had let rest for months, that he must eventually think of his 'glory and welfare' and that 'his time must not be wasted'. After Palmyra, he must promise to think of his future. Later Hester would tell him sadly, 'Why did I not abide at *once* by the determination I formed upon these sands? It would have been better for both.'[7]

To Bruce, this sudden talk of his leaving seemed cruel and unnecessary.

Chevening, Hester's childhood home and family seat of the Stanhopes, believed to have been designed by Inigo Jones. This 115-room residence so impressed the visiting Lord Rosebery in 1911 that the former Prime Minister crossed out 'Chevening' on a piece of letterheaded note paper and substituted 'Paradise'.

A partial view of Chevening's famous entrance hall, which when seen in full, is a hymn to weaponry, bristling with rifles, bayonets and daggers from an Irish militia regiment bought by the 2nd Earl Stanhope.

Lucy Pitt, Hester's great-grandmother, who brought together the Stanhopes and the Pitts when she married James Stanhope, a man twice her age. From their house in Whitehall, they made a formidable, glamorous political couple.

Regarded as the greatest politician of his time, William Pitt the Elder was known as 'the Great Commoner' and revered for leading the country through the Seven Years War. Hester idolized him and liked to describe herself as 'a chip off the old block'.

Hester, Countess of Chatham, Hester's maternal grandmother and namesake, was a memorable influence. Strong, resourceful and unflappable, her discretion and tact led Thomas Coutts to declare her 'the cleverest man of her time'.

Hester's shrewd Scottish-born grandmother, Lady Grizel Stanhope, ran Chevening with precision and fortitude. She introduced Hester to a lifelong love of plants and gardening.

Charles, 3rd Earl Stanhope, Hester's father. Politician, scientist and leading member of the London Revolution Society, Stanhope was a fierce champion of democracy and the French Revolution.

This portrait is widely assumed at Chevening to be that of Hester Pitt, the future Lady Hester Stanhope and Lady Mahon, Hester's mother. Renowned for her intelligence and beauty, she was at the height of her powers when she married, aged 19.

Charles, as Viscount Mahon, in a self-portrait showing him holding a painting of his mother Grizel. At a young age, he showed precocious talent and was considered a genius by his tutors.

Patriotic Regeneration. _viz._ Parliament Reform'd, a la Françoise. that is Honest Men (i.e. Opposition) in the Seat of Justice.

Democratic Leveling. _Alliance a la Françoise;_ _or_ The Union of the Coronet & Clyster-pipe.

As 'Citizen Stanhope', Hester's father was mercilessly lampooned by Gillray, who depicted him as an emaciated drunk. In this vivid imagined scene (above), Stanhope reads charges against a cowed Pitt, impeached for his crimes against liberty, with Charles Fox presiding as judge.

When Hester's sixteen-year-old sister Lucy eloped with a local apothecary, the scandal did not go unnoticed. Here, Gillray takes a dig at the republican lord 'pushing' his aristocratic daughter into marriage with a commoner, with Fox as the priest performing the ceremony.

It has often been suggested that this miniature painting is of Hester, made in 1810, the year she left England. Its authenticity is unconfirmed, however – another source suggests that it dates from the late eighteenth century and is of Hester's mother.

Hester as Hebe by the society painter Richard Cosway, in 1808. As an old woman Hester remembered her youthful beauty: 'My complexion was like alabaster; and at five paces distance, the sharpest eye could not discover my pearl necklace from my skin; my lips were of such a beautiful carnation, that without vanity, I assure you very few women had the like.'

Philip Henry Mahon, 4th Earl Stanhope. Hester's relationship with her eldest half-brother was always intense. As the once-close bonds soured, Hester developed a lifelong repugnance of him.

James Hamilton Stanhope became Hester's closest sibling after the death of their brother Charles. More morally conservative than Hester, he was no less brave. A soldier turned politician, James survived horrendous wounds in battle, only to hang himself after the death in childbirth of his beloved wife, Frederica.

Hester regaled friends with an anecdote about this bust of William Pitt the Younger, completed by Nollekens after the Prime Minister's death. She claimed she thought the shape of the nose wasn't quite right and that she took a small chisel to it and surreptitiously made the neccessary adjustments. No one noticed, she said, but the perfect likeness of Pitt's 'Chatham' nose was remarked upon.

With Pitt at Walmer Castle on the Kent coast, Hester found freedom and a sense of family. She revelled in being invited to voice her opinion when war stratagems were debated, and uncle and niece developed a strong symbiotic relationship. Pitt described Hester as 'a light in his dwelling'.

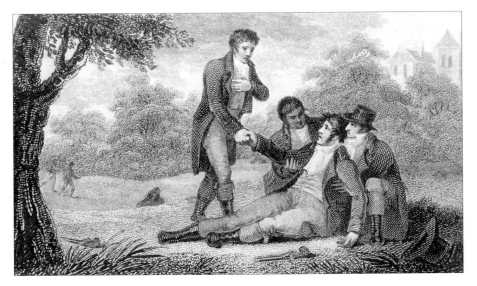

ABOVE: Thomas Pitt, Lord Camelford –
depicted here dying after a duel – was
Hester's first cousin and her first love.
Nicknamed 'the Cornish Hercules', he
was in every way larger than life. It was
he who gave Hester her taste for
weapons.

RIGHT: Another cousin, Captain
William Sidney Smith, was a national
hero who defeated Napoleon at Acre
in 1799. He was a great admirer of
Hester's and tried very hard to enlist
her into his special operations.

LEFT: Lord Granville
Leveson Gower,
pictured here with his
extended family, was
charming, politically
ambitious and one of
the best-looking men of
his generation – in
short, everything Hester
believed she wanted. She
was devastated when he
broke off their affair.

They had, after all, only just arrived in Egypt. His love for her had never been greater. He did not want to imagine his life without her. 'This determination has, as you may well conceive, hurt my feelings very deeply. Nothing under Heaven would ever have induced me to break off this connexion . . . because both my Happiness and Honour were engaged in it,' he admitted to his father. In a pique, as he had done before when she rejected his offer of marriage, Bruce began to lay plans for making his own tour, this time along the Nile to see the marvels of Upper Egypt himself – without her.

Hester seems to have been disappointed by Alexandria, thinking it 'hideous', although she was to write that she 'liked Egypt extremely, notwithstanding the narrow streets, the stinks and bad eyes'.[8] She would have known that Moore had been here, almost to the day, eleven years before, as part of the Anglo-Turkish advance against Napoleon.

She and Bruce stayed for ten days, making preparations for the journey to Cairo. She wanted to see where Moore had fought; the place where he had told her he 'had never seen a field so strewn with dead'. They trekked to the site at Canopus, near Aboukir, crossing Lake Idku on reed boats, then made their way to Rosetta on bad-tempered donkeys. Although they were impressed by Rosetta's lush gardens, their lodgings were depressing, infested with fleas which seemed to burrow their way into every item of clothing they owned. Once, Hester claimed, 'I found 180 on my clothes on undressing'.[9] Their blotchy skins and incessant scratching cannot have helped their mood.

'Celebrated as the Nile has been in ages,' wrote a disaffected Meryon, 'it had nothing to recommend it in point of beauty, and the water is the most turbid that can be seen.' They set off from the riverbanks of Rosetta on 9 March. They had hired two barques or *dahabeahs* – the boats the ancient Egyptians believed were used by their gods and by souls on their way to the afterlife – with billowing white sails above gaily-painted cabins no more than eight feet wide. By day, Hester and Bruce deliberately travelled apart. The women travelled in one boat, and the men in the other, laden with the bulk of their luggage.

Hester was grappling with her emotions, and wanted time alone to think. At first, they reconnoitred in the evenings, but then the men fell behind. The day before Hester's birthday, Meryon records that their boat 'ran aground' in the shallow banks; they were unable to catch up with her boat. Five days later, when the men reached Cairo, they had word that Hester had already settled into a grand mansion in the Frank quarter near Ezbekiya, and was expecting them.

Hester spent her thirty-sixth birthday alone. Within two days, she had introduced herself to Henry Salt, the British Consul-General, and his French counterpart, Bernardino Drovetti. Passing herself off as a young bey, accompanied by a Janissary guard, she rode through the streets, marvelling at the life that seethed within the city's walls.

During the short separation from Bruce, Hester's mood changed. The climate was not yet oppressive. She was excited by the great metropolis; perhaps the thought that she might see Boutin crossed her mind. But she felt remorseful for hurting Bruce. She did what many women do in times of emotional upheaval, when they feel torn between men and big life-decisions: she set about beautifying herself. First she made for the baths. Then she laid siege to Cairo's souks, to complete the transform-ation she had begun at Rhodes. Soon, merchants were hurrying to her rented house to tempt her with beautiful textiles, exquisite printed Aleppo, Tunisian, Ottoman and Coptic fabrics and delicate linens. This time she had no intention of being mistaken for anyone of low rank, or indeed, anyone other than herself.

In pioneering her own new look, Hester had an instinctive grasp of what concoctions of fashions and fabrics would suit her. She took the basic components of the dress of a Turkish bey, but made sure not to wear anything too bulky, opting for cinched-in waists and long, pantaloon-style trousers. In particular, she liked the Mameluke style. To everything she wore, she added her own subtle feminine flourishes, so that up close there could never be any doubt as to her sex – or her attractiveness. She experimented with new ways of tying turbans. Unexpectedly, she found they flattered her, emphasizing her elongated neck and cheekbones; in them she looked both more dramatic and authoritative.

She spent impulsively. Bruce had insisted she must, to replace at least the clothes she had lost in the shipwreck; they had estimated the value of her losses at between two and three thousand pounds. In no time at all, she ran through £600 pounds (about £30,000 today), acquiring new wardrobes for herself and Bruce, wanting to surprise him. They both needed new pistols, swords and a variety of triumphant-looking saddles to match their outfits. Nor was she able to resist delightful bed-linens, kilims, Tulip-era candlesticks and the idiosyncratic copper 'helmets' used in all the best Turkish households to keep food warm at the table. Business was conducted through interpreters, haggling conducted over sweet *café au lait* in small china cups.

But when Bruce arrived, he remained subdued, and responded to her with a new coolness. Now it was she who was made to suffer pangs of jealousy. At a dinner given for them by Drovetti, she was upset by the deliberate attentions he paid to one or two pretty young French women, and by learning that he had been invited to visit them – without her.[10] Several years later, she would reflect on how this rift between them then seemed to take on a life of its own, and tell Bruce: 'Perhaps God knew that had I been as happy as I once expected to have been, I could not have kept my word with your father and on purpose wisely made me otherwise.'[11]

Hester must have counted on the fact that news of her arrival would soon reach Mehmet Ali, the great Pasha of Egypt. The son of a humble Albanian merchant, he was neither Egyptian nor Arab, and made up for his lack of formal education by innate cleverness and immense determination. In 1801 he turned down Napoleon's overtures; five years later as Pasha, he politely but firmly ensured the departure of the British. By 1807 he had seen off the last of the British expeditionary forces. Increasingly, he was becoming too powerful for the Sultan, who nonetheless saw no alternative but to rely on him to quash two powerful groups who threatened the Porte's interests, the Mamelukes and the Wahhabis.

Everywhere in Cairo Hester could see evidence of Mehmet Ali's arbitrary power. Each night, every quarter in the city was locked and guarded and citizens were randomly searched. Apparently Cairo had been purged of the violent crime commonplace under the Mamelukes, but the city's sandy streets still reeked 'like a butcher's slaughter house', Meryon thought.

The Pasha had realized, just as Napoleon had done, that to achieve lasting authority in Egypt, he would have to break the power of the

Mameluke beys, the notables descended from Circassian mercenaries who had previously ruled Egypt and parts of greater Syria and Palestine for the Ottomans. Their cult of fearless horsemanship was legendary: they rode like Cossacks, they attacked with *djerids*, severing heads while gripping the reins between their teeth. The year before Hester and Bruce arrived, Mehmet Ali had overthrown the Mamelukes in a carefully planned, gruesome *coup d'état*. He had invited the Mameluke beys and officers to a grand banquet within Cairo's walled citadel and had his Albanians massacre them. The palace records counted 470 severed heads.

Next, with the backing of his *ulema*, he had sent an army, led by his eighteen-year-old son, Ibrahim Pasha, to suppress a revolt by the fundamentalist Wahhabis, who had seized control of Islam's holy cities, Mecca and Medina. Not only did the Wahhabis question the right of the Ottomans to rule over all Muslims, they had achieved the unthinkable by crossing the great desert into the Hijaz and seizing Islam's holiest shrines, massacring those who refused to join their faith. They desecrated the Kaaba in Mecca's Great Mosque – and closed down the Haj, a state of affairs which scandalized Muslims throughout the Caliphate, and which the Porte, who relied on the revenues from the pilgrimage routes, was not prepared to tolerate. In 1811 Mehmet Ali had underestimated them: the great Egyptian army led by his teenaged son suffered a humiliating defeat. Now, at the Porte's request, he was preparing a major offensive, determined to retake Mecca and Medina. Without yet making his intentions plain, Mehmet Ali intended to rule Egypt independently, and he had his eyes on Syria and Palestine too.

Mehmet Ali was 'curious' to see 'an English lady dressed in men's clothes'. Hester was summoned. Mehmet Ali sent her 'seven horses, most magnificently caparisoned' to convey her and her entourage. They rode up into the Citadel, whose mighty walls were built by Saladin, to reach Al-Gawhara Palace, and were ushered through a passageway into an attached summer house. Mehmet Ali was waiting for them in a tiny room, no more than thirty feet wide. Aside from his guards, he seemed to be alone, but soon they heard whispers and giggles from behind an upper screen, and realized they were being watched by his harem.

Mehmet Ali's wives and concubines jostled about for a better view, curious to see Hester dressed like a man, towering over their husband.

They all knew the Turkish expression 'a white woman for beauty, but an Egyptian for pleasure', but this white woman was unlike anyone they had ever seen. Somewhat provocatively, she was dressed in the Mameluke style, in purple Tunisian velvet embroidered with gold. In the afternoon light she looked luminous. That day Mehmet Ali gave her the nickname of *Meleki*, which can mean in Arabic both 'angel' and 'divine queen'.

They all thought the Pasha looked at first sight a disappointing figure, a 'mean-looking man of about forty-five, and dressed very plain'. Short, with greying hair and a straggling beard, Mehmet Ali had at first made little effort to be charming. Meryon thought that as he had been 'a common soldier' he would be 'somewhat embarrassed before an illustrious stranger like Lady Hester'. (Meryon did not quite take the measure of the future founder of modern Egypt and of the dynasty that would last until King Farouk was overthrown in 1952.)

Mehmet Ali questioned Hester closely, glad to find an opportunity to talk unofficially on subjects she had strong opinions about. He wanted to modernize Egypt, and to do this, knew he had to cultivate friends amongst the leaders of the West (although he had no intention of giving the British any chance of replacing the French). She later mentioned to Sir Joseph Banks that the Pasha informed her he was keen to experiment on the practicability of using steamships on the Nile, and hoped that through her father's contacts a suitable expert might be recruited to come out to Egypt.

At the end of the visit Mehmet Ali took her out across the Citadel, to show her the magnificent view of the entire city, the domes and needles of its mosques, waving a hand at the place where his own giant mosque would rise. He invited her to return after her tour of Syria, offering her a guard of a thousand men if she wished.[12] Though delighted at the thought, she turned him down, knowing she would be expected to pay for the honour. She glowed to Crauford Bruce: 'We have been better treated and more talked about than any people who ever visited Cairo.' Nor could she resist crowing about her success with 'the all-powerful Mahomet Ali' to Stratford Canning, attempting to smooth over their awkward confrontation. 'He was civiler to me than he was to anyone in his life . . . I rode with him, paid him visits when I chose, where I chose; I talked to him for hours together and everything I asked was done.'[13]

The mere fact that she was being accorded the sort of attention usually granted only to the highest-ranking British envoy caused only consternation amongst Cairo's diplomats. Soon she was being invited back to attend a special review of Mehmet Ali's cavalry, sitting in full view as his guest. Amongst the expatriate community in Cairo there was much jealous sniggering and gossip. It was said that Bruce had got himself all trussed up 'like a Duke's son', and that it was obvious they were lovers, although amongst the non-English, Hester typically introduced Bruce as 'her cousin'. Hester unnerved the Europeans – especially the women – by the way she was seen riding astride, considered very vulgar for a woman. There was a simple explanation: the magnificent horse Mehmet Ali had sent her was already fitted with a ceremonial saddle: there was no other way to ride. At the end of the evening, Mehmet Ali told her to keep both the horse and the saddle. Hester never rode side-saddle again.

More rumours began over her friendship with one of Mehmet Ali's lieutenants, the extremely handsome Abdin Bey. Word got around that when Hester accepted his invitation to visit him alone, 'naked girls were made to dance before her'. He presented her with two beautiful horses 'perfectly trained to the Mameluke exercise', and a delighted Hester described how 'to mount one of them is like a leaf in the air, for the horses capers and leaps about in proportion to the dignity of the rider'.* Whatever rift there had been with Bruce, it seemed to heal, and he put aside his plans to travel by himself.

---

* She had them shipped off to Britain, the first as a surprise present for the Duke of York, the second for Lord Ebrington.

# 8

## *Friendships*

Near the majestic medieval gate of Bab Zwayla, on the corner of Cairo's
Sugar Street, one of the city's small hidden architectural treasures is tucked
next to a jewellery shop and a grubby Turkish bath. Here you can see an
impressive façade: a slim-columned two-storey building in delicately
carved limestone, sensuous *mashrabiya* windows and a marble panel
engraved with beautiful calligraphy above a fountain. Peer closer and you
can see that the ornately-stylized grilled windows have an unusual motif,
that of a heart and a woman's breasts. The building is known as Nafissa
al-Bayda's *sabil-kuttab*, a charitable *madrassa* that in the last quarter of
the eighteenth century offered free education and clean drinking water
from a public fountain.[1]

Nafissa Khatun, the woman who commissioned it, was known as al-
Bayda, 'The White One'. She was the most powerful woman in Cairo at
the time of Hester's visit, and she quickly became a close friend. To the
Mamelukes, Nafissa was their Helen of Troy. Her exact origins were
unknown; she had been plucked from her family as a child and sold into
slavery. Her beauty was so extraordinary, she was delivered directly to
the Mameluke ruler, Ali Bey. Equally unusually, he married her. Her first
husband ruled Egypt for the Ottomans for a decade; her second was the
man who assassinated him and assumed his power. Murad Bey had been
one of Ali Bey's trusted lieutenants. With Nafissa's enormous wealth,
Murad Bey quickly consolidated his grip.

When Napoleon arrived, Murad Bey and another Mameluke, Ibrahim
Bey, attempted to face him down with some 33,000 men against

Bonaparte's 25,000, only to suffer a crushing defeat. Ibrahim Bey escaped, melting away with his own army, roaming throughout the Egyptian desert, Nubia and the Sudan. After the massacre of the Mameluke beys, Mehmet Ali formed a reconstituted corps of some fifty low-ranking 'French' Mamelukes, mixed-race mercenaries, many of whom had previously joined Napoleon's troops. In Cairo, at least, there were too few of them to pose any threat to Mehmet Ali.

Nafissa had watched Hester's reception at Mehmet Ali's palace with interest, and issued her own invitation. Her home in Ezbekiya, reached through the labyrinth of old Cairo, was a tightly-guarded assortment of linked houses. Everything about Nafissa fascinated Hester at first sight: her strong personality and striking appearance, 'like a captive queen', she wrote. Although Nafissa was 'not young', probably in her fifties, she was still careful about her looks; she hennaed her long hair and put kohl around her eyes. They spoke in French which Nafissa punctuated with Arabic. She had the type of gallows humour Hester adored.

As their friendship developed, Nafissa revealed more of her past. During the French occupation, after her husband and his army were forced to retreat south to fight a guerrilla campaign, she remained to protect her family and their vast empire of property and possessions. She had been careful to present a gracious face to Napoleon, inviting him to dinner and charming him while secretly sending her spies south. Once, in the dead of night, just before Turkish reinforcements were about to arrive, husband and wife had even signalled to one another; Murad from the top of Cheops' Pyramid and Nafissa from the roof of their house.

Hester learned a great deal from Nafissa and was also impressed by her humanitarian nature. While her husband was doing his best to cut down the French, she did not discriminate when it came to helping the sick and the wounded, and opened her house to abandoned French soldiers and deserters. Like many who witnessed it, she had been outraged at the way Napoleon had callously discarded his soldiers, as soon as they were incapacitated by battle or illness. She paid into the French treasury at Cairo the equivalent of almost a million francs, a sum she explicitly insisted must be used to meet the cost of returning his wounded troops to their families.[2] When Napoleon made his famously sudden departure from Egypt he left specific orders that Nafissa must be watched over and protected. He had every intention of returning, and must have guessed that if anyone could unite the Mamelukes and win them over to his cause, it would be Nafissa. Nor could Mehmet Ali touch her. The *ulemas* held her in high regard.

Nafissa was now living what she considered to be the life of a pauper. She had been a clever businesswoman, keen to apply her skills regardless of her fortune, creating a huge *wekala* or covered market, adjacent to her *sabil-kuttab*. It survived the French occupation, but under Mehmet Ali, her interests were now strictly controlled. Her husband was spared the violent death of the other Mameluke beys; he had died of the plague in 1801.

Hester quickly developed what she referred to as 'a real friendship' with Nafissa. She considered her 'the most charming woman I ever knew' and she felt almost as though she had rediscovered an older sister, or mother. After she left Cairo, Hester wrote that she wanted to return 'if only to see this woman'. It was Nafissa who opened a storehouse of information on previously unimagined subjects and suggested whom she might seek out in Jerusalem and Damascus.

Nafissa confirmed the rumours Hester had heard, that Napoleon still hoped to unite the Mamelukes and the Wahhabis against Mehmet Ali, with the aim of retaking Egypt. She took Hester to meet the Mameluke widows and bereaved mothers whose grief was still fresh. She instilled in her a great curiosity about the Wahhabis, describing their horsemanship, and their belief in the coming of a messiah-like figure called the 'Mahdi' or the 'expected one'. She also let slip to Hester that the mysterious Boutin had regularly visited her.

This friendship with Nafissa – though brief in person – was influential, and kept alive in letters for some time afterwards. Four years later, the 'White One' would die in her Cairo mansion, with few of her previous army of retainers, all her wealth gone.

Few of Hester's countrymen in Egypt impressed her. Aside from Misset, she was less than complimentary about the English consuls: 'It would be difficult to collect such a lot of rascals anywhere.' She preferred the French, some of whom had come out as Napoleon's *savants*, and stayed, thinking them 'infinitely more civil'. Drovetti invited the party to the opening of a mummy – a dissection – performed by a French surgeon, and they had watched enthralled as tightly-bound layers were carefully cut away, revealing a creature with 'well-preserved' facial features, hair and teeth.[3]

In one of her letters, Hester mentioned that in Cairo she began going to mosques to observe prayers, keeping her profile well-wrapped but taking off her shoes, sitting cross-legged on the mat, and putting on 'an air of solemnity and respect'.[4] No one seems to have accompanied her on these secretive missions, nor disturbed her.

By the middle of April, through Hester's efforts, her party had acquired a formidable entourage. She and Bruce each had a personal servant, valet and interpreter who went with them everywhere; in addition she took on a cook, two grooms for their five horses and two men to pitch tents. Abdin Bey gave her two French Mameluke bodyguards (each of whom had his own servant), fitting them out with pistols and swords.

She hired more horses and camels. She commissioned six Turkish tents, in green rather than imperial red, which might get them mistaken for the Turkish military. They were reinforced with leather and decorative appliqué in flower and jewellery motifs with patterned borders, topped with a brass star and crescent. At night, flickering with light from glass-covered candles, they would look straight out of one of Scheherazade's stories.

Just as they were making last preparations to leave, Boutin reappeared in Ezbekiya, where he rented rooms. She says nothing about the nature of her encounter with him. There is just one hint of some playfulness shared between them. This time, seeing her with her exquisite clothes and ambitious expedition plans, we know he made a rather taunting remark that she was now quite the 'Queen', because she later refers to it.

Hester had no evidence to support her teasing accusation the first night she met him, but she was utterly on the mark. He was one of Napoleon's most prized agents. When Boutin arrived in Egypt in the winter of 1810, his mission had been clear.[5] Napoleon's orders were to survey, in total secrecy, the strategic positions of certain cities in Egypt – Alexandria, Cairo, Damietta, and much of the Red Sea coastline – as well as Aleppo, Damascus, Jaffa, Tripoli and Acre.[6] He was to assess the political situation, and identify potential allies and enemies, and report particularly closely on the Mamelukes, the Wahhabis and any other warrior factions keen to resist Mehmet Ali and to fight the English.[7]

Napoleon was indeed angling after another invasion, planning to reclaim Egypt and Syria. He also dreamed of marching his armies into India. This time he intended to lay his groundwork meticulously. In Egypt Boutin was to pose as an archaeologist; in Syria as a newly-appointed diplomatic commercial attaché; his performance in both roles had to be entirely convincing. None of the consuls were to be told of his real activities. He was to report directly to Joseph Fouché.[8]

Shortly after Boutin's return, a wretched scene took place between Hester and Bruce, creating a more profound rift. Perhaps she argued that it was her duty to find out exactly what the French 'spy' might be doing; perhaps he disagreed and had cause to be jealous. Nevertheless, they decided to travel on together. Several years later, a woman in whom he had confided all the details of his history with Hester would tell him, 'You ask me for advice, but really I do not rightly understand what kind of advice you want. According to what you told me yourself she renounced you and even gave herself to others.'[9] From later events, it certainly seems possible that there may have been more to the unexpected flirtation with Boutin in Cairo.

On 20 April Bruce wrote to his father to let him know they would soon be in Syria, but that his thoughts had turned to coming home to 'live tranquilly in the bosom of a family which I adore'. As for his future, he wrote coolly that 'Lady Hester Stanhope is quite against the resolutions which I have formed, and although I shall always pay the greatest deference to her opinions yet on this occasion her arguments have failed'.[10]

The chance to pitch the tents came before they left Cairo. It was the end of April, already very hot by European standards. Hester's cousin Wynne and his travelling companion John Fiott arrived to join their party, elated from their intrepid travels. The pair had succeeded in reaching Palmyra, and could talk of nothing else but their scrapes, although of the Bedouin they had seen nothing. Hester questioned Wynne closely, extracting all the details: the equivalent of £30 had been the Arab guide's fee; they had taken no gifts for the Bedouins; they had no protection beyond their own pistols. She learned that in fact they had only managed to see the ruins from a great distance as their guide, who was from

Damascus, had been terrified they would all be killed by the local Bedouin if they ventured any further.

To celebrate their safe return, an expedition to the Pyramids was suggested. Hester intended to stay behind in Cairo for a day or two, and meet them there. On the night she joined them, she pleaded exhaustion, and went off to a house in one of the nearby villages where she had arranged to sleep. Wynne apparently joked to Harry Pearce that he was long overdue for amorous adventure; Meryon seems to have been the one deputed to arrange for a bevy of dancing girls to come along with them. He wrote, rather lamely: 'Not knowing how to pass the evening' they had decided to hire 'some dancing girls'. They were all young – Egyptians and a couple of Negresses. 'A blouse, with a girdle around their waist, was their only covering,' Meryon recalled.

That night the men sat outside their tents, with candles, drinking coffee and rose syrup and whatever wine they had managed to find in Cairo. They plied the girls with drink, while a trio of musicians played. Before them was the spectacular sight of the Great Pyramid of Cheops and a sea of desert bathed in moonlight.

The following morning, when Hester arrived, she sulked at signs of the hurriedly concealed orgy. She refused to accompany the men for a closer inspection of the Pyramids. Instead, she sat in her tent.

As they sailed down the Nile towards the port at Damietta they passed landscapes little changed from the days of the Pharaohs. They squinted through bright light across swathes of reeds, to make out mud villages and wallowing buffalo, and, from time to time, naked children splashing in the shallows. They saw colonies of huge hippopotamuses. Bruce's bad temper triggered full-scale confrontations almost every day. Meryon suffered the brunt of it but kept his lips angrily pressed together. Everyone assumed the lovers were having a private quarrel, and did their best not to add to any tension.

Around this time, something specific upset Meryon so greatly that he contemplated resigning. He alluded to the reason to his sister, but then fretted that he should not have mentioned it. In a later letter he told her 'with respect to whatever relates to my dispute with Mr Bruce, in God's name keep it an inviolable secret'.[11] The vehemence of Meryon's reaction suggests something highly confidential – probably requiring medical attention, and of which he disapproved.

It would soon become clear to Crauford that all was not well between his son and Hester. On one occasion, she evidently picked up her pen to write to him while an argument was still fresh; 'His taking it ill or well shall make no difference to me; I was not born to be any man's toady,' she scrawled angrily. Hester and Bruce chose once again to be separated during the day; her boat sailed ahead; his followed behind with all the baggage. She was agitated and wanted to confide her anxieties, yet the only person she thought might understand her anguish was her lover's father.

On 2 May 1812 she sat huddled on wooden planks, shaded from the sun, as they glided slowly down the Nile and wrote one of her longest, most deeply personal letters to Crauford. Once she had begun, the flow was unstoppable; the letter ran to twenty pages. Her words are heavy-hearted:

I have B's interest so much at heart and so much convinced that I have conscientiously [stood] by him in every respect, that I would not change my tone were I certain he would leave me in the desert tomorrow, and the time may come when he will thank me for my candour, and acknowledge I had right on my side.[12]

Quite apart from the new tension between them, she felt impatient and disappointed with Bruce. It was as though being with her was diminishing him, making him doubt himself. He had already admitted to her that he no longer wished to pursue a political career. Not long after their meeting with Mehmet Ali, at which he felt so maladroit compared to Hester, Bruce wrote to his father that he feared 'the inadequacy of my abilities to fill any public situation', which added to the 'present state of Europe, the corruption of the English Government, and a total change of my own sentiments have induced me to give up Parliament and to renounce public life altogether'.[13]

As Hester was well aware, Bruce stood to inherit estates in Oxfordshire, Gloucestershire, Buckinghamshire, Lancashire, Berkshire and Scotland as well as land in Hampshire and Dorset. It appalled her that he affected to 'rather despise' all 'country amusements' when she herself, she pointedly told Crauford, would be quite happy just to 'dig my half acre of land my two sheep & feed my horse', adding sharply that their company would 'be preferable to that of a stupid or vulgar man'. By now she regarded Crauford as a confidant and a friend:

> A man of B's fortune must acquire habits of business to manage his own affairs and to become a respectable private member of society and therefore to tell you the plain truth I am sometimes mortified that he will attend so little to my lectures upon this subject . . .

And she made no excuses for her high standards:

> If I had been a man, my love for fame wd. have been unbounded. I know it & I confess it, and had I been a Duke I must have been a Soldier to have been happy, but not only a General by name [but] a Cabinet General, I must have added to the theory of Lord Hutchinson the activity of General Moore . . .*[14]

Her description of the sort of man she felt she could admire did not seem to fit Bruce:

> I hate fops and conceited men, but I like a man to be well-bred and to know how to command those about him, besides I like to see a young man active, to ride, to walk well, to be handy and manly, to shift for oneself, that is to be covered in dirt, to eat nastiness and eat ill and to be always vexed in doing nothing, a military man for me, who makes himself comfortable in a place 7 feet square and who comes out so smart and so clean, and who seems contented and at home everywhere and who if he is worth a horse feeds it before he feeds himself.[15]

She did not think Bruce was ready for a political career. 'A young man wants a *foundation* first to build upon, and thorough knowledge of politicks [sic] before he becomes a politician. Foreign politicks are all very necessary, but one should first know the laws of one's own country and something of its rights and constitution, its resources and the disposition

---

* Both Hester and Bruce admired the military and political bravery of General Hutchinson, who succeeded Abercromby, and commanded the Anglo-Turkish force in Egypt.

of its inhabitants,' she wrote, evidently satisfied with her own grasp of these matters. 'Superficial knowledge and flash' was not enough, she warned. Crauford most certainly must have felt that his son had taken up with an extremely strong-minded woman equal to life's challenges.

Over the ten days it took them to reach Damietta, the weather became unbearably hot; there were dust storms and more arguments. Bruce had been all for changing their plans and remaining in Egypt.[16] But Hester had no intention of staying. Her heart was now being bitterly torn in a way she had not expected. She realized her hold on Bruce was slipping. But one look at his handsome head, his tanned skin and tousled beard still stirred her. 'I cannot but love him the better,' she wrote. She could forgive him his youth. He was still her 'sacred charge'.

On 17 May 1812 they arrived at the fortress seaport of Jaffa, today swallowed up by the sprawl of Tel Aviv. Ranged around a distinctive sugarloaf hill and walled citadel, the beauty of Jaffa's long curving bay and pristine sea, backed by groves of orange, lime and almond trees, took them all by surprise.

News had now spread that an English princess was making her way to Jerusalem. Now that she had added more servants, horses and a train of camels to her retinue, it did indeed bear a resemblance to a royal caravanserai. Rows of curious faces turned to see her. Hester despised the Governor of Jaffa – the coarse, openly-ambitious Muhammad Aby Nabut. He made a crude pass at her; she would later accuse him of being no better than a common rapist. But the Aga had his uses; he let her take two of his soldiers – at a price. He knew full well that even with them, she would not be safe in the biblical badlands.

In 1812, the vast Ottoman-ruled region of Syria consisted of the present states of Syria, Lebanon, Israel and Jordan. It was divided into five provinces or *pashaliks* – Aleppo, Damascus, Tripoli, Acre and Jerusalem – with each of the five pashas ruling over subordinate agas or governors throughout their territories. However, the open country between the triangle of Jaffa, Jerusalem and Acre belonged to bandit-like sheikhs who saw fit to extract a 'toll' from pilgrims or travellers. Such men were, commented Hester, 'according to the politics of the moment . . . either robbers or police officers'.

They had barely left Jaffa's outskirts before they found themselves at the mercy of most notorious bandit-sheikh of them all, Abu Ghosh, who commanded some three thousand men and was said 'to hold the keys of Jerusalem'. When he thundered up towards them, surrounded by twenty 'blacks, with ready pistols', they feared the worst. To Hester's astonishment, Ghosh announced that he had come to pay his respects, having heard that Hester was a relative of Sir Sidney Smith, whom he regarded as a personal friend. He insisted on escorting her party to Jerusalem and his four wives served them a feast.

The closer they came to Jerusalem, the more arid the land became, its scrub picked bare by goats and strewn with white boulders. Hester found it both forbidding and disappointing: 'This was the chosen land flowing with milk and honey that was to reward the sufferings of the chosen people?'[17]

The light was fading when they first saw Jerusalem, the sun sinking towards the west like a great flaming disc so bright it made their retinas dance. From a distance, picking their way along a barren mountain track, they could see only the city's crenellated walls. Then the Dome of the Rock hovered into view, with its great roof and beautiful blue and green Persian tiles inscribed with Koranic verses, and its crescent, which had long ago replaced the cross.[18] As was customary, they all dismounted and kneeled down.

In Ramleh – now Ramallah – the same morning, Hester had dressed with ritual care. She wore a tight-fitting crimson jacket and wide Mameluke 'trowsers', cinched at the waist and embroidered at the cuffs and hems with gold. Over that she wore a white silk '*burnooz*', a hooded cloak, tied at the neck with long decorative pendants and tassels. Around her head she had bound a length of white silk. Her horse was just as carefully groomed, the saddle and bridle chosen to match her outfit.

By the time the travellers reached Jerusalem's Bethlehem Gate, the eastern walls and cobbled streets leading to the Christian quarter were in darkness and almost empty.[19] There was a forbidding, lawless atmosphere; everyone about them was veiled or hooded. They stayed at a monastery near the Holy Sepulchre; the men were admitted to hutch-like rooms off a narrow enclosure and locked in at night in by Turkish guards, according to the monastery rules. Hester endured equally cloistered conditions in a small house a few steps away. Several persistent beggars kept a vigil outside on her steps. If Hester had hoped for an epiphany on the day she entered the Holy City this was hardly it.

Yet by morning the fate predicted for her so many years ago by the religious prophet Richard Brothers seemed to have come almost eerily true. When she emerged into the street astride her horse, she found a mob, convinced she had the means to shower them with gold. Nor was any formality lacking at the palace, where the Aga of Jerusalem provided guards to protect them while they were in the city, and gave them a courteous welcome. From his balcony, they surveyed what all Muslims called 'El Kuds' ('The Holy'), the Temple Mount, centrepiece of the messianic tradition for Jews, Muslims and Christians.

Jerusalem worked its strange, potent magic. Away from the crush of the canopied bazaars, they threaded their way through narrow, high-faced alleys, seeing brief flashes of life inside through half-open doors, dodging mules and gangs of sweating labourers laden with sacks. They could feel religion in every crevice, woven into the fabric of the city's life in its bewildering juxtaposition of faiths and collocation of shrines. Even Hester, with her sceptic's eye, was awed. She had always been resistant to religion, growing up with a disregard for Christianity that had shocked even her father.

> I never would be confirmed and they would not make me, although they tried over and over again. I said to them – I don't understand what it means – can you tell me? And then one day I made a very good answer to them. I asked 'What is it for that I am to eat the body and drink the blood in Christ?' and they told me it was to show our love for our Redeemer. I remarked that I loved my poor mother who was dead but I was not going to show it by digging her up and eating a bit of her flesh and drinking her blood. And as I would not do it out of love, I am sure it must be a disgusting thing to do for anything else.[20]

They were given a theatrical tour of the Holy Sepuchre (having paid the monks a considerable sum for the privilege). Each Station of the Cross was pointed out to them along the Via Dolorosa. They surveyed the hill of Calvary, and made a pilgrimage to Bethlehem the next day.

That year, Brothers may have heard of Hester's arrival in the Holy Land. Still incarcerated in a private asylum just outside London, he was preparing his great tract on 'the New Jerusalem', preaching the Messiah's return. He believed that the chosen people of God would gather in the great ancient cities of Baalbek and Palmyra, and from there, unite under their leader and converge on Jerusalem. In 1815, Brothers would be released into the care of his closest disciple, with whom he would live quietly until his death in 1824.

They followed the seacoast north, resting at Haifa, Mount Carmel and the tiny port of Tantura. Scorpions wriggled their way into their bed-linen and they had to fumigate their clothes to get rid of ticks. Hester was curious to see Acre, the final stronghold of the Crusaders in the Holy Land, the city associated with Napoleon's defeat by her cousin. In 1799 Smith had been in command of a squadron cruising off Alexandria and had sailed in to assist Acre's then-governor, Ahmed Pasha – better known as Djezzar, 'Butcher' – against Napoleon.* Acre had proved Napoleon's Achilles' heel. His inability to unseat Djezzar ultimately forced him to give up his dream of dominating the Holy Land. After the siege, Djezzar strengthened his defences with the help of British engineers to make the most impregnable fortress in Syria.

Hester was welcomed in a state reception at the palace by the new governor, Süleyman Pasha, and befriended by his chief aide, Malem Hayim Shaady, a brilliant and shrewd Jewish banker and one-time rabbi, who now embraced Islam. Under Djezzar the unfortunate Hayim had lost his nose, an eye and an ear, and narrowly escaped another of Djezzar's favourite chastisements; being slowly roasted in an oven.

While staying with the Austrian consul at his 'country' house in Nazareth, they met a mysterious traveller. Bruce had gone with the Spanish priests of Nazareth on an expedition to Tabaria – ancient Tiberias – to witness Mass on St Peter's Day, on the very spot, so went the legend, where Peter had cast his net. There, Bruce was startled to come across a man who addressed them in Arabic, introducing himself as 'Sheikh Ibrahim'. He wore coarse, mud-flecked peasant clothes, a rustic turban and beard; his legs were bare, 'thrust into old shoes, like inn slippers'. The stranger's blue eyes, rather Germanic face and athletic build struck Bruce at first as probably Georgian. Meanwhile, Bruce himself was being

---

* Sir Sidney Smith's old ally had also been a brutal madman. Tell-tale signs of those who had survived his brutality were missing limbs, eyes, ears and noses. The dazzling waters that lapped the edges of Acre's fortress hid entire villages of shattered skeletons: Djezzar once slaughtered all the women in his harem, to punish the few he suspected of infidelity.

sized up. The wild stranger turned to him and spoke in slightly accented English, making him laugh with amazement. It was Burckhardt, whose nickname amongst his new friends would instantly become 'The Sheikh'.

Johann Ludwig Burckhardt, anglicized to John Lewis Burckhardt, was Swiss but considered himself an Englishman. He had been commissioned by the African Association, co-founded by Sir Joseph Banks, to determine the source of the Niger river, a mission considered so geopolitically sensitive that he was to pass himself off as an Arab so as not to attract attention. In preparation he had already spent more than two years in Aleppo immersing himself in Arabic, and making increasingly bold excursions into the Syrian desert. Now he intended to travel into the vast stony wilderness that the Romans called *Arabia Petraea* to search for its ancient capital, lost to the world since the time of the Crusades. Astonishingly, less than two months later, he was to succeed. His miraculous discovery of Petra would be Burckhardt's legacy to the world.*

For all his erudition, he irritated Hester, or more likely, she was irritated by Bruce's enthusiasm for him. Burckhardt would later write to Bruce, telling him he would 'feel infinite satisfaction from another meeting with you'. Burckhardt commented that Hester and Bruce argued so passionately in his presence that 'no one could doubt that they were anything but lovers'.

Burckhardt, then twenty-eight, found Hester to be a forceful and ambitious personality. Although willing to credit her with 'a manly spirit and enlightened curiosity' he felt she was too eager to accept blandishments from the Ottoman grandees he made a point of despising. He told her she was deluded if she thought she had influence with them; they only wanted her gold and her presents. If she were more like him, he said, she would use whatever opportunities she gained to buy up precious manuscripts and antiquities and save them from crumbling to dust. Burckhardt made the mistake of lecturing and patronizing her, and thereby gained a lifelong enemy. He too had already been to Palmyra, but it had not been a successful journey: he was robbed and left to die. In everything he said and did, Burckhardt presented himself as an authority on the Arab world. His air of superiority grated on her, but she could not help envying his

---

* He would also be the first Westerner to stumble across the Great Temple of Rameses II and the Lesser Temple at Abu Simbel.

sense of mission. Still, he had no sooner arrived than he was ready to depart. With promises to write, he disappeared at midnight on 1 July, joining a small caravanserai heading into the Jordan valley.

Four days later, amidst 'the merriment and bustle of departure' for Acre as their own party headed off into the dark, Hester's horse lost its footing on a large stone and slipped. She was thrown from her mount, and then pinned to the ground by its weight. At first, seeing how much agony she was in, Meryon feared she had broken her ribs or pelvis, and that her vital organs had been crushed. The injury caused her lasting damage; she would be ever after troubled by a painful stiffness easily aggravated into shooting pains up her right leg.

From then on, she was always superstitious about departures.

Hester's intention now was to head directly for Damascus and Palmyra. They passed Tyre, the great city of the Phoenicians, famous for its stone – used in King Solomon's Temple at Jerusalem – and for the purple dye made from the shell of murex snails.

At first glance Sidon struck Hester as no more interesting than any of the swaggering, rather sullen port towns they had seen on the Mediterranean. Watered by tributaries from the Awaly river, its fields, usually fertile, with flourishing banana and tobacco plantations, were parched by a summer heatwave.

After Jerusalem, Acre and even Jaffa, there was little grandeur to Sidon's bulwark-like Crusader castle, which sat on a promontory lapped by salty breakers, and the town itself seemed to hold few surprises. As a rather jaundiced Meryon put it, Ottoman towns in Syria were getting to be 'much alike'. Invariably, the largest, most impressive building belonged to the governor; the souk was crammed into a maze of narrow alley-ways, where merchants arranged themselves in feline positions on tiny mats 'where an ink stand and two or three large bound account books are the whole apparatus of sometimes very extensive dealings'. The Muslims lived in the principal quarter 'in jealous stillness', the Maronite Christians in another. Separated from the rest by 'a few dirty lanes' lived the Jews, 'inaccessible from the stench and filth to any but their tenants'.

Nothing suggested to Hester that in just over a year's time she would make her home in these low-lying mountains visible from the coast, and that Sidon, far from being just another waystation, would become her closest, and last, link to civilization.

For Hester, the distinction between reality and fantasy was becoming blurred. If she needed any further proof of her own importance to those who mattered she found it in the letter from Emir Bashir Shihab II waiting for her in Sidon. She boasted to Crauford Bruce:

> The King of the Druses has had a palace prepared for us, his message to me was this, it is yours for a day or a year . . . B. says England owes us more than to any Ambassador, for no person (except Sir S. Smith) has made its name so respected or seen things so perfectly.[21]

The Emir had sent enough camels, mules and guards to bring them safely up into the mountains, a journey that took them several days, winding up through perilous, impenetrable-seeming tracks, passing towering hills, deep valleys and crossing streams through a necklace of mountain villages. One of these was Djoun, notable for its imposing Melkite monastery, Deir-el-Moukhalles, whose single tower pointed to the sky like a finger. To the villagers who watched them pass, Hester must have seemed a portent almost, from the outside world.

To Hester's eyes, in the first week of August 1812, Deir-el-Kamar, which sits in a commanding position over the Chouf foothills of Mount Lebanon, was not only a bustling boom town, but a portal to a strange feudal kingdom, whose very name means 'Monastery of the Moon'.

Two years before, Emir Bashir Shihab II and Sheikh Bashir Jumblatt, the leaders of the two ruling clans governing the Druze, had led a combined attack on Damascus, managing to claim back large swathes of territory, including much of the Bekaa Valley, Baalbek and Mount Hermon. Soon afterwards, the two Bashirs had defended Druze communities near Aleppo against the persecutions of a rival chieftain, and offered them sanctuary. With the support of both leaders, more than four hundred refugee families had uprooted themselves and were now newly settled in these hills.

Hester had learned that although the Emir was the ruler of the Druze, he was in fact a covert Christian, having recently converted in the greatest secrecy to the Maronite faith. The Emir, it seemed, was inclined to present his own beliefs as ambiguous, all the better to dominate his varied subjects, who included Druze, Maronites and Sunni Muslims. He had ruled intermittently since 1786, maintaining his grip by routinely cultivating allies – first Djezzar Pasha, then Mehmet Ali in Cairo, then a string of rebel sheikhs – then betraying each of them in turn. Now many wondered how long his alliance with Sheikh Bashir Jumblatt, whose religious pedigree was never in any doubt, could last.

Hester was immediately fascinated by the Druze people. They gave every appearance of being a breed apart, with their pale skins, fair hair that often glinted with gold and startlingly light eyes of blue, green or grey. 'The people are savage and extraordinary,' Hester would write, 'the women wear a great tin trumpet on their heads and a veil suspended from it, seeming very proud of these frightful horns.'[*]

They stayed at a medieval palace on the town's square, the home of the Emir's former murdered rival, Sheikh Girius Baz. The Emir's unfinished palace, a miniature city in apricot-hued stone at Beit Eddine, a mile away, was intended to be his statement of power. Once again, Admiral Smith's reputation preceded them, and they were impressed by the Emir's generous welcome. They marvelled at his palace, every interior surface decorated with a profusion of beautifully inlaid marble, with painted, gilded cedar ceilings and ornately carved doors. Hester's initial verdict on the Emir was that he was 'a mild, amiable man,' and she shrugged off the many stories about his periodic cruelty to his subjects.[†]

The friendship struck up between Hester and the Emir's supposed brother-in-arms, Sheikh Bashir Jumblatt, was more personal. Sheikh Jumblatt was uncommonly good-looking, tall and commanding, regal

---

[*] All Druze women were expected to wear the *tantur*, a unicorn-like horn, about fourteen inches in length (although some were as high as two feet) always worn with a veil, usually of black muslin, which could be twitched about as the wearer pleased. The angle of a *tantur* had a language of its own; some women wore them erect, others at a jaunty angle, or almost horizontal. They were also a vital status symbol, preferably made from silver, some encrusted with diamonds and precious stones. They were not meant to be taken off, even in bed, and the Druze invested them with a powerful erotic appeal. In 1812, to expose one's horn in public and not keep it shielded by a veil would be thought scandalous.
[†] The Emir would boast how he controlled his subjects: 'Every three or four years, they [the inhabitants] would rebel, although they never succeeded. I would kill, hang, imprison and beat without opposition to make them submit.'

on his white horse, with curled moustache, sceptre and his scimitar. His wealth exceeded that of the Emir fivefold: his annual income of some two thousand purses was in Hester's time the equivalent of £50,000. Hester wrote of her first visit to the Sheikh's palace at Mouktara:

> I am the first traveller he has ever allowed to walk over his palace, which has been the scene of several massacres. The two days I spent with him I enjoyed very much, and you will be surprised when I tell you that he judged it necessary to make one of his chief officers taste out of my cup before I drank, for fear of poison; but I am used to that; yet this man on his knees before me looked more solemn than usual.[22]

It would be largely due to Sheikh Jumblatt's friendship, and the understanding that she could rely on his protection, that she would return to this part of the world for good.*

Not long after they had returned to Deir-el-Kamar, Bruce was caught and beaten by Druze villagers while he was trying to eavesdrop on a *khalwa,* a place of religious retreat for the *uqqal,* which had always

---

* While researching this book, I travelled to Mouktara to meet his direct descendant, Walid Jumblatt, a charismatic modern-day warlord, a tall, balding man in his fifties, once famous for his leonine hair, with lidded, enigmatic eyes used to weighing decisions carefully. The once-renowned playboy turned militia commander during the civil war retains his own militia, and leads the popular Progressive Socialist Party (PSP.) He introduced me to his Syrian-born second wife, Nora, whose tawny, effortlessly glamorous good looks made me recall Meryon's diary entry: he had been struck speechless by the beauty of Sheikh Jumblatt's wife. Over sweet coffee laced with cardamom, we talked about Hester. 'Some people believe, it seems, that she and my great-great-grandfather were lovers,' he said, letting out a laugh as though this were a ludicrous thought. We discussed the Druze faith. I had read that the Druze were 'technically Shi'ite Muslims' yet their beliefs were characterized as 'a mixture of Judaism, Christianity and Islam, including elements of Gnosticism.' I had also heard that the faith was intended to be impenetrable to all but those among its closed circle of initiates, the *uqqal* or 'the enlightened ones' who made up only a fraction of the Druze. 'It is not a secretive religion, that is apart from the Secret Books . . .' he replied, and at this deliberately cryptic remark, I could not help but smile. 'You could say our faith is inspired by Neo-Platonism, and that in some aspects it reflects the teachings of Socrates and Plato, and the philosophies of ancient India, the Vedas . . . Like other cultures, like the Hindus and the Isma'ilis, we believe in reincarnation and transmigration, and in the coming of a new Messiah.' Few of the illustrious clan of the Jumblatts have had the luxury of a peaceful death. Walid's father Kamal was assassinated by the Syrians in 1977, like his father before him. Shortly before his murder, Kamal Jumblatt was quoted as saying 'The Jumblatts are usually killed – they don't die in their beds.'

included women in its ranks. Scurrilous conjecture was rife and had long centred on this, hinting that this mingling of the sexes must be to 'hold promiscuous intercourse'.[23] The *khalwa* was held on Thursday nights in a secluded meeting hall, usually on the outskirts of town. The *uqqal* were fastidious about making sure they were neither followed nor watched.

Sometimes these sessions included ceremonial inductions of would-be initiates, who would first have to undergo years of rigorous study and then prove themselves 'entirely trustworthy' and 'capable of extreme secrecy'. It was one of these ceremonies that Bruce was trying to spy upon when he was caught and beaten.

Bruce's disgrace forced them all to make a snap decision. He urged Hester to come with him to Aleppo. A civil war appeared to be looming. Whichever way they went, Syria was dangerously unstable. They heard that the Pasha of Damascus had ordered a series of assassinations, and that the Pasha of Aleppo was said to be among them. Meanwhile, the Wahhabis, under their leader, Saud ibn Saud, were massing across the desert towards Damascus, and it was rumoured they would try to take it. 'Above 40,000 Arabs are now at war with each other in these parts,' wrote Hester excitedly.[24]

She refused to change her plans. She was convinced that the Wahhabis would not dare take Damascus, which would unleash the full fury of the Porte. They agreed to part for a matter of weeks, perhaps to meet midway, and from there head westwards into the desert. She was adamant on one point: if the opportunity arose for her to go to Palmyra without him, she would take it; Bruce no doubt gave up trying to change her mind when she was in such a stubborn mood. She had a strong reason for not wanting to join Bruce, anticipating that John Barker, the British Consul-General for all Syria, would certainly try to dissuade her from making the attempt.

The Pasha of Damascus, Süleyman Sulahdar, had sent her two letters, one advising her not to attempt the journey at all, and the next, in the face of her continued persistence, warning her that she must enter the city quietly after dark and remain veiled while she was there. Hester was by now well informed about the 'fanaticism of the Turks in that town'. Violence had flared up all over the city; most Christians were careful to observe a twilight curfew and those who did not were often found with their throats cut. Hester behaved like one compelled to seek out danger. She craved the addictive surge of adrenalin. It would lead her where she wanted to go.

# 9

## Under the Minaret

On 1 September 1812 Hester rode into Damascus. She had decided she must make a memorable entrance and chose the moment just after the last afternoon call to prayer, when the light was at its most honeyed and the swallows dipped and swooped.

This time, she took even more care to dress magnificently. At her hip was a large Turkish scimitar, suspended from a red silken cord, and she wore an embroidered pouch with a prominently-displayed copy of the Koran. She had given the matter a great deal of thought, fully aware of the theatrical impression she would create. She deliberately wanted to inspire comparisons between herself and Zenobia, the proud and beautiful third-century warrior queen of Palmyra.[1] Zenobia's memory held sway over the Damascenes just as Cleopatra – from whom she claimed descent – exerted a fascination over Alexandria. As Hester rode through the great Roman archway – the Gate of the Sun or *Bab Sharqi* – the most ancient and symbolic of all the city's entrances, and up the street called Straight, she was unveiled, her fierce grey-blue eyes daring to be challenged.

Although Meryon, sent on as her advance guard, had found 'what was reckoned a very fine house in the Christian quarter', Hester immediately rejected it. Staying there, with the small number of other Europeans in the city, was unthinkable when she intended to keep her affiliations firmly in the Muslim camp. She wrote of this resolve to Sligo: 'I said to the Doctor: "I must take the bull by the horns and stick myself under the minaret of the Great Mosque". This was accomplished, and we found ourselves, for three months, in the most distinguished part of the Turkish quarter.'

> It was a glorious jewel of a house, with the *haremlik* or family quarters
> – six spacious rooms painted with frescoes with ceilings made of cedar
> wood – arranged around a courtyard garden, with its own melodious
> fountain.

For the next three months Hester would live 'under the minaret' at the southeast corner of the Umayyad Mosque. The city breathed through the ebb and flow of the mosque's bare-footed pilgrims, filing in through its vaulted arcades, across its great white marble flagstones under the glitter of its Byzantine mosaics. Within its enclosure, the severed head of John the Baptist was buried in a shrine. The tomb of Saladin, the great foe of the Crusaders, was also here, the stones of which were worn with kisses.

It was at the Umayyad Mosque that pilgrims traditionally gathered to set off on the *Haj* to Mecca. Usually the streets were thronged with thousands of pilgrims from Anatolia, Iran, Iraq and Syria. But the Wahhabis had barred the route to all Muslims except those who followed their creed since their daring seizure of Mecca in 1803. Many in Damascus believed only dire events could follow, that this heralded the descent to earth of the 'false Messiah' ad-Dajjal predicted by the Prophet Muhammad, said to precede the end of the world.[2]

Hester's imagination was fired by everything around her. She loved to listen to 'the beautiful language of Arabic', and now made a concentrated effort to learn it. She was close to the great covered souk, and loved its extraordinary, seething maze. She was forcefully struck by the elegance of the city's great palaces and *baits* or houses belonging to distinguished religious and merchant families. She rode out to see the early morning horse auctions, to visit mosques and the *madrassas*. Word spread that she was a *Meleki*, or 'queen'. She would nod and reply graciously, saying little but always in Arabic. 'It was generally supposed,' noted Meryon, 'from her fair complexion, that she painted [her face] white, and it was confidently affirmed, as her appearance was so little European, that although by birth an Englishwoman, she was of Ottoman descent, and had Mahometan blood in her veins.' As she passed through the crowded reeking streets, rosewater and coffee were sprinkled on the ground before her to perfume her way, an honour usually only accorded to the Pasha.

On the eve of Ramadan, she was given an elaborate welcome at the Azem Palace by the newly-installed ruler, Süleyman Sulahdar, and marvelled at how magical the city looked, illuminated by festival lamps and candles: 'Two thousand attendants and guards lined the staircase.' The walls and ceilings glittered with mock precious stones, gilding and tortoiseshell and mother-of-pearl inlay. She found the Pasha waiting for her, all alone, seated on a crimson satin *diwan*, a small, bird-like man, fine-boned with an elegant beard and long fingers. Their meeting was brief and to the point.

The Pasha was determined to show his force. On his orders, mutineering soldiers and any dissenting citizens were punished daily, as gruesome numbers of severed heads on pikes at the city walls attested. Two years before, the Wahhabis had advanced into the Syrian heartland, terrorizing villages across the Hauran, only two days distant from Damascus. Now they were back to continue their aggressive campaign, gathering up allies amongst many of the Bedouin, convincing them that the Egyptians and the Ottomans, as well as infidel foreign powers, had designs on their land.

Just as at Cairo, Hester inveigled herself into the graces of the 'head of everything military in Syria'. Aga Seyd Ismail, the newly-appointed commander of the Pasha's elite guard, invited her to inspect his 'wild and warlike' cavalry. It was a highly successful encounter.

All I can say about myself sounds like a conceit, but others could tell you I am the oracle of the place, and the darling of all the troops, who seem to think I am a deity because I can *ride*, and because I wear arms: and all the fanatics all bow down before me, because the Dervishes think me a wonder, and have given me a piece of Mahomet's tomb; and I have won the heart of the Pacha . . . I was even admitted into the library of the famous Mosque, and fumbled over the books at pleasure, books that no Christian dare touch or even cast their eyes upon.

Ahmed Bey, one of the wealthiest property owners in Syria, also made it his duty to make her stay in Damascus agreeable. He staged several sumptuous feasts, horse races and games of *djerid* in her honour. She was soon satisfied that she had seen all the marvels of every harem. She revelled in the knowledge that her behaviour broke every rule. Here, 'tho' sometimes followed by 2,000 people to my own door not a soul insults me,' she said, adding wryly that 'the women treat me with the greatest kindness, how different they are from English women'.

What surprises me so much is the extreme civility of the Turks to a Christian, which they detest so much more here than in any other part of the Sultan's dominions. A woman in man's clothes, a woman on horse-back – everything directly in opposition to their strongest prejudices, and yet never a smile of impertinence, [they] let me go where I will.[3]

The quality of Hester that most intrigued the city's powerful elite was her authority. She described how she was invited to meet 'a very great Effendi', the scholarly Kaia Bey:

He led me to a beautiful court paved with coloured marbles, with foun-tains playing among the orange trees and in a sort of alcove we found dinner prepared, or rather supper, for it was sunset. Everything was served in high style by black female slaves; a black gentleman. Immense gilt candlesticks, with candles nearly six feet high, were set on the ground, and great illumination of small elegant lamps suspended in clusters . . . The proud man talked a great deal, and kept my little dragoman nearly four hours on his knees, having fetched a great book to talk about astronomy, upon which he asked me ten thousand questions. In short, he kept me there until nearly ten o'clock, an hour past the time which, if any one is found in the streets, they are to have their head cut off – such is the Pacha's new decree. All the gates were shut, but all opened for me, and not a word was said.[4]

When Hester informed the Pasha of her plan to go to Palmyra, he insisted that she must not think of going without a large troop of his guards, although of course, this would be at her expense. She was coun-selled by her new friend, Aga Ismail, who told her bluntly how the Pasha was despised by many of the Bedouin, and even more so by the Wahhabis:

if she went with his troops, she would not only be alienating them, she would make herself an obvious target for attack.

Aga Ismail, who was himself no admirer of the Pasha, had strong connections with many of the Bedouin, and was willing to act as go-between. Soon Hester had a visitor, Nasir, the black-eyed twenty-five-year-old son of Sheikh Muhanna al Fadil, chief of one of the most powerful factions of the Anazeh tribes, the Hassinah. Called the 'Prince of the Desert', Muhanna was said to rule over forty thousand of his own men, with authority over some fifteen other tribes, who roamed the caravan routes around Palmyra, as well as Homs and Hamah and as far away as Baghdad and Busora (modern-day Basra in Iraq). Hester's curiosity would have been further piqued by the fact that Muhanna's tribe was renowned for breeding the finest Arab horses in the desert, the 'Nedgdi'.

A dinner was arranged. Muhanna proved to be formidable-looking, about fifty-five years old, and had fierceness written all over his features. In his black cloak, worn over a striped cotton shift, with a bright gold silk *keffiyeh* folded and secured on his head with an *agal* or headband, he looked every inch a desert king. Like most of the Anazeh men, he was short, with strong, aquiline features, and wore his greying hair long in thick, waxen braids. If Muhanna was taken aback to be approached by a lone Englishwoman, he did not show it. They agreed to communicate through Nasir, who was able to pass virtually unnoticed in Damascus, disguising himself as a common Arab in his sheepskin cloak or *abba* and sandals.

Hester heard about the terrible vengeance exacted by the Bedouin; their blood-curdling raids on sleeping caravans, and the dreadful intricacies of tribal revenge. An army of men and boys – as many as five thousand at a time – rode vast distances on their camels, barely stopping to eat or drink, then swooped in for the kill with terrifying war cries, their blades high, showing no mercy. She also knew what happened to pilgrims or travellers who strayed into their territory without paying the required tribute money: they were stripped of everything they had, even their clothes, and left to die naked in the desert. This was exactly the fate suffered by Burckhardt.

Nasir admitted carrying out such savageries dozens of times, though, he claimed, only against those who came armed against them. But he told Hester that she would be safe with the Anazeh: 'To you, the road is open wherever you choose to go'. It was agreed that before they embarked upon the expedition to Palmyra, Hester should first go into the desert to be welcomed by the tribe. This was a 'test', to see if Hester was physically strong enough to make the long, arduous journey.

Meanwhile, letters were flying between Damascus and Aleppo. Bruce pleaded with her not to expose herself to any risk. 'If any thing happens to you I will make a vow to pass the remainder of my days in the Desert,' he told her passionately. As Hester had predicted, the British Consul-General John Barker urged Bruce to convince her to give up the idea. When that failed, Barker proposed what must have seemed the chivalrous alternative: that they all travel together. He recommended taking a caravanserai from Aleppo led by another Bedouin chief, a friend of Burckhardt's, and the leader of a rather timid, small sub-tribe called the Sokhne whom Muhanna would have regarded with some contempt.

Even more annoying for Hester was Barker's proposal for them to travel in what he called a 'tartarvan', a metal cage covered with canvas and pulled by mules. With her plans already in place, Hester was furious. 'What an absurd idea,' she scoffed. She could not think of anything more vulnerable to attack: 'to be stuck upon a machine, the tartaravangers [sic] running away and leaving you to the mercy of two obstinate mules.' What was she made for, after all, if she could not ride like the Bedouin, on the 'swiftest horse one can find?' Almost immediately, Hester's scorn was vindicated: a large caravan of exactly the type Barker put his faith in was attacked between Homs and Damascus, and sixteen people were killed. 'Who is right?' she asked triumphantly, 'I, or the Consul-General?'

Hester had heard about an intriguing Frenchman said to have considerable knowledge of the desert, and sent Meryon with an invitation for him to come and see her in Damascus. Théodore Lascaris de Vintimille, self-described merchant and music teacher, lived modestly at Nebek, halfway to Homs on the Aleppo road. Not overly tall, at thirty-eight Lascaris was olive-skinned and well-built, with a mane of thick dark hair and lustrous beard, and he dressed in the rough clothes of an Arab peasant. He came from Piedmontese nobility, and claimed descent from a clan of Byzantine emperors. If his heritage seemed at odds with the obscure semi-poverty in which he lived, so was the fact that until Napoleon invaded Malta in 1798, he was a Knight of St John of Jerusalem.*

Lascaris had spent almost a decade in the Middle East. In Cairo, shortly after his arrival, he had taken a Georgian slave girl, Mariam, as his mistress, securing her freedom from one of Murad Bey's lieutenants. He so impressed General Abdullah Menou, Commander-in-Chief in Egypt, with his 'zeal, probity and attachment to the Republic', that his dispatches were forwarded to Napoleon. What was important to Hester was that he claimed to know the desert as well as any Bedouin, and spoke Arabic fluently. He knew Muhanna and Nasir. She could hardly believe her luck.

Hester claimed to like 'charming rascals', and often said she preferred a rogue to a bore. Now she had found one, unaware that he would contrive to control her. She considered him a thoughtful guest: he brought her fine tobacco to give to her visitors – and demonstrated the way he preferred it, mixed with opium, in powder form, worked into a paste with crushed cardamom, the Bedouin way. An addict himself, he knew its effects.

Hester decided that Lascaris was not only 'a very clever man' but that his 'very curious information' and his undoubted knowledge of the region would prove invaluable to British interests. She wrote to Oakes, with the suggestion that he be recruited as an agent:

> I have met an extraordinary person, Mr Lascaris de Vintimille. He is certainly a little mad but he has considerable talents and a perfect knowledge of Arabic; he is extremely poor but very active and well-connected . . . It might be worth while to consider and represent this subject to government as it would ensure them an agent in parts where few could live – I mean on the borders of the desert; and I can assure you, this in future would be of great importance for the Arabs are now so strong as to hardly be managed by the pashas, besides it would be an act of humanity to a once great man. The French are sending agents in

---

* At Malta, Napoleon had personally overseen the dismantling of the centuries-old Order, adding to his war chest an estimated seven million francs' worth in gold, silver plate and assorted treasure. All men below sixty were stripped of any personal wealth and expelled – all except thirty-four that is, considered by Napoleon to be too potentially valuable, and whom he was able to coerce to volunteer for his Egypt campaign. Lascaris was among them.

all directions (at immense expense) into the desert, and why do we not do the same?[5]

In her first dealings with Lascaris, Hester demonstrated considerable naïveté. It is difficult to tease out the truth in Lascaris's voraciously ambitious career as spy, double-agent and fantasist. According to Fathallah Sâyigh, the Arab dragoman whom Lascaris recruited and eventually let into his secret, Napoleon himself had approved his highly clandestine mission to penetrate the desert heartland shared by Syria and what is today Iran and Iraq. As Sâyigh tells it, his master's misson was to establish the best land route to India, and to determine whether the notoriously factional Bedouin might be persuaded to unite against the Ottomans, preferably under one strong leader.* In fact, at the very moment he met Hester, Lascaris was preparing to forge a secret pact between some of the most powerful Bedouin sheikhs, and had earmarked Muhanna al-Fadil and Nasir as the men most likely to lead the unified confederation of Bedouin.

But Lascaris was a freebooter, and his debts were pressing. He began to play an elaborate game, intended to outwit all parties, and take his money where he could. Unaware of his machinations, Hester struck a bargain with him. If he would accompany her, she would pay him a generous fee. It was time, she thought, to 'experiment on the good faith of the Arabs'. She wanted to be gone before Bruce arrived, so she could fulfil the first part of her agreement with the Hassinah without interference. But just as she was about to leave, Bruce arrived in Damascus, with a feverish Barker in tow. For the moment, she decided not to risk telling him of her plan with Lascaris, not wanting him to try to dissuade her, or worse, insist he come with her.

She delayed for two weeks. Just as she expected, Bruce felt uneasy living in the Muslim heart of the city; he found the atmosphere both fanatical and ominous. Fortuitously, Aga Ismail offered them a house in Hamah, a desert town of medieval *norias* or wooden waterwheels on the Orontes river halfway between Damascus and Aleppo. Leaving Bruce to

---

* In his *Voyage en Orient*, Lamartine would hold up the hitherto obscure Lascaris as one of France's unknown heroes, a man whose considerable ingenuity and devotion to Napoleon went unlauded, yet whose mission, had it succeeded, would have changed the country's destiny.

tie up their affairs in Damascus, and to join her with their entourage soon, she took the road to Hamah.

Hester told no one that she intended to go into Bedouin territory with Lascaris. She admitted the secret only to Crauford Bruce in a strange confessional letter dispatched on the eve of her departure: 'I have put myself into the hands of a man (who I pay dearly enough) and it is his business to see me safely out of the desert'.[6] She told Crauford not to think she is robust, even though:

> I have so much energy, it is my nature, it is the Spirit of my Grandfather, for had I one foot in the grave I could command an Army, even in Egypt. I am like one of Mahomet's mares, who he ordered to be kept from drinking 48 hours and when carried to a spring, the moment the *battle horn sounded* they refused the water before them and flew to their master.

She gave the impression of someone determined on banishment and atonement. 'I will take flight into the desert . . . amongst people who consider it ignominious to complain save to God. What I have suffered is at his pleasure,' she said. But, she added, 'My mind is superior to circumstances'. There was one last phrase she used, which did not suggest such humility: 'The Universe is my country!'

# 10

## The Desert Queen

On the road to Homs, Lascaris gave her the coarse garments worn by the Bedouin: a woollen *abba*, 'made of a sort of carpeting', and a sheepskin jacket, to wear as soon as they were safely out of Damascus. She had with her a small number of servants, those who could double as grooms, all of whom she had made sure had no wives or dependants.[1] Once they were in the desert, she stripped them all of their weapons – 'much against their inclination'.

Aga Ismail warned her never to wear women's clothes while she was with the Bedouin, telling her that if she appeared as 'only' a woman, her authority would be undermined. In fact, she had already caused widespread consternation in the desert. Muhanna's sworn enemy, Sheikh Duray'i, put it succinctly: 'What are we going to do about this English princess? After all, she is not merely a woman,' he said.[2]

From Homs they rode northeast to the small desert hamlet of Talbisah, to be met by a single Bedouin sent by Nasir. The next stage was the most dangerous, for they had to risk attack by a rival Anazeh tribe, the Fid'an, who were raiding the area on their way to Baghdad. 'Our horses never drank for two days, we rode from ten in the morning until after midnight without eating or drinking to get out of their district,' wrote Hester. When they arrived, their clothes and hair covered in filmy dust, Hester's joy and wonder at being welcomed by the Bedouin took her almost by surprise. When Muhanna told her that he and his tribe had waited for her in the desert, risking ambush, for twenty-four days, she was moved to tears. She was deeply impressed by the sight of the 'old king' among his nomadic kingdom of low-slung, black camel-hair tents and grazing livestock, and by the pride and resourcefulness of his people, whose most precious possessions were their horses. They were wild-looking, with sun-blackened faces, the men with long beards and long dark tresses, at ease with the swords and daggers slung about their bodies. 'These savages, guided by their own wonderful abilities, and who have reduced the wants of human nature to a mere nothing, [give] a most wonderful example of mental and bodily strength,' she would write.

At dawn she thought the sight of 'twelve thousand camels' coming to water more wonderful than anything she had ever imagined. She saw how children went about entirely naked and that women wore their 'lips [tattooed] light blue and [hennaed] their nails red and hands all over [with] flowers and designs', and weighed themselves down with as much heavy, jingling silver jewellery as could be swathed about them; and that both sexes smeared their eyelids with thick black kohl.

Equally, she fascinated them: her appearance, her air of confidence and her great skill and knowledge with horses. 'I had calculated upon what happened, that a woman on horseback dressed as a Bedouin, would be considered little less than a Prophet amongst them.'[3] Even if the Anazeh had never thought to imagine what form a white warrior goddess might take, Hester intended to show them. She considered that 'the power which so extraordinary a creature as myself was likely to gain over a savage people, as first only speculative' now presented her with an astonishing opportunity 'which may not come again these fifty years'. Hester quickly grasped what Lascaris had spent years trying to ascertain: the Arabs were willing to revolt against the Ottomans, but if they were to be motivated to join forces, they required leadership and the strong belief that they would be left to self-rule.

There was a formal welcoming ceremony in her honour. Muhanna presented her with an *abba* of the sort worn by his sons made with thick creamy wool with gold-threaded designs across the neck and shoulders, and a twelve-foot black ostrich-feathered lance. To Muhanna, she gave one of Bruce's new prize pistols, presenting to his sons great quantities of fine Damascus fabrics to be distributed amongst the family.

For three days, Hester and Lascaris joined the tribe as they marched towards their next encampment. She lived as they did: sitting cross-legged,

176

drinking camel's milk, eating from a copper tray with her hands and sleeping on woven rugs laid on bare earth or sand in a camel-skin tent, surrounded by camels, horses and men. It was a life both barbaric and dangerous, but she found herself adoring every moment of it. She woke with the tinkling of goat bells to a blue-tinged landscape and watched the desert creatures stir themselves in daylight's first glow. After a day of hard riding, she spent the evenings dining around a big campfire with Muhanna and his sons, smoking the *narguileh*. She found them wild and fearless, and discovered they loved nothing better than to talk and argue about the lineage of their fine thoroughbred horses, and on this subject, she thought them 'the most brilliant and eloquent people I know'.

Hester would say of the Bedouin that 'many people are afraid of them, but I am not'. She would say that they taught her 'the value of poverty and independence', and that they were '*my people*'. She vastly impressed the tribe with the nonchalant way in which she tamed one of their unruly horses. Her first attempt to ride a camel made them all laugh, when 'all those about me ran away in an instant, and left me with a troublesome beast who would not keep on his knees long enough for me to get up'. She quickly imitated the way they rode, using only the thinnest cord for a bridle, something only the most experienced riders will risk. True to his word, Muhanna, with a small army of 'a hundred lances', escorted them back to Hamah, promising her that in the spring, they would go to Palmyra.

Although brief, her first few days with the Bedouin gave her a glimpse of something she wanted desperately. She could not forget the extraordinary feeling of galloping through the open country, under flocks of hoopoe. 'I like my wandering Arab life of all things,' Hester would soon write to her cousin Wynne. '[There] is the danger of going with Mohanna, yet please God, I must go.'4

While in the desert, a small but telling incident soured her initial enthusiasm for Lascaris. She had rebuked him for something, in her usual manner, making it clear that in her employment she liked things done her way, and he had snapped, turning on her menacingly. 'Don't you know, Madam, that you are here in my power, and my power alone?'5

Lascaris's treachery had far-reaching implications. Hester's interests were certainly not his. As soon as he returned from this expedition,

Lascaris told his young dragoman, Sâyigh, that Muhanna was 'no longer useful for his purpose' due to the fact that he had acquired 'a number of new enemies that would prevent them from pushing east towards Baghdad'.[6] Then, without Muhanna's knowledge, Lascaris made overtures to Muhanna's arch-enemy, another Anezeh leader, Sheikh Duray'i of the Ruwalah, who was ambitious to forge alliances, expand his base beyond the banks of the Euphrates and to 'wage a war to the death' against both the Ottomans and the Wahhabis. Shortly afterwards, on 12 November 1811, Lascaris signed a secret treaty with Sheikh Duray'i and a number of allied tribal chieftains, who together controlled territory that encompassed much of present-day Iraq, right up to Basra.

Even more Machiavellian, Lascaris then went straight to the Pasha of Damascus, and offered him certain privileged information – for a fee. He warned that Muhanna and his sons were becoming too powerful: not only had they aligned themselves with the Wahhabis, they were too friendly with the governors of Hamah and Homs, all of whom threatened the Pasha's authority. He suggested that Hester's presence and her association with them might not be accidental and that 'no one knew her true intentions'.[7] Sâyigh would recall that around this time, Lascaris told him privately 'that something had to be done to stop her'.

Hamah, where Hester had returned to reunite with Bruce, was usually a delightful place. The town was famous for its waterwheels on the Orontes, its beautiful linen, latticed wooden houses, and indolent pleasures. Politically, however, Hamah was explosive, a hotbed of opposition to the Pasha's authority.

Only months before, a large-scale battle had taken place close to the city, with the Pasha's troops fighting the Wahhabis and assorted Bedouin tribes, foremost among them the Hassinah. Hester seemed to take a vicarious thrill in the lawless atmosphere. 'The cook cooks away with his pistols on,' she wrote. 'It is vastly amusing.'

Her new friends in Hamah, who included the Governor, Mully Ismail, Malem Musa Koblan and his son Selim, and Nassif Pasha, a renegade Ottoman, the son of the Grand Vizier in Egypt, were all under intense suspicion. About herself she said that now the Pasha 'washed his hands of me'. Meanwhile, Hester kept Lascaris under close observation, making him useful to her. She put him on her payroll as 'interpreter' and paid for him to winter alongside her, renting a cottage for him and his wife, in which she also billeted Meryon.

It would be an exceptionally cold winter, as Napoleon's soldiers in Russia would discover. Snow and ice trapped the waterwheels and froze the ancient fruit trees. On the plains, perishing winds froze scores of exposed Bedouin and their livestock to death, and flash floods destroyed a neighbouring village, killing fifty people.

However charming Aga Ismail's wooden house first seemed, it was never meant to withstand such weather. The river overflowed its banks, stranding much of the town; water and damp seeped in everywhere. Even their walls, made of mud and straw, threatened to collapse. 'Every room is a pond,' wrote Hester. They endured a strange sort of domesticity, consumed with the need to stay dry and warm. Their clothes and boots were caked with mud; clothes had to be strung up by the fire. Mrs Fry's hands chapped from so much washing; soon her lungs gave way to pleurisy. The alarming weather kept Hester and Bruce from riding for weeks at a time, and she fell ill too. Tempers frayed; they snapped at one another. Bruce described himself hunched over a battered copy of Adam Smith's *Wealth of Nations*, constantly dripped on from leaks in the roof.

Lascaris persuaded Hester to ask for the Pasha's permission to conduct an archaeological dig at Palmyra, and made a great show of securing the necessary *firman* on her behalf. (In fact, during his brief stay in Damascus, Lascaris agreed secretly with the Pasha that the archaeological dig would be the ideal pretext under which to set a trap for the Hassinah, so that the Ruwalah would know exactly where to attack.)

Hester knew her expedition would be expensive, as she wrote to Crauford Bruce:

It will cost about £100 for the protection of the Great Emir Muhanna el Fadel, his people and camels (for so many are wanted to carry water), £100 more, remaining 6 weeks at Palmyra at all events in the desert, keeping all these Arabs who come to visit us, giving them pipes and coffee, £300; presents to the different chiefs of 40,000 men – £500. To people who understand the subject, £1,000 could not be spent to better advantage, as I said before relative to our communication with India and other political objects.[8]

Rather grandiosely, she hinted to Crauford that the journey to Palmyra 'would be worth £10,000 to him' once it was done. Could Lascaris have hinted that he knew exactly how far Napoleon might be prepared to go to secure the land route to India? Bruce scoffed that whatever the incentive might be, it was 'an enterprise of so difficult a nature' as to be impossible. Hester was not so sure. She warned Crauford Bruce that he should let his friend General Hutchinson know that the British were 'behind hand with our information', that if they did not watch out, the Arabs would soon be courted by the French.

> My original plan in coming to this country was to procure a very just
> idea of the Arab character, their customs and their power, the latter I
> have always considered as important relative to our Indian possessions.[9]

Just before New Year 1813 Muhanna sent her a message, begging for her doctor. It was agreed that Lascaris should accompany Meryon to the Hassinah camp near Palmyra, an unappealing, risky prospect in the bitter, squalling cold. Still, all appeared to be going to plan until Meryon found himself detained by Muhanna against his will. He was only able to secure his freedom by arguing that Hester's fury if she knew would be so great she would refuse his escort, and then Muhanna would never see his money and presents. Lascaris had betrayed him, lying to Muhanna, telling him the doctor was a spy, and that they should never trust the English.

'Tomorrow, my dear General, I mount my horse with seventy Arabs and am off to Palmyra at last.' As she wrote these words to Oakes, Hester could hardly control her elation. Bruce added a playful echo of her ambitions: 'Who knows but she may prove another Zenobia, and be destined to restore it to its ancient splendour?'[10]

Despite all that Hester had said to Bruce about how this exploit might benefit him, they both knew that there was no particular glory to his presence. It was obvious that it was Hester's moment – and hers alone. She had prepared the expedition almost single-handedly. It was her couage and willpower that had got them this far.

On 20 March 1813 they set off to rejoin the Hassinah tribe, breathing in 'the air of the desert . . . so pure [even the horses] quite live on it', with Hester riding at the front flanked by Muhanna's sons, Nasir and Hamit. Although Bruce was sensible enough to see she had the upper hand when it came to 'management to keep the Arabs in good order', he could not resist a little sarcasm. He added a postscript in his letter to Oakes.

> . . . my Lady Stanhope is a little disgusted with the promised land and the Holy City. She found the Jews a nation of old clothes dealers, without imagination, without courage, without any of the qualities necessary to a great nation. She has decided consequently to transfer her Empire to Palmyra. The post of Prime Minister is still vacant, but perhaps . . .

Bruce had made no secret of his disdain for the Bedouin, thinking them untrustworthy as well as dirty. Eating anything cooked by a desert Arab disgusted him; he fixated on their black-rimmed fingernails. Equally, Hester knew Bruce would not impress the Arabs. 'He rides vastly ill for a man with so fine a person,' Hester had told his father.[11]

Hester had thought of everything, as her account of her entourage suggests:

> Forty camels, loaded with provisions and water and presents, twenty horsemen, the Doctor, Mr Bruce, myself and an Arab dragoman, a second dragoman, and a Mameluke, two cooks, a *caffagi* [coffee and *narguileh*-attendant], four Cairo *säyses*, the Emir Al-Akoar, a stud-groom, Mr B's valet, Madame Fry, two *sakas* [water carriers], my slave, two *ferrases* [tent-pitchers], with an escort of Arabs.

Hester kept her possessions to a minimum, and would have insisted that all of them do the same; she took only several changes of clothes – camelhair *abbas* and cotton shifts – and linen; essentials for her *toilette.* They had to take the threat of the Bedouin raids extremely seriously, and be able to gallop unencumbered. But she trusted in the Muslim code of moral conduct. 'Arabs seldom murder, indeed *never* unless provoked,' she asserted. About Bruce, she said: '*He* they might strip and send about his business'; she added, 'but me they would keep to sell'.[12]

By the time Hester set off, spring had breathed the bloom back into the vast bowl of the desert, flanked by a line of mountains as far as the eye could see. In the changing light, the stone-grey and amber landscape appeared streaked with delicate colours: rosy pinks, hazy greens and rust-reds. There were clusters of mustard flowers, blood-red poppies and 'innumerable, unknown, odoriferous herbs'.

It was not yet hot enough for them to ride at night, as the Bedouin did in summer. Still, the air scorched, the dry heat burned any exposed skin, and parched their throats and nostrils, making them long for the coolness of dusk. Each day they rode almost twelve hours, sometimes not stopping for water.*

The first night in the desert set a precedent for the rest. In the silent, empty wilderness, Hester slept apart from Bruce. For the polygamous Bedouin, despite the fact that divorce was widely practised, a woman's honour was a primitive thing: once gone, it could never be restored. Bruce had to watch, keeping his distance, as Nasir visited Hester's tent, supposedly out of courtesy and to go over plans for the next day's march,

---

* A few months later, when her advice on desert travel was sought by another venturesome Englishwoman, Mary Rich, then in Baghdad, who – dazzled by Hester's example – planned to journey overland with her husband to Constantinople, Hester told her: 'Imagine, Madam, a plain which never seems to end'. Hester – now the desert oracle – added, 'It will be in vain to seek a bush or tree for any *little purpose* and anyway you cannot stray from the party'. She offered her own practical solution, which was to have her groom carry a small tent 'about five or six feet in diameter' and a *pot de chambre*. 'Pitch up [your] tent . . . saying you wish to repose or eat' and retire, making sure to "order coffee for the people"'.

She recommended never being without a kettle 'to boil up bad water' and to never lose sight of one's own private supply of water and provisions, as well as 'a bag of lemons', with a few drops each day to protect against scurvy. She advised always keeping a close watch on their 'favourite' horses, and to 'lash a fellow up to them at night' with strong chains 'or you will lose them, I know not how'. No creatures were stealthier or shrewder than the Bedouin, when they wished to steal at night, she warned them. During the day, it was another matter. 'Our people,' said Hester, 'went out robbing every day'.

but then he would sit with her by the fire late into the night. Inevitably, tension built up. If Nasir sensed Bruce's increasingly hostile scrutiny, perhaps he guessed the reason for it. Bruce's instincts warned him something was amiss. He had disliked Lascaris, but he loathed Nasir. He tried to persuade Hester that they should turn back.

On their sixth night in the desert, without any warning, just after they had set up camp, Nasir and all his men leapt on their horses and galloped off, shouting that they had just heard that an enemy tribe was approaching. Bruce noted that Hester remained 'as cool as if in a ballroom'. She ordered everyone in her party to arm themselves and take up guard. They feared the worse: that Nasir had deliberately left them vulnerable to attack, and planned to use them as bait.

Refusing to let Bruce accompany her, Hester decided she would surprise the enemy herself, and distract them from the others; she rode off in the direction of the departed tribe, but in a wide circle, making sure she was plainly in view. Within a matter of hours, she saw 'some hundreds of Bedouin' galloping towards her on the horizon, their spears held above their heads.

Until her dying day she relished the memory of what happened next. She 'stood up in her stirrups' and charged at her attackers, riding 'like a Wahabee', without a shred of fear, 'dash into the middle of them'. At the very last moment, with an ear-splitting battle cry of 'Avaunt!' and her pistol ready, she tore off her *keffeyeh*, uncovering her face. At the very instant she felt sure she was riding to her death, she found herself looking into Nasir's face, and behind him a contingent of raiders from one of the Anazeh's affiliated tribes. 'The threatening yells of the assailants were suddenly changed for loud shouts of joy and admiration at the bravery of the stately Englishwoman and festive gun-shots were fired on all sides around her honoured head.'[13] Hester, who knew that the raids or *ghazus* were as much a sport as a means of income for the Bedouin, always credited this moment as her true initiation into the tribe. Only later would she learn the reason for the ruse.

That night Nasir revealed that all along Lascaris had told them that the English 'Princess' was not to be trusted. But they had now discovered his perfidy, and his pact with the Ruwalah. They had to make sure that she had not gone with them intending to lead them into a trap, as Lascaris had intended. A mutual respect was forged. From that moment on, there would be no more 'unpleasant scenes' with Nasir and he would tell Hester he was her Bedouin brother. But now, she was told, war between their Bedouin rivals was imminent. They would continue to Palmyra, but instead of staying six weeks as Hester had planned, they could stay only a couple of days.

On their way, they visited 'the tribes of the Melhem, the Beni Hez, the Beni something else and the Sebahs', wrote Hester. Muhanna had instructed Nasir to strengthen the tribal alliance. The spectacle of two thousand Sba'ah on the march was something Hester and Bruce would always remember. She had never seen a people as wild, bedraggled and impoverished as the Sba'ah, the men with matted ringlets, and women with heavily tattooed faces. They had pitched their black tents, their 'houses of hair', amidst an 'enchanting vale . . . upon beds of flowers of ten thousand hues'.

At last they reached the high pass overlooking Palmyra. To finally see the remains of this sprawling, once-legendary city with its magnificent ruins of temples, wide, colonnaded streets and triumphal arches gave Hester the sense that she had achieved something wonderful. It spread about before her, like a mirage. The ruins spanned three miles and the eye was caught by half-collapsed mansions, peristyles, sunken baths, a giant agora. In her mind's eye, Hester tried to resurrect it, imagining a city of unsurpassed luxury and opulence, its olive-skinned people wearing silks from India and China, anointing themselves with the finest oils from Mesopotamia; graceful warriors, with a queen as majestic as their capital.

The qualities for which Zenobia was idealized were those Hester could easily identify with. The Palmyrene queen was noted for the clear, commanding voice she used to rally her troops. Ancient historians mentioned her open preference for men. Her stamina on a horse was outstanding – she scorned the women's covered palanquins and even a man's chariot and would gallop alongside her men – and her bravery and daring were said to outstrip those of her first husband, Odainat, a celebrated general.* Above all Zenobia belonged to an Arabian tradition of formidable queens and was regarded by her followers as both prophetess and warrior, who rode as leader at the head of her army.

The welcome given to the Englishwoman was extraordinary. The Sheikh of Palmyra and some three hundred of his warriors swarmed out to meet her. Some were naked; others wore loincloths studded with leather, cowry shells and amulets. Hester found herself besieged by men 'armed with matchlocks and guns, all surrounding me and firing in my face with the most dreadful shouts' and feared they would pull her off her horse. The staged attack was all part of desert tribal etiquette; in return, they were expected to mock a ferocious response, with much display of horseman-ship and brandishing of lances on both sides.

Hester was familiar with Wood's and Dawkins' engravings of Palmyra's great monumental arch, a structure that retained a strong association with Zenobia. As she rode down the central colonnaded street towards it, she found that she was being welcomed in the ancient manner, like a victorious Arab queen. A row of broken columns stood nearby. A number of the tribe's beauties – 'most fancifully and elegantly dressed' – had clambered up onto the pedestals to strike theatrical poses with flowers in their hair and in their hands; they had wound garlands around the

---

* Determined to bring sophistication to her court, Zenobia surrounded herself with clever men: eminent scholars, historians and philosophers. She presided over a short but impressive flourish of building, completing the city's magnificent display of public architecture begun under the Emperor Hadrian less than a century before. Before long, Zenobia pushed the frontiers of her increasingly autonomous kingdom to seize the entire province of Syria, famously defeating the Roman general Heraclianus in a battle in which she commanded 70,000 Arabs. Then, to the utter amazement of Rome, she invaded Egypt, destroying Roman garrisons and conquering it within a year. In AD 270, she sent her armies into Asia Minor, seizing the strategic city of Bithynia, on the Bosphorus. Then she proclaimed Palmyra independent of Rome. No one had dared to challenge the authority of the Roman Empire in such a spectacular way, nor been so successful. The 'Queen of Victory' was eventually defeated by a campaign led by the new Emperor Aurelian, who hounded her to a line of battle on the Orontes river, near modern Homs, slaughtering her cavalry until the ground was thick with corpses of armour-clad men and horses. Zenobia herself managed to escape, but was forced to surrender and hauled off to Rome fettered in gold chains, paraded as a war trophy in a triumphal procession through the city, along with exotic and strange beasts – giraffes, elephants and tigers. Her once-great capital was ransacked in reprisal. Some accounts claim that in Rome Zenobia reinvented herself as a matron of means, and was granted a stately villa, near that of Hadrian, at Tibur, modern Tivoli. It was said she took a second husband, this time a Roman senator.

stone, which glowed a pinkish-grey. As soon as Hester passed by, each girl unfroze her pose, and jumped down to follow her, singing and scattering flowers over her as she walked. Then, as Hester recounted in a triumphant letter to her cousin Wynne, one of the maidens 'suspended over the arch, held a wreath over my head'.

> After having stopped a few minutes, the procession continued. The dancing girls immediately surrounded me. The lancemen took the lead, followed by the poets of the Euphrates, singing complimentary odes and playing upon various Arabian instruments. A tribe of hale Palmyrenes brought up the rear, when we took up our habitation in the Temple of the Sun, and remained there a week.[14]

Recalling her triumph to General Oakes, she told him that Brothers, mad or not, had looked into the future and seen her crowned 'Queen of the East'. Now, whatever way one might look at it, it would appear that she met her destiny.

'Her Ladyship visited everything,' Meryon reported to Sligo, 'climbing up into places almost inaccessible to a woman.' They stayed close to the Temple of Bel, in a mud-brick dwelling near the Tenemos Wall. Each day, she and Bruce explored the ruins, scrambling over collapsed masonry and crawling in through narrow passageways. In the Temple of Bel, Hester spent more than an hour gazing intently at the magnificent monolithic so-called 'Zodiac' ceiling, craning her neck by the light of her flaming torch to see its carved representation of Jupiter presiding over the heavens and the fortunes of men set amongst elaborate geometric patterns and fleurons of acanthus and lotus leaves. Somewhere, in the surrounding stone, she carved her initials with a small chisel. On the outskirts of the town she bathed naked in a pool which had been used by the Bedouin for centuries.

They stayed a week in Palmyra. Nasir's men captured four Bedouin from an enemy tribe allied with the Ruwalah, the Anazeh Fid'an, who had been spying on them on the city's outskirts. He had them stripped naked according to tradition, and bound as prisoners. Two of the men managed to escape nonetheless. Nasir insisted they had no choice but to

leave at once: the Fid'an would be back for the inevitable vendetta, probably having gathered up other tribes. They could all be slaughtered.

This time, Hester was not so trusting. She insisted on interviewing
one of the remaining prisoners herself. He told her that although 'they
were determined to have the head of the chief who accompanied us . . .
I need fear nothing, that everything that belonged to me should be
respected'.

Such were the orders given out to this powerful tribe by their chiefs
assembled in [the] neighbourhood of Bagdad [*sic*]. If I please I can now
go to Mecca *alone*; I have nothing to fear. I shall soon have as many
names as Apollo, I am the sun, the star, the pearl, the lion, the light from
Heaven, and the Queen, which all sounds well in its way.

Gloating over this, Hester was nonetheless aware that within a day or
two, the entire Fid'an tribe would be at their heels. They left at dawn the
following morning, and their return was not without drama. Hester gave
varying accounts to her friends; to one saying they were pursued by 'two
hundred horses', to another, 'three hundred'. Now she truly demonstrated
to Nasir that she had şabr – endurance. Hester remembered how hard
they were forced to drive themselves. 'I was twelve hours on horseback,
and when I got off, I stretched myself out upon the ground as if I had
been dead, not from fright but fatigue and want of water, and when I
drank, I was well and as cheerful as ever in a quarter of an hour.' They
learned that the Fid'an caught up with the Sba'ah, seen so recently outside
Palmyra, and beheaded their chief and carried off their prized mares.

More Bedouin streamed out of the desert see her: the 'Amoors, the
Hadideens, the Wahabees and a party of hunting Arabs that are dressed
in the skins of wild animals,' wrote Hester of the tribe she called 'the
Slepts'. (She noted that the Wahhabis had 'black slaves who are devils,
who are armed with a shocking crooked knife tied around their neck, to
rip up people and a hatchet under their pelisse to cut off heads.') Muhanna
welcomed Hester with a feast, killing a camel for the occasion, and
appointed her an honorary Anazeh emir, with 'the rights of the Desert'.

Hester would always have nothing but admiration for the Bedouin.
'They are the most singular and wonderfully clever people I ever saw,'

she told General Oakes. '[They] require a great deal of management for they are more desperate and more deep than you can possibly have an idea of,' she added. Her charismatic approach with them was based on a kind of trusting fearlessness, as she tried to explain. 'The thing is to look round one, free as the air of the deserts, to observe something like a flight of crows at a distance – to look proudly that way, move your hand, and in one instant see fifty lances spring in your defence . . .'

She added that the sheikhs wanted as many firm details about the great war as possible. They questioned her in detail about her opinion of Tsar Alexander, and she judged that they feared the Russians more than the Turks. 'They have got into their heads that the only power which can affect them is Russia. They were always thanking God I was not Empress of Russia, otherwise their freedom would be lost.'

In Hamah, she was welcomed by another magnificent reception. First, a corps of Delibaches rode out to meet them, sent by her friend, the governor Mully Ismail, barely able to contain his delight at seeing her alive and well. He had prepared a vast feast 'for three hundred people'. She estimated that there must have been a 'full ten thousand people assembled out of curiosity' swarming to the outskirts of town. Everyone had to see the new Zenobia. She mocked herself in a letter to her cousin Wynne: 'The Wonderful Woman in the Revelations Clothed with the Sun and the Moon and Her Feet with a Crown of 12 stars on her head is to be Mr B's Royal Consort.'

She was now considering ways to capitalize on her triumph. 'All Syria is not only in astonishment at the power I have gained over these people, but that I am returned safe from such an expedition . . . I am now, properly speaking, a Bedouin, having been admitted into one of the tribes.'

But although she tried to gloss over the humiliation of being duped by Lascaris, it rankled. 'He made me cry in front of everyone – I could not hide the emotion that his ingratitude caused me,' she confessed.[15] She had no intention of letting him get the better of her.

Sâyigh, Lascaris's sidekick, claims that on her return to Hamah, Hester set a trap for Lascaris, luring the unsuspecting Mariam to be her house guest. After some adroit questioning, Hester pieced together some notion of Lascaris's various desert projects and his possible paymasters.

Meanwhile, Mully Ismail came to her with a grave face: he had heard that Sheikh Duray'i was sending his son, Sayn, to present him with a letter from the Pasha that would bind him against Muhanna. An open declaration of war was expected. Hester asked that the young man be sent to her; and soon she wooed Sayn with generous presents for his father and the entire tribe; she also learned, by the bye, that Lascaris was with them at that very moment. By the time Sayn returned to the Ruwalah, Mully Ismail had brokered a truce. The plan so carefully set up by Lascaris had been foiled. Hester sent Lascaris a note, making it plain she knew exactly where he was and who his new friends were. She informed him that Mariam was with her, knowing he would have to come.

Hester never fully divulged her side of the story of what happened next, and whether an agreement was struck between them. But it was only a matter of time before Lascaris decided to betray his original paymaster and become a double-agent.

Hester's confrontation with Lascaris came just as Misset, the British consul in Alexandria, tipped off his superiors in Bombay that he was 'greatly concerned' that France might be trying to stir up a guerrilla rebellion among the remaining Mamelukes under Ibrahim Bey and the Wahhabis against Mehmet Ali. In his dispatch, Misset cited both Drovetti's and Boutin's recent journeys (in Upper Egypt and the Red Sea respectively), noting that they 'matched perfectly' the known movements of the Mamelukes and the Wahhabis. 'I have no doubt that Monsieur Drovetti, after having made contact with the Beys, sent Boutin to propose the terms of an alliance with the Wahabys,' he wrote.[16] It was his conviction that the French might be readying to provide both factions with arms and munitions; to counteract this, Misset urged immediate, secret preparations for an Anglo-Egyptian military strike. This was the dramatic backdrop to Hester's 'experiments with the Arabs'.

She gave tantalizingly few details about the Wahhabis she met in the desert, except that she had been left with the assurance that she would be welcomed in their capital of Darayya (on the outskirts of modern-day Riyadh) and that they told her about the 'imminent coming of the second Mohomet', about whom 'little was known and whose importance we are not aware of'. Bruce reported to General Oakes that he expected the newly Arabized Hester would now go on to add another conquest to her already impressive list of powerful male friends, predicting she would decide to 'form a matrimonial connection' with the man most feared and revered in the desert, the Wahhabi leader, Saud ibn Saud. 'He is not represented as a very lovable object, but making love subservient to ambition, they may unite their arms together and bring about a great revolution both in religion and politics and shake the throne of the Sultan to its very centre,' he wrote, mocking Hester's new grand scheme to infiltrate the Wahhabi kingdom.[17]

She was quite serious about this plan. At her request, a *firman* had been written for her by Muhanna al-Fadil, signed by five other Bedouin and Wahhabi chiefs at the convening of the tribes she had presided over, which praised her 'vision', her 'esprit', her 'knowledge' and her '*ṣabr*'. 'Mylady Hester Stanhope' was granted the freedom to roam wherever she pleased throughout their territory. It was her pass to the very heart of the Hijaz and with it she intended – without too much delay – to go to Darayya.

But she did delay, and within a year desert politics as Hester and Lascaris knew them would change. Saud ibn Saud would die of the plague. The Hassinah, under Muhanna and Nasir, would suffer multiple attacks by the Ruwalah and their ally, the Fid'an; many died and much livestock was stolen. Soon, the Fid'an would take up the mantle of power, and the Hassinah's days of glory passed.

It would be Hester's great triumph – and her lasting bitterness – that in her ambition to befriend and counsel the Arabs she was well before her time. Almost a hundred years later, the considerably more circumspect Gertrude Bell would make her mark, exploring, mapping and excavating these same lands, winning the trust of Arab sheikhs and chieftains, and providing vital intelligence to the British government. It was the sort of role Hester might easily have craved, except that, had she our benefit of hindsight, there would be no contest. In every way, she would have seen herself as laying the groundwork for Lawrence of Arabia.

While they were still in Hamah, Bruce wrote a draft for a commemorative tablet. Burckhardt had suggested it. Some kind of memorial, he said, should be erected for Hester in Palmyra, to mark the visit of the first European woman. Bruce's effort is a touching, schoolboyish rhetorical flourish:

The place was visited in the Spring of 1813 by Lady Hester Lucy Stanhope, an undertaking worthy of her refined Tastes, her comprehensive mind & her enterprising courage. She did not like other Travellers take an escort to protect her against the Arabs but put herself into their powers & by her virtues commanded the respect & admiration even of this barbarous people.

Happy we should be if we could indulge the hope that she was destined to emancipate this ill-fated country from the Thraldom of Despotism & to restore the splendour of this once celebrated City. It will not appear like flattery to those who know her character to say that if she had reigned at the period marked by its downfall, that altho' she might have been unable to have resisted the power of a Roman Emperor, yet unlike another illustrious female, she would have preferred Death to a disgraceful captivity & to the infamy of having sacrificed a Minister whose wisdom aided her counsels & whose genius reflected Lustre on her City.[18]

# 11

## Separation and Despair

Hester had made her bargain. She knew that she could no longer in good conscience prevent Bruce, now twenty-six, from making his way in the world. At the same time, she was in a vivacious mood, 'vastly improved, both in health and spirits', still basking in her brilliant success, and in contrast to recent months, ready to be amorous. Her feelings for Bruce appeared to shift between desire, irritation and protectiveness, and she candidly acknowledged that she confused him with her commands. 'I am telling B. to go & yet reasoning against it, not liking to part with him,' she revealed to Crauford Bruce while his son still shared her bed.[1]

A furious letter from Bruce's father had reached them. Once again, the damage was caused by Sligo, who had told Bruce's parents details about his son's romance they might have preferred not to know. The likelihood of Hester having fallen pregnant and miscarried while they were in Turkey seems to have been mentioned. To Crauford, the effect of hearing his son's mistress described through Sligo's eyes must have been jolting.* Addressing Bruce, but for Hester's perusal, he wrote:

---

* Sligo did not mince his words when he wanted to get his point across. In 1815, in Naples, thinking it might further a diplomatic career, he offered to spy on the bedroom antics of Caroline, Princess of Wales, then travelling in Europe. He boasted to William Lowther (1787–1872, the son of Hester's friend Lord Lonsdale) that he would be able to gather incriminating reports, having gained Caroline's trust. 'I don't know who is rogering the Princess now,' Sligo wrote to Lowther, when he learned she had dismissed a man amongst her staff who appeared to be a favourite.

I understand through Lord Sligo that you subsequently and earnestly pressed for a marriage, which Lady Hester peremptorily negatived, and I can enter fully into the motives that then determined that line of conduct . . . had I been on the spot I should have joined my admonitions and recommended an indissoluble union, now my friends, the period is gone by, the World is in possession of your misconduct.

Crauford's reprimand to his son was immediate and stern: 'Lady Hester has a sole and entire claim on you,' he told him, 'and if you was [sic] to forsake or desert her, I should depreciate [sic] you as an ungrateful and unfeeling, I can almost add, bad, Character.' This was a theatrical flourish Crauford knew would appeal to Hester, whom he termed 'the Heroine of the Drama', but he wrote in the knowledge that she was too proud ever to hold him to it. Worse for Crauford, Sligo's revelations had forced him to confess to his wife that he had known of the affair, but kept her ignorant of it.*

As Crauford predicted correctly, Hester preferred the moral high ground. He had given her another incentive to demand Bruce's immediate departure. General Hutchinson had offered to meet Bruce in Europe, a chance she was unwilling for him to lose. But Bruce, now equally stubborn, insisted he would not leave her. If they had to part, he argued that they could at least delay it. Surely Hester could return with him to Europe? He began to think of himself as a spurned lover, and informed his father that his affair with Hester was 'no common case'.

There has been no seduction, no binding promises, none of the artifices usually practised by the sex, but it is that of a woman who has refused marriage, the only compensation in my power to offer, and an honour to which I had no right to aspire.

---

* Hester and Bruce could not have known then that on 16 December 1812, 'dear old Sligo' suffered the indignity of a public trial at the Old Bailey, and was sentenced to serve four months' imprisonment at Newgate, in addition to a fine of £5,000, on charges of suborning two British seaman. Sligo simply assumed, as was hardly uncommon, that aristocrats like himself were entitled to a little bending of the law.

In the end, two factors would disentangle the lovers, who had weathered every other kind of peril together. One was money. The other was the plague.

At first it seemed possible they would not suffer the virulent epidemic that had struck Constantinople. But by late spring, bodies were being buried in mass graves outside Damascus, Acre and Tripoli, which alone lost seven thousand people. Only Aleppo and small settlements along the coast seemed unaffected. Hoping to escape the worst of it, they decided to shift camp to Latakia, a sleepy seaside town north of Tripoli.

On their way from Hamah, escorted by two of Mully Ismail's guards, they passed through the Jebel al-Sariya, the most striking scenery they had yet seen. Many dozens of Crusader castles perched perilously along these all-important mountain passes, like a line of stepping stones to Jerusalem from Tripoli and Antioch. The region was controlled by the Alawis and the Isma'ilis. The Alawis in these mountains were also known as Nusairi, meaning 'little Christians' (today their descendants, the minority Alawites, represent Syria's ruling clique).*

Just as at Deir-el-Kamar, Hester and Bruce were drawn by the enigmatic allure of these sects, but they were not welcomed as they had first been by the Druze. No doubt they were spurred by the challenge. The Alawis and Isma'ilis were regarded by most Arabs as heretical offshoots of Shi'ite Islam, and like their more powerful brethren the Druze, shielded the mysteries of their faith from strangers' eyes.

As they went on they passed mountain villages. There were fewer Alawis, and the people looked different: tall, sharp-featured, often light-eyed. These were the Isma'ilis. Although apparently at peace, the travellers were told that the deep-seated hatred between the Alawis and the Isma'ilis erupted periodically into skirmishes, even outright war. But for the moment, the Isma'ilis were weakened and outnumbered.

---

* There were wild rumours about the Alawi. Burckhardt recorded in his notes that they were said to adore 'the sun and stars . . . and the pudendum' and that he heard the men 'prostrate themselves every morning before their naked mothers . . . and have promiscuous intercourse with their females in a dark apartment every Friday night'.

Mully Ismail called them the 'Hashashins', and told dark tales of murder and treachery.*

Meryon reported that Hester 'thought they had so military an air she wanted to stay longer and observe them', adding, perhaps unnecessarily by now, that 'when she was intent of any plan which required much penetration and great conduct she generally chose to be alone'.[2] Insisting that Bruce and Meryon go on ahead of her, and refusing to fully explain her actions, she remained. The excuse she gave Bruce was the same as in the desert, that although these militant Isma'ilis were known for their vicious attacks on outsiders, she judged that as a woman she was unlikely to be harmed.

Two days later, arriving in Latakia on 22 May, she emerged insouciant from her mysterious meeting, having also ridden unprotected to present herself to an Alawi chieftain. To Bruce she told strange stories, of sacred fish and fertility rites. Meryon wrote in his journal: 'It was said she had completely gained the hearts of mountaineers among whom she encamped.'

Latakia appeared to be safe from the plague. All the same, no British ships of the line could be expected; even Maltese vessels, relied upon for all communication with Europe, stayed away. That year, the plague would kill more than 100,000 people in Damascus, and 300,000 in Constantinople.[3] A cycle of delay, anguish, doubt and self-reproach set in. The drama of when and how Bruce would go, and whether Hester would go with him, would continue for more than five months.

They rented a vast mansion, just off what is now Al-Quds (Jerusalem) Street. Just as at Damascus, all sorts of callers wanted to see the *Meleki*, curious to discover if she had influence and magical powers: merchants, pedlars, priests, self-styled sages and charity-seekers. 'I had so often heard the Turks say that she was a daughter of the Grand Signor by some

---

* As the Assassins, this militant branch of the Isma'ilis had carved out their own small empire between the eleventh and thirteenth centuries. Their heartland was Masyaf, twenty-five miles from Hamah, where their leader Rashid al-Din first claimed the title handed down to his successors, the Old Man of the Mountain. Their descendants still struck fear into their adversaries, renowned for centuries for their extreme daring and skill in completing political assassinations. Initiates into the brethren were served secret herbs – probably the 'hashish' (or *kaygusuz* as it was more commonly called) that gave rise to their name.

English lady, and the Jews convert prophecies from holy writ to her person,' wrote Meryon.[4] Questions were being asked about her faith. Did she favour the Arabs as many said, or the Jews? Or was she a 'Follower of The Book' (meaning a Christian), as the rest of her party were assumed to be? Everything she said or did – and what she ate – was watched closely.

By mid-June, an apparent lull in the epidemic prompted Bruce to set off for Aleppo so that he could cash more bills of credit with Barker. As soon as he arrived, plague cases cropped up there too. That month ten people in Latakia died of an unspecified 'vomiting' fever which may have been Asiatic cholera. 'They pretend the heat destroys it,' Hester wrote, noting that all Europeans in town 'hardly will put their head out of a window'. Meryon was 'in a vast fright'. He ordered them not to buy anything off the ships and to fumigate all letters by holding them over pots of vinegar or perfume on smoking braziers. Hester felt unwell, and blamed the 'unwholesome southerly wind'. She urged Bruce to leave Aleppo immediately, and suggested the Barkers get out too. Her offer to arrange two houses further up the coast at Suwediyah for them – Barker himself was unable to throw off a bad fever – was gratefully accepted.

In Aleppo, Bruce had been shocked to discover that they had no credit: their bank drafts had been returned, dishonoured. Having already borrowed heavily from Barker, they would now be forced to borrow more. Since Bruce took up with Hester, he had been paying bills of at least £2,500 a year (approximately £125,000 today). Now he was obliged to write to his father and ask him to intervene with Thomas Coutts – banker to all the Stanhopes and Pitts – on Hester's behalf.* Between them, he confessed, they owed £3,000, at least a thousand of that to Barker. He chose this moment to remind Crauford that Hester had lost possessions worth at least £4,000 in the shipwreck, and suggest that 'some remuneration' be made 'in the most delicate way possible . . . for she experienced

---

* In a letter sent from his office on The Strand on 29 October 1813, Coutts asked Hester to take a kinder view of his actions, claiming it was commonly believed in London that 'you and your suite had all been murdered' and that he had been warned 'by various hands' not to accept or pay any of their bills, 'as there could be no security against their having been forg'd, or what was more likely obtained by the Drawers by force!' He urged her to take out a 'Life Certificate' as soon as possible, advice which Hester seems to have ignored.

this misfortune by attaching herself to my fate'. Whichever way one looked at it, it was proving a very expensive affair.

While Bruce was away, another letter arrived from London, this time from one of his father's friends. Crauford was said to be very ill and possibly dying. Hester decided there and then that she must make him leave her, and that she would stay.

She was ready to set in motion a plan she had been musing on for some months, a calculated bid to construct a career. She wanted to prove the apparently impossible: that a woman like her could dazzle the world. She made an appeal to Sir Joseph Banks to consider her as an authority and a go-between with the Bedouin Arabs, who controlled, she informed him grandly, the 'great barrier between the Eastern and Western world'.[5] To impress upon him how great her influence was, she sent him a copy of the *firman* drawn up for her by the Bedouin and the Wahhabis. 'With your permission I should be happy to lay at your feet any information I may have amassed, considering it as the most certain mode of its becoming useful to mankind,' she said. 'I shall be able to receive any commands you might honour me with, which I shall execute with as much pleasure as exactness.' She hinted that she would like to go to Darayya with his encouragement.

She had begun to think of herself as a woman of action, someone with an ability to influence history. All the places she now spoke of hankering to see – what are now modern-day Iraq, Saudi Arabia and India – and that she felt were vital for the future, were wide open canvases.[6] Perhaps she feared that if she returned to Europe – and to England itself – she would soon feel, if not shrunken, then at least no longer larger than life.

She would give Bruce another compelling reason to go. She was always circumspect about exactly how she came upon what she described as 'a curious manuscript once belonging to the Church of Rome – an instruction where to find treasure hid at the time of the Crusades', some 'three million pieces of gold'.[7] Although undated, it looked at least two centuries old, and was said to be a copy of the much older original.

The location of what appeared to be the principal hiding place of this treasure was the ancient fortress of Ascalon (now Ashkelon), which had been bitterly fought over by Muslims and Christians, and which Richard the Lionheart had rebuilt as a stronghold during the Third Crusade. Because a chapel was detailed as the burial place for the treasure, the obvious deduction was that it had been hidden before the departure of the Crusaders.

She did not discount the possibility of it being a deliberate forgery that might 'make a trial of her eagerness about it . . . and thereby [prove] that this was her reason for travelling or that she was a spy'.* With this in mind, she reasoned that she would be better off buying the manuscript than refusing it, for during such suspicion-ridden times, it was less dangerous 'to be considered a treasure-hunter than as a secret agent'. The document certainly looked convincing, but there were few people close at hand she could trust to authenticate it.

She made Bruce promise to convey her plan to Robert Liston, the newly re-installed British Ambassador in Constantinople. They had the manuscript copied in the greatest secrecy, and he was to carry it with him. Hester's suggestion was that Liston should show it to the Reis Effendi, the Sultan's Secretary of State. Her offer was disingenuously simple: if the Porte granted her mission to excavate, she would deliver up anything she found to it, and claim only the triumph of discovery. Hester expected Liston would see this gesture as she did, as a shrewd exercise in diplomatic relations.

Bruce was devastated by her decision to stay. She 'possesses a spirit and sensibility which I never found in any other person,' he wrote to his father. 'Lady Hester has insisted upon my leaving this country immediately,' he wrote curtly, hinting at volatile disagreements with an obdurate lover. 'I can assure you that by consenting I have done great violence to my own feelings.'

---

* If this were indeed so, the strongest possibility is that Lascaris had something to do with it. Hester described the copy she had as being written in Italian, and smuggled to her in great secrecy from 'a dying monk' in an unspecified 'Frank monastery'. Later, she would acquire the original for a substantial sum. Lascaris had spent not inconsiderable amounts of time at three of the main 'Frank' monasteries on Mt Lebanon: at Antoura, where he befriended an abbot by the name of Gandolfi, whom Hester knew; at Deir-el-Moukhalles in Djoun and at Harissa. As he had already demonstrated, Lascaris was capable of highly devious deceptions. He also believed Hester – and certainly Bruce – to be rich enough for them not to suffer too greatly by being a little out of pocket on the deal.

When Bruce kept finding reasons to postpone his departure, Hester secretly made all the preparations for it. On 5 October Hester wrote again to Crauford, apologizing for her financial 'scrape'. She lectured him with a litany of reminders, revealing the degree of control she exerted:

> First about his health, his stomach nor head have never once been disordered for more than two years and it is not a little owing to my care. Tea is poison for him, and so is wine except in very small quantities, so are . . . spices of every kind. The complaint in his stomach is all irritation and his stomach being out of order affects his head. Sitting up late and rising late also destroys him, he loses his appetite and his looks, exercise he must take, and regularly, which he is not fond of . . .
>
> Don't let him make faces when he speaks, it is hideous, or twirl about like a bad actor on a stage. Pray sit him down regularly to business for an hour or two every day, if he does not get the habit of it now he never will, make him sort and arrange his papers constantly and keep his things in good order, there is nothing like it, and never to leave papers and letters about for servants to read or the key of [his] writing box in their possession . . .[8]

As she often did, Hester left what she really meant to say until her 'PS':

> It is only anxiety which makes me look into his failings so minutely, that the world may do greater justice to his virtues. A purer heart never existed.[9]

Before Bruce left, the lovers agreed that he would make over to her a portion of his allowance, an offer she told him she would accept, although 'I repeat, it shall not be permanent . . . I shall not draw upon your father, it would ill become me, or to allow that to be permanent which I accept only to prevent the world talking of my being left in a strange distant country ill provided for'.[10]

She would not stay more than a year, she assured him, which would give her enough time to dig at Ascalon. She promised she would gather literary, religious and other 'vastly curious' manuscripts, the sort they knew would interest Banks. They talked about Bruce following in the footsteps of his 'relation and namesake' James Bruce, and becoming a writer, and as his surety that they would see each other again before too long, he left behind his precious travel journals, and she promised to compile them and add her own observations.

Winter was coming. On 7 October Hester insisted he must go, telling him he could delay no longer. They had spent the night entwined, barely sleeping. All the arguments had been resolved; she had herself under tight control. Everything was ready.

They had agreed that first he should go to Aleppo, and then take the route north through Antioch. He had two men with him and assorted servants; the dragoman Beaudin would accompany them as far as Aleppo, and Hester's trusted Giorgio would return when Bruce had safely reached Constantinople.[11]

At the appointed hour, the horses were saddled. Bruce hoisted his last few belongings onto his mount. Hester could not bear to part in the house they had shared. Bruce bade farewell to the others, including Meryon, embracing him heartily with tears in his eyes, so that the doctor was touched, thinking him 'so amazingly affected at taking leave that I was afraid he would have retracted his intentions at the last moment'.[12] For three years, they had been almost inseparable.

She rode out with him a long way – some twenty-eight miles – through pine-scented, gorse-covered hills as far as the remote landscape around the Crusader castle of Sâone, where they had picnicked. By late afternoon soft layers of mountains rose eastward to Qalaat Samaan. Having long prepared for this moment, Hester was nonetheless unable to stop herself crying. They clung together one last time as though they would never part. Now Bruce had to be the firm one, turning away first. Giorgio grinned as he waved.

Hester had not imagined how lost she would feel at his leaving. As soon as he was gone, the empty landscape stretched ahead like a darkening abyss. Later, when she recalled this moment, the parting that she had always judged would restore her honour, she understood it was a death from which she never entirely recovered. Alone, stripped of her bravura, she asked herself whether she had been right to send her golden boy away.

\*   \*   \*

*'You have left your telescope behind you . . .'*

Loving words, reminders, entreaties and orders for commissions for 'the dearest creature' now followed Bruce on the road. Her first letters after their separation are imaginary one-sided conversations, tangled up in a way only lovers might excuse, suggesting by their intimacy the way she spoke to him in private. She told him she wrote from her bath – 'I, Philosopher in my Tub' – so he could imagine her face flushed and her hair wet, wanting to tell him little gossipy snippets that would make him snort, endearments so he would remember he was her 'angel'. 'As my poor heart is so full of affection for you, if I were once to begin to express its feelings, I should never end . . .'

For the first weeks, it was as though they remained physically connected. He still had her comb, she told him, 'the only one I can untangle my hair with'; she could still see his naked body in their bed. She told him he should wear flannel next to his skin – 'the cleanest thing possible as it soaks up all the perspiration' – and have Giorgio rub 'your legs from the knees very hard before you go to bed'. She imagined him being scrubbed in the *hamam*, reminding him that although he should let his beard be groomed, 'not the dear eyebrows to spoil them'.[13] His horse would tire; he must get a 'strong one' as soon as he could, and remember if either he or his horse tore a muscle or developed back pain, that 'in this country there [are] men who rubbed and pulled both horses and men well again'. Each day, he 'must have elderflower tea for breakfast, and a daily dose of barley gruel with a little milk and sugar'.

Even at a distance, Hester was a strict matron. She told him, 'remember if you should be constipated with hard indigestible food, 2 spoonfuls of castor oil when going to bed, or very early in the morning would be best for you'.[14] Doses of chicken broth, calomel pills and rhubarb powder were also advised – it is hard to imagine Bruce stopping for any of these.

Bruce had barely been gone a month when a letter from Sligo had reached her, announcing his intention to come out to Syria immediately. Passing the information on to Bruce, Hester hinted that Sligo might be harbouring some kind of amorous interest in her, and told him: 'The last letter I wrote Lord S. was a very *violent* one. I said if he persisted in his conduct I begged he would not come near me if he came into the country, for that it would pain me too much to see or argue with him.'[15]

She reported delightedly that 'Sir Sidney' had also written, and 'he is all kindness and calls me his great ally'.[16] He had also agreed with her course of action 'on the subject of the T' and promised her that 'everything I wish for & asked for shall be done as far as depends on *him* the first moment that circumstances will permit . . .'[17]

But November began with sickening news. Not one but two of Barker's little girls, Zabetta and Harissa, developed 'malignant fever', which was proving as deadly as the plague. Meryon could do nothing. They died within hours of one another. Danger came ever closer. Until then, coffins had been placed in the outskirts of towns for hasty burial; now, victims were simply wrapped in linen and turfed into the street by relatives too terrified to leave their houses.

Insurrection in the larger cities was becoming commonplace, and the pashas of Damascus and Aleppo used civil disorder as an excuse to indiscriminately dispose of their enemies. Soon Hester's friends Mully Ismail and Nassif Pasha suffered humiliating ends, and the women in their harems were raped and killed and their Mameluke servants massacred.[18] Earlier that summer, walking through the town's main square, Meryon saw a group of men, gruesomely slashed to death by razors, stakes driven through their bodies.

Hester was confident that in the Druze kingdom more enlightened measures were in place, both to control the unrest and the plague. She turned to Sheikh Jumblatt, who suggested the small monastery of Mar Elias, which lay within his territory, as a temporary refuge. It belonged to the Syrian Melkites (often referred to as Greek Catholics) whose presence was tolerated on Mount Lebanon. The Patriarch Athanasios, the Melkite religious leader, used the residence as a private retreat from the larger monastery near Djoun, but he had recently died. It was hers for as long as she wanted it for thirty pounds a year.

She announced her plans to Canning in Constantinople:

In about a week I repair to a pretty convent at the foot of Lebanon for the winter. The Pacha of Acre is come into that area to repair a castle, and the Prince of the Druses hunts within an hour of my habitation, so I shall often see him. We are great friends, he is a very agreeable man, and very popular in the Mountain. I am quite at home all over the country; the common people pay me the same sort of respect as they do a great Turk, and the great men treat me as if I was one of them. In short, I am very comfortable in my own way: part of this country is divine, and I always find something to amuse and occupy my mind.[19]

But on 15 November, the morning they planned to leave, Hester complained of pains throughout her body and an appalling headache. By the evening she was feverish, which worsened throughout the night into dreadful spasms of shivering. Meryon too began to feel unwell. For three days he fought fits of sweating and trembling; on the fourth he collapsed feebly into his own sickbed. Then both Mrs Fry and Beaudin sickened. The heartbroken Barkers sent their French doctor as well as an Italian surgeon.

Although all four patients were very ill, only Hester seemed beyond all help. By the time Meryon recovered sufficiently to realize he was neglecting his patient, he – too weak to walk – was carried in to see her. At first he thought he was looking at a corpse with a deep rasping breath. Any strength she had seemed supernatural; he had some difficulty restraining her during her violent seizures. Later, Hester seemed almost to relish the details of her ghastliness:

I was a monster larger at my knee joints than in the leg or thigh & my arm was enough to frighten anyone you could see the large & small bone & I looked altogether like a spectre![20]

For fifteen days Meryon barely left her side. Barker, having seen her, was convinced she could not possibly survive. He sealed up her papers and possessions, preparing to have them sent to her lawyer. Later he wrote to Admiral Smith, describing how bravely she behaved believing herself about to die.

I had an opportunity of admiring the force of mind, with which She encountered and defeated Death in a Conflict where the Doctors thought his triumph sure. The paroxysm were so violent each night as to render her continually delirious, but in the day, altho' the fever never left her,

she was generally quite composed, and gave me orders for her funeral
& the disposal of her effects, with a calmness and resignation that was
truly edifying.[21]

Meryon's treatment principally consisted in applying large numbers
of leeches to her body and lancing her glandular swellings. He immersed
her in the hottest water he thought she could endure, a 'native' treatment she was willing to try as an experimental cure. He fed her asses'
milk – the freshest they could find – by the teaspoonful, and slowly,
miraculously, she improved. Meryon was inclined to think at first that
she might have caught a 'modified' version of the plague – a 'secondary
or tertiary' disorder – but he later revised his opinion; it was 'beyond all
doubt' the plague.

Over time, Hester would recover. But her beauty – and some thought
her mind – was never quite the same again. Her lungs were damaged,
making her more prone to bronchial infections. The membranes of her
brain became inflamed during her frequent fevers; from now on, she
would complain of vice-like pains gripping her temples. 'Great have been
the ravages that this illness has made in her looks, and it will be many
months before her person can recover any of her *embonpoint*,' wrote
Meryon sorrowfully.[22]

Meryon commented that after her physical recovery, Hester underwent
a striking metamorphosis.

From that time her character changed deeply. She became simple in her
habits almost to cynicism. She showed in her actions and her conversation, a mind severe indeed, but powerfully vigorous. Scanning men and
things with a wonderful intelligence, she commented upon them as if
the motives of human actions were open to her inspection . . . Sometimes
she looked into futurity like the Sybil of old; and as she reasoned on the
great changes which were taking place in Europe, she scattered her
prophetic leaves.[23]

It was as though she had undergone a conversion, or had a glimpse
of something beyond life. Soon after her illness, she would begin to seek

out the esoteric and the mystical, which until now had only been only a mild interest with her. Soon it seemed to Meryon that the Hester he first met and the one he now knew were two different women. Her old playfulness, her boisterousness and easy habit of flirting seemed to vanish overnight, replaced by a certain bitterness and reserve. Her former gaiety would return only in flashes.

Hester's great vibrancy, her strong body and expressive eyes had made her appear an irresistible beauty to many men, some of them, like Bruce, much younger. That changed. Hester knew that her looks were not what they were even a few months before; that in fact now she looked her age in a climate where, as Meryon put it, 'women of thirty are gone in their wane'. For the first time, thin lines appeared around her eyes and mouth, and her hair had fallen out in clumps after her illness. She cut what remained short, but the insouciance of the last time she did so – when she had dared Bruce not to find her seductive in Rhodes – had vanished.

## 12

## 'The Queen Orders Her Minister'

When at last Hester set out on her sea journey to Sidon it was 6 January 1814. Weak and feverish, she had to be carried about in a makeshift palanquin. She left her horses behind, intending to send for them later. In Sidon she bought stumpy, sturdy mules to carry their possessions up from the coast. For the moment, the great horsewoman could only ride if she was held up by her armpits on both sides by servants.

By the end of January she felt well enough to ride up for a day to inspect Mar Elias to determine what needed to be done. Meryon was amazed to see how her energy seemed to return as she picked her way up the slippery mule track, eager to inspect the monastery as a 'skeleton to work upon'. Hester quickly performed miracles at Mar Elias. Discovering that, according to rather macabre tradition, the Patriarch's corpse had been immured in the convent, she had the little chapel sealed up. A small army of villagers was coerced into beautifying the monastery: scrubbing every inch, whitewashing walls, repairing chimneys, building outhouses, store-rooms and a wood-fired *hamam*. All the shutters and trimmings were painted her favourite Nile green. Into the kitchen went a new, capacious oven, shelves, plate-racks and cupboards. Over her bed was her prized mace. Around the property she demanded a 'stone and mud wall to keep out strangers and dogs'. Soon there would be stables for the horses; a chicken run and 'a gazelle house'. To Misset's dragoman in Cairo, she wrote gaily that Mar Elias would soon be 'an English fortress'.[1]

She had still not heard from Bruce, and worried about him constantly. (By now the plague had reached as far as Valletta, and she feared for her friends there too.) If she were to recover her strength – and her looks – she knew she needed rest and a careful diet. Isolation seemed the best precaution, so she stockpiled provisions to last for a year, and prepared to shut herself away from what she called 'ordinary society'.

Soon, her little farm consisted of two hundred chickens, some sheep and lambs, and stores of rice, wheat, figs, raisins, oil, candles and soap. She had taken on two local women to soap, scrub and massage her in her *hamam*: Mariam, a still-pretty mother of two beautiful daughters, and 'Hadjy', referred to by Hester as the 'old hag'. There was 'a little old man who twaddles about after poultry', 'a tall, strong Maronite for the asses' and also 'Pierre', a cook who had served in Napoleon's army.

The two rulers of the Druze kingdom welcomed Hester warmly. Presents arrived: a small caravan of camels laden with expensive and thoughtful gifts: healthy, glossy-flanked goats and asses to be milked and eaten; amphorae full of 'oil is that is like milk'; and more remarkably still, sheets of coloured and plain glass from Damascus, carefully wrapped in kilims, to be installed in her window alcoves to keep out the wind. It was the first glass most people on Mount Lebanon had seen in their lives.

Sheikh Jumblatt stopped by to see her, accompanied by his band of fifty men, as he passed on his annual tour of his territories. Although Hester wanted to see him, when she looked at herself in the mirror, she wavered. The ravages of her illness were still visible: she could not let a handsome man see her this way. When Sheikh Jumblatt was informed that she was indisposed, he was puzzled, perhaps hurt: he left a mountain garland of gifts for her: partridges and an antelope he had hunted himself in nearby hills, using the pistols she had given him.

Still with some satisfaction, she boasted to Bruce that the two Bashirs had told her that 'all is to be at my feet' on Mount Lebanon, and that she had been invited to meet the new Patriarch at Deir-el-Moukhalles in Djoun. 'If I go, the bells of the mountain are to ring,' she told him.[2]

Finally, early that spring, Bruce's letter reached her. He had heard about her terrible illness the moment he arrived in Constantinople, and told her he had almost 'fainted' at the news. 'I believe that the state of my feelings was but too apparent to the whole company. But I care not what they thought as it will always be my glory to have loved – and to love – the dearest and most wonderful woman in the World,' he told her.[3] It seemed miraculous, but he had narrowly missed the onset of the plague at every step 'from Yuzgat to Constantinople' and for that, he said, 'my Guardian Angel preserved me'. He offered to come immediately.

> If you should have a relapse and remain ill for any length of time, will you not allow me to come and join you? You well know what violence I did to my own feelings when I separated myself from you. It was only fear of displeasing you that forced me away. If you command I shall obey but no language will be able to express my sufferings. I should disregard the commands, the entreaties, or the threats which might proceed from any other quarter, but your wish shall be my law.[4]

There was more. 'I know not how it is that you . . . possess a power of fascination that all those who have ever known you are attached to you . . . I only think of my dearest Hester – all other considerations vanish before you – and altho' I feel conscious that I have now and then given you pain partly owing over which I had no control yet do me the justice to believe that no one can ever love you more than I do.'

Bruce reminded her of 'drawing upon me whatever was necessary for your comfort', telling her that on his return he expected his father to make him an allowance of £2,000 a year.

> Can I do less than make over one half to you? Do not, at least, deprive me of the satisfaction of making so proper a use of my money. £1000 will be more than sufficient for me: for I shall live very retired, and principally in my father's house.[5]

He told her:

> Now my dear love, I can enter into all your feelings; and I am sure that nobody can entertain a higher admiration for your lofty and dis-interested spirit than I do. Indeed, the more I reflect on your character, your talents, and your history, the more I am lost in wonder; and look upon you not only as the most extraordinary, but the first of created beings.[6]

This was all Hester needed to restore her equilibrium and resolve. She told him he must on no account return to her, nor must he trouble himself worrying. She was quite firm about her intentions to remain another year. As for him, while he was in Constantinople, she told him he would do well to cultivate Liston and his wife, Henrietta, who were great friends with her favourite uncle, Lord Grenville, but warned him to stay away from some of the expatriate Europeans, 'the horrid Jacobean set'.

Would she have picked up her pen to reply so uninhibitedly if she had known that Bruce had already embarked upon a passionate affair with a young French woman? Little can be discovered about the woman who signed herself Théophanie Escalon except that she was unmarried, sweet-natured and attractive enough to catch Bruce's eye the first week of his arrival. She was probably from a Huguenot family living in Pera, and he soon arranged lodgings to be near her.[7] Judging by the *tendresse* and regret of their letters, it was a tortured but physically ecstatic love affair.

Théophanie was merely the first of a string of women who would gradually help Bruce forget his ardent promises to Hester. But for the moment, however, he still felt 'bound to [Hester] by the most sacred ties'. He had his portrait made for her in Constantinople, sending it to her with a tender endearment that he would rather be in its place. In between his visits to Théophanie and thinking about Hester and his father, Bruce spent a great deal of time miserably retching and vomiting. The burden of expectation and uncertainty in all his affairs stirred up his old complaint, the stomach ulcer Hester had made it her business to cure.

Late in March 1814 Hester was thrown into agitation by the news that Vincent-Yves Boutin had just arrived in Sidon from Cairo, and was now in charge of France's commercial interests in both Egypt and Syria.[8]

It seems their mutual friend Nafissa may have tried to play match-maker, for she had asked Boutin to bring along with him a present for Hester, a pretty Muslim girl called Hanyfy, just thirteen (whom Meryon, with his eye for pubescent beauty, noted was 'exceedingly well-made'). But the human offering was sent up on a mule, to hand her new mistress a scrawled, curt note of a few lines.

Puzzled, Hester wrote Boutin not one but four letters over the space of as many days. Her first letter was lively and long, spilling over with enthusiasm to see him, adding with a possible hint of jealousy that she would look after 'your girl' with care. She told Boutin she would not mind receiving him 'at my little apartment in Sidon' (the set of rooms at the *khan* (inn) she kept for when she was visiting) but that due to the plague, she wanted to avoid the city, and also his host, the French consul Alexis Taitbout, whom she judged 'an irascible, untruthful drunk'. Instead, she pressed him to stay at Mar Elias, even though it would stir up gossip.[9] 'Come, a room awaits you, and you can stay as long as you need to get everything ready for your journey.'

As another enticement, she said she had something to tell him about Burckhardt, who was planning to explore regions south of the Sahara. She went on: 'I plan to tell you something important, that I know will interest you,' adding that she had been puzzling over some details which his 'mathematical mind' would be able to solve 'within fifteen minutes'.[10] Above all, she hoped he would trust her to offer him what advice she could about Syria. 'I have spent enough time in this country to count myself as one of its inhabitants, and to know a number of people who might be useful to you,' she told him.

Angling to find out where he planned to go, she asked if he might be soon passing through Tripoli. Perhaps he could ask the French consul there, who she added pointedly was her 'obliging friend', to send her some particular books? 'I don't like novels or French poetry,' she said, 'nor modern history, except anything to do with Louis XIV, Henri IV and the Empress Catherine.' What she particularly craved was 'anything on geography, botany, agriculture, politics and the history of different wars'. She planned to travel again before long, she told him, 'to Baalbek' and 'if the plague doesn't stop me, perhaps I will become a Bedouin again . . .'[11]

No answer made its way up the hillside. That she made this somewhat familiar overture, and expected a reply in kind, gives us every reason to guess that in Cairo there had indeed been a genuine spark of mutual attraction. She struggled to interpret his silence. She sent down another letter, this one impatient and haughty. She had heard of a fresh outbreak of plague near Sidon; if so, he would soon be quarantined, she warned:

Your situation there strikes me as rather pitiful, and of course, if you stay, you won't be able to make any journeys into the rest of the country. I'm not suggesting that you have to stay [with me] at the convent; I am too busy with my own affairs to try to understand someone so incomprehensible, but I can offer you a clean, pretty room in the village with a place for your mule . . . I'm not going to eat you . . . you are your own master to stay where you like.

She ordered Pierre to wait for three hours for an answer from 'Monsieur Vincent'. He returned empty-handed. That same night, she sent down another note – from 'the Queen'. This was a tongue-in-cheek, sinister tease. 'My Minister has his orders to return himself for an hour or a day, whichever pleases him.' She promises him that she will tell him some nice stories which will amuse him. Would he like to gossip with her in her garden pavilion? Or will she have to threaten him, perhaps with a nod to her executioner, to make him pay her a visit?[12]

Unintentionally perhaps, Hester ignored the real reason behind Boutin's reluctance to see her: Lascaris. By now, the French consuls, as well as Boutin, suspected that Lascaris may have been courting the British side at her behest.

From the time Hester returned from Palmyra, an order was put out to the French consuls in Syria – issued directly from Talleyrand – to file reports on her movements. For the moment, Lascaris was being watched closely, and so was Hester.

A few days later, she made one last try. She told Boutin that she had received a bulletin about a great series of French victories, sent to her by special 'tartar' from Constantinople, news she was sure Taitbout would not have until the next ship from Cyprus arrived in at least a week's time.[13] Neither of them could have guessed that at the very moment Boutin hesitated to see her, the sound of artillery fire had reached Paris, and the Allies had begun marching in.

This time, within two hours, Boutin turned up on her doorstep with his belongings, wan and dusty. Seeing his surly, handsome face, Hester felt a shock of excitement but realized in the same instant he was in a bad state; his eyes were raw and inflamed, he looked tired and worn. He had contracted ophthalmia from his constant exposure to sand storms in the desert. As she studied his face, his cloudy blue-grey eyes, she saw him weighing everything, as though trying to decide what she knew. A startled Meryon was summoned. He advised Boutin to try to avoid looking at bright sunlight, and gave him a pair of his own green spectacles.

Shortly before Boutin's visit, Hester said cryptically that Meryon had gone off to 'stick himself up in the village', a ten-minute stroll away. Whether she sent him away or not, he stayed there at his own expense. Meryon now exasperated her: 'He had no delicacy,' she complained, and plotted to find another doctor 'to serve me in all capacities according to my taste' as soon as she could. Is this a hint that Meryon had been unable to hide his disapproval that she wanted to invite the Frenchman into her bed?[14]

Undoubtedly, Hester found much to admire about Vincent Boutin. She thought him brave, honourable and extremely clever. He could be silent; in her later letters to him, she teased him that he was 'the master of listening'. Did he tell her that in Siwa, he had been beaten and imprisoned by the local chieftain? Or that he had been back to Arabia, and seen the Monastery of St Catherine? Did he add that he had been as far as Yemen, to the Red Sea port of Mokha and the Hijaz? And that at Yambu, he had unexpectedly found one of Mehmet Ali's sons, Toussoun, waiting for him, barring him from going any further into the interior to Medina or along the coast to Mecca?

Hester left him in no doubt of her great partiality for the French people. She certainly admired Boutin and believed him to be a man of honour and courage, even if she held his supreme commander at fault for brutalizing Europe. When she had been in Constantinople, Hester had clearly been charming and persuasive enough to sway the consul, Latour Maubourg, around to her point of view, and in Cairo, Drovetti and several of the French *savants* had been taken with her. In her presence once more, away from what was being said about her, Boutin seems to have softened towards her too. Every indication points to the development of a sudden and intense attachment – an infatuation – at least on Hester's side.

In the end, Hester would find out about his past. He had grown up near Nantes, where at the Oratory he was befriended by both Victor

Hugo and his prefect, Joseph Fouché, who later recruited him. Having interrupted his engineering degree in Paris to enlist, he had served under Marshal Ney and General Kléber. After being wounded in the left knee by an Austrian musketball at Wagram, he turned his talents to establishing routes, surveying for bridges and devising defence reinforcements. Fast-tracked by Fouché, Boutin had been issued various roles; that of a diplomat in Constantinople, and a commercial attaché touring Algiers and Tunis. In Algeria, where Boutin spent only fifty-three days in 1808, the coastal map he drew up was so detailed and exact that by 1830, when the French invaded, it was still the best available. Unassuming he might pretend to be, but the former officer had been awarded the highest possible honours in France and Turkey.*

Boutin seems to have tried to bore her, even to make her laugh, telling her she had no idea how desperate French merchants were to improve cotton and silk production, and that Syria was their next great hope. But as he glanced at her, he caught the disbelieving, slightly mocking expression on her face.

Typically, Meryon drew a discreet veil over the entire incident, not mentioning the fact of the visit to Mar Elias, noting however that the Frenchman arrived in Sidon on 28 March and 'left the province' on 6 April. Yet Boutin took one of Hester's horses and one of her servants for his journey.

On the same day Boutin left, Hester dashed off a breezy letter to 'dearest' Bruce from her rooms at the *khan* in Sidon, where just a week before she had refused to go. She seemed unusually cheerful. She mentioned that 'the very agreeable Mr B' had arrived, but that she 'only saw him for five minutes'. Therefore Hester deliberately misled Bruce about the timing and extent of her relationship with Boutin. Why? She seems to have expected to see Boutin soon; over the coming months, her letters would pursue him, suggesting numerous rendezvous.[15] As he rode towards Aleppo, Boutin did not yet know that his mission was over. One

---

* In 1807, the former Sultan Selim III had decorated Boutin with the Order of the Crescent for his role in designing the construction of new sea fortifications that proved highly effective in repulsing the British navy's attempt to bombard Constantinople, having breached the Dardanelles, telling him, 'You have saved my capital.' In 1809, Napoleon had made him a Chevalier of the Legion of Honour for his efforts in Algeria.

week later – although the news would not reach Syria for many weeks – Napoleon abdicated.

The plague struck again, in early May. Meryon was called to the sickbed of an old man in Abra who 'went to bed at 2, and by 8 was a corpse'. Within the space of several weeks, Meryon noted thirty cases of infection and twenty deaths. Immediate quarantine took effect in the kingdom, and Emir Bashir informed Hester that she should take any measures necessary to uphold it. But she was unable to stop many of the villagers from panicking, and some escaped to the hills, which were riddled with ancient caves; later their bodies would be found picked over by jackals. Within the next two months, some 360 people in surrounding villages died.[16]

Soon Meryon retreated, fearing for his life, and ceased trips to the homes of those afflicted. Hester visited some of the distressed families, and tried to do what she could for them. She was deeply traumatized at the suffering around her. 'God knows why he thus afflicts mankind,' she wrote.

> I am so anxious about this subject I never felt the least afraid when I visited these people, I tell you quite the truth, but when I found the poor mother had made holes in the earth to bury her children, I could not stand that, yet I behaved well till I came home, and then I threw myself down in the corner.

In desperation she decided to try out a 'serpent's stone', a bezoar, said to be from India, on a twelve-year-old boy, who she was certain was close to death.[17] 'It struck me that this stone might be useful in the plague, in sucking out the venom of bubos [sic], which would not break,' she would later report to Banks; 'at first I had experiments made by Turks, but as I feared they might deceive me, I was determined to interest myself in its effects.' She had a 'Turkish barber make a slight incision' on one of the boy's buboes, noting that when she applied the stone, it 'stuck like a leech', clinging there for four hours, after which, as though sated, it fell off. Following the instructions she had been given, she placed the stone in a glass of warm milk; 'it discharged its poison, the milk turned sour'.[18]

Within a day, the boy improved; he was the only one in his large extended family to survive the plague. It did indeed appear to be a miracle. She made copious observations with the intention of interesting Banks, with the hope 'that if there is ever a Society established to investigate the nature of the plague and to make experiments upon it, that you will admit me'.[19]

As the plague abated, she continued adding to her papers for Banks. She was by now desperate to be assigned some kind of official role, and she trusted him to recognize that she wanted to gather information, not for 'public conversation' but so her discoveries 'might rest with an unprejudiced, honourable set of men'. This was another strong hint. Hester particularly craved something she knew Banks could bestow if he was so minded: admittance to a society of scientists and travellers like the African Association.* She would soon tell Banks she had heard that Burckhardt had by now reached the Kingdom of Dongola in Nubia: 'Some day or other I shall follow his footsteps in that part of the world.'[20]

She tried to woo Banks with assertions that she intended to preserve for posterity the traditional method of creating the famous Damascus blades, 'made from aerolites and lumps of a particular metal' – 'in case the technique was lost'. She informed him she was growing him a tree from a cutting of what she had been told was 'the mandrake tree spoke of in the Scriptures'. Then there was a strange fish, a type of carp that she had been told could be found only in certain high mountain springs within Isma'ili and Alawi territory, and that for six weeks in any given year they gave off strange excretions. 'I am almost ashamed of speaking of their *qualities*,' she told Banks coyly. 'These fish render the water so dangerous for any man to drink . . . for he becomes positively *mad* for women.' At that time of year, she reported, the Pasha of Damascus sent up his guards to prevent villagers from drinking from the spring – but they were not always successful. Now, she informed Banks that 'a most active and clever French traveller who has lately left this neighbourhood and whom I knew in Egypt' had promised to bring her some of these fish; soon, she told him, she would send them on for his collection.[21]

---

* Hester was only 105 years before her time. In 1913, after almost twenty years of debate, the Royal Geographical Society admitted women as Fellows for the first time.

This is revealing. Whatever tensions and undercurrents existed in her relationship with Boutin, he was obviously the sort of man she felt she could ask to find her a rare, aphrodisiacal fish. That such a search would take him deep into dangerous, politically contentious territory was another matter.

By 11 May she had sent a number of letters but still had nothing from Boutin. She wrote again, enclosing a news bulletin Barker had sent her. She summarized it: Lyon had fallen; General Blucher 'was paying heavily for his preceding victories' and the plague was raging in Constantinople and Smyrna. She ended with a playfully menacing flourish:

> If you do not send me your news, I will cut off the heads of my Arabs for giving me nothing but uncertainty.
>
> Adieu
> Hester-Lucy Stanhope
> P.S. The Queen orders her Minister not to pay attention to vague reports unless he receives her permission.[22]

This time, Boutin responded immediately. He was in Aleppo. His letter was sharp, bristling with annoyance. 'Apparently, Mylady, circumstances call me away to the Persian coast,' he wrote coldly, and quite misleadingly. 'Knowing you are surrounded by your allies, who I hope are more faithful than ours, gives me great pleasure. I see nothing of any great significance in any of the bulletins that your consul obviously accords so much weight. One has to consider the overall picture.'[23] This was a new tone, as though he had learned something distasteful. Hester sent this letter back to him, gleefully underlining the last sentence, writing on the top, 'That's why, you naughty boy, I cannot wait to see you again'.[24]

But she knew immediately that he referred to Lascaris, whom he had quite clearly expected to see. Lascaris had gone missing. The word was that he had fled from Syria to Constantinople. That she had apparently deliberately neglected to tell Boutin of her dealings with him suggests she did indeed have something to hide. Now she replied, somewhat defensively, 'I was once very taken up with your man, but I hardly need to make excuses when it is you who has benefited by my doing him a service.' It is not clear, from the curious ambivalence of this remark, quite what she means. How exactly did she suppose Boutin might benefit from Lascaris's disappearance? Given the fact that she had confided her plans for her intended excavation to Boutin, and wanted to rely on his advice, had she also proposed that he assist her? Or was there far more than this at stake, as later events would suggest?

Now the subject was raised she protested her innocence. Lascaris had deliberately placed her in danger and embarrassed her, she explained, and the 'whole incident' with him was something she had decided to put out of her mind. She did feel some sympathy for the man, she insisted, but was quick to belittle him: 'He is quite crazed, his brother in chains, almost dead.'[25] She suggested to Boutin that if he went to Hamah, perhaps he might learn something of his whereabouts from Mariam, 'the woman who calls herself his wife'.

Her answers would not satisfy Boutin. He now began to wonder how much, if anything, she had discovered about his own true mission.

A few days later, on 23 May, she wrote to Boutin again, as though unable to suppress the desire to tell him things, however inconsequential. She sent him packets of news bulletins, perhaps trying to cheer him up by saying: 'I think you will find the Allies very badly placed'. But any hard news was delayed by months. Although in Europe the game of war appeared to be over, the Queen and her would-be Minister had not yet reached a checkmate.

The fact was that shortly before Boutin's arrival in Syria, Lascaris had made John Barker a startling proposition: a trade of accurate information in return for money, British protection and a passport. His behaviour suggests he was already under suspicion. If this betrayal became known, he would be arrested, and face imprisonment or worse.

Barker referred to the 'Lascaris plan for the conquest of Syria' when he forwarded Lascaris's papers to Admiral Smith, judging him to be the best person to evaluate what appeared to be either so optimistic a plan that it bordered on fantasy or a highly ambitious blueprint for invasion.[26*] Some time in early 1814 Lascaris left Syria on a filthy, over-crowded Greek ship, heading first for Smyrna then Constantinople. He had enough money for his passage out (and the promise of more at a later date) and the prized provisional British passport. He left Mariam behind and deliberately neglected to tell her where he was going.

When Barker informed Hester of what he had done, he was tentative, uncertain whether she would approve of his actions. He assumed she knew nothing about it. But her reply indicated the opposite, for she hints that she had forced Lascaris to confess to her. 'My politicks are all upon a grand scale and I seldom agree with other people [but] . . . I am not the least displeased with you for having proposed what you did and you judged right as to fact, for I know all that can be known upon the subject you allude.'[27]

This is indeed a curious remark, open to several different interpret-ations. Some time later, another (no longer surviving) letter from Barker would reach her and she replied:

> . . . I knew all that you have told me, and much more, yet it is all useful, very useful, therefore all you hear in conversation, do write to me, because it gives me an opportunity to compare it with my own information and leads also to the discovery of lies, but I have been so prudent and *close* about this business.

The question of what Hester knew (and what others thought she knew) lies at the very heart of her romance – and her rift – with Boutin, and the strange triangle with Lascaris.

In the shadowy race for influence between the major powers, even the apparently improbable cannot be discounted. Both men were arch-deceivers;

---

* The plan proposed that Napoleon's advancing army arrive at the mouth of the Orontes, where 'a trusty individual, provided with a secret signal, was to await the arrival of the armament, in order to guide the army to Mar'ash'. This is modern-day Kahramanmaras, in Turkey – not far from the Syrian border, north of Antioch, and over the years a frequent stop on Lascaris's criss-crossing expeditions. The city was chosen as an ideal position from which to stage operations; Lascaris noted that plentiful forests nearby could supply timber for the construction of a flotilla, which the troops would use to transport themselves down the Euphrates. In the second stage of operations, Bussora (Basra) was to be fortified. From here the longed-for expedition to India would be mounted.

Boutin the more conventional and convincing in manner. Lascaris's man, Fathallah Sâyigh, swore to his brilliance; yet others were willing to believe he was almost insane. It is impossible to ignore the possibilities of double-cross. Might the Lascaris plan have been nothing more than an elaborate hoax? To what extent was Hester, at least at the beginning, an unwitting victim and stooge?

That June news reached Hester of Napoleon's exile. She brooded over what would become of France. She wrote to Boutin in Aleppo, trying to be consoling, referring to the fact that the Paris mob, despite being enraged by the Allied advance, had not meted out dreadful punishments to Napoleon's family. Surely having Talleyrand as Prime Minister could not be the country's worst fate, she suggested: 'France will always be France, she will cure herself and heal her wounds. Perhaps now we will have peace!' In her opinion, she told Boutin with some severity, Napoleon 'no longer merited the confidence of his people'.

But she misjudged her audience. Boutin, a lifelong Bonapartist, found the news that the empire was lost bitterly difficult to accept. As far as he was concerned he shared Napoleon's views, that Talleyrand and Fouché were traitors. Whatever Boutin said on this subject in his reply to Hester, it alarmed her. Now this time she thought he was the one who was indiscreet. 'For God's sake, be careful – your country demands it and those about whom you speak, order it,' she told him. Hester was sure that a talented, distinguished man like him could thrive in the new France if he was willing to play chameleon politics, and evidently tried to counsel him to see sense. She entreated him to see her.

His reply has not survived, but Hester's response shows she made another overture, and was rejected. 'If all men knew how to value constancy like you do, unhappy women would not exist, or at least very few would be unfaithful.' It is almost certain that Hester tried to interest him in the possibility of working for Britain. But her hurt is that of a rebuffed lover.

Before she received this disappointing blow, Hester had been anticipating a reunion. Tired of waiting, she had decided she would go to Aleppo herself. It seems she had intended to break her rule, to dress as a woman again, to entice 'Monsieur Vincent' – Boutin – for she asked Barker to send her silks and linens, 'in the French style'.

It gave her no pleasure to know that her 'worthy cousin', the Duke of Buckingham, would be accompanying Louis XVIII back to Paris.* Barker pronounced himself flummoxed as to why she wanted to come to Aleppo, or stay in Syria at all, when she could 'go and partake of the universal rejoicings on the Continent' at the Allied success where, with a cousin like hers, she would find herself right at the heart of events. 'You say you would go to Paris were you me,' she replied, 'because it is probable that the King knows that Lord B. and I were always like brothers and sisters (till I visited Arabs and Turks which he does not like) [but this] is in my mind a reason for keeping away . . .'

Despondent, Hester turned her thoughts to those she felt truly loved her. She had last heard that James, now a major, was fighting under General Graham in Wellington's army in the Peninsula; nor did she know where Bruce was. She had received a letter from Sligo, now in Paris. 'As he likes the French as much as I do, he would not have enjoyed witnessing the distress all this must have caused individuals,' she wrote, adding poignantly, 'I always think of women when I hear of armies and battles, having suffered so much myself for the cause of Glory.'[28]

* It had been the Duke of Buckingham's late father, the Marquess, who had 'spent £25,000 a year' on the Bourbon family when they took refuge in England, when, as Hester put it, 'no soul could ever have supposed they would return to France . . . now that *is* English liberality'.

# 13

## A Chained-up Tigress

On 14 June 1814 a British sloop sailed into sight, firing rockets up into the night sky. The inhabitants of Sidon were terrified, convinced that the Porte had ordered an attack. But it was merely a welcome salute for Hester. Her letters to Liston and Admiral Smith had resulted in an astonishing coup. She now had a warship at her temporary disposal for her proposed excavation.

Captain Forster, wearing his gold braid and epaulettes, trooped up the mountainside to see her. He was astonished to find that Hester had a tigress 'tied up in the yard, well-secured' at Mar Elias, sent by Emir Bashir's son Hassan, as a joke after he heard she was hankering after tiger skins.[1] Although she was enjoying the novelty of owning such a beast, she could see it might be impractical to keep her. 'I think it will go off with the Ship, as the sailors say they know how to make it quite tame,' she wrote.[2]

There was one insurmountable problem: Forster had arrived just in time for the hottest time of year, and the plague risk had still not abated. She cursed Bruce, whom she had trusted to tell Liston on her behalf 'all about the T' and that he should delay sending his ship until the following spring. As it was, Forster stayed for a week, his visit proving to be nothing more than a glorified mail drop. He offered her passage out of Syria, and gave her time to consider the offer again while he made a survey of the coastline around the proposed dig sites, although it was obvious nothing could be done about the expedition for the time being.

On 1 July, after a farewell dinner at Mar Elias for all his officers, Captain Forster sailed away, taking the tigress, and a great quantity of letters and presents from Hester. For Banks there were several large boxes of plant specimens, as well as the precious 'serpent stone' and the 'extraordinary' fish, pickled in jars and fetched by Pierre the cook.

Hester mulled, mostly bitterly, over her latest crop of letters. She had been glad at least to know that James was safe, and in London, appointed aide-de-camp to the Duke of York. (He did not tell her how badly wounded he had been at San Sebastián: a musket ball had shattered his shoulderblade, and driven so far into his flesh it could not be removed.) He was full of concern for her health, suggesting either that he come for her or that he meet her in Europe, and promised to send her £500 'for her European wardrobe'. He told her that the Duke of York had been so distressed to learn of her predicament that he had ordered him to accompany a frigate to fetch her.

But if Hester believed that even those closest to her were willing to treat her as they had before her affair with Bruce became publicly known, she was mistaken. When James returned to London, he had immediately sent a servant to Crauford Bruce to ask for any news of his sister, but he pointedly and repeatedly declined any face-to-face contact. It does Crauford some credit that by contrast, he did his best to be welcoming, extending what he hoped would be a well-received compliment about James's sister. James was not mollified. He left a curt note stating that he had no wish to discuss Hester, nor any wish to add to the 'unfortunate publicity' of her affair. He returned Bruce's letters to Crauford, all unopened.[3]

In general, it must have struck Hester by now that her bid to achieve recognition was – by and large – ignored. Instead, she was increasingly seen as an object of pity or ridicule. Crauford Bruce beseeched her, with what he believed was genuine compassion:

> Leave then the Convent in Syria and quit the Country of the Turks and of the wandering Shepherd Tribes . . . you must gain ascendancy wherever you are and with whoever you associate, because of the superiority of your genius and Talents . . . give them then this benefit in a better region and not waste your excellent qualities in the burning Sands of the Desert.[4]

The prospect of Hester remaining in Syria bothered Crauford, and he had written his son a series of confidential letters on the subject. By cruel chance, they had been forwarded to Hester by mistake. Their contents turned her stomach. She found herself referred to as though she were some kind of awkward moral encumbrance that had to be carefully negotiated. Crauford was willing to make a provision for her, but only if Bruce promised him that the affair was at an end, which he had not done. To add to her sense of injury, there was mention of salacious gossip about her.

Furious, she wrote what would be her last letter to Crauford, apologizing for reading what was not meant for her eyes, but determined he should neither pity nor patronize her: 'I am sorry to find that B. has been complaining to you of my situation & circumstances, neither deserve a thought since I am separated from your son.'

> If I have not resigned yr. son in the way most advantageous to himself it is not my fault, three years constant inopportunity upon one thing & another, have not left me the free agent I *once* expected to be . . . Notwithstanding I have kept my word with you. His scampering after me to God knows where, will derange his own plans . . . and besides make my own assertion of having *forced* him away be doubted by those who would otherwise believe it. I tell you very fairly that whilst I am within his reach you will never get him to think of marriage & take care for the present how you converse on that subject for if you make him angry, he will perhaps say something that will displease you, something that he may find difficult to recall . . .[5]

With some piquancy, she hinted that Bruce was deliberately concealing something from him, something she was certain he would not like. If prodded to anger, he might reveal the truth, even though he knew 'the misery this would inflict upon me'. Was this a reference to the miserable secret they had shared at Therapia?

Hester sent Bruce his father's letters, with certain sentences furiously underlined by her pen. After her great sacrifice in giving him up, it infuriated her that Crauford utterly failed to credit her 'for not having acted the *base and interested part of other women*'.[6] As for the gossip, she told

Bruce that it was all 'very tormenting stuff'. She had never concealed the fact that she already had a history when she met him, and did not attempt to deny it now. 'I know human nature better than you do,' she wrote, and had experienced '(for a short time) that love for dissipation, which you have never felt . . . and affect to despise'. She signed her letter self-mockingly 'the Nun of Lebanon'.

Bruce's actions at this time, and his letters to his father, suggest Hester was never far from his thoughts, despite his entanglement with a mysterious second woman. He had promised James and others, including Sligo, that he would bring Hester back to Europe safely if she did not come of her own volition; in fact he rather staked his reputation on it. By the end of summer Bruce would seek out 'a beautiful and large dwelling' close to a forest outside Vienna, paying rent for six months in advance and informing its owner that he would return with a female companion.[7] But the romantic bolthole would remain empty until the following April, dust-cloths draped over the furniture and the windows tightly shut.

Hester still seemed to be counting on a rapprochement with Boutin. Her allegiances always came from her heart, and now it seems hers had been stolen away by a Frenchman, whose bitterness at the fate of his country became a creed she would adopt. She informed anyone who cared to listen of her strongly partisan views. She thought France 'the fountain of elegance, of esprit and every thing charming. If France was no more, the world would become so vulgar that it would not be worth living in.'[8]

But the world *was* vulgar, and gossip and innuendo often passed for fact. If, as seems likely, Boutin sought out the abandoned and bitter Mariam, he would have interrogated her about Lascaris. Mariam resented Boutin, who Fathallah Sâyigh told her was fresh from the Englishwoman's bed, with his upright, infuriatingly honourable manner, such a contrast to her once-gallant husband who had left her almost penniless. The gossip she put out about Hester was of a deliberately low sort: that she slept with any man who took her fancy, and put them to work for her, spying for Britain; and that she had also tried to seduce Lascaris.[9]

Boutin's letter to Hester from Hamah has not survived, but it probably did not stoop to repeating such allegations. Judging by the strength of her reaction, however, it deeply disappointed and hurt her. 'The Queen' was apparently unable to inspire a chivalric feeling in 'her Minister', and she felt humiliated.

Hester's temper could be volatile, but now her behaviour struck those around her as unbalanced. 'A louder rap at the convent gate than usual; a quick step across the court – were sufficient to throw her into a state of agitation. Every stranger was a messenger, and every disappointment made her sink into a lowness of spirits,' observed Meryon. This was new. So were her sudden 'transports of rage'.

Meryon had no notion of what so distressed her. As soon as she received Boutin's damning letter, she decided she could not bear to spend another hour in the confines of Mar Elias, and that they must leave immediately for the mountains. In the rush, her instructions were confused. Whenever she made a journey like this, she always expected to have her bed ready and tent pitched in a sheltered spot. This time her bed was left behind and the tent was not where she thought it should be, sending her into a fury. 'She was no longer herself,' wrote Meryon, and afterwards claimed this was the start of her 'fits of temporary insanity'. Having exhausted herself, she began to sob uncontrollably. As he moved to comfort her, she suddenly switched into the tone of voice she used to order about a servant of the lowest order, and barked at him to bring her a drink. Meryon had faced many dangers on her behalf, but felt himself unable to stand this humiliation. Attempting to maintain his dignity while mounting his mule, he rode back to Abra, inclined to quit her service there and then.

Hester's actions are suggestive of some kind of nervous breakdown, and certainly despair, but also great anger for which she felt she had no other outlet. By the time Meryon made his way to Hester's mountaintop destination, everyone around her was cowed. When she finally sent for Meryon, after making him wait for two days, he noted she was 'calm and composed, and all was forgotten'. Writing up this incident, Meryon tucked his notes into a folio over which he wrote 'Lady Hester's journey to Meshmushy in 1814, in which she is mad'.[10]

At thirty-eight, Hester feared she might never again find love, nor the laughter and affection of children and grandchildren. Her devil-may-care, damn-them-all philosophy had always driven her on, and assumed some suitably ambitiously triumphant outcome. Only death, perhaps, was a preferable alternative: that attitude had certainly given her the freedom to do as she pleased.[11] But now she was irritable, her mouth tasted bitter. Even she did not recognize the stranger she was becoming.

It was easy to see why Hester saw 'Meshmushy' as she called it (it is Machmouche today) as a perfect retreat over her troubled summer of 1814. At 930 metres altitude, the air is fresh and pine-scented. She stayed just outside the village, at Roûm, a place known for its wild thyme and honey, in two adjoining houses which the Emir had allowed her to take over.

Hester arrived on 29 July 1814 and stayed for ten weeks, dividing her household and bringing Hanyfy, leaving Ann Fry to swelter at Mar Elias. The climate agreed with her. She rested, ate well and contemplated the perpetual snows of Mount Lebanon, and seemed to adopt a more philo-sophical attitude to her troubles. By the end of summer she felt in perfect health, able to report that she had 'grown fat and looked better than I ever had ever done [sic] in Syria', and that she had begun to ride horses again.

She was charmed by the beauty around her. 'I found out a little Mount Olympus covered with trees, vines and goats, and at the top (three hours high) a sort of temple in a grove of the largest oaks I have seen in Syria.' This place, which she called the Peak of the Santon, became her favourite retreat. It was almost on the edge of a precipice at Nabi Micha, near Jezzine, with views across jagged cliffs, striated river gorges and forested valleys to the Anti-Lebanon range, to the Bekaa, Nabatiyah and to the picturesque ruins of the once-great Crusader fortress Qalaat esh Shaqif, or Beaufort Castle. She camped in a domed tomb there dedicated to the Shi'ite saint el Khizr, 'the man dressed in green'.

Regretting her earlier angry outburst at Bruce, she picked up her pen again, wanting to undo some of the damage. This time she was calm, her words softer, sadder, even caressing. 'For my sake, take care of your-self, perhaps we shall meet again in this world, but it must not be for the *present* and when we do, not *as before*.'[12]

> The most unhappy moments are passed, and I now contemplate my own
> conduct and prospects with great composure, but not so your agitations

if you give way to them. I know I have reacted right, for your happiness and advantage, and for my own comfort.[13]

She remained hungry for all news, and was in the habit of sending Beaudin to Sidon twice a day to bring her letters and information. In what would appear to be a reference to Boutin, she asked to be sent news of 'the French fortress', and whether it was true 'it had begun fiddling with the ports of Cyprus'.[14] Evidently she learned his whereabouts.*

On 23 August, she felt compelled to write to him again, berating him for whatever he said that so upset her the previous month. 'What a disagreeable letter, Sir, truly incomprehensible,' she told him.

> You are about to leave and you don't have the decency to tell me where you are going? It is obvious that everything you told me about Aleppo was to stop me from returning . . . but don't you realise that if *my will* dictates something, neither heaven, air or earth will stop me pursuing it . . . If you reproach me for making war with you, it seems to me that you love it more than peace. I have never been able to find a just cause for war, and if it seems to you that I have behaved outside the law, am I now wrong to berate you for this cold, untrusting feeling that now exists between us?[15]

The next day, she sent another letter:

> It seems that I will not see you again, at least not in this country, but I cannot help but send you at least some words of consolation. Please don't tell me you are inconsolable, but thank Providence that Paris was not burned, and consider all the horrors that might have taken place but did not, then perhaps you will not feel so miserable. I did not become a Philosopher out of apathy, but out of resignation . . . If France was able to recover from all the horrors that brought in the Revolution, surely it can endure a peace that will at least offer some respite, and the chance

---

* Hester's references appear cryptic, but later become plain. She wondered about what news Boutin was sending to the French consul in Cyprus, someone she was aware held considerable influence in Paris, 'Chevalier' Regnault.

to contemplate all the remarkable sacrifices it has demanded of its people. Nothing can deprive France of its energy and ability to recover from misfortune . . .[16]

Then, as a sad rebuke, she added: 'Do you think you would have been more spirited, had more righteousness and integrity, been in a better state to dazzle, and add to the glory of your country, if you had the same weakness as a man as I do as a woman? Just know that wherever you go, my thoughts will go with you.'[17]

There were more shocks in store. A letter from James arrived telling her that their sister, 'the beautiful Lucy', had died in childbirth on 1 March, aged thirty-four, leaving her husband Thomas Taylor with seven children.

No sooner had this tragic news reached her, than she received the much-delayed report that Francisco de Miranda had been imprisoned for almost two years at La Carraca, the notorious jail in Cádiz. The Spanish had finally caught up with him. A great deal had happened to him in the intervening years, about which Hester had heard only patchy accounts. Not long after she left England, Miranda had returned to Venezuela, linking causes with Simón Bolívar.* Now, Hester learned what Miranda's friends in England had known for almost a year. Bentham in particular had been devastated by Miranda's capture and imprisonment, for he had hoped his friend might become 'one of the mainstays of South American liberty'.[18] Another of Miranda's old allies, Nicholas Vansittart, now Foreign Secretary, could not risk offering direct help, for fear of

---

* With Bolívar in tow, Miranda had canvassed his old allies Nicholas Vansittart and William Wilberforce, and found a reluctant patron in Wellington's brother, the Marquess of Wellesley. Covert financial agreements were struck. On 7 July 1811 Venezuela announced its independence to the world. Soon Miranda would tell Wilberforce optimistically that they were on their way to abolishing the slave trade. Within six months of his arrival, on 3 April 1812, Miranda was proclaimed Generalíssimo, but he was soon deeply unpopular. He had sworn to create a utopian new society – and its newly-minted constitution, based on the American Constitution and the French Declaration of the Rights of Man, certainly looked immaculate. But almost immediately there were summary arrests, torturing and hangings. Miranda was unable to stop the slide into civil war, and it would be a cruel irony that the title he had struggled so hard for would fall to Bolívar instead, *El Libertador*.

having to answer embarrassing questions about the surreptitious funding of foreign revolutions.

For the moment, all Hester could do was ask James to make discreet enquiries. It seemed Miranda had an advocate in Gibraltar, willing to smuggle letters to him, a Peter Turnball. She soon gathered from Turnball that it was only due to the not inconsiderable risks taken by a man who would become Miranda's last confidant that any letters reached his friends at all.* Miranda must have asked her for money. Only with liberal bribes could life in La Carraca be made remotely tolerable; only then could he hope to smuggle letters out and in, ask for books, writing implements and news from the outside world. But Hester had little available cash. Turnball discreetly advised Vansittart, and may well have hinted to Hester too, that if a sufficiently large sum of money were raised, in the region of £1,000, Miranda's escape to Gibraltar and into British protection might stand a good chance of being secured.

Without a doubt it was Miranda, and the hope she had of helping him if she could, that explains her sudden announcement that come spring, she intended to go to Valencia, which was not so very far away from Cádiz. She intended to keep her promise to Bruce about gathering up manuscripts and curiosities, but she had apparently lost her taste for all her other plans, including the proposed dig. And she was quite sure everything was over with Boutin.

From her mountain eyrie, she informed Bruce that she intended to set off in the coming spring, first to Constantinople 'to see Mr Liston', then to Valencia. She gave him instructions for Coutts to prepare letters of credit for her at Vienna, in Italy and Spain, 'particularly the southern part', as well as Gibraltar and Malta. It seems she was keeping her options open. Trying to be firm, the pain and confusion in her voice are plain to see:

> Therefore it now stands that we never must live together again, I shall always be your sincere friend for it is not in my power to feel indifferent

---

* This was Pedro José Morán, a devoted, low-born Spaniard who managed to attach himself to Miranda as a general functionary. Morán attested to the fact that a great many letters addressed to Hester reached a certain Señorita Leonor de Flores living in Calle San Cristobel, and later at the Calle de San Francisco de Asís in the adjoining Isla de León, but as to how many of them reached her in Syria, it is hard to say. Who Señorita de Flores was remains a mystery.

to you, but I will never from this moment ever have any more consul-
tation with you about your line of life, or any thing in common with
you. Should we ever meet again I shall consider you as Lord S[ligo] or
Lord anybody whose family do not support me and who neither have,
nor shall assume, the right to make me responsible or interfere with me
in any way . . .

In short I am sick of it all, and I never falter at anything, but end it
at once, it is for your advantage, and my happiness, but I shall always
love you so tenderly that I feel I cannot ruin you, which I should do . . .
were we to be again on our former footing. I am vexed to death as you
see and if you wrote me a cross unkind letter you will kill me, if not I
shall be composed and feel I have done (what I wish to do) my duty
most religiously. If nature has organized me so strongly I cannot help
it. I can never be happy when pestered and when I feel I am not a free
agent . . .[19]

# 14

## 'I Will Be No Man's Agent'

By October 1814 Hester felt strong enough to indulge her curiosity about parts of the country she had not seen. She had another reason. Unexpectedly, Boutin had replied, subdued and somewhat conciliatory, letting her know he was heading for Damascus. On that front, it seemed, all was not lost.

On 16 October, two days before setting off, she sent him an impulsive note, suggesting he meet her at Baalbek. 'You absolutely must come,' she told him, almost pleadingly, adding: 'You will find there is nothing beautiful to see in Damascus, only the Turks and their harems.'[1]

Once again she crossed the Bekaa valley, turning left at Zahle instead of following the route to Damascus. This time she travelled with mules, tents and all necessary provisions, wanting to stay well away from villages for fear of the plague. She wanted to see Baalbek, ancient Heliopolis, or 'City of the Sun'.

A horrendous storm pursued them to Baalbek, where she pitched her tent for two weeks in the shelter of the great Roman Temple of Jupiter, larger than the Parthenon, still being completed when Zenobia's city was at its height. She did not know whether Boutin might come. She waited. At night she slept in the moonlight and the shadows thrown by the forest of columns, amid torrential rain and cold winds. She felt none of the joy of exploration she had associated with Palmyra. Emir Bashir had offered to meet her in Baalbek, but he too stayed away when he heard news of the plague sweeping the Bekaa. Meryon scribbled a poem in Latin in charcoal, awaiting Hester's approval to be chiselled on the temple's inner wall, a suitable distance from Bruce's initials, which he had carved two years before.

> How many names, else never to be known
> Live for a while, inscribed upon this stone!
> But Hester, thine oblivion shall not fear: –
> Fame will transmit it, though not written here.[2]

She was not amused: off it had to be scrubbed. She told Meryon witheringly that she had hardly turned down famous poets and painters to relax her rule 'that she had never consented to be praised in verse or portrayed in painting' to go against it with such a scrawl.

It continued to rain torrentially as they wound their way up through the forests of Mount Lebanon, with snow flurries dogging their way. But the sight of the Wadi Kadisha, the 'Holy Valley', awed all of them. An ancient haven for ascetics and mystics, Kadisha was a crucible for outlawed sects and strange heresies and a birthplace for saints. Maronites had come here to escape Byzantine persecution, leaving behind their homes on the Syrian flatlands and seeking sanctuary in the folds of Mount Lebanon, and there were also Greek Orthodox, Nestorians and Abyssinian Coptic monks here too, sheltering in the shadows of Ottoman rule.

They rested for a day at Bcherre, a Maronite hamlet of churches, monasteries and hermitages clinging to the side of the mountain. The place made her uneasy. Here in the Qanubbin Gorge, warriors thrived alongside hermits. For the first time Hester heard the Druze overlords discussed with open hatred. Men fingering their daggers looked at her with disrespect. She was more cautious than usual. For the first time she veiled herself and hired additional guards to prevent people looking at her as she passed. A few miles beyond, from a high mountaintop sentry-post once used by the Romans, there were clear views down into Alawi country.

They pitched their tents at Ehden, not far from the Cedars, the ancient grove whose wood was said to be prized by Solomon, now buttressed by deep ledges of snow. The chieftain, Latouf el Ashy, 'who spoke a little

French', struck Hester as more welcoming to foreigners, and she was glad to find someone who had met Bruce.*

At Ehden she welcomed the arrival of Selim from Hamah, whom she had asked to accompany her on her travels. Hester obviously liked Selim, and took to fussing over his meals and generally indulging him. Meryon commented cryptically that the young man was 'the strangest compound of talent, frivolity, liberality and libertinism that I ever met with. He was the most wayward of mortals.'³ Others described him more bluntly as 'debauched'. Hester revealed to Bruce that she was deliberately cultivating Selim, who 'tells me very interesting things these last two hundred years' and 'has a fund of information very difficult to get at'.⁴ Some of the Alawi's sacred books and manuscripts had fallen into Selim's hands after a raid was made against the sect some years before, and Hester was now able to buy them. It gave her great satisfaction to know that Burckhardt, whom Selim had met when he travelled through Syria in 1810, had begged in vain for these very same manuscripts.

Hester was intrigued by what she had heard about the Monastery of St Anthony Koshaya, which overlooks the Qanubbin Gorge. Not only had it produced Bibles in Syriac script on the first Arabic printing press, it was widely believed that miracles were worked here. Bodies buried in the soil here never decomposed. And after a night chained to the altar in a stone cave, the mad – those thought to be possessed by the devil, epileptics and the mentally ill – were cured, or so the legend went. 'The Devil or somebody comes in the middle of the night and snaps the chains asunder,' she reported.

The monastery endeavoured to keep everything female – and therefore distracting to contemplation and chastity – from straying into its inner chambers, a rule that extended even to goats, chickens and cats. Hester, however, insisted on a visit. She arrived at the monastery, deliberately riding a female mule, demanding to pay her respects to St Anthony,

---

* Bruce had been drawn to Ehden by reports that in 1469 Abyssinian priests settled here for what was generally thought to be some mysterious purpose. They had been sent by their king, who claimed descent from Solomon and the Queen of Sheba, and built a monastery, Deir Habache. But in 1488, they were expelled from the valley. In small chapels and nearby grottos just outside the village, they left behind frescoes, geometric inlays depicting wondrous beasts and inscriptions in Ge'ez, the tongue of fifteenth-century Abyssinia.

announcing grandly that the Sultan himself had given her permission to see all places of interest on her tour of his empire.

That night Hester dined with the monks at the head of the table, drank their wine, and endeavoured to prod them into theological debate. Donning a monk's rough robe, she visited the chapel, its pillars carved from monolithic rock, an unseen river rushing loudly behind its walls, and the sacred grotto, with its manacles and its simple wooden cross. Hester had not expected to be moved by the monastery, but it was the one place in the valley, surrounded by men, and alone, where she felt stilled and peaceful.

Next, Hester stayed for a month in Tripoli, arriving a week before Christmas. She was careful to be escorted in by the governor's armed guard in full daylight. At first, she claimed only to want to spend a few days resting, visit the *hamam* and arrange money matters. But she had good reason to expect Boutin would pass through the city on his return from Damascus.

One of the most perfectly preserved medieval cities in Lebanon, Tripoli was once a great centre of Arab learning, famous for its *madrassas*. Its library, said to have rivalled that of Alexandria, was burnt by the besieging armies of the First Crusade. Its coastal skyline was clustered with Mameluke mosques and minarets, curved archways and cupolas of medieval *khans* and marbled *hamams*.

This time, Hester was willing to stay within the confines of the Christian quarter, and rented most of the Capuchin monastery, while Meryon, Selim, Bertrand and the rest of her party stayed in a large house provided for them by the governor.

The French consul, Charles-Edmond Guys, heeding Talleyrand's direct-ive about Hester, dutifully reported her activities: her long rides around the massive, sand-hued ramparts of the city's Crusader fortress and into the surrounding countryside. In particular he marvelled at the impres-sive ease with which she was granted an audience with the governor, Mustafa 'Berber'Aga.[5]

The Porte considered Berber a dangerous upstart too popular to remove. The son of a mule driver, whose rise had been swift and brutal, he was now so fearful of assassination that he travelled with an armed guard of sixty men. He had a disconcerting habit of scanning the crowd with his piercing eyes: if he thought a person looked suspicious or guilty, he ordered them to be immediately seized and taken away to be summarily executed. Observing him at close range, Hester wrote: 'He [is] indeed a sanguinary tyrant,' and later observed: 'He made a noise sometimes like the low growl of a tiger, and his people knew that blood must flow . . . it was his custom, when the fit was upon him, to send for some poor wretch from prison and kill him with his own hand. He would then grow calm, smoke his pipe and seem for a time quieted. But he was a shrewd man and a clever pasha.'[6] By now Hester seems to have become as pragmatic and unsqueamish about gratuitous bloodletting as her father had been about the Jacobins in France.

'Odd people from all quarters' seemed to turn up in Tripoli, Hester noted. She collected one of the more intriguing ones, an Italian doctor, Balthazar Volpi, who had spent several years travelling in Syria, thinking him a useful recruit for what she now called her 'little family' of employees. The accusation levelled at Hester by Mariam Lascaris – that she paid men to gather information for her – was true enough. Volpi would return with her to Mar Elias and travel on her orders for the next three months; afterwards they could see what arrangement to come to. She now had five able-bodied, quick-witted and multi-lingual men working for her, not counting Meryon. What precisely did she have in mind?

Meryon offers an alternative insight into her thoughts at that time:

Lady Hester spoke to me of a plan, which she had been turning over in her mind, of forming an association of literary men and artists whom she proposed inviting from Europe for the purpose of prosecuting discoveries in every branch of knowledge, and of journeying over different parts of the Ottoman empire. In fact, she aimed at creating another Institute, like that which Buonoparte led with him to Egypt, of which she was to be head. Chimerical as such an undertaking would be for an individual, unless of great wealth, it must be allowed that a society so made up [could] combine all the requisites for thoroughly investigating the arts, sciences, statistics, geography and antiquities of a country unknown, like Syria. For a while, her mind was entirely engrossed in this new scheme.[7]

Perhaps memories of Miranda had brought back the old enthusiasm she had felt in his company for reshaping the world.

It was the prospect of looking for valuable manuscripts that drew her to visit a *madrassa* to see Sufi dervishes and to befriend their sheikh and chief theologian, Sultan Ibrahim. Locals nicknamed them 'white butterflies' for the way they whirled themselves into a trance with their rhythmic chanting. Whatever Sheikh Ibrahim told her about the main tenets of Sufism – of the hidden otherworldiness of life, of the possibility of transcendence and enlightenment – was enough to create a lasting fascination. She announced her intention to make herself a student of Sufi teachings, and as a demonstration of her goodwill, gave a generous donation to the *madrassa*, striking up an arrangement for a succession of dervishes to come to instruct her at Mar Elias over the coming months.* Soon, Hester would tell Meryon that the Sufis 'are all like my brothers'.[8]

When there was still no sign of Boutin, she decamped to a small Cistercian convent on a windswept headland a few miles from Tripoli, Deir Natour, 'Our Lady of the Watch'. Meryon noticed that Hester had been behaving oddly again. She was by turns expansive, wanting to talk about her new plan, then brooding and quick to go into another of her ferocious rages.

One morning he found her weeping, surrounded by opened letters from a packet that had just arrived. One letter from Vienna had stirred up long-buried pain. It was from Sir Sidney Smith, who told her he had seen both Bruce and Granville Leveson Gower at the Congress of Vienna. (Hester had told Bruce he must 'call upon Smith without loss of time – He will tell you whether I am right or wrong in some of my ideas'.) Hester must have imagined them both caught up in the extravagant celebrations, concerts, balls and soirées. Several months before she had toyed with the idea of going herself, as her instructions to Coutts indicated.

Meryon sat with her, afraid to touch her, but letting his hand rest on her shoulder. She broke down, wanting to talk. '[She] told me it was better that he should not write as they were much more comfortable

---

* Hester's offer was clearly highly unusual. There was no easy way to become an initiate; at the very least most Sufi disciples had to serve their master for three years, often undergoing all kinds of humiliations as well as intense study.

separate,' Meryon recalled, adding that Hester confided: 'Perhaps God does it to punish me. I have been as wicked as most people but Bruce's beauty is not like some I have loved. If you had seen Granville you would indeed have seen a beautiful man. He was beyond all other men I ever saw.'[9] Hester usually kept her own affairs very private. But that day she told Meryon of the suicide attempt she made shortly after the love affair with Granville; how he had broken her heart, and left her so that she did not care what happened to her. In any case, she made it clear that her present uncertainty and sadness were triggering painful memories. It was also her way of trying to explain her behaviour on the day they set off for Machmouche.

> When I have made up my mind to any thing, it costs me no longer any pain: it is whilst I am wavering. Thus it was when you left me last year. On the first night I was very much agitated but on the next day I was as tranquil as you see me here. So it was with Lord Granville. Had I thought he disliked me or was tired of me I could in a moment have resumed my firmness and tranquillity of mind, but it was because I saw him suffering that I too, became a martyr to my feelings. And even to this day if he happens to see any one who was intimate with me at the time of our intimacy together he turns pale and is ready to drop.[10]

What did Meryon say to comfort her? Hester must have felt desperate to confide in him. The thought of Granville coming face to face with Bruce unnerved her. But Meryon had no idea how her emotions were also bound up with Vincent Boutin, nor how her uncertainty over him contributed to her despair.

It is a very curious thing that while Hester craved a vital role in regional affairs, she appeared to spend the best part of the next six months rebuffing her cousin's repeated, vigorous offers to 'claim me for his own', as she put it. Of all men, Admiral Smith took her capabilities perfectly seriously. He now invited her to become his unofficial ambassador extraordinary, not just in Syria but in Africa too.

Smith had taken himself to the Congress determined to persuade the assembled politicians to put an end to the practice of enslaving Christians in Ottoman and Barbary territories. He was itching to invade Algiers, the traditional clearing house of captured European slaves, many of them women and girl-children sold into harems. Now he wanted to apply martial force to the campaign. To Hester's bemusement, 'Sir S.S.', as she called him, had been writing to many of his old friends in Syria to drum up their support, and he was, she noted, always 'thanking them for their civility to me'.

That summer, as part of Captain Forster's cargo, Smith had sent her 'some very long letters' and 'five hundred papers and bulletins' proclaiming his cause that he wanted her to circulate throughout Mount Lebanon and Syria. His plan was quite specific: to recruit Hester and let her do his work for him. She sent Barker one of Smith's letters, which she told him had to be 'seen to be believed'.

> He has therefore wildly taken it into his head to employ me as his agent and wants to send me to Barbary; after that to repair to Leghorn to meet him. He knows no one else to deal with semi-barbarous people but me – a fine compliment, you will say, but as I said before '*I will be no man's agent*'.[11]

First of all, Smith wanted her to use her friendship and influence with Emir Bashir to convince him to put together a contingent of soldiers for the military action he planned against the rulers of Barbary. He tried every kind of flattery: 'He calls me Queen and the Comet of the Desert,' she confided. Smith would have been appalled by what Hester had done with his precious bulletins. She made a bonfire of them, telling a startled Meryon that she would rather be 'first in [my] village, not second in Rome'. Then she sternly rebuked Smith for not sufficiently thinking his plan through, for she believed it could only result in a débâcle.

> Grant that the Emir Bashir has 1,500 men at his disposal and that he is ready to make them over to you – have you taken the right method of enlisting them? No. What you have proposed to be done will risk his head. Give troops to be at the disposal of a European power without the Sultan's leave through the Pasha of the district – a thing impossible!

How did he propose to fit them out, she asked? Surely he realized that he must make them wear 'Turkish colours?' she demanded. 'Otherwise you are making rebels of them and [ensuring that] no nation ever [has] to answer for them.'

For her time, Hester held remarkably progressive views. The passion and intensity with which she championed the Arabs she had befriended, her empathy and admiration for their way of life and her genuine belief in their importance and equivalence, went far beyond what might be seen as enlightened in the early nineteenth century. As a girl she had joined the boycott of West Indian sugar (and therefore cake and puddings) in support of the abolitionist movement. She had admired Wilberforce, and certainly seen a good deal of him during her years with Pitt (although probably not forgiven him for his censorious denunciation of her uncle during the scandal over embezzled navy funds in 1805). She declared herself an ardent follower of the Abbé Raynal, the philosopher and historian whose powerful humanist treatise about the economics of slavery made such a strong case for abolition that he was forced to flee into exile.* But she did not share Smith's crusading Christianity; if anything she poked fun at it, teasing him for wanting to make rescue missions to the harems of Algiers. 'Suppose the Turks were to take it into their heads to be scandalised by all the street walking ladies of England!'[12]

Although she admired and loved her cousin, Hester worried that at the highest levels, Smith was seen as a figure of fun. She confided to Barker that she thought his older, gauche, spendthrift wife had ruined his chances of a truly illustrious career. Not wanting to rebuff him altogether, she promised she would put his request to the Emir, and ponder on it a little herself, then see what could be done. 'We will suppose the plan to be a flexible one, and only argue the mode of execution,' she told him non-committally.

Yet Hester certainly used her cousin's name freely as she travelled, and

---

* The Abbé Raynal's book, *Histoire philosophique et politique des établissements et du commerce des Européens dans les deux Indes,* had apparently been a point of common enthusiasm and agreement between Hester and her father. The book had been written in collaboration with Diderot, and along with a book written by Lord Stanhope's great friend and correspondent Condorcet, *Réflexions sur l'esclavage des nègres,* and the Société des Amis des Noirs helped bring about abolition in France in 1794.

it brought her many friends. Her next visit was to a wealthy Druze noble-woman, Syt Habûs, who invited her to stay a few days at Choueifat, just outside Beirut. Syt Habûs had achieved what most would have held to be impossible: she was the only woman in the Druze kingdom – and perhaps the whole of Syria – to preside over the administration of her own and several neighbouring villages. She was also said to be a highly knowledgeable *akal*, initiated into the higher orders of Druze faith. They had been joined by Sheikh Jumblatt, who had not seen Hester since her illness, and from this time onwards, their friendship deepened.

News that the Kapugi Bashi demanded her presence in Sidon now reached Hester. The Kapugi Bashi, Dervish Mustafa Aga, was one of the Sultan's lieutenants, the military commander of the Janissaries, and a 'Lord of the Stirrup'.[13] In the structured Ottoman military hierarchy, the sudden appearance of such a man in the provinces usually meant only one thing: that the arrest – and certain death – of someone notable or powerful had been personally ordered by the Sultan. This time, it was soon known, up and down the coast, that it was Hester he had come to see, and that he had brought with him a troop of a hundred slave soldiers from the Barbary coast.

Hester's wish was granted precisely when she had lost all desire for it. A year after receiving her dispatch outlining her plan for the proposed dig, the Sultan gave her his blessing. The original manuscript was now to be examined by the Kapugi Bashi, who had orders to go ahead with the excavation if he was satisfied. On 28 January 1815, the Kapugi Bashi arrived at Mar Elias and was her guest for three days. His verdict on the manuscript's authenticity was positive. He now invested Hester with 'greater authority over the Turks than was probably ever granted even to any European ambassador,' placing himself under her command.[14] She was given *firmans* ordering the pashas of Acre and Damascus as well as all the governors in Syria to provide whatever assistance she might need. One of the three sites marked out on the manuscript was Sidon, and to the Kapugi Bashi it seemed the obvious place to start. But Hester was adamant that they start with Ascalon.

Though she had been away almost uninterruptedly since the previous summer, Hester would stay barely two weeks at Mar Elias. It seemed cramped and uncomfortable, her clothes took up almost one entire room. The garden was a mess. This twist in circumstances had caught her unawares, and she felt ill-prepared. Her finances were already stretched. Boutin had not come. All that had stood between her and departure from Syria was to finalize plans with James, who had obtained leave and was waiting for definitive instructions from her. Now that would have to wait.

She did not have much time to consider how the expedition was to be financed: while she dawdled, she knew the Sultan's men were waiting for her at Acre. She decided she must take the Sultan at his word, for the Kapugi Bashi relayed that '[he ] had already condescended to say that their obligation to me should the thing not succeed is the same as if it did'. The truth was she had no real guarantees from anyone. It was a critical misjudgement for a woman who considered herself a scrupulous planner.

Explaining that she had been bound to secrecy as to the reason for her important visitor, Hester wrote to Barker to tell him that she was about to mount an expedition and be away for several months, and that even though 'the Porte desire that it may cost me nothing' she anticipated she was going to need at least at least 12,000 piastres (about £650) which was going to be for 'public purposes' and for which she would have 'every right to reimbursement, as you will see when the affair is explained to you'.

Barker complied instantly, telling her that everyone in Aleppo was agog with gossip about what she might be up to. Most Arabs were convinced the Kapugi Bashi had come to accompany her to Jerusalem on some holy mission. His own guess was that she had taken it upon herself to prosecute 'some ancient *privi public* claim of Sir Sidney's' on the pashalik of Acre. Hester had written to Barker about the cautionary saga of Smith's ongoing battle with the government for reimbursement, 'because he could not produce bills like a tradesman' yet he had spent 'two thirds of his private fortune on its service'. *

---

* Hester had let a confidence slip to Barker about Smith's affairs, telling him: 'Poor Sir Sidney is totally *ruined* . . . his finances were not in a good way and during his absence his wife finished the business'. In one of his many confidential letters to Hester, her cousin confessed that he had only managed to scrape up the resources to go to Vienna by selling up his London household and was flat broke. Later, on St Helena, Napoleon would tell Las Casas that 'I am sorry I spoke ill of Smith. They tell me he is a good fellow. His government does not appreciate his services in Egypt and Syria.'

It was a state of affairs she had no intention of repeating. She told Barker that her mysterious mission 'will be an honour to me if it does not ruin me like Smith'. When she sent Meryon off on a rushed mission to Damascus to buy horses and everything that might be needed for the excavation, she gave him instructions that he spend no more than five thousand piastres, telling him that every expense for the excavation must be scrupulously noted and evidence retained for it. She added: 'I will then send in my bill to the government, by Mr Liston; when, if they refuse to pay me, I shall put it into the newspapers and expose them'. 'I will send in my bill to the government' was one of those phrases that stuck, to be repeated with amusement and derision.

In the middle of this new, perplexing development, Vincent Boutin surfaced unexpectedly, and his contact with Hester coincided with the few weeks that Meryon was away. Perhaps the Kapugi Bashi's arrival was an irresistible lure. Perhaps the hurt in her letters had touched him, and he realized that he had misinterpreted her impulse towards him. Or perhaps he wanted to confront her. Whatever happened, something took place to heal the earlier breach, and shift the nature of the relationship, which is reflected by a new tone when referring to him in her letters.

When Meryon returned from Damascus, he noticed that she looked serene and more youthful. The lines 'that mark a frown, a smile or a grin, and the workings of her mind were not visible in her lineaments'. She wore the look of 'serene calm, when she chose to disguise her feelings', he noted. She also told him she intended to buy a prize thoroughbred black stallion from Damascus, but would not say whom she intended to give it to.

One thing is certain. Before he left, Boutin trusted Hester enough to leave behind a large number of bags and possessions he would need for his onward journey; he obviously intended to return.

From this time on, Hester hinted strongly to several friends that she and Boutin had become at least as close as lovers, that she near-worshipped him. If she felt obliged to hide the relationship, assuming correctly that James – and especially Bruce – would be shocked by it, she did not bother to conceal that she enjoyed his company and admired him. She would tell Sir Joseph Banks that Boutin 'had neither the levity nor the flattering manner of a Frenchman, and was not the least handsome, but had a look which

242

seemed to embrace every object and seize every idea'. Her claim that she did not think much of his looks may well have been a deliberate ruse to defuse speculation they were lovers. To Bruce, who knew exactly what Boutin looked like, she was willing to say later that 'even if he had the form of a monkey, with such a mind' he would have still been remarkable. She thought he had both 'courage and resource . . . in the highest degree', and that for his 'talents and integrity he was a man in ten thousand'.

When Hester was happy, she became impatient for action. Suddenly she was overflowing with ideas and enthusiasm. Quite apart from her excavation, she wrote Barker a hurried, excited note saying she had some ideas for books and that she hoped they would command a tidy fee. One was to be all about Arab horses; this she intended Barker should draft up and then she would add her own flourishes. 'Let me have the rough copy and after that have it written out fair and pretty drawings made,' she told him, confident that the Duke of York would arrange for its printing. The other book was to be a collection of Arab folk tales that she intended to have translated and write up herself, and imagined a little illustrated book, perhaps called 'Abdallah' or 'The Damascus' or 'Syrian Story Teller', would 'fly about like wildfire', predicting that 'histories of this kind, with a few peeps into a harem when a husband is out, with a fine description of coffee cups, precious stones, and gold and silver stuff furniture, fountains, slaves and perfumes will enchant the *bon ton* and no fine lady or fop will be without [it]'.[15]*

She informed Barker that she intended to visit him soon to go over her manuscripts. No question about it: Hester was in good form.

On 15 February 1815 she set off for Acre, accompanied by the Kapugi Bashi's army, banners flying. On that same day, Boutin wrote a letter to his brother, a simple assurance, merely telling him he was well, that spring was 'beautiful' and he soon intended to return 'to the bosom of my country'. Everything about those two words – '*ma patrie*' – had so far defined his life. Whether he would pay the price for that love of country with his life will probably always remain a mystery.

\*   \*   \*

* Sir Richard Burton's translation of the Arabian Nights, when it came out in 1885, was an instant success.

This time the excited crowds welcoming Hester at Acre were enormous. There was a mood of curiosity and expectation. She was given royal honours, referred to as 'Her Felicity, the Emiry'. Men wore ceremonial *benysh* headdresses in her presence and made the traditional gesture of deference as they nodded in her direction, touching the tips of their fingers to their lips and kissing them, lowering their eyes.

But during the month she spent in Acre, she had plenty of time for doubts and worries. On the day before her thirty-ninth birthday, her spirits faltered. She had not heard from Boutin, and this time it seems, she had been very sure that she would.

She wrote Bruce an anguished letter from her room in the stone citadel – 'The pomp which surrounds me makes me low.' She was beginning to have misgivings about the treasure mission, but now felt there could be no turning back. Hayim, whose opinion she valued, raised a niggling doubt that others might have got to it first. She had heard from Sligo and others that Bruce intended to come for her, and she demanded he must not:

> All I entreat is, do not come near me. I fear so much meeting you again that I shall not go to Europe as I intended this year, when you have seen enough of the continent, it is then time for me to come there.[16]

She did not want to reveal what a gamble she was taking. The Kapugi Bashi had already intimated he expected a large payment, and offended her by asking her to give him Hanyfy. She had felt forced to offer him money instead of her slave-girl. (She wrote to Bruce that to give her 'to this man, who I know will make use of her for his own purposes on the road; it is a disgrace, I cannot do it'.) In the end, she would pay the Kapugi Bashi some £1,500 for the expedition, money that was largely forwarded to her by Barker and lent to her by Hayim.

Overall, the entourage swelled to some two hundred men, with 'two troop of horse, a division of Albanian infantry, tent-men, watermen, lamplights and all the extraneous retinue of an Eastern prince'. With her, she also had some trusted lieutenants of her own choosing: Selim's father, Malem Musa Koblan, but not Selim himself (whose company she had decided was too risqué); Catafago, the Austrian consul and her one-time host at Nazareth, and the now-returned Giorgio as her dragoman. Süleyman Pasha provided twenty more tents, to add to her six from Cairo. The one reserved for her was a vast double tent, green on the outside, studded with gold flowers and stars. She was given the Pasha's private *takhterwàn*, a gaudy palanquin covered in crimson cloth, with six gilded globes, which glittered in the sun like nineteenth-century versions of mirrored balls, dangling in front, as though to amuse a bored child. Hester refused to be carried in it, and rode her mule.

She made a great show of respecting her Muslim hosts, making a rule that none of her party could drink wine. For the first time since she had been up in the Kadisha Valley, she veiled herself and ordered Ann Fry to do the same. She behaved like one under surveillance, knowing her letters were read. 'My zeal for the services of the Sultan, my master, has induced me to leave my convent in the season of storms . . .' she wrote in one such deliberate display of allegiance, typical of most of her letters to England while she was on the road that month.[17] Hester was capable of writing one thing while intending quite another, when she saw fit.

At midnight on 18 March, a stranger arrived at their camp, demanding that Hester see him. An Italian dressed in a British naval uniform introduced himself as Don Thomaso Coschich, special envoy to Admiral Smith. He had come all the way from Vienna to present her with a sheaf of private dispatches, with an offer Smith was certain she could not refuse.

In a letter dated 8 December 1814 Smith told her that all his hopes rested with her. His plan for action against the Barbary States had been submitted to the emperors of Russia and Austria, to the King of Prussia and Talleyrand, 'who all thought highly of it,' he told her. To her astonishment he informed her that Emir Bashir's word had been secured by the freelance 'Mr Fiott' (the same Mr Fiott who had accompanied her cousin Wynne to Palmyra, and travelled with her and Bruce to the Pyramids). Now the 'Emperor of Morocco' was also in accord, but as for the new Dey of Tunis, he hoped she could make a journey on his behalf 'to see what sort of man he is'. He hoped in any case to rely on her persuasiveness and charm in delivering his private letter and presents to the Emir. Afterwards, he promised, the *Undaunted*, the same frigate that had carried Napoleon to Elba, would come for her, and she could then sail to Tunis and return to Italy. When all that was done, Smith told her that he and his family hoped to welcome 'dearest Hester' very soon.

The next morning, Hester ordered a temporary halt in order to deal with this new crisis. She had Coschich wait as she drank coffee and pored over Smith's letters in her tent, breaking the seal of every one. As she reached the main part of his letter to the Emir, she snorted at his obtuseness:

> Mr Fiott, an English gentleman, has informed me that you are ready to furnish me with 1,500 men. I just now have occasion for them, to subjugate the Barbaresque pirates who impede the transmission of corn from Egypt to Christendom; so Captain Ismael, Mahomet Ali's envoy to Malta, told me. I have enclosed a black cloak for yourself or for the officer you may choose to appoint Commander of your Troops.

Hester was astonished to see that there was no mention of how Smith or the British government intended to finance the borrowed army. She looked with dismay and some distaste over the presents Smith had sent: ornate but battered Persian pistols for his old friend Abu Ghosh, a dressing box for Emir Bashir's wife, a King James Bible for the public library in Jerusalem, a portrait of the Pope to grace the Holy Sepulchre, and a black satin *abah* emblazoned with Smith's crest. 'He seems to have known as little of the dress of the country as he did of its politics,' she fumed. 'A satin *abah* could be no more worn by a man in Syria than a pair of chintz breeches by a man in England.'[18] As for the pistols, she knew that the only weapons worthy as gifts 'for any Turk or Arab' had to be English-made, preferably brand-new.

Although she was careful to be polite, her reply to Smith revealed her anger. She felt he had acted presumptuously without realizing the implications of what he was asking. It was unthinkable, she told him, to assume he could co-opt the ruler of one small province into war on another, when they were both part of the same empire. 'Such a thing could only be done by direct application to the Sultan,' she advised (although again, she knew the letter would be read). She also told him that in her opinion, although the Druze army 'would fight well on their own dunghill' they had never travelled. There were other complications, too. With a large number of his troops gone, the Emir would leave himself unprotected. He had powerful enemies. 'Take care how you sink that which you have gained [here],' she told Smith. As for his suggestion that she leave Syria on the *Undaunted*, she would not do it, she insisted.

She had other reasons to feel annoyed. Hayim soon informed her that when Coschich arrived at Acre, he had not only exaggerated the urgency of his mission, which was 'to convey Lady Hester to a place of safety', but also openly speculated that 'a declaration of war between Russia and Turkey, in which England would take part' might be in the offing. (That January, when the Congress of Vienna looked close to collapse, Castlereagh had secretly agreed to side with Metternich and Talleyrand against Russia and Prussia, who were determined to claim vast portions of territory.) As a diplomatic envoy Coschich proved himself to be as spectacularly indiscreet as Smith himself.

Hester's actions indicate a degree of fear. To avoid any suggestion of her own complicity, she laid the matter before the Kapugi Bashi and showed him all the letters – Smith's, her replies and her letter to Barker – 'in order to set his mind at ease on a subject which would otherwise have excited a multitude of suspicions'. Had she said nothing, she reasoned, he would have had every reason to think her 'an emissary or a spy'.

As she explained to Barker: 'What a business Sir S. was nearly making! And what a scrape he might have got Mr Liston and me into.' She had no alternative, she added, but to submit to 'the propriety of stating to the Duke of York the *whole* of the affairs in which I am now concerned'. She told Barker not to forward her any more of Smith's letters. As soon as Hester felt she could write more freely to Barker, she was more explicit. 'I am very angry with Sir Sidney yet I have been laying my *ground* to save him. In 20 or 30 days the Tartar sent to Liston will return, we shall then know his pleasure.'[19]

Hester's quick judgement was soon borne out. In unequivocal terms, the Pasha of Acre soon informed her that if Emir Bashir had gone along with such a plan, he would have felt duty-bound to mount an operation against it. Hester could soon justifiably congratulate herself on acting 'with profound *policy*' and saving 'I may say the Emir's head, *a war with the Pacha*, and every other sort of evil owing to one of Sir S's imprudent freaks'.[20]

Although his contemporaries were not always so complimentary, Smith's inventive approach to warfare, especially through espionage and clandestine operations, would one day be credited with inspiring the work of the Secret Intelligence Service and the Special Operations Executive in the Second World War.[21] That Smith actively sought Hester's advice, and would continue to ask for it, tells us a great deal about his opinion of her acumen.

# 15

## The Broken Statue

Hester reached Ascalon on April Fools' Day, an apt day for fools' gold. At Jaffa the governor, Muhammad Aga Aby Nabut, joined her entourage, which she accepted in the spirit of unity, even though she found him personally despicable. A small tented city went up at El Jura, just outside Ascalon's walls. Word went out to the surrounding villages for men to work the site, to be paid 150 piastres a day, with three meals provided. Overnight, a hundred applicants turned up.

To separate themselves from the rabble, Hester and Ann Fry, barely recognizable behind their veils, decamped to two cottages in the evenings. By day, Hester issued commandments from a tent by the site. Hester had heard Sligo talk all about his amateur excavations, and absorbed some of his observations, mostly about how to keep the workers well fed and protected from the sun. When they arrived at Ascalon, she and all her new 'lieutenants' rode all around the ruined fortress which was enclosed within two miles of walls, scrutinizing the map and comparing it with what they saw. The ruins had been stripped of all marble and stone, plundered by Djezzar to rebuild his city after the siege of Acre. Hester was dispirited to find that all around the site where they judged the treasure might be – near the wall, in the southeast corner – the earth showed signs of earlier disturbance.

Having studied the topography of the site, she identified a set of columns near a semi-circular wall, as described in her manuscript. She used no particular method; she simply ordered the men to dig. Human skulls and bones, broken marble pillars, Corinthian capitals, delicate shards of pottery, phials and vases were all unearthed, as they searched for the hidden treasure. After a week of digging, a cry went up. A mutilated but extremely fine statue of a headless man was found, almost seven feet high, its limbs hacked off on one side. Its shoulders bore the symbol of a thunderbolt, and its breastplate was decorated with Medusa's head, placed on the goddess Athena's shield. Hester gazed at the exquisite statue, and at the long-haired monster with its terrifying eye. The statue was of Serapis, widely worshipped at the time of Alexander the Great, alongside Zeus, Jupiter and Dionysus, and believed to be an incarnation of Osiris.

On the ninth day fresh hope was raised when the underground crypt marked on the treasure manuscript was found. An 'extraordinary kind of trough' was uncovered, too small to contain remains, and as Meryon put it, 'fit for no purpose easily conceivable except for hiding treasure'. But the lid had been broken off. It was empty. It was difficult to tell when it had been disturbed, but Hester was increasingly convinced that it may have been the real object of Djezzar's wholesale plundering of the site. Nor could she reject the possibility that some other person, who pretended innocence, might have found it more recently. For the first time, Hester heard the rumour that the detested Muhammad Aga Aby had paid a recent visit to the site. By now Hester had begun to wonder whether the entire venture had been deliberately engineered to embarrass her.

She ordered the beautiful statue, the first artifact of its kind ever excavated in the Holy Land, to be shattered, and thrown into the sea, 'precisely', she later explained, so that 'such a report may not get abroad and I lose with the Porte all the merit of disinterestedness'. Although it seemed a gratuitously destructive act, for Hester it was a calculated tactic to appear oblivious to personal gain. To Barker, she referred to the destruction as the 'crime I have committed'. With some defensiveness, she later claimed to Oakes and others that she thought it crucial to show she was not seeking 'trophies for my countrymen'. She felt herself, as Meryon put it, surrounded by 'the surmises of doubting minds and the malicious reports of evil-disposed ones'.

The tented city was dismantled and the excavation abandoned. By 17 April they were back at Jaffa, where a desultory search was made at one

of the other sites marked for treasure, Awgy.* But this too proved disappointing.

Another visitor had sought her out on her ill-fated treasure hunt and he
would soon become an inmate of her house. Meryon described him as
'around sixty, grizzled, uncombed, very dirty', dressed in 'a long threadbare Spanish cloak' with a Bible gripped tightly under his one good arm.

Pierre Loustaunau had been a military freebooter in India for almost
twenty years, first fighting against the East India Company for Ranjit
Singh, then with the Marathas. He claimed that Tipu Sultan had made
him one of his generals, and that he had won, and lost, a fortune in
precious stones. At the age of fifty-eight he had left his family in the
Pyrenees, with a view to making another fortune in India. But he had
instead lost everything in a shipwreck off the coast of Palestine. Now he
wandered about, much like an Indian sadhu or holy man, claiming that
his brush with death had given him the gift of seeing the future.

Hester's first impulse to dismiss him as a madman was stayed by two
things. Firstly she had a taste for strange-fated Frenchmen with detailed
and unusual histories to relate, and secondly, she could not help but be
intrigued by his boast of prophecy. He had addressed her as 'la Reine',
telling her he assumed she was on her way to Jerusalem, where, he intimated, her future audience with the Almighty awaited. He told her he
had charted her arrival and read her what he said were relevant passages
from his dog-eared Bible. He was no penniless vagabond, he told her,
but 'a noble traveller' who wanted to place himself at her service. He
urged her to believe him: Napoleon had escaped from Elba, and soon
the world would see great and terrible events unfolding, and she must
play her part.

It was indeed true that Napoleon had sailed away from Elba on 26
February, arriving near Antibes two days later. Either the lugubrious
Loustaunau did indeed have the gift of foreseeing, or more likely, he was
craftily guarding the news Europe already knew. It is by no means implaus-
ible that the old general picked up this rumour fresh off the Jaffa seafront;

---

* This site, about twelve miles northeast of Jaffa, was called el-Khurby and would reveal, in an
excavation more than a century later, the remains of a Philistine city.

yet the news was not otherwise reported in Syria for some weeks. Hester found him too intriguing to dismiss, and had told him he was welcome to come to Mar Elias when she returned.

It was not long before more news was relayed from Europe: Louis XVIII had fled, Napoleon was back in Paris and war was about to break out once again.

'I would rather live in the East in a blue shift than in England with all the vulgar unnatural comforts of what is called a fireside. It is not affectation but to my taste I think England one of the most disagreeable countries I ever was in.'[1]

These were fighting words. But Hester was once again uncertain what she should do. She lingered in Acre, in no hurry to return. It seems likely she had some kind of communiqué from Boutin. Despite the disastrous expedition, her letters show her to be in a suddenly optimistic, expansive mood.

She had turned her mind to another potential career prospect. Five years earlier, she had talked with the Quakers, Joseph Fox and William Allen, about the prospect of establishing a Lancaster school in Venezuela. Since then, Fox had written to her twice to ask after her plans, and at her request, Allen had kept her informed of the progress of the Royal Lancasterian Society.[2] Now she finally wrote a much-delayed reply, telling Fox she believed she was in an ideal position to consider establishing a school herself. She had not decided where she might go, she told him, but 'in the Sultans dominions, I have been universally well received, and have had every advantage which belongs to both Man and Woman, having sometimes passed for one, sometimes the other'.[3] In due time, she intended to send him 'my Plans for extending The Lancaster mode of Education in the East'.[4]

Hester knew that one of Lancaster's main beliefs was to provide a non-sectarian, broadly Christian, education.* Fox was probably rather bemused by her dismissive attitude:

---

* Despite her own decidedly patchy formal education, Hester had evidently impressed Fox as being a strong believer in Lancaster's principles of mass education, and also that girls should be encouraged into the classroom.

The superstitions of the Christians and their want of principle is quite terrible; interest is their God, tho' they talk eternally of our Saviour. With such examples how can youth turn out well? – therefore I am more indulgent towards young sinners than I should otherwise be.[5]

She had also set herself to work for Sir Joseph Banks, who had pronounced himself 'charmed' by her letters and pressed her to send him samples and descriptions of Middle Eastern remedies.* She enthused about the ease with which it was possible to grow the Mandragora plant – to make the drink Cleopatra had supposedly concocted – and described its strange scent. She told him that at Acre she had come across a wonderful 'uplifting medicine' used by the Sultan and all the Pashas, and 'unknown in Europe'. The recipe 'cost me £40 in presents and a great amount of flattery, and the promise of several sorts of English cheese,' she told him, and enclosed Hermodactylus leaves, roots and flowers, and a powder she had prepared for him to mix into a paste. She forwarded him a long, highly detailed treatise on the plant, almost certainly adapted as a dictation from Süleyman Pasha's chief physician, which she offered as a foretaste of her proposed dictionary of plants. Throughout Egypt and Syria, she told him, Hermodactylus was used for 'affections of the brain and joints of phlegmatic constitutions'; 'mixed with aloes, it cures the pain in the thigh'. She added that 'with ginger and pepper it is a strong stimulant to the Sport of Love, exciting sexual activity, infused in milk and taken as a draught, it increases the secretion of semen: mixed thoroughly with saffron and eggs and applied externally it cures painful inflammation of the bones.' Hermodactylus, she told Banks straight-facedly, 'might also prove useful in the government, as its effects are wonderful'.[6]

---

* Evidently Banks had asked her opinion about how to treat his painful gout, knowing how closely she had monitored Pitt's health. Turkish and Arabic doctors were worse than useless on the subject, she told him: 'None of them know the meaning of gout'. Only one Turk she had ever met had it, Mully Ismail – who 'drank very hard'. She suggested he 'live like a Turk for a time' and 'get out the way of great dinners' and take 'plenty of exercise without heating, and to live a great deal in the open air'. It would be best, she insisted, if he converted a room in his house into a Turkish bath and set himself a regime of regular massages. Hester made it clear that on this subject of the *hamam*, she was an expert. 'If you should wish for a compleat treatise upon Turkish bathing I will make one out for you.'

Hester had by now consoled herself over the missing gold, and her self-confidence did not appear to be dented. Had she not succeeded in bewitching the reluctant Boutin, the most stubborn of all her sovereign subjects?

She was able to send her packets, boxes and letters on a British frigate. She decided to send Giorgio to London as her agent. Soon, dressed in new English clothes, he would swagger down Jermyn Street, carrying out her orders and enjoying making a show of exaggerated deference to the ladies. He had orders to carry out what she called her 'commissions' and she wanted Fox to arrange for him 'to attend some of Joseph Lancaster's lectures' so that he could report back in detail. He was also to find a replacement for Meryon, who had asked to return to his studies and his family.

She was anxious to stockpile gifts, and she knew exactly what was needed. Giorgio was to buy 'all sorts of cheap trinkets, very pretty, as well as silver gilt snuff boxes and mock stone necklaces etc'. He was to obtain 'the best little painting box' available 'for Monsieur Vincent, painter to the Queen of Palmyra,' she wrote in a playful reference to Boutin.[7] In addition:

A print of horses for Selim and coloured prints (not good quality) or cheap watercolour drawings of women and English soldiers on horse-back and a print of the Duke of York on horseback for Amin Bey put into a frame. English gunpowder for Ahmed Bey and Amin Bey. Large green fans for the sun . . . and some handsomer ones for the Jewish wives . . . I should also like to have a book about Stowe for Mr Barker and a butterfly executed by Randell & Bridge in fake stones for his wife to wear in her hair.[8]

Giorgio was also to be taught to sing 'the Duke of York's march' and 'the March in Bluebeard' so that he could amuse her circle when he returned.

That summer her friends in Malta and London would open her distinctive wax seal and be charmed and amused by her presents: tiger skins for their saddles, perfumes, daggers and glass from Damascus, cases of 'Meshmushy' wine, pots of aromatic honey, Druze, Bedouin and Turkish clothes, and 'boxes of soap like that used by the Sultan's women' from Tripoli. To her relative General Richard Grenville she sent a beautiful white goat, one that had been wild and grazed 'upon aromatic herbs which can certainly have some effect on its blood', whose milk, she promised him, would help his illness. She could not bring herself to write to Bruce, but instead wrapped several fine Damascus swords in a bolt of cloth for him.

She sent Lord Lonsdale a gift as a mark of gratitude for his generosity at a time when she had needed it, nine years before: a beautiful Egyptian statue, a fragment from the masonry of a temple.[9] It came from Byblos, and was of the unveiled Isis, on her knees, bending towards an altar.

When Hester heard the news that Napoleon was once again ruling France, she must have wanted to speed the news to Boutin but if she sent any letters, there is no trace of them. Instead, there is every possibility that soon after this news reached him, he let her know he intended to see her again, for at this moment she changed her plans. She had been preparing to leave again for Tripoli and Antioch, but she now stayed. As for Boutin, if he heard the news that Napoleon was back in Paris, with Fouché reinstalled, he might safely assume that his orders remained in place.

Hester was distracted to learn that two Abyssinians (or 'Habashees' as she would call the Ethiopians) had sought refuge at the Monastery of Deir-el-Moukhalles, much to the consternation of the priests. They were from Tigray, in the north of Abyssinia, and they had been attempting a pilgrimage to Jerusalem. The beauty of the Ethiopian woman proved too unsettling for the priests, despite the fact that the monastery offered shelter to women in a small convent within its grounds. 'Knowing that she would be very uncomfortable there, I have taken her and her brother to reside with me as long as I remain in this country, which seems to make them very happy,' Hester wrote.

Hester felt an affinity with them. 'Like me they were shipwrecked . . . and lost all their property,' she told Banks. In fact they were not brother and sister, but lovers who kept up the pretence so they could be together. Hester was sympathetic. The woman, Turinge, had left her husband and two children behind in Tigray; she was the sister of two important provincial governors.[10] Hester sat with them, communicating in Arabic and what little Amharic they managed to teach her. She was touched by how gracious they remained despite their adversity, and by the unshakeable power of their belief.

She thought Turinge's lover Musa 'a very intelligent man'. He showed her 'a little New Testament in his own language, written upon Gazelle's skin' and told her tales about wars waged in Abyssinia that she found 'beautiful, although too savage'. On their behalf, she wrote to Lord Valentia, who had undertaken an expedition to Abyssinia and written a book on the country, hoping to interest him in their plight.[11]

She hoped Boutin might return to see her beloved eyrie at Machmouche. She rented three cottages that summer, instead of her usual two, excited at the prospect of 'wandering among the rocks and precipices and in beholding the beautiful and magnificent views'. She took the black stallion she intended for him. She called him Aba El Hastar – 'Slave of thy Will'.

Turinge and Musa were preparing to return to Abyssinia – with money, provisions and horses supplied by Hester – but they wanted to wait until after the heat of summer. A grateful Turinge promised gifts of horses and sky-coloured robes from Tigray, even expressing the wish that Hester educate her own children. Having gained their complete confidence and questioned them in detail, Hester concluded that there was far more information to be gained than that contained in Lord Valentia's travel book, which was then the only source of information about that country for the Western world. She hoped Musa might prove 'a sort of Arabic dragoman, a confidential person to accompany any future enterprising person who might visit that country'.

In fact, she had decided that person would be her and that Abyssinia would be her next project.

The first sign that something terrible had happened to Boutin might have been easily missed. A silver watch made in Paris did not turn up every day in the Damascus souk. The one which surfaced some time in July 1815 had a particularly bloody story to tell; it is a measure of how effective her spy network could be that she heard of its presence at all. When, months later, Hester finally held his watch in her hands she knew with absolute certainty that he was dead.

The imaginings started then. She tormented herself, wondering whether in the last moments of his life he knew he was about to die, imagining the swift upward thrust of a dagger beneath his ribs, or worse, if he had been set upon from behind, his throat sliced like an animal. When she shut her eyes, the horrific images multiplied. In her dreams, she sought his face, but saw only his headless body.

First she alerted all the French consuls in Syria – and the ambassador in Constantinople – but was disgusted to find they had no plans to investigate further. 'Had a dog been massacred, all the European consuls could not have shown more apathy than they did,' she would say.[12] She made a forceful appeal to both Süleyman Pasha and Mustafa Berber, arguing that if her friend's death went unavenged, the murder would set a precedent, and no European traveller, including herself, would be safe in Syria. At the same time, Hester acted on her own initiative and sent four of her men, Pierre, Beaudin, Volpi and one of her Druze horsemen, disguised as poor itinerants 'at the risk of their lives, to go into different parts of those horrible mountains to ascertain facts I wished to be got at,' and had to 'bribe them pretty high'.

A year later Hester would tell Ambroise Firmin Didot, a diplomat from Constantinople, that Boutin had left her house at Mar Elias 'a few days before he was assassinated'. Given the mysterious circumstances of his death, her assertion is a vital piece of evidence. If this was true, then she was referring to some time during late May and early June 1815.

The possibility of her complicity in his murder has preoccupied at least one of Boutin's biographers. Perhaps her use of the term 'a few days' was an elastic one; she was never cross-examined. The thought that she might have had Boutin killed in a jealous pique perhaps, or as a way of striking against the enemy, is intriguing. What if, for example, he repudiated or mocked her, and her obsession with him hardened into hatred? We can never entirely know the truth about the last time they saw each other alive. But nothing in Hester's behaviour or her letters suggests anything other than her devastation and bitterness at having him snatched away.

At Mar Elias the sight of his bags, some containing carefully marked-up antiquities, his heavier clothes, his drawing equipment, and his glasses, was unendurable for Hester. Overcome by remorse, she felt somehow responsible for his death.

Her mind filled with images of him. Amongst the things he had left behind she found a locket, with a tress of golden hair and a carefully-folded love letter. But now his ghost seemed to belong to her as much as to anyone else.

How long did it take for her to discover the truth? Each of her four men gave her slightly different accounts. What is certain is that Boutin's ill-fated journey began in Hamah, at least a week's travel from Mar Elias. An undated letter from there informed Henri Guys, the French consul in Latakia, to expect him soon, and that he intended to travel through the Jesr al-Shurghur pass, directly through Alawi and Isma'ili country.

After spending the night at the ruined fortress of Shaizir, Boutin and his Egyptian dragoman Ali vanished. 'Despite all the advice given to him at Hamah, he was determined to make this crossing and see the country with his own eyes,' Hester would later say.

Another account places Boutin in Tripoli three weeks before he ventured into the mountains, and claims that he had visited Mustafa Berber at Hester's urging, and offended the governor by turning down his offer of an escort.[13]

As with any murder investigation, suspicion falls upon anyone who might have had a motive. Who might have leaked information about Boutin's intended route and the contents of his luggage? Somehow a rumour spread that he had with him a bag of commemorative coins from Napoleon's Egypt campaign, which was never recovered. But what kind of spy would make himself such an obvious target? Curiously, just as Boutin's trail went cold, Lascaris turned up in Syria again. Might he have played a part in Boutin's death?

From Tripoli the consul Charles-Edmond Guys informed his uncle in Aleppo that Lascaris had been apparently sighted in Hamah, that he planned to go to Jerusalem, or to return to Piedmont, the place of his birth. Guys relayed the same information to Talleyrand, adding that Mustafa Berber had launched a search for Boutin's killers and that Hester had instigated this turn of events, and that it was quite clear to him that she had formed 'un grand attachement' to Boutin. In other words, he had no doubt that they were lovers.[14]

One by one, her men returned, and at last Hester learnt what had happened to her missing Frenchman. Their accounts of Boutin's last moments she found so horrifying that she said her 'fortitude would have been insufficient to have borne me through the business, had I not reflected, that in me, and me only, rested the power of revenge'.[15]

The remains of Boutin and his dragoman were found between Beirut and Byblos, near the river of Nahr al-Kelb, outside a small village in the flanks of the steep mountains above coastal Jounieh. They had been beheaded, their bodies cut into pieces and scattered. However, further north, near the village of El-Blatta, a confession was extracted from a woman under threat of torture by Mustafa Berber's henchmen. She claimed that the men had in fact been set upon on their way towards the port town of Jeble, as they made their way down from the mountain fortress of Margat (Qalaat al-Marqab). This was Alawi country, but the surrounding valley was controlled by the Isma'ilis. The implication was that the perpetrators intended to shift the blame for the murders outside their territory.[16] The woman's claim that the murderers were motivated by simple robbery was never contested.

It is easy to guess why Boutin might have wanted to see Margat, the so-called Castle of the Watchtower, one of the most impressive of the Syrian fortresses. It had been rebuilt by the Knights Hospitallers using French-inspired architectural techniques. (T.E. Lawrence would later say it resembled 'an unrestored Carcassonne'.) It was to Margat that Richard the Lionheart came when he arrived in Syria to begin the Third Crusade. Bruce had been curious to see this fortress too. When Hester later told Bruce of Boutin's murder she would remind him that before he left her in Latakia, she had pleaded 'with tears in my eyes' for him to keep well away. 'When I entreated you not [to go] . . . you scolded me.'[17] She gave Boutin the same warning. But soon, she herself would return to those same mountains, taking the black stallion, El Hastar. She wanted to be close to where he had been, and ride where he had ridden.

# 16
## Renenge

News of Waterloo reached her in August. She opened every letter that came her way 'with great emotion', dreading what news it might contain about James. Anxiously, she scanned the names of the wounded and dead in the *Gazette*, only to find that in some cases, cruel errors were made about some of James's closest friends. It would be several months before she learnt that James was safe and in Paris. Almost to her own surprise, she confessed to feeling a tremulous 'attachment' for Wellington, for not pretending 'to disguise that our loss is excessive'. Peace had been achieved: the wars with France had lasted almost uninterruptedly for twenty-two years.

She wanted to defend the losing side. She told Barker that his jubilant letters about the British victory and the Allies' behaviour concerning France '[make] me low-spirited and furious'. She felt intensely bitter towards Napoleon. Why, she asked, had they not 'at once put an end to a man who has cost us lives of thousands and tens of thousands, and who has brought our resources to the lowest ebb'.

She felt 'excessively upset by all the empty bigwigs who have arranged things so ill upon the Continent'. If it had been her grandfather she thought at least he 'would have humbled France in the way she deserved'.

France was offered a treaty no nation ought to have signed and no honourable one ought to have tendered. England had everything in her power. The strong ought to be magnanimous. The weak only are unjust and cruel and willing to take every undue advantage over a fallen enemy.

Unable to bear the rabble of her household at Mar Elias, she made a journey to Beit Eddine, taking up the Emir's standing invitation to be his guest. After the usual pleasantries, he invited her to take coffee in one of his many chambers, the air heavy with the scent of cedarwood, the shutters drawn against harsh daylight. For the first time she found him distant. She told him both about the Barkers' sad loss and Admiral Smith's 'private situation', the debts he had already incurred in his enthusiasm to go ahead with his Algerian plan. She miscalculated. The stories the Emir had heard about her friendships with Bedouin sheikhs and rebel generals, but especially reports of her growing friendship with Sheikh Jumblatt, did not please him. He stared at her with a complete absence of emotion, and in that moment she sensed that there was nothing about their apparent friendship she could take for granted.

Whatever the circumstances of Boutin's murder, it created a dilemma for the three pashas who divided this mountainous territory between them. In Tripoli Berber needed little excuse to mount an attack on two communities he regarded as both heretics and potential insurgents, but his willingness to put himself at Hester's service was not shared in Acre or Damascus. Still, despite warnings that the guilty men must give themselves up or the entire population would be punished, no one put themselves forward.

In a remarkable feat of arm-twisting, with many letters to Malem Hayim, Hester threatened she would appeal directly to the Sultan himself if necessary. Finally Süleyman Pasha promised he might consider taking action the following spring. He told Hester she must be patient and trust his word. In the meantime, Hester laid her plans carefully, and fumed at Barker. 'Why will you Consuls restrain me from a natural impulse of revenge?'

At the height of summer, she sent Meryon to Egypt. The British consul in Alexandria, Misset, whose health was fast collapsing, had asked for him, and she had agreed that the doctor could amuse himself a little by travelling afterwards.

By coincidence Burckhardt had also pitched up at Misset's, just returned from his adventures in Arabia. He had achieved the impressive feat of penetrating Mecca and Medina, and gone into the Hijaz. He too had survived the plague, which had permanently weakened him.

After some wine was drunk, the men were in a bantering mood.

Burckhardt could not resist trying to prod Meryon into making indiscreet revelations about 'Queen Zenobia'. How could he put up with such a capricious and demanding woman? Blushing, Meryon admitted to a 'profound adoration', then cursed his use of language. (The truth was that although he might have once had certain fancies, he no longer thought about Hester as an object of lust or attainment.) Burckhardt jeered. What of other men who had tried to get into her bed since Bruce? Might they all expect to end up like Boutin, at the bottom of a gully? It was cruel, malicious – perhaps jealous – talk. Burckhardt admitted later that he went too far and was 'very free' in his comments about Hester, but then, he confided to a fellow traveller, she really did think too highly of herself and 'had more foibles than a lady in men's clothes should be guilty of'.[1]

Having taken up the opportunity to travel with Burckhardt, Meryon would scrupulously report 'every word' back to Hester; this soon earned him Burckhardt's lasting scorn.

Meryon was still in Egypt seven weeks later when Hester's man Beaudin turned up with the news that Hester had sent him in a great hurry to secure Boutin's property which was 'in deposit' in Cairo, before the news confirming the Frenchman's death could reach the French consul. Hester undoubtedly hoped to find valuable secrets, and was prepared to go to extraordinary lengths to get to them first. Was this the act of a possessive lover or a scheming rival? Beaudin also had a cryptic message from Hester: 'Find out about the Brotherhood of Luxor'. Hester had discovered something she thought was an important clue to Boutin's death, but she was biding her time.

Judging by Meryon's response, he thought Hester's efforts on Boutin's behalf were too vigorous. The rumour that they had been lovers was being widely bruited about, and he urged her not to intervene, telling her that 'the French consuls were bound to sift it to the bottom'. As a result, he noted that 'the only effect of my exhortation was that she never said anything more of the matter to me'.

When at last she had them, Hester contemplated Vincent Boutin's belongings laid out on her floor. No doubt she read through his notebooks, looked at his sketches and paintings and examined the ancient papyrus scrolls he had brought back, some of which threatened to disintegrate into dust at a touch.

Boutin had a collector's eye. There was a magnificent basalt head of a woman, her eyes half-closed and feline. Hester ran her fingers over a great many stones chiselled with impenetrable symbols; shells from the Red Sea; billowy white ostrich feathers; she picked up each object as though it might be charged with some hidden message. There were Egyptian statuettes, scarabs, hieroglyphs, reliquaries and amulets; Coptic crosses; ornate Arabian swords inlaid with jasper and gold, ancient Greek and Roman coins, cornelian and agate. When she came across a gold bracelet bearing a delicate pattern of horses, her eyes filled with tears.[2]

All this Hester sent on to Boutin's brother, Joseph, via Constantin Guys in Aleppo, including a bag filled with pieces of gold, which she always claimed she resolutely did not touch. As for his maps and notes, all that is known is that she later informed Joseph Boutin that '12 or 13 packets of papers' had been sent to the French government. There is no record of Vincent Boutin's bodily remains being returned home, nor of a burial in Syria. The possibility remains that what was left of his body was given to Hester, at her request.

Another mysterious tragedy took place. Musa – Turinge's lover – returned to Mar Elias, leading a riderless horse. The couple had left at the end of summer, and been gone only a matter of weeks. All Hester would say about it was that Turinge had 'died upon the road'. If Turinge had died of a fever, surely Musa would have told her, but it is probable that his lover's beauty was her undoing. If they had been attacked, and she had been raped, this alone might explain his unwillingness to mention the details. Of her death itself, Musa would say nothing, only shake his head, as though it was too awful to relate.

At first Musa insisted on camping within the grounds; later he resumed sleeping in the room he had shared with Turinge. The spell of peace and the charm they had seemed to bring with them had been replaced by a terrible oppressiveness.

At the first hint of winter, Hester wrote of her turmoil to Sir Joseph Banks. She could not restrain herself from giving him a long description of how remarkable the Frenchman had been. Boutin was 'a philosopher and a philanthropist, and a great writer' and 'had he but lived to have published his travels, those of *other* travellers would have ceased to be read,' she said, in a deliberate dig at Burckhardt.

> His death has excessively affected me for we were great friends! Nobody knew him in this country, not even the French, for they were not the sort of characters to please him, his silence generally offended people extremely, and they chose to fancy him ignorant because he never talked of himself, and stupid because he did not listen with interest to a pack of stuff called by some people information . . . Such a character must be a severe loss to his friends, and to his country, which he loved from the bottom of his heart.[3]

She mentioned to Banks that Burckhardt had asked her in one of his recent letters 'by what magic principle' she had succeeded in winning such influence with the 'proud Moslims of Syria'. She made it quite clear what she intended to do, adding, 'He may now ask how I prevailed upon them to set fire to the haunts of these ferocious people and to cover the mountains with troops and to revenge the death of this poor man in a way hitherto quite unprecedented.'[4] It was to be her form of retribution, she told Banks, 'for the sake of Europeans in general who may visit or reside in this country' and 'to pay a tribute of respect to the memory of a lost friend'.[5]

By the time he returned from Egypt, Meryon saw that Hester had changed again. Gone were the passionate enthusiasm and renewed taste for life that Boutin's impromptu visits had re-ignited. Letters to and from all the French consuls in Syria came and went. He thought she had a new ruthlessness about her, a tendency to engage in damning rants. She talked of dark conspiracies and secret societies seeking to consolidate their power in the new Europe.[*]

She lost her sudden interest in femininity; all the Aleppo 'stuffs' would

---

[*] Meryon came to hear of certain goings-on in his absence. He noted in his journal that an 'enterprising young Russian' by the name of Otto de Richter had come to see Hester, though he had no idea what his business with her might have been. Some time afterwards, he wrote, a man matching de Richter's description was seen in the bazaars of Sidon, so eager to rid himself of a quantity of silver 'Napoleons' – coins marked with a Jupiter holding an eagle – that he accepted a fraction of their value. Might these have been the same coins said to have been in Boutin's possession? If so, how had the Russian come by them? There appeared to be some kind of link, but Meryon, for one, was not about to raise the subject with Hester.

be sent on as gifts. From now on, she claimed, 'I dressed as a common person, except when absolute necessity required I should be otherwise.' Although she had emerged from the 'extreme lassitude' she had been in at first, she still hardly bothered to dress or get out of her bed. Now she stayed awake half the night, reading, writing, usually in her bed, but sometimes in her garden, so she could observe the night sky.

In the meantime, General Loustaunau had settled into Mar Elias like a tenacious weed. At his prompting, a magus-like figure appeared and also took up extended residence: Yusaf Metta, a Syrian Christian doctor who claimed to have spent a great deal of time in Persia, and introduced himself to Hester as a practitioner of the Chaldean arts. Metta corroborated what Hester might otherwise have decided were Loustaunau's half-crazed ramblings, and soon she was calling him 'the best of all Christians'.

Metta immediately captured her interest by announcing that her arrival had been predicted in an unspecified secret book. *Which* book was for her to discover, he said in his usual mysterious way. Yet it was he who procured it for her:

A European woman will come and live on Mount Lebanon at a certain epoch. She will build a house there, and obtain power and influence greater than a Sultan's. A boy without a father will join her, and his destiny will be fulfilled under her wing. The coming of the Mahdi will follow, but be preceded by war, pestilence, and other calamities. The Mahdi will ride a horse born saddled, and a woman will come from a far country to partake in the mission.[6]

The source of this Arab prophecy, which apparently originated in Damascus, has never been satisfactorily identified. Hester, although by now fairly fluent in Arabic, could not read the script, and would not have been able to verify the validity of what Metta translated for her. Nonetheless, this prediction, wherever it came from, struck Hester as adding a new dimension to that of Richard Brothers, especially with its mention of the Mahdi. For the Mahdi's mission to be complete, he would have to enter Jerusalem; the clash of civilizations would begin. Those who knew of this prophecy claimed that this event would follow the distintegration of the Ottoman Turkish Empire, and added the description of a Christian or a Jew who would 'first ride through the holy gate which leads to Mecca'.[7]

Was she willing to consider that this was all just mumbo-jumbo and skulduggery, or even a malicious hoax? Did the thought occur to her that like the treasure manuscript, it might be too perfectly calculated to appeal to her love of mystery? Who disliked her enough and knew her well enough to play such a prank? Meryon wondered who could possibly gain from planting the idea in Hester's mind that higher powers were calling her to her destiny. Only someone sufficiently determined to set a trap in order to expose her to ridicule.

By the end of February 1816 Hester's tense mood was not helped by the intrusion of a visitor, William Bankes, Bruce's once-ardent friend from Cambridge. An erudite scholar about to make his name as an explorer, Bankes had spent the best part of the previous year in Egypt, and now intended to make his way in Syria.[*] He arrived on her doorstep beaming, swathed in a turban, wearing exotic robes and scarlet boots, regaling her with his tales. To her distaste, he gave her a letter of introduction from Burckhardt, and also let drop the fact that the Swiss traveller planned to return to Syria to make another expedition up into the mountain homelands of those same inscrutable mystics who had killed Boutin.

In a letter to Bruce informing him that Bankes was with her, Hester conceded that he could be 'very civil' and 'a great talker' but said his 'vast deal of impudence, volubility and put-on naiveté' irritated her.[†] (Like Byron, Bankes may have jarred with Hester, perhaps for the same reasons, especially if he did not conceal his preference for adolescent boys.) 'He does not suit me, he bores me,' she told Bruce petulantly. 'He is naturally very mean, and wishes to see everything and wishes it to cost him nothing.'

---

[*] Bruce would hear of his friend's exploits in Egypt with envy, and wished he had followed his first instincts and travelled there more widely himself. Instead, it was Bankes who sailed up the Nile to Abu Simbel and visited the sacred island of Philae. At Giza, he explored the sarcophagus chamber of the Great Pyramid, and worked through the night copying inscriptions by candle-light. Bankes's fascination for ancient Egypt would lead him to become a pioneering Egyptologist and an early exponent of what would become the science of epigraphy.

[†] Bankes went on to become the Tory MP for Cambridge University, and a notable collector of art and antiquities. He later fled Britain in 1841, fearing he would be charged with sodomy, after he was caught with a guardsman in London's Green Park, and eventually settled in Venice.

She was not in the mood to be a charming hostess, feeling brittle at heart; she wanted only 'very, very philosophical persons' about her.

Still restless, not confiding any of her inner drama, she left Bankes at Mar Elias to spend her fortieth birthday alone, camping near Gharife in the Chouf mountains. She wrote a series of little prayers in French; perhaps she said them aloud. She felt terribly alone, as her *Prayer for Suffering* shows:

Oh God have power and mercy
Listen to the prayers of your humble creature whose heart is low
Speak of the suffering of the universe, offer some consolation to the soul of
　　your afflicted slave
But if it is your will that we should suffer
Grant us the force and the courage to fight the grief and inspire us with
　　resignation
And his decree shall be for the past
The present and the future.[8]

In *Happiness*, she asked God 'to cast again your protective glance, so that our happy nature does not desert us'. She had kept her grief entirely private until a kind and loving letter from James, now in Paris serving with the occupying forces as divisional quartermaster-general, evoked an emotional response:

I have never yet said anything to you of the distress the death of a Frenchman in this country has caused me. I feared you would reproach me for liking [him] much too well and I did not want to have any fresh disputes with you, but as the exertions I have made to avenge his death will probably reach you sooner or later, I might as well tell you the truth, that I have acted in this affair as I have ever done in those which interest me deeply. I thought this man one of the cleverest men I ever knew, as well as the best principled, and that is enough.[9]

Hester remained afraid of James's anger, and she decided this was as much of the truth as she could tell him; that in her preparations for avenging Boutin's death, she was about to act in the only way she could for a man she had not been able to stop herself from loving.

Meanwhile, an anxious and travel-weary Elizabeth Williams had arrived in Syria, having taken up her invitation to join Hester once more. At thirty-one, the still-pretty Elizabeth was tight-lipped about a failed engagement, but it may have been a strong impetus for her to want to leave Malta. At Montagu Square and up until the last time Elizabeth saw her, Hester's insouciant sense of adventure and fun, and the fact that she was always surrounded by dashing men, must have given the younger woman hope that she might find a better kind of future by following her mistress's example.

Although glad of Elizabeth's presence Hester could barely conceal her annoyance with Bankes.* Still, she did not want him to suffer Boutin's fate. When he announced his intention to go to Palmyra, she insisted he take Pierre with him as his guide, giving him private sealed letters of introduction in Arabic to her remaining friends in Hamah and to Nasir. Unknown to Bankes, she had struck an agreement with Nasir concerning all future friends of hers coming into the desert: 'If there comes to me a great man, on whom I can rely, and whose word you can trust as my own, who wants to live amongst you, to see your mock fights, or a camel killed and eaten, to ride on a dromedary in his housings etc. I will send him with two seals, but if it is another sort of person, I will send him with one.'

By the time he reached Hamah, Bankes had wormed the information about this coded signal out of Pierre, and was curious to know how Hester had described him to the Bedouin. Having opened the letters and had them translated, he was disgusted to find he had been accorded one seal, which he took to be an insult. What Bankes did not know was that Hester's agreement with Nasir specified that anyone who claimed to be a friend of hers but had no letter at all could be treated – or mistreated – as he saw fit. Angrily, he dismissed Pierre.

---

* Bankes sealed Hester's disapproval by trying to lure Meryon away. He asked him to accompany him as his amanuensis (to become, in effect, his ghost-writer) due to his own 'miserable indolence about writing'. He did not intend to pay him a wage, merely his travel expenses. Predictably, Hester was not impressed, and although she advised Meryon to take up the offer if he wished, in the end his loyalty to Hester, and perhaps his fear of incurring her wrath, prevailed.

Bankes appeared to be in luck: the new Pasha of Damascus, Hafiz Ali, was in Hamah, and he made a direct appeal to him. Within a day or two, he had his official *firman* which supposedly guaranteed his safety with the Bedouin as far as Palmyra.

But after several days in the desert, Bankes was ambushed by Nasir, who demanded 'a ridiculous sum', then forced him back to Hamah. Having grudgingly negotiated a fee and finally reached Palmyra, Bankes found himself at the mercy of Nasir's younger brother, who kept him prisoner until they agreed that Bankes would pay for the privilege of copying inscriptions from the ruins. The entire adventure had proved perilous, time-consuming and very expensive.

It was Bankes's belief that Hester had vindictively set out to humiliate him, to prove her own dominance 'over the unruly sons of the desert'. Some months after he had been her guest, he told Barker that even if this was 'an opinion never to be forgiven', he thought she was 'not at all a woman of talent' and that he believed she wanted to 'do all she can to thwart and obstruct me'. As usual, Hester seemed to have an unerring knack for making enemies who could do her reputation maximum damage.

When Bankes returned to London, he took great pleasure in finishing off what was left of her respectability, entertaining society with accounts of her household with its resident mystics, dervish masters and various Turks and Jews, whom he referred to as her 'supplicants'. He took particular pleasure aping Loustaunau, her resident millenarian, who claimed that 'She' was destined by the Almighty to play a great part in the world. Bankes maintained that whatever intelligence she might have, she squandered on obsessions with prophecy and arcane mysteries, and jeered that the last he heard, she had become a Druze. He repeated gossip from Burckhardt alleging that she was convinced she would shortly become 'Queen of Jerusalem', a fantasy that he asserted had now 'taken full possession of her mind'.

It was true that Hester wondered why others sought her out to prophesy that her future promised to fulfil a strange potential for greatness, and she certainly wanted to investigate these prognostications. As for being Queen of a future kingdom, it was not a belief she took literally. If she considered the possibility that her influence might indeed come to resemble that of a kind of leader, it was certainly one of the few dreams left that she could still believe in.

Shocking news about Bruce arrived from Paris. Hester learned that he had been arrested that January by Fouché's Ministry of Police, incarcerated in a cell in the Prison de la Force, interrogated with 'a great number of very insidious questions', and charged with planning a Bonapartist conspiracy to overthrow the government. At the time of his arrest, he had written hopefully to his father: 'The most severe punishment they can inflict is imprisonment for two years and the minimum three months.' In fact, the charge carried the potential for the death penalty.

The trial of Michael Bruce, and that of his two compatriots, was about to become the sensation of the British newspapers in 1816. *The Times* and the *Morning Chronicle* carried almost daily coverage (and noted an impressive number of attractive women crammed into the public seats of the Palais de Justice). On both sides of the Channel, he became an instant celebrity, known as 'Lavallette Bruce'. There was widespread sympathy for the men, especially for Bruce, whose impeccable French and Grecian profile in the dock were much admired.

The story of how Bruce came to be a central figure in the daring and successful escape plan for the Bonapartist Antoine Lavallette takes some unravelling. Lavallette, at forty-seven, had served Napoleon for much of his professional life, as aide-de-camp in Italy, Syria and Egypt. For thirteen years, he had enjoyed a comfortable, influential sinecure as postmaster-general, but on the return of the Bourbons he had been found guilty of conspiracy and usurping power, and sentenced to the guillotine.*

---

* The day before Christmas Eve 1815, just as he was due to be executed, Lavallette had pulled off a daring escape from the high-security Conciergerie. It was generally assumed that Lavallette had immediately been smuggled out of France, but in fact he remained in hiding in Paris. It seems to have been Napoleon's stepdaughter, Hortense de Beauharnais, who urged Bruce to enlist two friends of his, Major-General Sir Robert Wilson, and Captain John Hely-Hutchinson of the Foot Guards, and together they crafted a plan in which Lavallette, dressed as a British Guards officer, was to be spirited away in a series of carriages, including Bruce's, through military checkpoints and into Belgium. Everything went smoothly, and Lavallette was a free man. The arrest of the three Englishmen came about only when Wilson, unable to restrain himself, described the entire affair in a letter to Lord Grey, and entrusted it to his supposedly loyal valet, who turned out to be in the pay of the Bourbons.

Bruce gallantly claimed complete responsibility for the affair, and his conduct under pressure won him the lasting respect of Hester's brother James. Amid the earlier violence and upheaval of the Allied advance, they had already had an emotional reunion in which their former differences were put aside.*

It was James who wrote to Hester with news of Bruce's predicament, but the letter reached her on 15 April 1816, only eight days before his trial was due to begin. Immediately, she wrote to Louis XVIII himself, and to her influential relatives, the Marquess of Buckingham and Lord Grenville, begging for their intercession. To the King of France, she made a personal and eloquent plea.

The charges laid against Bruce could not have been more serious. Before a packed courtroom he proclaimed his innocence, maintaining that he had been motivated only 'by the commiseration which [Lavallette's] case had excited in me, the adventure of his escape appeared to me to have something romantic and even miraculous about it'. But as the trial intensified, great masses of Bruce's personal papers – 'letters from the East, notes upon my travels, translations of speeches, and speculative essays which had no more to do with the Politics of France than those of the Politics of the Moon' – were paraded as evidence, and Bruce found himself accused, to his astonishment, of plotting 'to overturn the whole Political System of Europe'.

The stance taken by the British government on Bruce's position was murky. Liverpool's administration took a very dim view of pro-Napoleon Whigs and Radicals, some of whom had argued that Napoleon deserved a fair trial rather than summary exile. Lord Bathurst, now Secretary for War, was willing to barter the freedom of the three men if Louis XVIII secretly agreed to pardon them in the likely event of them being condemned to death. But this was by no means certain. Indeed, on the day the trial began, Wellington wrote spitefully to Lady Caroline Lamb that 'your Dandy from the desert, or rather deserted dandy is not hanged

---

* James Stanhope wrote to Crauford Bruce that his son 'was not a military man and violated no laws but those of the country he was in. A cool head and a calculating heart might have left Lavallette to perish, but in the moment so applied to, I believe few honourable and feeling men would not have acted as he had done . . . I consider Bruce as the soul of honour.'

yet; but there are hopes he may be so if justice is done, by the end of the month'.[10*]

Hester was gripped with uncertainty over what the outcome would be for Bruce. Even before she had heard this latest news, she had written him a remorseful letter, asking him to forgive her anything she had said which hurt or misjudged him. When, for her fortieth birthday, she had returned to a place of significance to them she referred to as 'the old Spot', she told him, 'My heart always turns (even in its despairing moments) to *that spot* where providence saved two beings, who tho' deemed to be separated, I still hope will never forget by what ties they were once united.'

'I wish my tears could blot out what I wrote in agony of mind,' she had written, revealing that she had harboured 'black misconceptions' and 'suspicions' against him, not helped by his own 'horrid silence'.

Perhaps it was also her way of apologizing too, in case he should judge her for what he heard about Boutin. She had informed him about 'Le Boutonné'; that 'he is no more, the dagger of the Assassin ended his existence', and admitted that it had 'afflicted me vastly'.[11]

She told him then that she had changed her mind again and now planned to leave before winter and get 'to dear Rhodes . . . and to France in the Spring if things remain quiet'. She hoped James 'would not oppose my plan of returning to a place where I have set my heart upon spending the remainder of my days, and of cultivating the minds of some little beings in a humble situation of life which hereafter may prove faithful and useful followers of those I must ever love . . . this class of person is much wanted in the world . . . clever, honest, honorable men, which I

---

* Thirty-year-old Lady Caroline Lamb had arrived in Paris with her husband William, their marriage apparently enduring despite her well-publicized affair with Byron. Fanny Burney, who was in Paris at the time, described how the auburn-haired Caroline deliberately upstaged every other woman, dressed 'or rather not dressed, so as to excite universal attention and authorize every attention in staring . . . for she had one shoulder, half her back and all her throat and neck displayed as if at the call of some statuary for modelling, a heathen goddess'. She flirted outrageously with Wellington. The next man to get the same treatment was Bruce. The day after she first met him in Paris, Caroline Lamb wrote him a pert little note, addressing him as 'Mr Bruce' and suggesting he call on her personally to 'give me the answer' about whether she and William could come to his dinner party the same night. Soon she was determined to seduce him, calling him 'Monsieur, The Bruce' and 'He of the Desert'.

hope my élèves will turn out.' (Bruce may have wondered about her obscure reference to 'useful followers' and puzzled over what little minds she intended to shape. Perhaps a clue can be found in a line from one of her letters to Joseph Boutin, whom she asks to visit, and inquires wistfully, 'whether you have a child who resembles his uncle?')[12]

Another Englishman arrived at Mar Elias while she was in this state of turmoil: James Silk Buckingham. He and Bankes could not have been more different and Hester took to him immediately. 'He looked very much like a Mahometan' in his dress, but he was a handsome farmer's son from Falmouth in Cornwall, with clear white skin and light-blue eyes. He was restless, energetic and determined to make his name by combining his compulsion for exploring with writing, and his ambition clearly impressed Hester. He was also entirely broke, with no credit to speak of.

He had travelled some way with Bankes, who noted condescendingly that 'he begged to be permitted to accompany me, offering to be any use to me in his power by taking down notes or memoranda or ascertaining bearings for me. I consented to this, specifying distinctly that there must be no publication on his part.' With no encouragement from Bankes, Buckingham had written to Burckhardt with a proposition that the three of them should compile a book on 'Nubia, Egypt and Syria, particularly the countries east of the Jordan'.[13] But self-taught rather than Cambridge-educated, Buckingham was not a member of the club. Burckhardt was then feverishly working up his vast notes into tomes that would be published posthumously, and Bankes had no intention of diluting his discoveries by collaborating with a chancer like Buckingham. The irony is that of the three of them, it would be Buckingham – with his prodigious multi-volume accounts and lectures about his travels – who went on to win popular fame. He became the Mark Twain of his day, and went on to found the *Calcutta Journal* and *The Athenaeum*.

Buckingham later wrote an effusive description of his nine-day stay with Hester, giving us a sympathetic and admiring view of her world. He arrived at two in the morning to find her wide awake in her garden, and charmed her with his ship-boy's knowledge of the stars. After travelling rough, he was grateful for her hospitality. Years later he was still touched at the thought of her morning breakfast table, set with roses and glass, 'tea and coffee in the English style'. From her kitchen, he thought meals were 'a happy medium between frugality and abundance'; her house itself, aside from its divans and cushions strewn about, was 'furnished in the English manner', and notable for its 'clean and unostentatious simplicity'.

He described Hester as 'rather above average height, with regular and delicately formed features, a soft blue eye, fair and pale complexion, an expression of habitual pensiveness and tranquil resignation which was rarely disturbed except when her countenance now and then lighted up with the indignant feelings that always followed the recital of some deed of cruelty and oppression'. He described spending afternoons joining her in 'walks or a ride on horseback', seeing how she enthused over beautiful horses and her 'small stud of Arabs'. He observed that she spent a good deal of time writing, and that her secretary 'wrote from dictation for several hours in the middle of the day'.

> The evening was almost invariably passed in conversation, and so powerful in my recollection, even at this distant period, of the pleasure this afforded me, that I could use no terms which would be too extravagant in its praise. The early association with men eminent for their talents as well as their power; the habit of intense observation on all passing events, the abundant opportunities, afforded by years of travel to apply those habits to the utmost advantage all these added to a remarkable union of frankness and dignity, gave a pecular charm to the conversations of this highly accomplished and amiable woman.

So stimulating did Buckingham find these conversations, he 'felt extreme regret' at leaving. 'I had scarcely ever before concentrated so much of highly intellectual pleasure in so short a space of time,' he wrote. She made sure he had clothes, gave him a sturdy horse and one of her men to help guide his way, and enough money, food and medicine for his journey. She felt the need to explain her actions to Barker, knowing that Bankes ridiculed Buckingham as a squandering rascal only interested in 'the vanity of becoming an author [and] to the expectations of a great profit from his book'. Such criticism particularly annoyed her since she had decided Bankes was a parasite himself, and had a 'rich man's' lack of sympathy.[14]

Meanwhile Burckhardt gleefully crowed to Bankes that he had heard how 'Queen Zenobia, or Semiramis, as you like to call her, is dreadfully angry with you for having slighted her advice, and is making free with your name, almost as free as she did with mine'. The battle lines were drawn. Hester would wage an on-off campaign against Burckhardt until the end of his life, and he soon called her 'that evil woman' who 'if one does not humbly submit to her orders, kiss her hand and permit her to dominate one completely, one exposes oneself to her malicious tongue'.[15] Bankes was more than willing to take his side.

However, a grateful Buckingham made literary salaams. He would later recount that some weeks after his stay at Mar Elias, while travelling from Damascus into the Hauran, he heard first-hand how the story of Hester, spun into a fairy tale, had seamlessly entered Arab mythology:

> When the King's daughter, Bint-el-Melek, entered Damascus, all voices exclaimed, 'The city of Damascus, the great gate of pilgrimage, and the key to the tomb of the prophet, is taken from us; her glory is fallen, her might cast down, and her people forever subdued. An infidel has entered on horseback and rebellion is subdued by her beauty.[16]

So the Arab story began, and her adventures at Palmyra were related:

> When they reached the broken city, the princess was taken to the greatest of all palaces, and there gold and jewels were bound round her temples, and all the people did homage to her as Queen by bowing their heads to the dust. On that day Tadmor was richer than Sham, more peopled than Stamboul; and if the princess had only remained it would soon have become the greatest of all the cities of the earth, for men were pouring into from all quarters, horsemen, and chiefs and *munujemen* (astrologers); the fame of her beauty and benevolence having reached to Baghdad and Ispahann, to Bokhara and Samarkand, and the greatest men in the East being desirous of beholding it for themselves.[17]

More visitors came and were welcomed, yet she was now so worried about her fast-accumulating debts that she fretted even over the cost of feeding them. Two eminent Abyssinians, a priest and a prime-ministerial aide, had come looking for Turinge and Musa; the priest presided over a sad little ceremony commemorating Turinge's death. They stayed for several weeks to rest and prepare for the journey home. In return Hester subjected them to detailed questioning about their country. She was gratified to learn that 'Wellety Selassy [*sic*]', the Prime Minister himself, had invited her to come as a guest to his country. With some regret, she let the handsome Musa go, and with him, the possibility that she might accompany him to see Aybssinia for herself.

Still grieving for Boutin, Hester saw herself as a cold and lonely heroine, unleashing her revenge by stealth and force. 'I suffer more than you can know, for both the past and the present,' she wrote to an unknown correspondent in French.[18]

Finally, she received word from Acre and Damascus that their soldiers were on their way, and immediately sent two English pistols to Berber in Tripoli, with a note: 'In my country, when a gallant knight goes to fight a just cause, a lady must first give him a sword.' By her own account, in the middle of June 1816, five thousand troops under Berber's command swarmed up into the mountains, first sacking the Isma'ili stronghold of Masyaf, the seat of the Old Man of the Mountain. They terrorized more than thirty villages, burning houses and fortresses alike. The heads of fifty-two chieftains were sent as a grisly tribute to Berber. Other sources report that in total some three hundred were killed. Hester had exacted her revenge.

It was just the sort of exploit guaranteed to make Sir Sidney Smith envious. Yet the Knight Liberator would not have been so pleased at the fate of many women and girls caught up in the reprisal. Meryon noted that 'several women were sent to Tripoli as slaves'. As for the rest, it seems safe to assume that the soldiers sent in at Hester's request did what soldiers often did, and that there were also those who were raped and killed.

## 17

# 'I Am Done With All Respectability'

Like an omen, as the massacre began, locusts swarmed over the mountains around Mar Elias, filling the sky for several days with a dense, dark, mile-long cloud, leaving the landscape stripped and bare. The green shutters were closed against them, but never quite shut out the terrible beat of their wings.

Hester was not ready to quit the country, even if her heart was heavy. From her hilltop, all she could do was hope Bruce would be safe. Nor could she do anything in the meantime for Miranda, but she must have imagined them both in their prison cells. She felt she had promises to keep, to Bruce and to Sir Joseph Banks. To this end, she intended to pre-empt Burckhardt in his quest in the Syrian mountains to find 'compleat and valuable treatises' and she was anxious for Barker to send her his clever younger brother, to be her 'amanuensis' and help her make sense of a mountain of papers and notes that needed writing up.

Despite the heat, she made swift plans for escape when word reached her that the Princess of Wales had reached Acre on 2 July 1816. Hester guessed what savage fun the caricaturists at home would have at her expense if she were to meet Caroline, the two would-be queens at logger-heads to upstage one another.

If Süleyman Pasha and Malem Hayim expected a queenlier version of Hester, what they got was a poor parody.* Undoubtedly, Caroline had

---

* A recent observer had described Caroline, Princess of Wales, as wearing a scarlet dress, cut low at the front and back, reaching only to the knees, exposing expanses of plump flesh. She had 'a wig, (curled at the sides nearly as high as the top of the bonnet), artificial eyebrows, (nature having denied her any) and false teeth [and] appears very ignorant and coarse in her manners, and indelicate in her conversation. She walks, bows, twirls a stick and gesticulates like a man.'

been inspired by the stir of excitement generated by Hester's travels, and wanted to see the Holy Land for herself. She was travelling with a small entourage, including her current lover Bartolomeo Pergami, and intended to make a pilgrimage to Jerusalem. Snubbed by Hester, Caroline certainly felt the need to outshine her, and make her own mark as 'Queen of the East'. She deliberately rode into the holy city on a donkey, hoping by this symbolic act to stir up religious fervour. In Jerusalem, she founded a holy order in her name, investing the men in her travelling party as Knights and naming Pergami Grand Master.

Meryon and Elizabeth were left behind, instructed to greet the incoming 'Meleky' if she arrived as threatened. On 18 July Hester sailed for Tripoli, her bed strapped to the deck, along with her dragoman Bertrand, El Hastar the black stallion, and a donkey. The hull was crammed with her five servants.

At Tripoli all the eminences – Mustafa Berber, the Patriarch of Antioch and the European consuls – came to greet her at the docks as she stepped from her boat. Aware of Caroline's sartorial gaffes, she took care to dress like a queen, in a splendid black and gold *abah* with crescents and tassels, and her servants rushed to get her carpet to unfurl in front of her. She had no intention of having her own stock lowered by the Princess of Wales.

She met with 'Chevalier' Regnault, the new French consul, privately. He had come to Syria from his former post in Cyprus, where he had earned a reputation for being ruthless. Regnault told her bluntly that in his dispatch he had designated Boutin's death as suicide since he had deliberately put himself in harm's way and travelled without an escort. Hester judged Regnault as perfidious. But by now she was practised at playing the game. She knew he would be more useful as a friend than an enemy, and turning her charm on him, invited him to Mar Elias.

To her astonishment, Lascaris turned up out of the blue in Tripoli, claiming he wished to beg her forgiveness, pleading with her to keep his visit a secret from Regnault. She had not seen him since their argument in Hamah. He looked gaunt and desperate. If he was distressed by the news of Boutin's death, she did not mention it, but whatever he said appears to have been persuasive enough for her to put aside her earlier suspicions of him. 'He made me cry for an hour by the excess of his grief and the excuses which he made me – so much so that I, who hardly ever shed tears, was astonished at myself.'

Lascaris had obviously sought Hester out for a reason, but whatever they discussed was never revealed.* Shortly afterwards, however, Lascaris left Syria for Egypt, where miraculously he was granted British protection.

Hester spent some days as a guest of the Barkers at Suwediyah. The adjoining houses she had first suggested to Barker as a refuge three years before had been transformed under his direction. Their talk of simple things – how to engraft chestnut trees, the beauty of the Bengal rose, the correct care of French quinces – cemented the frayed friendship. Barker's sensitivity to her feelings is evident in his anecdote about a conversation they had late one evening in the garden. She had been in a particularly nostalgic, talkative mood, remembering an evening in London that stood out for her above all other nights – it may have been just around the time she met Granville. She described how everyone had admired one particular woman for her 'wit, sprightliness and beauty' – how all the men wanted to dance with her – and asked him suddenly, a little flirtatiously: 'Who do you think she was?' Caught somewhat off guard, Barker thought for a minute and replied, 'I suppose it must have been the Duchess of Devonshire,' and he saw a look of intense sadness cross Hester's face. 'No,' she said, barely whispering. 'It was me, it was *me*.'[1] Soon Barker would ask Hester to be the godmother to his daughter, whose name she picked out to be 'Hester Isabella'.

For the rest of the time, Hester simply disappeared into the northern Syrian mountains; for more than two months, she went missing, travelling on her own business, she told Barker.

Antioch was then a city of red-roofed villas and shuttered balconies, laced with cobbled thoroughfares and bazaars. Its Acropolis was still

---

* For reasons that become important later in this story, it must be mentioned that Lascaris had recently been seen in Smyrna in the company of Napoleon's disgraced general, Lallemand, who had tried to follow Napoleon into exile on St Helena, but instead had been imprisoned on Malta. After two months in prison, Lallemand had escaped, and when he met Lascaris, was on the run, having been condemned to death *in absentia*. The fact that Lascaris himself chose not to escape to America, as Lallemand did, is telling. He behaved as though he was still on a mission.

preserved. Hester rented a small cottage outside the city, close to its famous ancient relic, a giant head of a Sphinx carved in the rock. As Gertrude Bell later put it, 'her featureless countenance is turned slightly up the valley, as though she watched for one that shall yet come out of the East'.

It was up into that valley, past strange purple-flowered Judas trees and up into stark bleached-out limestone landscapes of the northern highlands, that Hester rode on her black stallion. She took only her dragoman Bertrand with her, knowing she was putting both their lives at risk. She came to seek out the mysterious sect known as the Yezidi, who lived in seclusion at Basofan, near the famous Stylite pillar of Qalaat Samaan. They spoke Kumanji, a dialect of Kurdish, and as a people had ancient roots in the mountainous borders shared by modern-day Syria, Iraq, Iran, Turkey, Armenia and Georgia.

She saw heavy-browed and fierce men, with long untrimmed moustaches and hair woven in plaits and twisted up behind their ears, like Vikings. Some of the old men wore conical caps. The Ottoman Turks had persecuted them for centuries, calling them 'devil-worshippers'.

Hester decided to risk making her pilgrimage to the Yezidi despite the recent slaughter of their heretical brothers and sisters, the Isma'ilis and Alawis, further down the coast. If anything it required more courage than her Palmyra exploit as she was alone and utterly unprotected. She stopped at every village to announce herself, informing them that it was she who ordered the reprisals against their distant neighbours further south, but that otherwise she meant the people of the mountains no harm.

The semi-nomadic Yezidi were the most enigmatic of all the sects she had yet encountered, and it was said they had magical powers. Something extraordinary must have occurred while Hester was with the Yezidi, although she never spoke explicitly about it. She later told Meryon that she spent precisely 'seventy days' with them, and that she afterwards regarded herself as an authority on their beliefs. If she had been permitted by the Yezidi sheikhs to witness one of their religious ceremonies she would have been one of the very few – perhaps the only – outsider to do so.

The Yezidi invoked astral spirits or *jakshas*, and their rituals involved the *kocak*, the caste of dancers who reached an ecstatic trance-like state through whirling Sufic gyrations and sometimes by self-inflicted wounds, so that dancing and bleeding became one: the fiery manifestations were said to show themselves in human and animal form. It was said that if a Yezidi sheikh drew a circle in the dust around you, you could not break out of it.

Hester hinted at only one detail to a trusted friend several years later, that during the ritual she had witnessed a manifestation which had altered her consciousness.

Whatever else she discovered during this time, it profoundly changed her and deepened her interest in what she termed the 'secret philosophy' of the ancients, and in the existence of another world, in which divine and spiritual beings were revealed as real. She learned that, like the Druze, the Yezidi believed in reincarnation, and that humans are gradually perfected over a succession of lives, a concept reflected by their description of it and in the symbolism of their rites as *kiras guhorin*, or 'changing the garment'. She saw that their worship involved ritual fire, their prayers always offered in the direction of the sun. When she returned to the coast, a different Hester emerged, one who was beginning to cast off her old world for another known only to hermits, magi and priests.

At the end of September 1816 she gave Meryon advance instructions to prepare the usual expedition to Machmouche, and went straight there. The route up towards the peaks in early October was already heavy with snow.

By now, good news at last reached her about Bruce. In the end, after he had been imprisoned for almost seven months, Lords Grey and Grenville appealed to Castlereagh, the Foreign Secretary, who was able to apply pressure. At the end of July (when Hester was in Tripoli) Bruce and his two friends had been summarily released and ordered to sail for England.

However, he had returned home to the devastating news that his father's bank had crashed on 2 July. Among the partners, the debts amounted to half a million pounds. The financial nightmare left the already ailing Crauford Bruce a broken man. His lawyers set before him the miserable task of signing away the prosperous businesses he had spent his lifetime building up, and he was forced to put the family properties up for sale. It was naturally a great shock for Bruce to discover that the fortune he had always counted on had vanished overnight.

For this reason, Bruce could take no comfort in the fact that on his return to London on 1 August, he was eulogized in an editorial in that day's *Morning Chronicle*. At Brooks's Club, he was made an honorary member and given a standing ovation as he walked through the door, his hand vigorously shaken by friends he had not seen in some eight years. Even if he felt little better than a pauper, he had a hero's welcome.

Had Hester and Bruce met at this juncture in their lives, they would have been able to openly discuss certain confidential matters, to which she alluded as being 'for your private ear only'. Even before his arrest, she had expressly warned him about putting himself in danger of 'committing himself in a political way, at a moment like the present'. Hester would destroy all of Bruce's letters. But many of hers survived, and they are riddled with crypticisms.

A great deal had taken place in Bruce's life in two and a half years. A question mark hangs over whether he joined Sligo on his Naples-bound brig over the summer of 1814, and stopped off at Elba with a view to seeing Napoleon. Théophanie Escalon, the woman with whom he had a brief affair in Constantinople, wrote to him that October: 'They say you have been to the Island of Elba, if this is true then I shall be very interested to hear all that you can tell me about your meeting with Napoleon.'[2]

In a private letter from Elba, Sligo reported that he first caught a glimpse of Napoleon as he was returning from his drive, and noted his popularity.[3] Is it possible that Bruce decided to take his chance and achieve what Hester could not?[4] Shortly beforehand, he had written to Hester suggesting an alteration to 'the plan' (presumably her Napoleon plan) and she had been very cross with him for apparently trying to put it in motion. 'I am like my grandfather, I must act alone or not at all,' she had scolded. In view of later events, the matter of whether a specific communication was made is crucial

If Bruce had indeed taken the initiative and travelled with Sligo that summer, and managed a meeting, he would have been well ahead of the queue.[5] He would have come with a glowing reference from his new friend, the linchpin of the Bonaparte dynasty, Hortense de Beauharnais, the 'Queen of Holland'.* Hortense was Josephine's daughter; Napoleon had arranged her marriage to his brother, Louis (from whom she had separated), and her son, Louis Napoleon, the future Napoleon III, was then six. In Paris, invitations to her private parties and dinners were much sought after. Tsar Alexander was an admirer, and so was Wellington. Nonetheless, Hortense had instantly warmed to the well-travelled, handsome Bruce, and asked him back repeatedly.

At the same time as Hester was following Boutin's movements around Syria, Bruce had embarked on a new affair with Aglaé Ney, Hortense's close friend.† She was married to Marshal Michel Ney, who, having played a prominent part in Napoleon's campaigns, lost little time in aligning himself with the Bourbons. When Bruce met Aglaé, she had a grand title, Duchesse of Elchingen, and was the mother of four boys. She was also jealous, not only of the women Bruce might see when he was not with her, but of 'that woman in Syria'.** By the following year, at the height of his trial and its aftermath, their affair was so advanced that she expected him to marry her.

---

* Hortense de Beauharnais wrote of 'Mr Bruce, a young Englishman whom I had met several times . . . pleased me on account of his simplicity and idealism, and his account of the journey he made in Africa [sic]'.

† Aglaé Ney was pretty, petite, dark-haired, full-bosomed, with a somewhat acquiescent, conventional nature, and a modest royalist background. It was said that her mother had once been a chambermaid; but then Ney himself was the son of a blacksmith. Her marriage had been arranged by Napoleon after he noticed her in Hortense's company, and thought she would make an ideal foil for Ney, one of his more curmudgeonly and unpopular marshals.

** Aglaé Ney wrote to him: 'Is it a good thing or a bad one to know you? The agitation I have suffered since that mutual confession, does it do me more good or harm? It is midnight and I am thinking of you! And your image pursues me ceaselessly . . . why have you shown so much interest in me? My poor heart, bruised by so much anguish, opened too quickly to the temptation of such sweet comfort, perhaps the generosity of your own has deceived it about its real feelings!'

Secret meetings were arranged by agreed signs, such as Bruce holding his cane a particular way, or Aglaé placing a pin against her teeth, and letters left behind an ormolu music box in Hortense's salon, or delivered by their personal servants, the latter method sending Madame Ney into a frenzy. 'The most dangerous thing, which was also the sweetest, is to stay with me in the evening when everyone has gone,' she wrote. When they were in public, she told him, 'You must also humour the Grumbler, talk politics to him and do not be surprised if I appear sulky, because I prefer to remain silent than to speak of other things than those that are occupying me entirely.'

Bruce had returned home in October 1814. His father was apparently no nearer death than the last time he had seen him. Three weeks later, he returned to Paris, picking up where he had left off. The 'delightful' evenings 'at the Queen of Holland's' continued, and it was soon spread about that he was Hortense's lover rather than Aglaé's. (It is revealing that when Hester heard the gossip that Bruce had become the Queen of Holland's lover she did not reject the possibility but considered he had been intentionally targeted, so that he might be 'deliberately mixed up with [the Bonapartists'] intrigues'.) Bruce had certainly softened his formerly rigid stance on Napoleon, and by now could claim many friendships within the former ruler's old circle.

Bruce, along with Hobhouse, was one of the few Englishmen to remain in Paris during the Hundred Days, caught up in invigorating discussions and erotic distractions, and attending parties full 'of all the Ministers and Grandees of the Empire'. At this time or earlier, Bruce was approached by Fouché, who despite his spectacular past treacheries had been reinstalled as Minister of Police. It seemed Napoleon had been casting about for a go-between in his final attempts to negotiate with the Allies, with a view to preventing the war that would lead to Waterloo. Napoleon's Minister for Foreign Affairs, Caulaincourt, had met Bruce and evidently liked him. Someone had suggested that the Englishman might be tailor-made for the job. Bruce later explicitly confided to his father: 'I was under the protection of the French government and had procured a regular French Passport from Monsieur Fouché himself.'[6]

Bruce felt sour at the Allied victory and Napoleon's second fall, and particularly resented that the French people once more 'had the Bourbons forced upon them'. In those tense last hours, Bruce had immediately made his way to see Caulaincourt, who had been huddled with Napoleon, along with other loyalists, while he vacillated about what to do in the immediate aftermath of defeat.

Many of Bruce's friends feared the backlash of what would become known as the Bourbon 'White Terror', the persecution of the Bonapartists. Hortense had been given only a few hours to gather her belongings and was banished to Switzerland. Fouché, who managed to retain his position of influence under Louis XVIII as provisional governor, did nothing to refute the rumour that she had led a conspiracy to help Napoleon

LEFT: William Noel Hill fell in love with Hester soon after she began living with Pitt, and later proposed. When Hester left England she promised Hill, then a diplomat in Europe, that she would come out to see him. She never did.

BELOW: Romance burgeoned between Hester and General Sir John Moore after a meeting in July 1807. Their letters reveal a great attachment and Hester's grief at his death was profound; to the politicians who came to call on her, she behaved like a war widow.

BELOW: The flamboyant revolutionary General Francisco de Miranda – depicted here in prison – did much to help Hester recover her enthusiasm for life after the deaths of Sir John Moore and her half-brother Charles. He told his friends she was 'the most delicious woman I have yet encountered'.

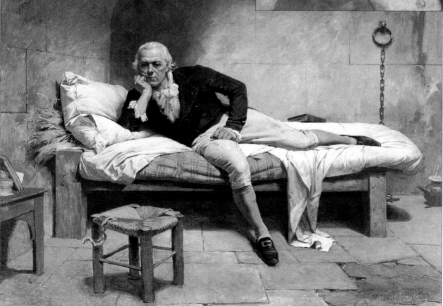

LEFT: Charles Lewis Meryon, Hester's long-suffering doctor, became the ultimate Boswell to her Johnson when, after her death, he published a six-volume opus recounting her life and adventures. Bred in Rye and educated at Oxford, Meryon's shy manner belied a will of steel. He never fully understood Hester, but faced many dangers on her behalf and their destinies remained entangled to the last.

RIGHT: When Hester met him, Michael Bruce was twenty-three, the son of a rich nabob and undeniably good-looking. For both it was a *coup de foudre*; their bohemian living arrangements in Athens and Constantinople became the talk of London. He left her only when she ordered him to, a traumatic separation that haunted them both.

LEFT: Howe Peter Brown, 2nd Marquess of Sligo, was a Cambridge contemporary and friend of Bruce. He, Hester and Bruce soon settled into a workable ménage, travelling around the Mediterranean on Sligo's brig, but there were tensions and jealousies.

ABOVE: At the end of 1810, Hester took a six-month lease on a three-storey mansion in the charming fishing village of Therapia (now Tarabya), on the shores of the Bosphorus. For much of that time Bruce and Sligo were travelling, while she was 'engaged in solitary work'.

RIGHT: Artistic talent ran in the Stanhope family and Hester enjoyed drawing, although this is one of very few sketches by her that survives. She sent this to Crauford Bruce to show him the all-encompassing robes that Turkish women wore.

Mehmet Ali (with pipe), the great pasha of Egypt, once fought as part of the Anglo-Turkish force led by Hester's cousin Sir Sidney Smith, and he showered Hester with attention and presents when she visited his palace in Cairo. The son of a humble Albanian merchant, he made up for his lack of formal education by his innate cleverness and immense determination.

Hester felt a spiritual affinity for life in the desert, acknowledging that it could be both barbaric and dangerous. It was above all a place she felt alive. She would say of the Bedouin that they taught her 'the value of poverty and independence'.

LEFT: The remarkable explorer John Lewis Burckhardt, known to his friends as 'The Sheikh'. He discovered the ancient capital of Petra shortly after meeting Hester and Bruce in Nazareth, and they were among the first Europeans to hear of it. He credited Hester with 'a manly spirit and enlightened curiosity', but their ambitious natures ultimately clashed.

RIGHT: James Silk Buckingham struck Hester as 'very much like a Mahometan' in his dress. Hester befriended him when he was a broken-down traveller, earning his lasting admiration.

LEFT: A comical self-portrait of the Polish Count Waclav Seweryn Rzewuski, who came out to Syria and Arabia on a horse-buying expedition funded by Tsar Alexander. He shared a love of the esoteric and the equine with Hester, and both were made honorary emirs by the Bedouin.

Abva. Couvent abandonné dans le Liban près de Seide, restauré par Esther ; elle y demeure l'hyver. (Mav Elia)

Rzewuski's sketch of Mar Elias, Hester's residence at Abra.

The mountain village of Djoun presided over chalky hills, deep valleys and mountain streams. Hester's fortress here was an impressive testament to her determination: it took just under two years to build and she lived there for almost nineteen years.

ABOVE: A letter to Meryon in Hester's handwriting. The hundreds of letters between them spanned long periods when he was back in England and Europe conducting her business. Much of their correspondence was encoded, and they developed a complicated cipher intended 'to bewilder into what hands the letter might have fallen'.

ABOVE: Meryon lived to be ninety-four. He nurtured great literary ambitions, but apart from his book on Hester his efforts failed to find favour with publishers.

LEFT: Lucy Meryon as a young woman, with her hair done in the latest fashion and wearing the gold earrings sent as a gift from Hester.

This whimsical portrait of Hester in old age, strolling with her pipe
in her garden, was drawn from memory by the young nephew
of the British consul Joseph Abela in Sidon.

escape from Elba, an accusation Bruce pronounced 'absurd and unjust', although he himself would later be accused of being involved.[7] Bruce ignored all warnings that he too should leave.

When Louis XVIII drew up a list of nineteen men to be arrested and tried by court-martial for aiding and abetting the Emperor, the first name on the list was Marshal Ney. At the bottom was Count Lavallette.

Like an idealistic lawyer taking on a first big case, Bruce had taken up the defence of his lover's husband, doing everything in his power to have the charges overthrown.* On 21 November 1815 in Paris, the trial of Marshal Ney began. After the majority verdict was returned at two in the morning of 7 December, he was immediately shot. By taking such a visible part in Ney's defence, Bruce acknowledged that he had 'brought upon me the anger of the Duke of Wellington'. Just as Hester's movements were watched in Syria, he too found himself followed by both French and British agents.

Late in 1816, Hester read a short announcement in a French newspaper that Bruce was to marry a Miss Fanny Crosbie, a young Englishwoman who had been living in Paris. Hester had no way of knowing that the engagement, if there was ever any substance to it, was not in fact about to result in a marriage. In France, Aglaé Ney, too, had been caught out by the news. Heartbroken, she had called off the affair by letter, and Bruce, by then in Brighton, had not protested, finding himself again the object of the newly-separated Lady Caroline Lamb's attentions.

From James, Hester heard the news of Bruce's release and Crauford Bruce's ruin. He had received her letter, with its admission of grief over Boutin, and having heard of her exploits was far less loving. He told her angrily that he had not lent her money to fund adventures in the Syrian mountains, and that all those who wanted to help her were losing patience with her, particularly the Marquess of Buckingham. He informed her that their relative, Lord Temple, who was fast thrusting himself up

---

* Bruce became intent on publicizing the injustice of Ney's trial, asserting that it was a direct violation of Article 12 of the Convention of Paris. With the help of Caulaincourt, he drafted letters for the Prime Minister Lord Liverpool, Wellington, Lord Bathurst and the Prince Regent, all written out in Bruce's best handwriting and signed by Aglaé. That summer, Bruce did everything in his power to sway opinion against a guilty verdict.

the political ranks, had been particularly incensed by the 'malevolent aspersion' spread about concerning her relationship with a Frenchman. 'Bring that woman home by force and I'll lend you whatever assistance I can,' he had bellowed. He warned her they were all thinking of hiring a brig to come and get her.

Hester's love for James metamorphosed into rage for meekly allowing her to be spoken of so insultingly, for not standing up for her, but above all, for hinting that despite all her qualities, she had behaved like a whore. What use was his 'admiration and veneration' if 'the only time I wanted his assistance he chose to desert me and find fault with my conduct?' Hester was resolute. That was enough. She could never – would never – return home.

Her pride was somewhat restored by confirmation that in the desert at least she was still revered. Two Bedouin arrived to present her with a colt from Muhanna al Fadil – and with a letter asking her to intercede on their behalf with the new Pasha of Damascus. They had been at war with the pashalik ever since she left them, and the Pasha's soldiers had killed one of Muhanna's young sons, and now they wanted Nasir's head. Like a voice straight from the desert, the letter begins:

> To our dear Sister, the Syt Hester, whom may the Almighty save, and whose days may he prolong unto us, whom she has breathed upon – this letter with our most profound respect, comes greeting – Amen, O God of the Universe! Next, shouldst thou, our sister, inquire after us, thy brother, we praise be to God, are well, but ever anxious after thy perfect safety, which is the sum of our wishes and prayers . . .[8]

'We wait for the commands of your Felicity,' he told her.

She picked up her pen and wrote what was to be her last long letter to Bruce, telling him that she wanted to settle anything between them that might lead to bitterness before ceasing to communicate for ever. Any financial promise he had made her was now 'absolutely void', she told him, and she would never have accepted any money from him if she had known the grievousness of his father's troubles. She was sorry for her past haughtiness and anger towards his father, she said, conceding that his only crime had been 'not knowing how to deal or act with sufficient delicacy towards a being, who to him, might appear incomprehensible'. As it was, she wanted Crauford to know that 'the strange creature is as much hurt as any of his best friends at what must cause him uneasiness'.

Crauford Bruce's bank was hardly the first or last to slide. The country was bankrupt. In 1815 the national debt stood at £834 million. Interest on this was crippling taxpayers, and a dangerous amount of paper credit had caused massive inflation.

She told Bruce he must understand that for her the past three years of trying to interpret his true feelings with so few letters from him, and his apparent failure to keep his promises, had kept her feelings 'in a constant state of agitation':

> I feared you no longer had any friendship for me, and if it was sheer neglect, it raised a feeling of anger, if not contempt in my breast, that any man, who professed to have feeling, could thus tamper with that of another. Had I loved you less, I might have been more cool, but coolness is a quality I never had, nor shall, I fear, possess until I am interred in my grave.

She had accumulated a great many papers for him including 'the Bible or the Koran of the Akal Druze'. In addition, she had acquired 'the most valuable treatise on horses by the Imam Ali (the Prophet's son-in-law I mean), a most scarce and highly prized work, and many other vastly curious manuscripts I am almost certain no one has ever got hold of before'. She was still having them copied and translated 'under my own eye', which was no small task, but would send them on to him when they were complete, she promised, 'on a man of war', so they should 'not be fumbled about with'.

As for the future, she told him: 'Do not be uneasy about me in any way, or fancy your marriage pains me,' adding pointedly that 'for your mutual happiness, you must correct your temper'.

She gave him a few last words of queenly advice:

> If I might be allowed to say a word in advice respecting your future public career, I should strongly recommend your taking no part for the

present, and before you mix in politics, to become well acquainted with all parties, without any way committing yourself, and to make the *real* constitution of England your study – for at the moment, she appears to have *none*. But the present state of things cannot last. The infamous system must crumble into dust and hurl those with it, who either fabricated or upheld it. Then is the time for exertion; and for uncontaminated persons to come forward, acting on the principles of my grandfather.

But she knew she was digressing, falling back into her old habit of lecturing him once again.

'Adieu! Farewell my once dearest B! I must call you so no more – but I shall never cease to pray for your prosperity and your happiness,' she wrote, warning him too that 'I am done with all respectability'. With that she brought to an end the love affair that had preoccupied her for almost seven years.

In November 1816 Giorgio returned from England bringing with him Meryon's replacement, Dr Newberry (chosen for her by the Marquess of Buckingham) and twenty-seven trunks, including the all-important presents intended to reinforce her influence. Feeling sad, she opened the parcel containing the Smith, Warren & Co. paint-box she had meant to give to Vincent Boutin. It was the latest model, adorned with the image of a helmeted goddess, to whom an angel was perpetually kneeling, offering her the box, as two black slaves looked on. Wrapping it in Aleppo silk, she placed it in a cupboard where she would not see it and wept.

It was time for Meryon to leave. He was exhausted by the constant uncertainty and drama of his life with Hester, and yearned to see his family. All the same he felt a compulsion to lay his plans before her, to be of what service he could, and to come clean about something he had kept hidden all from her all these years, the secret he had not yet admitted to his own parents: the existence of his daughter Lucy. His sister Sarah had taken her into her own family as a foster-child when she was a toddler, telling only her husband the truth. To his astonishment, Hester was not in the least shocked. Instead, the thought of his little motherless Lucy appeared to make her pensive. She told him she wanted to pay for a year of Lucy's schooling, a gift she was sure would please him more than any other present she could give him.

On 18 January 1817, released from seven years of service, Meryon departed. As he left his little house in Abra, the villagers swarmed about him, pressing his hand. Hester gave him wine and honey from Roum, and a lambskin pelisse which he would tell her became 'my bed, my coverlet, my sea-cloak, my everything'. Elizabeth pressed on him 'cold pastries of gazelle-venison, tarts and plum cake, cold fowls and some other good things'. It would take Meryon almost five months to reach England as he could not afford to be particular about his passage. From Beirut, he sailed to Cyprus, staying there for six weeks, recording everything with the elation of a free man.

It was Meryon who sent Hester the news first of one death, then another. In Cyprus he saw an article in a newspaper published out of Trieste: her father had died shortly before Christmas 1816. Despite all the time that had gone by, they had never exchanged a single letter. Some time afterwards, from Malta, having sought out Peter Turnball at her request, he forwarded Hester the news that Miranda had died of a massive stroke on 14 July 1816.

Lord Stanhope had been unwell for months, his limbs and organs painfully swollen. The cause cited on his death certificate was dropsy, the all-purpose term for cirrhosis of the liver or cancer. Earlier that year, James, who by now had returned to London, broke his own vow, and twice begged to see him. When Sir Joseph Banks came to see his ailing friend, he was horrified to discover that James had been turned away. Instead James saw his father only as a corpse, and acted as one of his pall-bearers, along with his widowed brother-in-law. Chevening was left in a ramshackle state. All its 'aristocratical' trappings had been removed, its vast rooms left unheated and turned into chaotic workstations; the innards of the great house unravelled with his fireproofing treatments.

Their stepmother Louisa had been replaced by the dark-haired Mrs Lackner ('Wally'), their father's mistress, a pianoforte player who had originally come to Chevening to teach the mistress of the house, but ended up stealing away the master. Banks suspected that Wally's parsimonious management was a ruse, judging her 'naturally anxious to make a purse', and was of the opinion that she had 'starved him to death'.

To the disgust of the Stanhope children, 'Wally' did very well out of their father's will, inheriting £5,000. Shortly afterwards, she left for her native Prague.

Philip Mahon, now the fourth Earl Stanhope, was living in Vienna, away from his wife and young family, and was about to move to Paris. In April 1817, stirred up by old bitterness, Hester wrote to him, addressing him stiffly as 'Stanhope'. She still despised him. 'The precariousness of our days upon earth has induced me to write you these few words, not as a mark of respect to the *now* head of the family (for I disown all heads of families unless they have *hearts*) but in the hope that if ever you can feel, it will be at this moment when, if you will move your conscience to speak, it will dictate to you the true and only means of repaying past conduct.'

The reason for her hatred was something they were both aware of. 'It was wishing to eradicate, if possible, from your character, the seeds of that abominable vice (a vice unknown to wild beasts) which occasioned the rupture between us.' It is easy to jump to twenty-first-century conclusions when looking at a letter like this, and it is curious that her brother did not burn it.

Now he was to inherit their childhood home where once, she reminded him, she had sworn 'never to forsake you, until I had extricated you'. If he reflected on his past behaviour towards her, his guilt would surely be 'intolerable and embitter the remainder of your life'. As it stood, she made it clear: 'There is nothing in common between us'. Perhaps he would become 'respectable', she told him, and 'merit the favour of Heaven, by doing that which is most acceptable in the sight of God – becoming the father of those who surround you'. If this was not a literal reference (that he may have sired an illegitimate child is not improbable) it was certainly intended to remind him that being son and heir carried responsibilities. She wanted him to 'forgo a little pecuniary interest and take with a grateful heart what your poor parent left you' and act with 'duty and forbearance' to provide what he could so that 'those who were [once] supported by him should feel his loss as little as possible'.

As for herself, she wanted nothing from him, merely to ensure that he 'place in Coutts's hands' the inheritance willed to her from Charles's estate that for legal reasons was now to be released, a sum she expected to be some £10,000.

With that money, Hester intended to buy back her pride. She notified Bruce with a letter that was no more than a paragraph, entirely to the point, with no endearments. 'The death of my poor father will put me in possession (next December) of a certain sum of ready money. I have therefore ordered Mr Coutts, when he receives that money, to replace in your father's hands every shilling placed by him or you, to my account since you left me. This is my irrevocable determination so save yourself the trouble of combating it as it will be useless.'

She had cut her ties with Bruce and said her piece to her eldest brother. Now all her commitments and debts, emotional and otherwise, were severed and settled.

That same April in Cairo Lascaris died suddenly. Dysentery was suggested, but no one believed his death was natural: poison was almost certainly the cause. He had turned up in the city in December 1816, and despite the fact that an arrest warrant had gone out for him, it was quietly dropped when the French consuls discovered that he now travelled on a British passport and was under British jurisdiction. When news reached Roussel, the French consul in Alexandria, that Lascaris had recently been to see Hester, he regarded it as significant enough to be cited in a dispatch to the Duc de Richelieu, Talleyrand's successor.[9]

For some months Lascaris had earned a living teaching French to Mehmet Ali's young son Ismail Pasha but had also, some said, been filling his head with dangerous ideas. Roussel reported to his superior that Lascaris had been trying to persuade Ismail Pasha to revolt against his father, by taking renegade command of the Bedouin and the Wahhabis in their military clash against Mehmet Ali's elder son Ibrahim Pasha. The British, Roussel reported, were 'very aggravated' at Mehmet Ali's successful consolidation of power over the Persian Gulf and the Red Sea, and Roussel believed Lascaris was acting on their side.

Roussel reported the ex-consul Drovetti's extreme panic on hearing of Lascaris's death, and how he 'seemed to behave like a madman', and that he confessed 'his great fear that he too would be poisoned like Lascaris' for he knew for certain that 'some of his own agents had sold themselves to the British, and were now his enemies'.[10]

Although Britain and France were no longer at war, covert rivalry remained intense. The British suspected that it was the French who had Lascaris killed. There was a scuffle between the rival consuls to gain possession of the dead man's private papers: Drovetti went so far as to summon Fathallah Sâyigh from Syria, insisting that if he had any of his master's manuscripts in his possession, he was prepared to 'purchase them at any price'. But the British consul in Cairo, Henry Salt, secured them by force.[11] Whatever those papers contained, and what became of them, remains a mystery.

Hester's comment on Lascaris's death was ambiguous. 'Poor man. It was not Napoleon that he was so much attached to, it was to him that had the *portefeuille*'. Whatever his secrets and lies, it seems that Lascaris took them to the grave.

# 18

## Mr Koand's Spy

Hester found herself in a predicament. The Anglo-French rivalry that began as a military clash over Egypt was evolving into a much wider race for political influence. The fact that she had organized a reprisal on Boutin's behalf had not gone unnoticed in France, both among the Bonapartists, and those who had speedily 'pulled down his eagles and put up the arms of France'.* The possibility of using herself as a lure for counter-espionage had obviously crossed her mind, and may indeed have formed the basis of her one-time 'Napoleon plan'. She believed herself capable of outwitting even the ablest of men. Even if she had rejected Admiral Smith's offer, she welcomed his praise that she knew how 'to make short work of things, and *always of a blackguard*.'[1]

She told her friend General Anderson that she had just written to the East India Company, to explain the Ascalon 'scrape', and to offer her services.

> I wrote to India to state how I had acted in this country under a variety
> of circumstances, what was my real situation and influence, and if a
> humble individual like myself could get on thus, what would a respectable

---

* In 1816, Hester was thanked publicly for her role in avenging Boutin's death in the Chamber of Deputies in Paris, and much later, an article dated 29 April 1830 in the *Courier Français* also paid tribute to her great hospitality to the fallen French hero, and 'the use of her influence to ensure the assassins were punished and the restitution of the colonel's property'. While Lascaris was given a simple burial in Cairo (the expenses paid for by the British government), Boutin would have his name remembered by a street in Paris and in his home town of Loroux Bottereau, near Nantes, and a column erected for him after the French invasion of Algeria.

agent do if appointed upon this coast? This strengthened my opinion that I was but doing justice to myself and good to the public not to neglect every opportunity of increasing that influence I had gained. And if I should not be even able to pursue the system I had begun and not to allow it all to slip through my fingers, and if unable myself to pursue the system I had begun to have the satisfaction of making it over to someone else who would be invested with regular power as well as being provided with necessary means to accomplish the work I had begun. If India did anything for me, very well. If not, poverty never alarms me, God is generous. Allah knows.[2]

It is tempting to imagine the East India Company official who received Hester's overture choking into his tea at the thought of Chatham's grand-daughter announcing her willingness to be an agent.

To support her petition, she prepared confidential files detailing all Syria's leaders and people of influence, including the Bashirs and Mustafa Berber but also Malem Musa and Selim, who might possibly be sought as allies or agents, with observations on their strengths and weaknesses. (Only Sheikh Jumblatt presented a challenge, she thought. She thought him quite his own man, unlikely to be 'bought'. 'It is difficult to find any present suitable for a person who already has everything money can buy.'[3]) She told Anderson:

> I hope that no sensible, unprejudiced person will think money ill spent in having acquired a knowledge of the people who command the whole tract of country, in conjunction with the Wahhabis, which extends from the borders of Syria to the Persian Gulf and from the Isthmus of Suez to the Straits of Babel Mandel.

Yet as she pointed out, '*money* alone will not do, they must have influence [and] every body here has implicit faith in my word'. However, the letter she sent to Bombay does not appear to have survived, nor has any reply been recorded.

Her earlier aspirations to set up a school, to write books, and her other speculative ideas, seem to have paled somewhat. She made her offer more explicit to the Duke of York. She wanted to be commissioned to operate in some unofficial capacity, as his ear to the ground on Eastern matters, or as a spymistress. She asked to be sent 'sound-headed' and 'admirable men' – future empire-builders – to help train them up, and make something of their position.

She had hinted at her ambitions in her last letter to Bruce, telling him she envisaged that in the near future, Syria and Arabia – and even Abyssinia – might become a source of major economic wealth for whatever empire claimed them first. The challenge she saw in these countries was similar to those faced long ago by her ancestor Diamond Pitt, whose dealings with the East India Company had forced it to change and adapt.

> Ever since my arrival in this part of the world, I have considered it much more politically important than it has generally been supposed to be. I have looked upon Syria (including the Desert) as one of the keys of India, and Abyssinia as a little India, at least as a future market for her commodities when it should become civilized.
>
> With respect to Syria, I am convinced that there is no tyrant, whether Napoleon or Alexander, who may spring up in Europe, who will not cast a longing eye towards India. It was indisputably, one of the great objects of the former; and will, time and place convenient, be the same of the latter. Syria then and a host of Arabs [sic] which may be seen to belong to it, appeared to me to be most important – important as far as keeping up an interest with the inhabitants and acquiring all possible knowledge of the country as well as the disposition of the people, in order to be prepared for whatever may take place. This has been my aim, and without risking being accused of exaggeration or conceit, I believe I have succeeded ten times better than any other European.[4]

Hester was obviously manoeuvring for a role as powerbroker, promoting herself as willing and able to resume her activities in the desert and rally the Bedouin Arabs.

When it came to intelligence, Hester boasted to Meryon, still in London, that she was 'a chip off the old block'. Her grandfather had taken a very personal interest in spycraft. He 'liked to write and do things which no human being would dream came from his hands,' she said.

I once met with one of his spies, a woman of the common class, who had passed her life dressed in man's clothes. In this way, she went as a sailor to America, and used to write him letters as if to a sweetheart, giving an account of the enemy's ships and plans in a most masterly way, in the description of a box of tools, or in something so unlike the thing in question that no suspicion could be had [of] the meaning of the contents.[5]

From her time with Pitt, Hester was familiar with the way the Foreign Office, the Admiralty and the War Office collected information, through official channels and other highly ingenious routes. She had her own well-informed contacts; she even had her own apprentice spies. She had good reason to believe that she might be as capable as any professional agent. For the moment, she took on several new men, all of them noticeably handsome – an Arab by the name of Hassan Logmagi and a well-born youth from Cairo, Michael Ayda, whose uncle had been a general in Napoleon's Egyptian army, and whose family fortune had been confiscated by Mehmet Ali – and put them to work.

At first her requests to Meryon were merely errands: letters to be hand-delivered, money matters to be arranged with Coutts and others.* Soon, however, Meryon found himself admitted into the parlours of the grandest houses in London on Hester's service. He took tea with Lord Grenville at Whitehall, and unravelled parcels of specimens before Sir Joseph Banks at Soho Square. He would commiserate with Banks over news that Burckhardt had died suddenly in Cairo that October, apparently of dysentery. Meryon met the Generals Anderson and Oakes, the latter now back in England. He saw Hester's other Grenville uncle, Sir Richard Grenville. He was summoned to Brooks's by Lord Ebrington and he breakfasted with the elderly Coutts, now eighty-seven.

To Lord Lonsdale, Meryon delivered precious statues in person. As a

---

* Meryon's first weeks in London were taken up with her urgent plea for books, and he spent a good deal of time pestering the booksellers at Hatchards in Piccadilly. She had asked for the best Arabic and Persian dictionary available. Also at her request, into the box went a Hebrew grammar, tomes on astronomy, medicine and gardening; Volney's *Ruines*; Thompson's *Suetonius*, and Sterne's *Sentimental Journey*, and clipped items in the newspapers he thought might interest her.

matter of honour, now that Hester had some money from her brother Charles's inheritance, she reimbursed the £2,000 with which he had long ago paid her brothers' debts. Lonsdale, one of the Lords of Treasury and a Commissioner for Indian Affairs, was exactly the sort of powerful friend she wanted to keep.

Meryon visited the Duke of York at the Horse Guards, and admired the full-length painting he had commissioned of Hester's gift mare.[6] The Duke wanted to know everything about Hester's life in Syria. 'Would she not be in more comfort at home amongst her friends? Is Lady Hester attached to nothing now in England?'[7] When the Duke enquired after the cause of her breach with James, Meryon tried to be discreet, telling him that she was 'more rooted there than ever' due to what she considered to be the 'plot' to get her home. He reported that as far as he knew, the idea had been abandoned, and James remained as dear to her as ever, he said diplomatically.

In the months to come, the Duke of York promised to take Hester's interesting proposition to his brother, the Duke of Sussex, who remembered her well as a superior rider on shared hunts. In the meantime, the Duke of York sent her an exquisite silver inkstand, to encourage her to write to him.

Over the summer of 1817, Meryon went to the village of Chevening as Hester's spy. If Hester had the vain hope that she might inherit even a modest sum, she was disappointed. Nothing was left to his surviving children and grandchildren, nor to any of his faithful old servants.

Meryon met Varley, Stanhope's old friend, whose title of blacksmith hardly reflected his essential role in so many of the Earl's experiments over some thirty years. Varley took him to the edge of a field to look over the hedgerows to Chevening House. It struck Meryon as vast and almost monstrously impressive.

He asked: 'Have you left Lady H well? I have heard what a pitch of eminence she has reached in Arabia.'

'Have you, sir?' I replied, 'and from whom?'

'From Lord Stanhope,' rejoined Mr Varley. 'He used to tell me all about her as she went from place to place. Perhaps your ladyship will be surprised to learn that her father followed her movements with so much interest.'[8]

For the moment, the estate was unoccupied. The new Earl was in Paris with his family, and had not yet returned.

Meanwhile, Meryon worked at St Thomas's Hospital and completed his studies. With money Hester allocated for the purpose, he installed his daughter Lucy at a respectable girl's school near Petersham in Surrey run by the same 'clever and pretty Lisette' who had left Chevening abruptly around the time of Ann Fry's mysterious pregnancy. Hester had hinted that Lisette, too, had been in a similar predicament but that she had gone to Paris, a brave and unusual move in those revolutionary times.

He felt a twinge of nostalgia when Elizabeth Williams wrote to give him an account of life at Mar Elias, of Tabitha, with whom he had shared tender moments, enquiring after him – 'she looks, poor girl, very miserable' – and of the majestic views and pine-scented air at Jebba where they had spent the summer. She told him that Giorgio had returned to the Greek island where his family lived and had been replaced by an Arab called Salan. Elizabeth continued, 'I should say I had never seen her in better health in my life than she is at present.'[9]

Hester had a compelling reason for staying away from England. The way in which certain members of her family had taken to referring to their unpredictable, strong-minded relative was disturbing. It was very easy to label a woman mad in the early nineteenth century. A new breed of privately-run asylums tucked away from public notice in rustic surroundings made it more convenient than ever to discard a difficult wife or child, or sibling. It was frighteningly common for a sane person to find themselves accused of lunacy, and for doctors to be found to make damning assessments. Once confined, an inmate's attempts to seek legal protection and redress became almost impossible.

It is unlikely that Hester would ever have thought that her relatives might consider such a drastic step, but for one powerful factor: her brother, the new Earl Stanhope, now an ultra-Tory MP for Midhurst. He had influential contacts, and she was quite sure he would use whatever means he could to control her. It is telling that she asked Meryon to find out what was being said about her, not only among her friends, but by people on the street. His answer was not encouraging:

I will tell you in a few words what is the state of opinion concerning yourself as far as I have been able to learn. The common people think you eccentric and half-mad. A higher description of persons talk of your being disgusted with the world and wonder how you can live without society amidst Barbarians etc. Others picture to their minds Eastern pageantry, horrid wastes, burning deserts, Circassian beauties and all the visions that fancy reasonings at a distance can create.

Such are [the opinions] of the Mrs Coutts's and the half-initiated, and as [Sir Francis Burdett] very justly said to me, I hope that Lady Hester does not give herself the trouble to ask herself what nine-tenth of the world says of her, whose opinion good or bad is not worth having and whose wrong-headedness no one would set right in a hundred years. I assured him you did not, nor cared perhaps but for the opinion of 8 or 9 people in England. Last of all, those such as General Grenville, Lord Ebrington etc. Such persons consider you as the Phoenix of the age, consuming itself in its own fires. They will not allow the Turks to have any intellect nor (although this is a point observed that on yr account I never discuss with them) the French any virtues. On the expediency of yr remaining where you are or of the reasons which induce you to do so up to this time, not one of them will be fully persuaded, and I do not find that on this head, an angel would convince them.[10]

In trying to establish her real standing in the eyes of those men she did admire, Hester knew she was asking a great deal, but she intended to stick to her resolution. Yet Meryon warned her that almost all her friends in England were 'determined to think you act imprudently in yr. affairs. Prejudice, total ignorance of the people you are among, short-sightedness, blinds them.'

Meryon saw Bruce, and thought him still his old handsome self although 'rather thin'. Any old rancour between them had been cast away.

Speaking of Hester, Bruce was at times visibly upset, and at least once, got up and paced about in distress.

> At his own moving we had a long and interesting conversation on past affairs. He was much agitated. I told him yr mind was tranquil and that in repaying the money, you felt like the independent person you had always been. He said his conduct towards you had been uniformly respectful. He added that he always had but one feeling respecting you and if it would serve Lady Hester he would even now take a journey to see her. For his sentiments of respect and regard [whole line crossed out in Meryon's journal] would still and ever would remain unaltered. Other conversation passed. I then represented to him kindly how sorry you were that you had made him shed so many tears and thus soothed somewhat his feelings which this discussion had agitated considerably.[11]

Meryon's account of the conversation indicates that Hester had revealed to him her specific grievance against Bruce, which was that she had relied on the promise that he would send her a portion of his allowance, and in the anticipation of it, had got herself more into debt.* Bruce clearly felt bad about 'the violation of his promise' and confessed he had hoped to set everything right with Hester but that his father's bankruptcy had taken him completely by surprise.[12]

Although cordial, the meeting was not a prelude to a friendship, but a settling of scores. Meryon would see Bruce again, but they would never again talk so openly of matters of the heart.

As well as enrolling in law studies, Bruce was now determined to make a go of politics, and had convinced Sir Francis Burdett to act as his patron. Some months later, Meryon described going to Covent

---

* In 1814, when he was in London, Bruce had tried to keep to his side of the bargain with Hester. Anticipating that his father was not going to make any kind of reparation payment for her shipwreck losses, Bruce came to a private agreement with Coutts, so that Hester could be forwarded a £1800 Letter of Credit, using his own 'verbal promise' as surety. He also agreed to pay Hester £600 a year out of his own allowance, scaled down from his original offer. In a letter, he told her that should he die, his father would consider it 'a sacred duty' to pay her, for the rest of her life, £800 a year. That was not the way life turned out.

Garden to see Bruce make a speech. 'Facemaker has been playing a most conspicuous part at the hustings,' he would tell Hester, whose nickname for Bruce combined affection, contempt and sexual innuendo (for 'making faces' was colloquial usage for having sex). 'He spoke well and some of his sentences were elegant and forceful.'[13] The would-be candidate flinched before the notoriously raucous inner-city crowds.

> I could understand that Bruce was a favourite with the people, if indeed these remarks were not made by emissaries of Sir Francis's Committee, planted amongst the people to damage the Tory candidate's cause. One man said he was an excellent speaker and had a pretty French accent, another that he must be a clever fellow who could contrive La Valette's escape from prison, a third that he was very graceful. The women said he had very nice white teeth (which was quite true), the men called him 'a dammed [sic] good-looking fellow' and there was after that a cry of 'Bruce, Bruce, let Bruce speak!'[14]

While casting about for a seat to contest, Bruce would also find another distraction in the form of the woman he would propose to three weeks after their first meeting: Marianne, the attractive, dark-haired widow of a prominent war hero, Sir Peter Parker. His marriage would follow within the year.*

Hester needed no official sanctioning to dabble in espionage and subterfuge herself, for this is certainly what she began to do next. The

---

* Captain Sir Peter Parker had been a lieutenant under Nelson on the *Victory*. He died near Baltimore in 1814, singled out for posthumous praise in the House of Commons as 'the gallant Parker' who led his men in battle even while he was dying of his wounds, and buried in Westminster Abbey. Marianne was modest and respectable, with good connections, but it was by no means the glittering match Crauford hoped for. Bruce left a shambolic note announcing his intention to marry, enclosing Marianne's letter, on his father's breakfast table and fled. He had no money, and Crauford was in no position to make a settlement. Against the wishes of both families, in August 1818 they married in secret; soon to rent their first home together, No. 34 Grand Parade in Brighton. Bruce became step-father to Marianne's two sons. Their daughter, Marianne, would be born a year later.

many dozens of letters between Hester and Meryon dating from this period employ a complicated cipher of codenames, metaphors and references, to 'jumble things up on purpose' and to 'to bewilder into what hands the letter might have fallen'.* Meryon's adoption of her coded names and deliberately obscure style can be seen in these extracts from his letters to her, from 1817 and 1818:

When I delivered the message to Mr Tall-Wheel, he said, remarking on the words, 'The man whose palace is a snuff-box, that must mean S' (the name of a personage who warms his bottom before company). Now as I am almost sure you meant no such thing I hasten to inform you of it lest he should go and commit you by saying of one person what was intended of another. I did not hint my suspicions to Mr Tall-Wheel because I did not feel sufficiently confident I was right. I know a place that looks very much like a snuffbox not in London but where one Mr Khi-yat lives. Mr Tall-Wheel asked about John Bull who has been recommended to Slim Serpent's Father by Slim Serpent.

And another:

Respecting other matters as touching Facemaker and the like, they are no more open to conviction. Heather, who to my mind, thinks better on these subjects than anyone with whom I was called on to converse, will write to Mr Kocub shortly, as I know the opinions that he entertains on politics, religion and other important matters.

---

* In Hester's code, 'A' was sometimes Anderson (and other times America, which she also referred to as 'Yenky Dunia'). James was simply 'J', and Chevening 'C'. 'Tall-wheel' was Banks; 'Leviathan' the Marquess of Buckingham; 'Whale' Sligo; 'Heather' Sir Francis Burdett and 'Scribe' Hester's lawyer, Alexander Murray. Lonsdale became 'Master of the Egyptian Figure'. 'Mosquito Net' was Ebrington; 'Castor' Lord Glastonbury and 'Pollùx' General Grenville. 'My Son' was the Duke of York; Coutts was 'Gownwearer's Husband' and he and his wife became 'The Canker and his Lady' or 'January and May'. The hated Burckhardt was 'Serpent, the Fat' and Bankes 'Slim Serpent'. The names go on; some are impossible to puzzle out. (Place names were sometime coded too: the State of Virginia became 'Bintra'). Even Meryon was perplexed: 'I'm afraid I shall deserve the appellation of stupid for not understanding who you mean by Sultan's Mother,' he wrote plaintively.

'Mr Kocub', it soon becomes apparent, is Hester's codename for herself.*
Sometimes, far less often, she also referred to herself as 'Um Nijem', or 'mother
of stars'. Meryon is 'Stutterer', 'Tabitha's master' and sometimes 'the quiz'.

Hester was formulating an idea which was really just a variant of her
original 'Napoleon plan'. It was one she felt would do no disservice to
the true patriots of either country. But she had changed her focus. Now
her aim in appearing to align herself with the French was to secure the
position she wanted no matter what, that of powerbroker and leader
among the Bedouin Arabs.

Ali Bey el Abbassi, whose real name was Domingo Badia y Leblich, a
Spanish-born scholar and explorer, was someone Hester had been making
discreet enquiries about for more than two years. One of her visitors,
Ambroise Firmin Didot, then a junior diplomat at Constantinople, had
presented her with a copy of *Travels of Ali Bey in Morocco, Tripoli, Cyprus,
Egypt, Arabia, Syria and Turkey between the years 1803 and 1807*, published
by his father in Paris in 1814. Badia's account of his adventures in Wahhabi
territory, his meetings with the Wahhabi leader Saud ibn Saud, and his
journey to Mecca undoubtedly impressed her. He described the terror
instilled by the Wahhabis as they rode into battle with their 'long, floating
hair' and the way many of them bore scars on their cheeks which signi-
fied that they had 'declared themselves slaves of the House of God'. She
had passed on to Bruce Malem Hayim's comment that 'B[adia's] talents
were remarkable' but that 'some little circumstances obliged him to leave
the service of *his master*, who otherwise liked him extremely'. The master
in question was Napoleon.

In her dealings with French diplomats, Hester manoeuvred between
staunch Bourbons and those more sympathetic to the republican cause.
Among the latter was Firmin Didot, whom she personally liked.

There were certainly those who genuinely wanted Napoleon rescued,
but there were also others who might have wanted to see the former
Emperor escape so that he might be disposed of once and for all.

*   *   *

---

* By her own definition it meant 'planet', and seems to have been one of the many sobriquets she
acquired from her time with the Bedouin. '*Kaukab*' was apparently a Bedouin word for the 'star
of destiny'. It is also curiously similar to the words used by the Yezidi to describe a *koassa* or
prophet, but especially *kocak*, or an initiated adept, a 'dancer to the heavens'.

Much to his surprise, Meryon was soon bombarded with requests to 'take all possible means to enquire about America, North and South'. Hester boasted, '[There] I shall be everything for the sake of my grandfather, the climate only is the objection, but in Virginia I believe it to be good enough. In short, take measures to find out all you can about that.' But, she cautioned to Meryon, 'Not a word to James about America!'[15]

Next she demanded to be sent tracts on 'South American Emancipation', and ordered Meryon to present himself to 'the minister from Buenos Ayres [sic] who lodges at Albany' and make discreet enquiries about 'setting oneself up in Buenos Ayres and Chile' and 'pose as a prospector, to enquire the price of passage, of passports, permissions etc'. But shortly afterwards she told him that 'America and all that was kiddup [Hester's slang for a lie] because I knew letters were read'.

Before Meryon could recover from his confusion, she sent him off to see Miranda's old friends and advisers, among them Bentham and Vansittart, now Chancellor of the Exchequer, as well as his private secretary, Tomás Molini, who was to be pressed for his contacts in South America. Vansittart – or 'V' – would become one of her trusted go-betweens. Meryon could never quite understand the nature of some of his missions, which sometimes involved handing over letters, and mused that this might be deliberate obfuscation on Hester's part.

In late spring 1818, out of the blue, Meryon received a mystifying command. 'Wait until you have received my letter . . . I find that the Kocub has given particular orders to the Stutterer to become, without loss of time, a Freemason. Study hard at our new trade and get rank as fast as possible in France as well as in England. Better, said the Kocub, sell your shirt than not obey.'[16]

Hester's sudden fascination for Freemasonry was all about power and the monitoring of intelligence. It is telling that almost all of the men closest to her had Masonic allegiances of some sort. Foremost among them had been her father, and it was no accident that in his crackdown on sedition, Pitt had introduced legislation to make the activities of the Freemasons more transparent. The Duke of Sussex, whom Hester knew to be mulling over her unorthodox suggestions, was none other than Grand Master of the United Grand Lodge of England. Miranda had founded his own South American lodge in exile. Meanwhile in France, ritual initiation tended to be regarded as an essential career move from Talleyrand down.

Hester had a compelling reason to want Meryon to become her pliable Masonic 'mole'. She intended to make use of the way in which affiliations could be discreetly tested out and messages sent under a guise of organized secrecy. She knew there were highly clandestine groups forming within established Freemasonry, especially in France, but they had spread to England too, and she was desperate to find out about them. Hester's earlier observation that powerful secret societies were at work fomenting political changes in Europe was entirely accurate, and she is likely to have heard about it from someone who was on the inside.

General Loustaunau had told her about the spread in popularity of the reformed Masonic order of the Rite of Misraim. It was known to attract former Jacobites who wanted to see the return of republicanism. Another was a new order, the one she had referred to as the 'Brotherhood of Luxor'. This was the Rite of Memphis, formed by Bonapartists faithful to the Eagle. She was certain Boutin had been a member.

Within four months of receiving Hester's instructions Meryon had presented himself to a lodge in North London and studied 'the trade'. On 24 June 1818 he was admitted 'to the Castle Inn Kentish Town via a lodge of Frenchmen'. As a teenager Meryon had been sent across to Boulogne for three summers in a row, and spoke excellent French; he told Hester that he preferred the French lodge to the English one 'who make this sublime mystery a motive for guzzling and think only of the dinners the meetings lead to'. He added meaningfully that 'J. assured me that you would be perfectly satisfied with the seat he now held'.

'An ill-natured person would perhaps call the role I now fill in England that of a spy,' he wrote to Hester around this time. He observed that certain friends of hers were trying to distance themselves from him, and as her 'confidential instrument', his own motives were being questioned. 'Pollux', General Grenville (the Duke of York's great friend and the head of his household for many years), confided to him that he did 'not know what to do about Lady H's letters' and that 'J wanted [him] very, very much to burn them'. Grenville fretted that after his death 'they will almost certainly fall into others' hands, but I should not like, in case any reflections concerning pecuniary arrangements should ever be cast upon her character during her existence or on her memory hereafter, that these authentic documents should be wanting to prove how wrong-fully she has been accused'.

Meryon warned her that 'contrary to your injunctions of secrecy' whatever she had written 'respecting "A"' was in danger of being leaked, and told her that 'the knowledge of this has induced J. to request him as well as Pollux to burn your letters'. The identity of 'A' – which we will see takes on great significance when later events unfold – is never revealed.

Meanwhile, in a separate development, she had Meryon order large supplies of pistols and blunderbusses as a favour for Emir Bashir from the Duke of York's favourite weapons manufacturer, Messrs Dobson & Co, and the payment for them was brokered through Coutts.[17] But there was much more at stake than buying political goodwill with Emir Bashir, and whatever it was, it involved plans sufficiently momentous to make Lord Grenville very nervous indeed.

In 1818 a bizarre and ingenious plot by French Bonapartists to rescue Napoleon from St Helena was under way. Hester's awareness of it, and possible involvement in it, has only been revealed by a careful reading of Meryon's letters and by putting together pieces of information from other sources.

As a result of his new contacts, Meryon informed her that he had dined with 'a Colonel of the Guard over Bonaparte at St Helena'. It was reported that the former Emperor, on his optimistic days, was fond of making grandiose pronouncements that a new government would come to power in Britain and release him. Then he would sail for America, and even considered he might lead Venezuela, Chile and Peru into independence. 'I shall mould Latin America into a great Empire,' he would say.[18] (Suddenly all Hester's confidential exertions to gather information about South America take on the air of a plan.) But he was also fond of announcing that if he could return anywhere it would be Egypt, 'the geographical key of the world'.

In the same letter Meryon dropped an innocuous line of apparent gossip about a French landlady. 'Madame Bertrand is always wanting carpenters for little jobs.' This was in fact a piece of inside information. General Bertrand and his wife Fanny had chosen to share Napoleon's exile, and of all the women around Napoleon at Longwood on St Helena, she was closest to him. (It would seem that in his remark, 'carpenters' was a rather obvious reference to 'Masons'.) Along with this, Meryon sent Hester a picture of Longwood, and an atlas, telling her 'by cutting the edges of the sheet no 24 of this atlas all round you will come at it easily; do the same to map no 14 and 29'. Whatever the meaning of these instructions, they are too obscure now to understand, but he was either spelling a message or suggesting directions.

There were other clues in his letters. He reported that he had been to see one of James's old friends, one Harry Dillon, seemingly unimportant except for the fact that Fanny Bertrand was also a Dillon from the same Franco-Irish family. Hester had a message for Harry Dillon, that he should remember that 'the wife of Murad Bey was my friend'.[19] General Bertrand had been in Egypt as Captain of Engineers, and would have known, or known of, Nafissa.

Around the same time, Meryon evidently communicated something to Hester which he later wrote in the margin of his journal: the name 'Ali Bey' and after a single dash, as though there is a link, 'the Count Las Casas, St Helena'. As one of the last Napoleon stalwarts, the Count's presence on St Helena was well-known. As for Ali Bey el Abbassi, or Badia, the diplomat Didot Firmin reported that he was 'extremely anxious' to meet Hester.

More intriguingly, in their coded interchange, Meryon makes mention of 'the man with a sort of Brutus look, a dignified and unbending manner who bid you adieu on the pier at Ramsgate when he embarked for Holland'. There are not many candidates who match the description of this mystery man, whose message to Hester was that 'those who called upon him are set on to call'. But there was a man who did, a certain Captain Tom Johnstone, a former smuggler and Channel pilot, a blue-eyed charmer said to have a way with 'ladies, horses and dogs'. Johnstone once worked for her father and Robert Fulton on the development of his submarine prototype. While Hester was at Walmer, he was hand-picked for a key role in the planned covert operation that was to have been launched against Napoleon's armies at Boulogne, led by Sir John Moore by land and Sir Sidney Smith by sea. Hester later went to watch the sea trials. Johnstone had indeed gone to the Netherlands shortly afterwards. After Fulton left for America, Johnstone (on Smith's emphatic recommendation) had been secretly commissioned by the Duke of York to continue the construction of an adapted submarine prototype at an obscure location at Wallingford on the Upper Thames.

There is no satisfactory explanation as to how the Bonapartists singled Johnstone out, nor who suggested him, but that year Johnstone was reportedly offered £40,000 if he would agree to transport his submarine out to St Helena at an agreed signal. Once in the open sea, it was to be towed by a sailing vessel to the South Atlantic, and then ferry Napoleon to a waiting ship.[20]

In his reports to Hester, Meryon alluded to her new mystery correspondent in Marseille, one Monsieur Guerin, also known as 'the Old Figure'. Meryon had been advised by one of his shadowy new acquaintances that Guerin was someone she should flatter more assiduously, 'to keep up his attention which otherwise might flag' and suggested 'it would be well if you were to desire Mr Regnault to write a few lines to him in praise of his conduct towards you'.[21]

All these intriguing fragments add up to one strong possibility. Hester appears to have been trying to gather information for others with whom she was hoping to ingratiate herself. She had Meryon obeying her commands, often months after receiving her instructions. Sometimes he inserted little notes in books, once he sent her letters hidden in a locked cabinet, with a secretly-sprung compartment, sending the key in a separate dispatch.[22] Meanwhile she was pulling her own strings as deftly as she could, never giving more information to any one party than she thought necessary. Whatever she laid out in letters to the Duke of York, General Grenville and James, among others, does suggest that there was a plan, and that a trap was indeed being set.

Over the summer of 1818 Regnault, the French consul in Tripoli, informed Louis Molé, Minister of the Marine in Paris (Napoleon's former finance minister who now headed the French equivalent of the Admiralty), that all was going according to schedule. 'Following the instructions of the Arab traveller who had an urgent and specific wish to become acquainted with Milady Stanhope, I shall return immediately to see her,' he said, adding that 'Milady is known in these parts only as queen and heroine'. Regnault had 'made known to her the true motives of this traveller', he added.

When Hester met Badia, she would have seen a man who could certainly pass for Arab nobility. As 'Othman Bey el Abbassi', he presented himself as a descendant of the Abbasids, and cut a princely figure. Whether he came with news from 'Count Las Casas' or not, Badia had come to talk about desert politics, and the building of a new Arab alliance.

Earlier that spring, the minds of everyone in Arabia had been seared by a major military strike against the Wahhabis led by Mehmet Ali's son Ibrahim Pasha resulting in the razing of their capital Darayya to the ground. It was not only the Wahhabis who died: the general population were also horrendously brutalized, their villages torched. For many Arabs, the usual attitude of resigned sufferance was replaced by intense hatred towards the Ottoman overlords. In the power vacuum, there was a clear opportunity to build new alliances with the Arabs, and this was why the French were so suddenly interested in Hester, and willing to see her as an asset.

Those acting for Bonaparte hoped to secure a platform for him to stage a brilliant comeback. This tallies with what Lascaris had been attempting to do in Cairo, and his efforts to turn Mehmet Ali's youngest son against him. It helps explain Boutin's mission in Syria. It certainly explains Badia's intentions in Mecca. The theory was obvious if audacious: if Napoleon escaped and managed to get to the Syrian coast, and an army were primed to support him, it was he who might lead the war against the Pasha.

Hester faced a choice: either she could help the Bonapartists and find herself a role in unifying the Arabs, or she could inform on them to the British – or the Bourbons. Whatever she did, she must have reasoned that she would gain great leverage.

A clue surfaces in an unsigned quatrain addressed to Hester, apparently from the Duc de Rivière, the French Ambassador at Constantinople, some time between 1817 and 1818. It is a very curious and ambiguous work that appears to be an invitation to reciprocity. It was intentionally mysterious and had a hidden meaning:

> *Ne verse pas des larmes, ma chère et belle marquise*
> *Tu seras l'héroïne de toutes mes entreprises*
> *Je prie trois dieux pour toi, et si ton héros meurt*
> *À eux laisse mon âme, à toi je donne mon coeur.*

(Don't let your tears fall, my precious and beautiful marchioness
You will be the heroine of all my enterprises
I will pray to three gods for you, and if your hero dies
Leave my soul to them, and to you I give my heart.)

The 'hero' to her heroine appears most likely to be Badia.

'Our heroine is being an angel,' Badia wrote to Regnault about Hester, on 16 August 1818. 'She will tell you what she has done. She is very digni-fied about the glorious role that awaits her, if destiny has its way.'[23] That some kind of extraordinary complicity has taken place is clear from this letter, which Badia wrote from Damascus, shortly after seeing her at Mar Elias. It is also indicated by the careful laying of plans for Badia to meet Hester about which Regnault had closely informed Molé at the Ministry of the Marine. Hester would later mention to Meryon that around this time the Duc de Rivière came from Constantinople to see her.

Now the story gets more complicated. It is possible that Badia was willing to play for both sides too, something Hester had taken the trouble to enquire about. He wrote to Sir Joseph Banks in 1814 to signal his willingness to work for Britain 'in the interests of science and explor-ation'. Banks no doubt considered his offer carefully, and passed it on to be reviewed, as indicated by a note he wrote in the margins: 'The present would be a favourable time for an attempt, because in the event of peace an Englishman will go nowhere without having a Frenchman at his back to counteract him.'[24] Whatever the 'glorious role' Badia had promised the 'new Queen Zenobia', Banks's analysis of the new dynamic between France and Britain lay at its core.

Seven days after he wrote his letter about Hester being 'an angel', Badia was fatally poisoned. He had taken a common remedy – powdered rhubarb – to stave off what seemed to be a mild fever. It was given to him by his host at Damascus, Chaboceau, a French doctor who was known to every European, including Hester. A question would linger over whether and how it might have been tampered with.

By the time Badia's symptoms worsened, he had already left Damascus and gone into the desert, intending to join the caravan to Mecca. By the time he reached the walled medieval village of Zarka, near Mezerib, agonizing pains ripped through his gut; he began to vomit dark coffee-like granules of blackened blood.

On 23 August Badia wrote to Regnault: 'It is indisputable that this remedy contains poison, though poor C. will doubt it. I will send you the rest of the papers. If I save myself the question is finished,' he said, 'but in the event that I perish, send this letter and the contents [of his bag] to Molé.' That same hour, he wrote to Hester, sending her the packet which still contained traces of the mixture, urging her to send it immediately to Molé. Clearly he trusted her to investigate his poisoning, and he trusted Molé, but not necessarily Regnault. Hester burnt the letter. She hid the packet away, too afraid to send it. Such was her paranoia and fear, she later said she saw potential assassins everywhere.

All the same, she tried to retrieve Badia's belongings. She sent one of her men out into the desert to discover what he could, but was told that everything had been turned over to the leaders of the village where he died. Even so, she appealed to the Pasha of Damascus, arguing that Badia's property should go to his young son in Fez, but she was unsuccessful.[25]

Hester would later say she felt sure 'his murder had been ordered'. She knew that it was rumoured that Mehmet Ali had been furious at the publication of his journeys, and she knew that many believed he had ordered the deaths of both Lascaris and Burckhardt, for the latter's death had struck many as being suspiciously swift too. But she believed he had been killed 'for *other* reasons' which she was too nervous to discuss.

Both she and Regnault in their separate ways behaved as though they were in shock. If Regnault had received Badia's letter and the precious papers he said nothing of it for some months to Molé. Instead, in October, the consul lightly mentioned that he had once again been to see 'Milady' – who had 'told him a great deal about the Arab traveller' – and that he 'had the satisfaction of having established the most desirable correspondence between the two illustrious strangers'.[26] He stalled, and did not report the 'sad news' of the death of 'Hagi Ali Abou Othman' until 9 November.[27]

The already shady circumstances of Badia's death were further complicated by the presence of another equally mysterious figure. The Polish cavalry officer Count Waclav Seweryn Rzewuski had seen the ailing Badia onto his Mecca-bound caravan from Damascus. He had heard Badia muttering under his breath: 'It is all part of a great chain. I cannot break it. I will never speak of it.' Rzewuski had ridden out to stay by his side some days later as he died.[28] In the last hour of Badia's life, Rzewuski claimed that he said, 'The immense chain has been shattered,' and that it was as though a torrent had been released. He began to talk about Napoleon, with whom '[Badia] had often shared intimate and secret conversations', especially those concerning 'le Grand Orient'. (The 'Great East' was also the common name for the French Masonic lodge.) He said he had received a large payment from France, arranged through Regnault.[29] He talked of Lascaris. He spoke of his conviction that if Napoleon could not complete his 'cause', then Tsar Alexander would 'soon prove capable' of taking it on.[30] Certainly Napoleon had tried to lure the Tsar with his vision of a combined march on India as early as 1808, and it was often rumoured that a secret alliance had been made to revive the undertaking.[31]

Rzewuski would later write, with deliberate mystification: 'It seems that he was poisoned by people who sold themselves to "A" . . . Hester knows it.' Was this the same 'A' whose involvement had so perturbed Lord Grenville? Or did it stand for 'Angleterre'?

All that is known for a fact is that three men sent into Syria, Egypt and Arabia on secret missions by Napoleon had crossed Hester's path, only to die mysteriously soon afterwards. In each case, all sides vied to get their hands on the dead man's secrets, none of them more eagerly than Hester.

Hester's reaction is hard to gauge. Everyone was tight-lipped; the French gossiped among themselves and blamed Badia's death on the English, who in turn claimed it was another sad case of dysentery. If her plans had been placed in jeopardy, she gave no sign of it. She intensified her secrecy and communicated as little as possible with anyone.

She summoned Meryon, demanding he come out at once. 'A year of your time is all I want, or perhaps a year and a half at most.' She offered to pay all the expenses of his journey, and he was to take a circuitous route through France, Switzerland and Italy. But this time she bound him to total secrecy; he was to tell no one, especially not James, she

312

emphasized. If anyone asked, he was to say he was going to Europe for a year for his own reasons. Regardless of whether Badia's death was a setback or a gain, Hester behaved as though her plan had only just been set in motion.

Shortly after Badia arrived, Hester received an invitation to meet with a delegation from the 'Koreysh' (Quraysh) tribe, who lived around Mecca. Where she met them is not clear. The Quraysh were held to be the descendants of Muhammad, and Badia had advised her that they, more than any other tribe, would prove a dominant and powerful force. There was a belief among many Arabs that any great caliph or leader among them could emerge only from the Quraysh, from whom the Prophet himself had come. It was with their blessing that he had intended to seek what he hoped would be the new alliance's foundation stone, the approval of the Sherif of Mecca. That this influential tribe now turned to Hester meant that she was given an extraordinary opportunity.

Hester's reaction was not level-headed. Badia's death seemed to have unhinged her. By the end of 1818 she claimed with messianic fervour that the Quraysh were her 'new family' and that they too predicted wondrous things for her. With great excitement, she informed Meryon that:

> The Kocub is now as I have understood, generally acknowledged by the sheriffs [sheikhs] to be related to the green turbaned race, and is combined with all that has been written . . . Here without any stir on my own part, there come from various quarters, dervishes, priests, rabbis, Druzes [*sic*] and all descriptions of people saying I am the Messiah or the forerunner of him. Am I a fool to admit of the possibility to wait to see what it all means?[32]

Bankes had painted a caricature of a God-obsessed Hester. Now she was genuinely exhibiting what others might term delusional behaviour. It becomes understandable in the context of the extraordinary hero-worship she received from 'the famous tribe of Koreish [*sic*] subdivided into many tribes, and which are a mixture of Hebrew blood' who were the subject of 'an ancient prophecy'. Meryon later tried to explain how Hester came to be an honorary 'Koreysh':

From this tribe of Arabs sprung Melek Seyf, a great conqueror . . . and somehow the story had taken root that Melek Seyf was her ancestor [and so] as tribes, like clans, [they were] all one blood. This story repeated over and over again, became current among the servants and in the villages, and the maids were accustomed to say 'Yes, my lady, they may be princes or emperors who come to see you, but your descent is higher than theirs, your ancestors were Melek Seyf and the seven kings'.[33]

This was not an idea she had tried to impose; it was her 'Koreysh family' who told her that they were willing to claim her as one of their own. Hester embraced the notion that descendants of these early Semitic Arabs had found their way to Britain and the Celtic nations.* She was unable to contain her wonderment at the news, telling Meryon:

The person to whom you once gave an eiderdown counterpane [she means herself] turns out to be the heir of the herdsman David. Her education has been a good one for her future situation, when she will have to act the Malem (master) like her father and great-grandfather.[34]

That year, Hester witnessed the birth of a secret new alliance in the Syrian desert. It was presided over by the Quraysh and she would refer to it as the Alliance of the Abouache, in which tribal sheikhs pledged their willingness to fight against the Ottomans. A glorious new caliphate was envisaged. Hester believed with all her soul that their triumphant campaign would lead them to a great era of self-rule, and an enlightened Western ruler would enter the nation as a friend, welcomed by the Arabs. Her own closest Arab friend became Dayr, Muhanna al Fadil's son-in-law, a tall, slim, boyish-looking man with an unusual eloquence of manner.

She was now even more compelled to probe into such prophecies as Metta and the Quraysh themselves had presented to her. 'The disciple's eyes have been opened,' she announced. Now she finally felt she understood her purpose.

---

* The idea was hardly new; it would later be termed British Israelism.

She invited a stream of Arabs and Jews, scholars and practitioners of all kinds to parse over old manuscripts to try to discover the source of the Quraysh's prophecy. She believed she found it in a medieval Hebrew manuscript, *Nevi'im Ahronim* or The Latter Prophets.[35] Meryon would later describe the particular emphasis she placed on a passage 'about Mount Lebanon, another of a woman who should do a new thing and turn a man about'.

> The meaning of this she strained by applying to herself and a great personage, whose name she was not at liberty to divulge. Other passages, to which she drew attention, were to show that hitherto none of the signs indicative of the true Messiah had been verified. Therefore, he was yet to come.[36]

In trying to picture Hester as she was seen by the Quraysh, we can draw on the eye-witness account of an Arab noblewoman from Baghdad, Amira, the daughter of Emir Abdullah Asmar. She described Hester as 'a tall and splendid figure, smoking a narguileh, dressed in a long saffron coloured robe with red stripes, fastened at the throat with a gold aigrette' and 'unmistakably womanly', despite being 'attired as a man'. She spoke Arabic 'with great fluency'. She created a magnificent scene when she got up to say her farewells, and turned to her 'spirited charger, putting her foot in the stirrup and vaulting nimbly into the saddle . . . [she] started off at a rapid pace, galloping over rock and mountain in advance of her suite with a fearlessness that would have done honour to a Mameluke'.[37]

Early in 1819 Hester retreated to her 'Chapel of Santon'. She appears to have been lying low after her recent dealings with the French. It was here that Count Rzewuski, the mysterious companion at Badia's deathbed, came to seek her out. He had already identified her as knowing who ordered Badia's death. Hester had every reason to regard him with great wariness.

But by the time he came to pay his respects to 'Esther Malek', as he called her, Rzewuski too was himself an honorary emir with the Anazeh, which put them on a very unusual footing and suggested they had shared motives. When he wrote to her with a special message that he had 'learned to esteem [her] in the deserts of the Neged' and believed she would respect his 'soldierly exploits' and that he now sought her out 'in the name of purity and freedom', she understood that he was a trusted member of the 'Alliance of the Abouache'.[38]

Rzewuski had come to Syria and Arabia on an expedition funded by Tsar Alexander and his sister, Catherine, Queen of Württemberg. The Tsar and he had strolled in the Hofburg Palace gardens to discuss his mission at the Congress of Vienna. A former Captain of the Austrian Hussars, and a veteran of battles against Napoleon, he had come to buy pure-bred Arab horses for the imperial stables and the military. He had concentrated his horse-buying efforts in the grazing lands of the Nejd, the vast plateau that had been the Wahhabi stronghold.

Hester and Rzewuski greeted each other in the traditional Bedouin manner. On his horse, he 'knocked on the door three times with his lance'. Hester's housekeeper Hannah 'kissed his cloak and touched her forehead with it', and then led him to a tent which had been prepared for him.

> When he dismounted, Mamelukes took him under the armpits and another carried the train of his cloak, and he was thus put on a carpet laid on the ground. They then bustled about pulling off his boots. A Mameluke knelt with a basin and washed his feet. Another raised his Bedouin kefieh and washed his head. A third put a basin on his crossed legs and the Emir washed and soaped his beard and hands, not neglecting from time to time to let escape some words of the pious formulas for the ablution. Finally he wiped himself and everyone saluted him with respect, asking him how he felt and repeating to him expressions of the pleasure they had in seeing him, and those which they put in the mouth of their august mistress.[39]

When he was summoned, Rzewuski, 'wishing to give pleasure to Esther, went barefoot to her, in order to become in her eyes a true representative of the desert where Esther was cherished'. He was filled with respect at the sight of 'the Idol of the Children of the Tents'. He thought Hester 'an inconceivable being, a woman admirable in every respect'.

Esther wears the clothing of men and the cape of an Emir often adorns her shoulders. She is tall, slender and well proportioned. She has a noble and gracious bearing. A dignity that inspires veneration rules her deportment. A sweet but imposing look, an assured but agreeably sounding voice. Her smile has something of enchantment. A touch of melancholy reigns in her fine blue eyes, in which, however, all the fire of genius and passions shine when she is animated. Her courage is unfailing.[40]

He describes how Hester received him, standing on her divan, a foot off the floor, so that she gave the impression of extraordinary height.

The Emir gave her the Bedouin salute with two fingers. And, not forgetting his rank, he got on the divan and placed himself in the angle opposite the one where Esther was. Both thus placed on the same side at the end of the room, they sat down, Esther two seconds before the Emir. Such is the usage among the great who visit each other.

On that day Esther had put on her white emir's cloak, which the Prince of Tedmor, Mehannah abou Nasser, her great friend, had brought her from the pilgrimage to the Holy Ka'abah. The customary greetings and questions took several minutes. Coffee and the 'narguilé' were served.[41]

Rzewuski spent nineteen days with Hester, all the while admiring 'the romantic and solitary place [she] has chosen as her retreat'.

Esther lent extraordinary grace to everything she did, and knowing how much charm a beautiful spot can have in solitude, she went herself to choose the place where the tent which she had prepared for me should be put up. On my return, I found carved on the rock beside it the mark that she knew was dear to me. She nicknamed that rock the 'Rock of the Mark' (*Hadjar an-Nîshân*) and the Arabs adopted this name to identify it.[42]

Rzewuski made a drawing of Hester's design, which shows what appears to be a tree, linked by its upper branches, and with three trunks. It represents her Arabic name, given to her by the Bedouin, and is also a tribute to the Quraysh, who worshipped Al-Uzza (Venus, the morning star), whose sanctuary was represented by three trees.[43] His own insignia is striking, an elaborate calligraphic emblem that on close inspection is clearly a two-headed serpent.

Hester's respect for Rzewuski seems to have won over her initial distrust. She allowed him to build a cottage and a large stable on the crest adjacent to Mar Elias, referred to by Hester's servants as 'the Count's house'.[44] They must have discussed Tsar Alexander's future ambitions. Given her comments, she believed he was the sort of man who might succeed in the East where Napoleon had failed. She was not ready to commit an opinion about who the next great leader in the world might be, the man to whom the secret alliance might be trusted, but she doubted he would come from Britain. Rzewuski returned to Mar Elias at least three times. But almost as soon as he had come into her life, to dazzle and entertain her, Rzewuski, and his horses, were gone – back into the desert.[45]

Hester's original desire to serve her country was now subverted by fierce, desert-bred prophecies. In her meetings with the Quraysh she felt she had been given a glimpse of God and the meaning of her existence, and it changed her entire outlook. Her view was at once harsh and simple.

> All sects have predicted the coming of a Saviour or Messiah; this event, it is foretold, will be preceded by the overthrow of most of the kingdoms of Christendom; the work has already begun and we may soon expect its completion. For is not the world in a state of revolution? Have not kings been driven from their thrones? Hundreds and thousands of distressed persons will come to me for assistance and refuge. I shall have to wade up to [my waist] in blood; but it is the will of God and I shall not be afraid.[46]

It was with these absolutist thoughts in her head that, in 1819, she received news of the insurrection in Aleppo, and watched over coming disturbances and assassinations in Europe.

In the meantime, she continued to educate herself. She studied the Koran alongside her slave girl Hanyfy with the imam at Sidon. She maintained her interest in the Druze faith, and in Sufism; her lessons with her dervish master from Tripoli went on as before.

Sheikh Jumblatt had sent her a beautiful white mare with a black tail and mane, which she named Asfura, 'Winged Bird', and rode as her favourite. Accounts vary of how she came to be given another outstandingly beautiful mare. Some say it was sent by her friend Ahmed Bey in Damascus, others that it was a gift from Emir Bashir. Either way, the mare had produced a foal of equal beauty, except that it was born with a spinal deformation, 'with her back hollow, like a saddle'.

Hester thought the foal matched Metta's description of 'a horse born saddled'. Both animals became her precious charges, each tended by a groom, exercised twice a day, and housed in specially-built quarters well away from curious eyes. She gave them Arabic names, and nicknamed them Lulu and Laila, one grey, the other chestnut. The questions of who might fulfil the other aspects of the prophecy, the fatherless boy she would raise to be a great man, and the 'woman from a far country' expected to join her in the mission, remained, as yet, unanswered.

For Meryon, the timing of Hester's request to join her, and the deception involved, were deeply awkward. He had acquired a mistress, 'Mad Narcisse', whom he met in early 1818, not long after she had been discarded by Hester's friend, the second Earl of Lonsdale, Lord Lowther. Pierre-Narcisse Chaspoux had been a dancer at the Paris Opera, and had come to London hoping to improve her fortunes. When she met Meryon she was three months pregnant. He assisted at the delivery of her (and Lonsdale's) daughter, Fanny. She took rooms next to his at a Warwick Street boarding house and they lived together, first as neighbours, then lovers.

He had barely signalled his acceptance of Hester's offer before he was deluged with fresh orders. He was to prepare her shipment of goods, including the weapons, and see them off at the port.* He was to look around for someone to be his successor after he returned. Newberry had

---

* Meryon was kept busy with preparations for his departure. In the hope of raising cash for herself, Hester had sent Meryon some 'old and valuable Arabic manuscripts', including a life of the Prophet Muhammad, which he was to offer prominent book collectors. He was to order specific presents. She wanted a mechanical clock for Süleyman Pasha, a musical snuff box with dancing figures in Turkish costume for the Emir Bashir and 'a gold repeating alarum [sic]' watch for Sheikh Jumblatt.

been a disaster, and almost cost her Sheikh Jumblatt's friendship.* She even asked him to seek out General Sir John Moore's brother, James, to see if he would come out to her.[47]

She gave him orders to bring with him Miranda's eldest son, Leander, then fifteen. Left bankrupt and harassed with the massive tangle of Miranda's affairs, Sarah Andrews had welcomed Hester's suggestion that her boy come out to her for a time. Vansittart, the chief executor of Miranda's will, apparently endorsed the idea. Did Hester think he might be the 'fatherless boy' of Metta's prophecy, or did she intend to shape him as the first of her agents? She gave Meryon orders that Leander must use the pseudonym Frederick Seymour on their travels to avoid his true identity becoming known.

Meryon left England (and a distraught Narcisse) at the beginning of winter 1818. He spent several painful days at Rye, but was unable to lie to his own father, although they both agreed his mother should be spared the truth until his safe return. For the rest of his journey out, he tried to follow Hester's orders. In Paris he was to 'lie low' and spend his time familiarizing himself with Masonic lodges. Her message concerning Paris was cryptic: he was to find a few good books, 'Confucius or something of the kind . . .', also some 'masks of Asia and Africa'. (Hester's future letters make it plain that 'Confucius' was the agreed codename for Sir Sidney Smith, and 'masks' meant spies or soldiers. A later letter from Smith to Hester confirms that he saw Meryon at this time.) He was to travel via Rochefort to seek out Loustaunau's family in Tarbes in the Pyrenees, then go to Switzerland to find her some servants: she hoped he might find 'the widow of an *enfant de la gloire* or an orphan child'.

Meryon was nothing if not painstaking. He would tell Hester that he

---

* Newberry was on his way home, greatly disgraced, she informed Meryon. At first she thought him 'vastly civil and obliging', even 'bleeding me twice in one day'. But over the summer of 1817 Newberry made a terrible blunder with Sheikh Jumblatt's wife that almost cost Hester her valued friendship: he diagnosed pregnancy, when in fact she had a prolapsed uterus that required urgent surgery, and prescribed tonics that worsened her condition. 'I found out when he began to practise that a boy of twelve years old knew more of women's complaints than he did. The most common disorder he seemed never to have heard of which is scarcely credible,' wrote Hester disgustedly. Newberry was a former ship's surgeon, with very little experience of gynaecological complaints and none of Meryon's instinctive tact.

spent two months in Switzerland examining the qualifications of no less than '83 persons' who applied for a position with her. But he said:

> The bare mention of Syria put half to flight and the other half pretended to ground upon the distance of that country, the dangers of a long navigation, the fear of pirates, plague and numerous other chimeras and they had such exorbitant demands that my disgust knew no bounds.[48*]

Nonetheless, he hired a housekeeper, a *femme de chambre*, a manservant, and a 'little girl who is 13 and a half years old and pretty', the latter willing to work 'for your protection only, and in the hope of some cast-off things'.

In Turin Hester's old suitor William Noel Hill invited Meryon and Leander to dinner, taking them to the Opera and to meet the royal family, and entrusting him with a letter for Hester, his first communication to her for many years. By the time Meryon had got his entourage from Genoa aboard a ship to Cyprus, he was in knots of anxiety, worrying Hester would not like 'Pauline, Marie and Louise'.

But Hester had no time for such trifles. She sent Meryon firm instructions. 'Never mention the name of the author of the expensive Atlas,' meaning, of course, the murdered Badia. 'If named, with or without his title, affect total ignorance about him.' She continued her warning. When he reached Sidon, he would be in danger, she said, but did not elaborate. 'Be very dry and silent' with all Arabs and Turks of any authority, she cautioned, and 'say that a report of my death has alarmed you and that you came to see what it all meant. For God's sake, avoid all appearance of mystery.' Then, she added: 'Not a word of Sherka to any of the Brotherhood you may meet'.[49]

Hester knew exactly who the 'Sherka' were, and so did Meryon; it was her nickname for the Masonic followers of the Rite of Memphis, and whatever she was up to, she did not want them to know about it.[†]

---

* In his *Travels*, Meryon noted that a malicious report found its way into the English newspapers, copied from the French, stating that Hester had surrounded herself with a tribe of small children, of exotic heritage and religions, and was educating them herself. There was an insinuation that at least one of them might be her own child.

† The nickname Hester used for them is curious and presumably quite deliberate. Sometimes she uses 'Sherka' or 'Sharka' – both spellings meant one thing, the state in Abyssinia that had been loyal to the Emperor during medieval times.

Hester was waiting anxiously for a sign. She hoped Meryon might bring her news from London and Paris which she could act on. Whatever he brought, it was not what she wished for. The most urgent communications were from Coutts, about the bad state of her finances. Meryon noted 'the feverish greediness which with she received all reports of insurrections, revolts and political changes', for these no doubt heralded the great event she hoped for.

Hester felt listless and bad-tempered. Depressed, she skulked in her *hamam*, smoked her pipe, and had her resident barber, Mustafa, bleed her.[50] Meryon was horrified, and also startled when she told him she was conducting research into potions containing venom from snakes and scorpions, believing that mixed with blood, they might produce an elixir.

When Meryon saw how the new arrivals were to be housed, he was shocked. The type of huts they had been assigned were barely good enough for cattle, with nothing but rank-looking rugs on the floor meant to serve as beds. Hester had neglected to bother much about where the new arrivals should be accommodated. She kept Leander waiting four days before she would see him, and the boy, who had expected 'to come to a house where he might find cheerfulness and European manners and customs', instead observed that 'everything was mysterious, and that pleasure and diversions were not the predominant feature at Mar Elias'.

She did not summon the servants for seventeen days, and when she inspected them, only the man seemed good enough. The women, 'pinched up in stays', were clearly unsuitable, 'for how could they even ride or be active with such horrid things about them'. Their miserable faces, after nights of lying awake in terror of scorpions and rats, using their own luggage as pillows, irritated her, and she regarded them with suspicion. Not one of them would stay to see in the winter.

Hester was desperately agitated. Her friend Süleyman Pasha of Acre had just died, and ominous shifts in power were brewing. His replacement was Abdullah Pasha, a ruthlessly ambitious stripling, and not long after he took up his post, Malem Hayim was found strangled to death. One by one, her old contacts were sliding away. She heard that Mustafa Berber from Tripoli would not last long, and that the new Pasha in Damascus would soon be ousted.

Meanwhile she was greatly worried by the growing schism between

Emir Bashir and Sheikh Jumblatt. She now began to regret her earlier efforts to sweeten relations with the Emir. She warned both Meryon and Leander that these were 'poisoning times'. She told them 'not to pick up stones in the river bed (lest they might be thought as prospectors) and not to talk to peasants in case they were spies'. She also refused to let Leander go to Sidon or travel in the countryside by himself, which he bitterly resented. There was no talk of his education. Only in retrospect did Hester's secretive reasoning strike either of them as anything but paranoid. She never let on how fearful she was for their safety, in case they left at once.

What sent Hester into another of her spectacular rages was the news that the East India Company had sent one of its own men from Bombay to Darayya, a hapless individual called Captain George Sadlier who termed the Bedouin 'hordes of robbers'. Sadlier's official report on the prospect of forming any kind of alliance with the Bedouin went as follows: 'To attempt to argue with them on principles of justice, right or equity is ridiculous; and to attempt to insist on their adhering to promises or agreements is equally fruitless.'

Through no particular fault of his own Sadlier botched everything he did, and failed to gain the respect of a single Arab. His mission to map out a deal with Ibrahim Pasha for a combined Anglo-Egyptian force to police the pirate-ridden Gulf coast was unsuccessful. As far as Hester could see, all the British had achieved was to signal their willingness to side with a hated tyrant. Meryon had not delivered the highest level of support from England that she had desired; but worse, a complete incompetent had been sent in her hoped-for place, and no doubt confused her own Bedouin allies. Hester began to fear that Mehmet Ali intended to invade Syria and that as things stood, he would face little resistance.

Hester's frustration at not being able to put her grandiose and ambitious plans to work was immense. Why was it only foreigners – and the French – who could appreciate her, she ranted to a helpless and uncomprehending Meryon, to whom she only ever told a fraction of the story.

Whatever was said between Hester and Meryon about St Helena and 'the man with the sort of Brutus look' was not recorded. She subjected him to long interrogations about his meetings, and barked at him for not carrying out her instructions delicately or persuasively enough. 'If he had used his head,' bargains might have been struck, she raged, and berated him for using his time in Paris 'going to the opera and running to the Louvre to look at pictures'.

Hester's hopes had been so high, and she had thought herself so close to realizing them, that she felt deeply betrayed. She began to crumble into a kind of grief. Once Elizabeth called Meryon down from the village, telling him she could not bear to see Hester in the state she was in. She was 'wringing her hands and crying like a child'. She hurled dishes and plates against the wall, screaming 'Go away from me, the sight of all of you is poison to me. Good god, that people who are millionaires should have let me rot here and not once have offered me any assistance. Never will I go to England, to France I may but if ever they come near me, I'll stab myself or blow my brains out. I have bought a poniard for that. Don't think I am mad when I say so for I mean it,' she sobbed.[51]

When she was calmer, she confided to Meryon: 'May God only grant that I die in my senses, for what can my nervousness be? It is like gunpowder. If anything sets fire to me I go off in an explosion, and am no longer mistress of myself.'[52] After she had raged for what appeared to be several days, a calmness, almost an apathy, overtook her. She intended to retreat from 'anybody I ever knew', she claimed, except perhaps 'a few French servants and some French generals'. Hester had begun to see that her future might not hold in store the realization of any much-hoped-for dreams, that it might be bleak and miserable.

At other times, she was ready to consider the tide might yet turn in her favour, and someone for whom she could adapt her plans would materialize. These thoughts gave her renewed energy. She was willing to consider that Napoleon's seven-year-old son, now called the Duke of Reichstadt, but popularly known as *L'Aiglon*, might in fact be 'the one'. Meryon described how she considered sending him to Vienna with her Arabian horse Asfura as a gift, and had composed a letter, 'the precise wording of which I forgot, but it was to this effect: My Prince, I send you a young Arab mare called La Fleck. She will carry you faster than soaring eagles and lead you to glory and victory.' Hester had then mused aloud on her scheme for Napoleon II: 'If he is at Vienna you must find out where he walks, and go there, tying up the colt in a negligent sort of way,

you will present the letter to him, being sure to say out loud that his attendants may hear that it is from me.' The message, the horse and the fact
that Hester had sent it would apparently be enough; those close to him
would understand, she implied.

For the past two years Hester had tried to ignore her spiralling debts.
She had always felt something would come along that would magic away
her money problems. It was then that Meryon, aided by Elizabeth, began
to go over Hester's accounts, trying to establish exactly how much she
owed, a complicated business given the amount of unpaid interest on
loans, taken out in a bewildering array of currencies. Hester had turned
to moneylenders for credit, and did not appear to be disturbed by their
high rates. She owed large sums to merchants for supplies and commod-
ities in at least four Syrian cities. As they went over the account books,
Elizabeth confided details of all the money that had gone 'to soothsayers
and enchanters'. There had even been an American, she told Meryon,
who claimed to be able to contact the spirit world with his 'mysterious
box'. He had stayed 'a day and a night inside with her Ladyship' while
she and the other servants were ordered to stay away.[53]

Meryon, who knew little of Hester's other dilemmas, thought that it
was 'neglect of all her relations and the failure of her projects [which]
preyed on her mind and brought on these paroxysms of phrensy which
were so frightening to witness'. On another occasion, after he had examined her, noting silently the crescent-shaped marks showing frequent
blood-letting, she said something in a harsh voice which he found
profoundly unsettling. 'How would you know anything about my health,
when I have deceived you for six years?' It was a chilling rebuke that ever
afterwards caused him to wonder what it might mean. Hester knew exactly.
Six years before, Vincent Boutin had ridden back into her life and taken
over her heart. As for her own true allegiances, she held them just as
close.

## 19

## The Sun At Midnight

The inmates of Mar Elias – the ill-adjusted Swiss servants – staged a mutiny. All were unhappy with life under Hester's roof and terrified by reports that the plague was advancing once again. Only the youngest, Louise, now fourteen and distractingly buxom, wavered. She and Leander had been caught together in bed, forcing Hester to make a decision. First she insisted Meryon accompany all the servants back to Switzerland. She was firm about Leander, telling Meryon she intended to keep him with her and 'train him in such a manner as to make him tread in the path of honour and virtue'. But Leander too staged a revolt, and Louise refused to leave without him.

Meryon did not protest when she told him he would be more useful to her in England – and on the journey home.[1] On 1 August 1819, he and his subdued party of three servants left. Hester washed her hands of the young lovers, leaving Elizabeth to try and counsel Louise and Leander as best she could. She made arrangements for them to travel separately back to Europe. As Leander's temporary guardian she found someone who could accompany him – a middle-aged English Jew passing through Syria on his way to Jerusalem, who promised to see him safely home. She gave him to a stranger's care, with only the money for his passage, knowing he might be forced to live on his wits. He was seventeen.

Her bitterness at how badly things had gone wrong was not assuaged by a letter from Sir Sidney Smith written from Paris in January 1820. Much to the amusement of some of his superiors, Smith was now in the grip of his own grand obsession, nothing less than the restoration of the Knights Templar. He had proclaimed himself Grand Prior for England, affiliating himself with a 'restored' Ordre du Temple, which itself had evolved from a shadowy, highly contentious branch of the French Freemasons, the Chevaliers de la Croix.[2] He told Hester he was waiting, 'ready to do any duty when it may be put on me'. He used a code she was familiar with, and described how he intended to counter Napoleon should he escape:

> Now to revert to and restore the chain of our correspondence – you will have seen very soon after the arrival of my handkerchiefs, that I was not far out in my calculation that the person supposed to coop up in an island in the Mediterranean and who is really so now in one of the Atlantic, would 'bolt' and be seen on horseback again at the head of his hat who were so impatient under their inactivity and the quiet rule of a peaceable chief . . .[3]

'Handkerchiefs' meant his men; 'hat' meant army. Smith obviously allowed for the possibility that Napoleon's 'bolt' might again be successful, and he told Hester that he thought that if it was, he would probably 'go to Africa and there rally his Parthians and Mohammedans and others of his creatures'. Of course, this came as no surprise to Hester.

Smith reasoned that 'as [Napoleon] would have contrived to put African volunteers in motion, my idea [was] to counteract him on that ground by Levantines of that same stuff' who might gather at 'points of rallyment'. He had sent his 'handkerchiefs', he told her, who 'did not commit the profession 'til displayed in their proper place'. Tsar Alexander had offered 'two regiments of *Chasseurs* [elite cavalry], then in Finland, each of 3500 men if I should send for them, but the whole was so soon over that these circuitous assemblages ceased to be necessary'.

He asked her to write to him through the incoming British consul Peter Abbott in Beirut. They were on the brink of another great disturbance in Europe, he was sure of it, he told her, 'in Lisbon, Madrid and Nantes' it would be all the same – 'despotism, anarchy and military usurpation' would 'follow each other like the phases of the moon'. Evidently he was of the mind that this was as it should be, for it would lead to momentous events. He entreated Hester: 'Now that you are an enlightened being, pray give me your Ideas.'[4]

Hester's reaction was curt. The idea for counteracting Napoleon's phantom army was not in all truth his; it was simply a response to the Lascaris plan, and the fact that he had thought of it was something she gave herself credit for. She may have felt marginalized, and once again considered his ideas and plans badly thought out. For all she had given up and lost, she had not done it to become one of his 'Pocket Handkerchiefs'. She recorded her opinion of his letter by informing Robert Liston at Constantinople that she thought it 'a rhapsody of nonsense, which I did not choose to answer'. Was this true or was she dissembling? There are no other surviving letters between them.

By this time she had another 'Chevalier' in her life. Captain Jean-Baptiste Loustaunau, ex-officer of Napoleon's Imperial Guard, wounded at Waterloo and honourably discharged, had come to find his father. He was swarthily handsome and young, barely into his thirties.

Jean-Baptiste told Hester he had prepared all the necessary papers with the consuls and intended to travel on to India with his father before he lost his wits completely.[5] Old Loustaunau had always insisted to his family that they had a fortune waiting to be claimed in India. The young Captain, too, was pressed for cash. But he showed Hester an affidavit from the family lawyer concerning a remarkable stone, a spinel ruby which Loustaunau *père* claimed had been given to him by 'the Mughal Emperor, in return for saving his son's life'. The ruby, which weighed fifty-five and a quarter carats, had been subjected to scrutiny by experts in both Paris and London, who had pronounced it 'a stone without price, for a crowned head'. Quite where the stone was, and why the Loustaunau family was not already living off the proceeds of it, is not clear. A likely explanation is that, among other things, Jean-Baptiste had come for his father's signature to release it.

Jean-Baptiste did not leave, as he had told everyone he would. First he had announced he would stay only a few days, then a few weeks more. By spring he was caring for Hester's horses, and in her bed. His continued presence in the household became a point of consternation for the new

French consul in Sidon, Monsieur Martin, who mentioned the subject in three dispatches to Paris over as many months. He wrote to his superior: 'I cannot neglect my duty by not reporting that M. Loustaunau *fils* has put himself into Milady Stanhope's service, and is acting in all ways as though he regards himself as beyond the reach of the French authorities. Perhaps these are Milady Stanhope's orders, but it strikes me that a Frenchman should not enter her service without our approval, and that to the contrary, he should lose his rights for any consular assistance, should he need it.'[6] Martin suspected that 'Milady Stanhope' was making use of Jean-Baptiste as her spy or messenger. He was observed turning up in Tiberias and Acre and, Martin noticed, he 'was constantly coming to Sidon'. Martin went further, and confided to his superiors that he was sure Hester was trying to win over Abdullah Pasha, the new Pasha of Acre, to the side of the British.

That Jean-Baptiste, whom she always refers to as 'the Chevalier', became Hester's lover is certain; exactly whether, and how, she loved him is not. There is little in her own words from this period that allows us to see him through her eyes.[7] She had announced to Meryon: 'Gen. Loustenau's son has been with me since Jan 1820. He is indeed a gentleman!' Someone who saw them together, Ferdinand Perrier, was rather more explicit. He claimed that Hester had said 'that Jean-Baptiste bore a strong resemblance to a young English officer she had once loved'. If this is true, it may have been Camelford she was reminded of. Perrier claimed that Hester's attachment to Jean-Baptiste was almost instant, and that very quickly she became intensely passionate and possessive about him. 'She looked at the lines of his hand, and the shape of his feet, and claimed that she saw it written in the stars that their fates would be inseparable, that he was in effect, hers. She wanted to stop him from going to India,' he wrote in a later memoir.[8] This rather startling claim makes for a good story. But was it the truth?

On 28 August 1820 Martin reported that he had heard of the sudden death, 'that morning', of 'M. Loustaunau *fils* chez Milady Stanhope'. The death of the young man who, aside from his war injury, had appeared to be in good health just a week before was, on the face of it, mystifying. Hester would say that he was careless about what he ate, especially now that it was the height of summer, and that against her strict orders he was always picking things up in the market at Sidon. Acute gastritis was blamed. It is from Perrier that we know that Hester obtained permission to bury her lover in her garden, and that 'each day she went to his grave, placed fresh flowers there and stayed for a long time absorbed by her own private thoughts'.[9] As for Old Loustaunau, now exiled to one of Hester's cottages at Abra, he refused to believe that his son was dead, and would say he had merely gone away, and would return.

One event stands out in the short time between Jean-Baptiste's arrival and his death. On 15 June 1820, the Comte de Marcellus, aide to the Duc de Rivière, the French Ambassador in Constantinople, arrived at Mar Elias to see Hester. That day the young 'Chevalier' had been nowhere in sight. Marcellus described entering one of her rooms, 'with crossed lances and arrows on the walls, tiger skins on the divans' and 'a huge painting of a wild horse approaching a great torrent of water'. His eyes had darted about and immediately fastened on 'a portrait of Bonaparte, almost hidden from sight'. She ushered him into her garden and served him 'white apricots in syrup with spices unknown in Europe; figs, bananas and sorbets . . . I would never forget the meal offered by an Englishwoman to a Frenchman at a picnic in Lebanon,' he wrote. Their conversation lasted until two in the morning. He claimed that she told him that she had 'lived for three months with the Druze, in secret grottos where they devote themselves to their religious ceremonies'.[10] She had 'acquired the Arab taste for solitude', she told him, a comment rather at odds with her evident stamina for conversation.

She confided her suspicions over Badia's death to Marcellus, telling him this was the first time she had dared speak of it, and handed over the packet with its suspected traces of poison. But when it was later subjected to analysis in Paris the results were deemed inconclusive.[11]

The presence of the packet in Hester's house shortly before Jean-Baptiste's death has to be noted. Someone who wished the young man dead might certainly have had the means to do him harm. It was said that Jean-Baptise had a quick temper. It is also curious too that no more mention is made by anyone after this time of Hanyfy, Hester's pretty servant girl. No one, it seems, enquired into Jean-Baptiste's death, or thought it suspicious.

Old Loustaunau appointed Hester the executor of his son's will. She would soon claim in a letter she wrote to the French consul at Rhodes, Monsieur Le Doux, that he had entrusted her not only with power of attorney for his son's legal matters, but for his own also. 'I have full power to act for the whole family in their business interests,' she wrote on 20 October 1820.[12]

As for the all-important 'famous ruby', she was concerned about the lawyer who had been holding it in trust, and suggested he should 'inform me by letter as to any details which he thinks *I ought to know*. It would be even better if he would come here. He would be very welcome and I think I could convince him that he had every reason to be pleased with the conduct of the business. But in this case he must be careful *not to speak to any living soul* (the C's father knows nothing about this letter) of the object of his journey.'

The matter was so pressing that she planned to go to Rhodes 'as soon as weather permitted'. In the meantime, she urged him to send her condolences to the Loustaunau family and to tell them that she would try 'to extricate them from the painful circumstances from which they now suffer'. She warned that 'above all, they should be careful and say nothing about their affairs to anyone'.

Then she turned to the subject of her dead lover. 'I have said nothing about the last moments of our friend. You would feel it too much, and I do not like to tell you my thoughts on this sad occasion. So many years devoted to glory and to France, the reward, a prison, loss of health, sorrow, death!!! He was, now and again, of a hasty temper, but with all that the man was so thoroughly sincere and goodhearted that anyone who did not appreciate his merit or grieve over his cruel fate as I grieve over it, must be a monster.'

Whatever had happened to Jean-Baptiste, Hester certainly seemed to have plans for the ruby.

Meryon arrived in London early in 1820, just in time to find everything changed. King George III had just died and George IV was on the throne. Meryon was able to tell Hester that 'Mr Vemetpicket' [Vansittart] had 'smoothed his way in Europe' and that he had been able to see 'Castor and Pollux' [Lord Glastonbury and Lord Grenville] on her business almost immediately. Whatever this matter was, it also involved the intelligent and brilliant barrister Henry Brougham whom Meryon told her had 'found out everything to do with your affair'. Meryon relayed Brougham's answer to Hester, careful to keep it cryptic:

> The results so far he said was that people stuck at half and he asked me whether you wished at all events to have the business done. I answered that I thought so. On Friday I called again and found that other but no better offers had been made. Mr Brougham said he would write to you himself, that it would be useless for me to know the steps of the business. He should manage the affair and then when it was done he would apprise me of it.[13]

Regardless of what 'the business' was, Hester appears to have received a sum of money in connection with this affair. Whatever she was paid, she insisted to Meryon that she wanted it *now*, not later.[14] Hester told him: 'You understand that you will let Mr Brougham know that nothing James can now offer me will alter my determination'. Brougham – the future Lord Chancellor – also made his business to find out from Meryon whether Hester 'had anyone in Marseilles, aside from the Old Figure'.

On his way home Meryon had followed Hester's instructions. She had put him up for a job, 'to finesse a delicate arrangement'. He was to know only a few details, and that the Duke of Sussex wanted it conducted 'with the utmost secrecy'. In Geneva Meryon was entrusted with escorting two ladies, one an Englishwoman (described as having 'met with some misfortune' which was more than likely a reference to a pregnancy) 'and for whom a subscription had been raised'. The other, more of a girl, was 'the natural daughter of the Duke of Sussex'. Sandwiched between the two mystery females, Meryon proved to be an ineffectual warden. As they crossed France by carriage, it became so appallingly icy and hazardous that the pregnant woman refused to leave her fireside in a lodge in Dijon and announced she intended to wait out the winter there. 'As I could not take the young one without her, I left them both behind,' Meryon reported balefully. His 'supposed desertion of the ladies' would not go down very well with the Duke of Sussex.

In any case, Meryon had emerged from this encounter with a letter for Hester from 'Madame B'. It would appear that a great many parallel secrets added up to a hidden picture. It is certainly interesting to know that over the winter of 1819 Hester's correspondent Fanny Bertrand had persuaded her husband that she wanted to leave St Helena. Her decision seemed to throw Napoleon into a crisis. Madame Bertrand (whom he had called almost besottedly 'Madame Shrug' on account of her wonderfully expressive eyebrows and shoulders) was not a Frenchwoman, he raged, but 'a whore, a fallen woman who slept with all the English officers who passed her house . . . the most degraded of women'. She was deserting him, he ranted. Some accounts indicate that Fanny did in fact leave St Helena. Other sources place her back on the island in 1821 shortly before Napoleon's death, and record that she asked him to see her, but he refused. Shortly before she wanted to go away, Fanny had asked Antommarchi, the underqualified medical assistant assigned as Napoleon's doctor, to examine her for an unspecified complaint. Was Fanny Bertrand the woman Meryon had left in France? It is tantalizing to think so.

As for 'the business' Brougham referred to, it almost certainly concerned Napoleon's escape plan. It is only from a personal anecdote related some years after the event that we learn that towards the end of 1820, on a moonless night in November, Captain Tom Johnstone was apprehended by officers as he attempted to tow a submarine out to the open sea. A waterman, Charles Greaves, saw the craft being towed down the Thames 'not being able to sink, as the water was not deep enough'. Johnstone got as far as London Bridge, when a detachment of police officers forced him to stop, and seized the vessel, 'and taking her to Blackwell, destroyed her'. The entire incident was hushed up, no charges pressed, nothing ever made public.[15]

Two months later, Hester informed Meryon that she had sent her prized 'milk-white' foal – 'the horse destined for Him' – to the Duc de Rivière in Constantinople, 'who would send it on to France with a letter'. Nothing is known about the person this horse was sent to, nor why she decided to present it to 'Him' instead of Napoleon II. Nor can we guess whether the intended recipient was a full-grown man, or even a newborn.

A year later, on the night he died, on 5 May 1821, Napoleon would twice ask Marchand, the friend attending him, 'What is the name of my son?'

\*    \*    \*

One account of Hester at this time reveals her to have been in apparently 'much improved' spirits. Barker and his wife arrived in Syria at the end of 1820 and called at Mar Elias. (Neither of their one-year-old twin daughters survived the journey back; but another child had been born en route at Marseille.) Barker thought Hester seemed jovial. But he confided to the American missionary Joseph Woolf that 'she is undoubtedly crazy'. He told an anecdote about how they had reached a conversational lull at one point, and she had suddenly turned to him, and said in a low voice so that his wife could not hear, that he must find a way of leaving Aleppo within the year, for old Loustaunau had told her 'terrible things would happen' in both Aleppo and Antioch and that 'both cities would be utterly destroyed'.[16] It was a warning she would reiterate the following year. But Barker, and those to whom he repeated her dire words, had reason to recall them. In August 1822 Aleppo – and the countryside as far as Antioch – was devastated by a massive earthquake, with utterly catastrophic loss of life and property.

Increasingly, the more Hester felt thwarted by the limits to her power and influence, the more she turned to things religious and supernatural. 'It ever was an object with me to search out why I came into the world; what I ought to do in it, and where I shall go. God has given me the extraordinary faculty of seeing into the futurity . . . I may thank God for my sufferings, as they have enabled me to dive deeper into the subject.'[17] She had faith that she was in the right place.

A fate watches over me; and you may believe me when I tell you most sincerely that I would not change my destiny, however unhappy it may appear, for that of thousands of others; because, although I have been miserable at times, I have had always had a little to command, if not of money, of a *something* which others seek for their whole life with their pockets full and never get it. It is not my *rank* which has procured me this, for higher rank than mine is totally devoid of it. What it is I cannot explain; but finding friends here and there in the world, and having the power to knock down single-handed my enemies and never to feel a dread of failing anywhere. God fits the back to the burden.[18]

Hester's evolving philosophy would be called by those in her future fiefdom *dyn es Sytt* – 'the Lady's religion'. She became a convert to the power of the unseen world and of cosmic forces, but not to any single faith. She was fascinated by the mystical dimensions of Sufism, attracted by the Sufi notion that there were those who might attain, in a single mystical communion, '*jadhba*', a state of religious ecstasy in which they would feel the presence of God, to experience 'the sun at midnight'. She invited Kabbalist Jews to instruct her, and interpret texts for her.

To one visitor sent by Captain Jesse, a lifelong associate of her old friend Beau Brummell, she expressed 'her partial belief in the Koran', namely in the coming of the Mahdi and in the '13th Imam, the Saviour', so it would appear she had fastened upon the Shi'ite 'Twelver' tradition. (He was struck by the way she was conversant with all the Muslim names for Biblical figures, and referred for example not to Moses, but to Moussa; Ibrahim for Abraham and Husrat Esau instead of Jesus Christ. It is also possible she was deliberately trying to shock him.) 'The Mahometans look for the advent or reappearance of another who will convert the whole world to the faith of Islam and reign on earth for a time of great prosperity and happiness; the end of this period and the world will be simultaneous,' he reported her as telling him.

To another listener, she indignantly rejected any suggestion she held Muslim beliefs. To yet another she said she wholly approved of the description given by the Druze of God as 'the One, the divine Unity, who is infinite and unlimited and perfect', and many of her comments make it clear she had been closely studying Druze scriptures. For all her ranting about Christianity, she often said how she believed in the Christian virtues of charity and benevolence and 'still acknowledged the Holy Scriptures as inspired writings'. Meryon would attest that she 'quoted from them as such and may be said to have looked into them oftener than into any book'.

When Ambroise Firmin Didot visited her, he found her tight-lipped on her beliefs, except to say that she was happy to be living 'in the neighbourhood of the greatest metaphysicians the world has produced'. Her dragoman Bertrand told him he was convinced she was contemplating founding a new religion. 'She has come to believe that only by an alliance between Islam, Christianity and Judaism might mankind be saved from the coming apocalypse that the ranting Prophet in her backyard is constantly saying is nigh,' he told Firmin Didot.

She came to believe in the transmigration of souls, and in an unseen world filled with spirits, who watched over and guided the actions of men.[19] She considered 'the air we move in and the earth we tread on as filled with delicate and aerial beings', he observed, who rewarded 'the gentle and the sage' and punished the wicked and even the clumsy. She also believed in angels 'of different degrees, from the highest down to the devil'.[20]

She used the Turkish almanac, the Ruzname, with its minute measurements governing days and nights, in conjunction with an astrolabe. She would not budge until she felt the timing was auspicious. Wednesdays become her Sabbath, the day she regarded as unlucky for anything except seclusion, shutting herself up on Tuesday nights and not emerging for twenty-four hours, and 'talking to the stars and spirits'.

Astrology, and the belief that each person was born with what she called a *nijem* or star, also formed part of her faith. She apprenticed herself to a series of masters, some of whom came to live with her for long periods. She had the idiosyncratic notion of a caste system – or sliding scale – of stars, awarded like marks of merit, although some, she noted, 'might tend to beauty, but be no good in other respects'. She believed each person's star carried vibrational attachments and antipathies to everything in creation (and so they might find themselves inexplicably attracted or repulsed by others). 'From nature,' she said, a man will possess 'certain qualities, certain virtues and vices, certain talents, diseases and tastes'. She would say that 'every man, born under a given star, has his aerial spirit, his animal, his bird, his fruit tree, his flower, his medicinal herb and his demon'. No man's star was ever identical to another's, even those born in the same hour on the same day, for 'there may be varieties in the same star, occasioned by the influence of other stars, which were in particular position at the hour of a man's birth'.

She would also study a person's face, and 'the shape of the head, body and limbs', and form conclusions about every aspect of his character. 'I have learned to know a man's star by his face, but not by astrological calculations, as of that trade I have no knowledge.'[22]

There was such a thing as 'sympathy between the stars of two persons', she thought, 'or, in other words, of the star of another being good for you', proof of which 'is when a person puts his finger on you and you don't feel it'. A person whose star is bad for you might do this and you would 'shudder all over'.

There were those, she would say, who could only do well under the guidance of another's star. 'What was Lord Grenville without Mr Pitt? With him to guide him he did pretty well, but as soon as Mr Pitt was dead, he sunk into obscurity. Sir Francis Burdett has never been good for anything since Horne Tooke's death. So long as Napoleon had Josephine at his side he was lucky; but when he cast her off, his good fortune left him.'

Her own star, she believed, was the sun. 'When the sun is a person's star, it attracts everything.'[22]

As for magic, she would say 'it has to do with the devil'. It was only a matter of time before she described herself as bartering, 'by compact' and by fixing 'a certain price' with evil spirits. She claimed to possess 'means which I know to be powerful enough to bring devils under my command'. She would talk wonderingly of *djinns* and *nafs*, which could appear as serpents, dogs or cats, or even take human form; of the *zaubarah*, a dreaded whirlwind which could rise up in demonic form as sand or dust; and of evil charms 'which can effect the most diabolical purposes'. She would claim that she could 'feel' the 'evil eye', and could herself bargain with evil spirits, and that 'my star, more powerful than that on which they rely, renders their magic useless'.[23]

A cynic would say she cultivated the impression that she possessed formidable powers as a means of exerting control over people and events. Certainly the myth that she had supernatural gifts allowed her to intimidate and 'keep in awe' those around her whom she might otherwise find hard to control. But certainly some of the questions Hester posed about Islam, about religion and the spiritual world, now seem, if anything, more in step with our own time than her own.

# 20

## Djoun

When Hester first saw what would become her future house, it was no more than a few stone-built rooms set around a small garden surrounded by olive groves amid the wilderness. The Deir-el-Moukhalles monastery nearby often suggested it as a waystation for its more unorthodox visitors. Indeed this was where they had banished Hester's friend Turinge, the beautiful Ethiopian, and her lover Musa.

Some accounts say Hester bought the land outright from Sheikh Jumblatt, whose family had always acted as protectors to the monastery. Meryon thought it belonged to a Damascus merchant, who charged her £20 a year for it. Today the monastery Fathers say she leased the land from them, for which she paid an annual fee. The records of these transactions were carefully kept but went missing during Lebanon's civil war, along with much else.

Hester's fortress took shape first in her mind's eye. Before the foundation stone was laid, she imagined it. After carefully examining all vistas from the top of the hill, she made quick sketches which she later refined. First, her own bedroom would face the sea, and be steps away from the garden. She would have her own bathroom, a *hamam* naturally, and her own separate kitchen and store-rooms. The servants' quarters would be well away from hers, so she would never have to hear their squabbles.

Nor would she ever again be embarrassed by the expectations of visitors. There would be plenty of rooms. Indeed, she now relished the chance to divide her guests into two classes. She would have accommodation for 'first class strangers' and 'second class strangers', each with their own

store-rooms and gardens. Everything would be constructed in such a way
that connecting passages between certain wings or sections could be
locked when she chose. Therefore, strangers might stay under her roof,
yet never be aware of each other's presence.

Her own quarters would have a secret entrance, and there would also
be a latticed screen, through which she could observe visitors in her salon
without being seen. There would be 'two pavilions, with trap-doors in
the floor, leading to steps which descended to a room underground' and
led to passages that ended at a concealed exit in the open country. It was
exactly the sort of complicated design puzzle that appealed to Hester,
and a great indicator of her love of secrecy.

Construction began in late 1820. Hester was anxious it be finished as
quickly as possible. Where did the money come from? There had of
course been the mystery payment finessed by Brougham. Even if she still
had debts, it may not have presented a problem. In the East, long-standing
indebtedness between someone thought to have considerable where-
withal, like Hester, and merchants and moneylenders, could be seen in
a favourable light as part of an ongoing relationship; that she was building
such a house signalled her intention to stay. No records about financial arrangements for its construction have survived. There is also
the possibility that Hester had obtained some kind of payment from the
transaction on old Loustaunau's spinel ruby, for his family in the Tarn
are known to have received payments some time shortly after Jean-
Baptiste's death.

Villagers who came to work for her at this time testified that she was
a generous benefactress. Any woman expecting a child was given two lira
and two amphorae of wine, as well as clothes for her newborn. She always
gave preference to local farmers and artisans for their produce and goods;
stories began to circulate that unwed mothers, the sick and elderly would
never go away from her empty-handed.

Ayoub al Moussawba, a stone-master from Djoun, took on a team of
a hundred men and set about turning Hester's drawings and plans into
reality. The main section of the residence was finished by the end of
1821. The villagers referred to it as her *qasr*, or palace. There were two
main wings, separating her own quarters from her retinue's accommodation, with twelve bedrooms, not including those for the servants. Her

own suite consisted of five rooms, built with larger and more decorative stones, including several salons and a *diwan* open to the air. Inside the labyrinth of passageways and chambers were entwined around four inner courtyards, some open to the skies. 'Arbour, covered with Jasmine,' she wrote as part of her instructions. It was duly created.

There was a series of 'offices' and store-rooms, pantries and china closets. A cistern was installed, suggesting some kind of lavatory system. There were warehouses filled with huge amphorae of wine and olive oil, granaries and a dairy, as well as three store-rooms for ammunition and weapons. A 'prison' cell was located between her wine cellar and her 'carpenter's store'. There were separate quarters – 'extra muros' – for 'Doctor's rooms and pavilions', and rooms for her 'Secretary' and 'Major Domo'. Water was drawn from a huge well and a system of clay irrigation pipes was devised.

Lulu – the sainted horse – had her own stable, the other horses and mules were stabled together. Cows, camels and other livestock were kept at a distance, yet still within the perimeter of the encircling walls, which were ten feet high. To all appearances, she intended to be able to withstand a siege.

As for her garden, Hester's imagination flourished unchecked. She wanted to have 'covered alleys, serpentine walks, summer houses, pavilions and arbours'. She asked Meryon to find her a Scottish gardener. ('I like the industry and the frugality of the Scotch and their sober way of living. I consider myself half a Scotswoman,' she mused.) She wanted plants from the New World as well as the Old.

When Meryon saw her list, he groaned. 'An evergreen oak, a sweet bay, the great magnolia, the beaver tree, calmius, an andromedus, the tupolo tree, the white cedar, the plantanus, crimson flowered horse chestnut, the yellow, the hydrangea and all sorts of American creeper or any other trees or plants and state which type of temperature they grow,' she began. She wanted 'horse-chestnuts, beech and American firs; the common laurel, willow, mountain ash, lime trees; laburnum and rose acacia – acacia of all kinds'. She requested scarlet sweet peas in quantities; hollyhocks; sunflowers and periwinkles, heather of all varieties, rare and common; a quantity of lily of the valley, snowdrops and heart seeds. He should also purchase raspberry, gooseberry, moss and strawberry seeds.

She ordered Meryon to inveigle himself into the garden at Chevening with Brampton the steward (now that the new Lord Stanhope was again out of the country), to make sure he got cuttings of cherry, peach and fig trees. She wanted 'green peas, asparagus, all kinds of potatoes, turnip seed in quantity for the garden and for the cattle, red and white clover, different kinds of meadow grass, oat-grass and some peat for tangled roots which would grow in either sandy or moist loose ground which might be cut up with some earth roots and served for feed . . . acorns I must have in great quantities'.

Over the coming months Meryon would painstakingly collect everything she asked for and ship it out. It was as though Hester longed to re-create the garden at Walmer or Chevening. 'The grass which thrives well on the Kentish chalky hills would do very well here,' she wrote wistfully.

At a certain spot in her hillside garden, commanding views on all sides, Hester ordered a grave dug. Jean-Baptiste's body was disinterred, and his remains re-buried.

Leander Miranda would finally reappear in London at the end of 1821. He suffered many 'privations' due to 'having so little money in his pocket', but had managed to get to Geneva, hoping Louise might have returned there.

That year, between them, Hester and James paid eight hundred pounds to the Miranda family, money it would seem they could ill afford. 'Poor Miranda!' wrote Hester, who had evidently got over her temper, although she still thought him a 'troublesome cowardly molly-coddle'.

The news that James had married Lady Frederica Murray, barely twenty to his thirty-two, pleased Hester, although she knew now he would be unlikely to come out to Syria, as she had hoped. James had made a modest name for himself as a Whig politician. He was then representing Fowey, and would soon take up the Dartmouth constituency. For once, life seemed charmed for James; he was deeply in love with his wife and a child was on the way. Hester's nephew, James Banks Stanhope, would be born almost exactly nine months after the wedding.

Having married into a very wealthy family, from the outside it might be assumed that money ought not to have been a problem for

James. 'He is even good at keeping old Coutts quiet for the present,' Hester wrote approvingly to Meryon. 'I wish him happy with all my heart.'

Elizabeth Williams had come to Hester, her face lit up with happiness and expectation. She had fallen in love with Massad, an accomplished, handsome Arab from a respectable family in Beirut whom Hester had hired a few months earlier as a translator. Under her roof, they had become lovers. Now they wanted to be married. Elizabeth hoped that Hester would be generous, as she had been before, and perhaps, with her connections, be some help to his future career. But Hester's reaction was harsh. She called Massad in, and he, poor man, expecting to be congratulated, was instead told to pack his bags. As for Elizabeth, Hester told her she would have to choose. If she left with Massad, she could have nothing from her. She warned that if he wanted to divorce her, she would have no protection, and might find herself soon forced to beg or worse.

Elizabeth made her choice. She stayed. But whatever was left of the old friendship between them died that day. Why was Hester so deliberately cruel? Did she truly believe she was acting in the younger woman's best interests? Or was she simply unwilling to let Elizabeth have her chance at lasting happiness, which she herself had been denied? Shortly after this incident, Hester revised her will in Elizabeth's favour. But whatever light there had been in Elizabeth's eyes was extinguished.

As for Meryon, almost simultaneously he learned that he was to become a Fellow of the Royal College of Physicians and a father for the second time. Narcisse was pregnant. Unwilling to marry her, he immediately wrote to Hester, not explaining his reasons, but asking for his old position. 'Recall me to your side and I shall think the voyage back as nothing.' (He did not mention that James had struck a private deal with him, offering him an annuity of £300 if he promised to stay with Hester until the end of her life.)[1] While waiting for her answer, he accepted a position as travelling doctor to Sir Gilbert Heathcote, who intended a lengthy stay in Italy. Narcisse followed him part of the way to Paris and in November 1821, she gave birth there to Meryon's son, the future artist Charles Meryon. Meryon made arrangements for thirty pounds to be paid to her each year, but otherwise kept away. The existence of his son was something he would always keep a secret from Hester.

Just as Hester congratulated herself on a job well done at Djoun, Syria began to slide into dangerous instability. Rivalry intensified between the pashaliks. From Acre, Abdullah Pasha demanded higher than usual tributes and taxes, and sent troops into his territory to bully and brutalize. Many thousands could not afford to pay, unless they agreed to allow their families to be sold into slavery. Hundreds rebelled.

Hester herself was asked for a loan of 'a hundred purses' as 'an act of friendship'. She disliked Abdullah Pasha, but regarded him as a horse she was committed to backing. She gave him 'sixty purses', equal to some 30,000 piastres, expecting him to honour his promise to pay her back 'within thirty-one days'. She would always say that it was this loan, never repaid, that precipitated her debt crisis. Every other time, she had always managed, with some creative borrowing, to establish a financial equilibrium. But no longer. It would be also be an unpaid debt that Abdullah Pasha owed Mehmet Ali – some 60,000 purses – that would soon give Egypt's ruler the ideal pretext for invasion.

You can smell the gunpowder in Hester's letter to Meryon in April 1821:

> A terrible civil war has broken out in this country – about eighty thousand men in arms in Mount Lebanon, troops and inhabitants. You can have no idea of the state of things and next month all will be bloodshed from one end of the country to the other . . . Mouktara is deserted and left with bare walls, and poor and rich are flying from one place to another. Twenty-two villages have been deserted, not a goat to be seen for a day's journey. Night and day, for some days, troops of people of all descriptions came to ask advice of me and protection. I gave them all the same answer: that I would not meddle with the politics of any party and would only assist those who were too helpless to fly to a distance.

She described some forty merchant families from Damascus who sought shelter at Deir-el-Moukhalles, but had come to her when they saw the state of the monastery. 'The priests have been spit at and [some] have had their heads cut off. The poor old patriarch is actually dying of fright and perhaps is now dead. The confusion and alarm is beyond what you can imagine.' She told Meryon she had taken on a freelance Italian surgeon to do what he could for the injured, and that now large numbers of Albanian soldiers were congregating around her fortress in the hope she might employ them. (She did not tell him the terrible scenes she had witnessed with her dining table used as the surgeon's slab for amputations, and how one room had done duty as a makeshift morgue.) Some of them 'have shot one another in disputes and have shot people out of fear'. She had hidden what priests she could, she told Meryon, and helped one of the Fathers at the monastery to escape undetected to Abra, where for the moment 'he is in your old house', until he could be placed in greater safety.

In 1822, Abdullah Pasha renewed his attempt to annex Damascus. In the chaos Emir Bashir lost his authority, but quickly regained it after making a secret pact with Mehmet Ali in which he agreed to become his ally in exchange for weapons, money and a reinforcing army. The deal thrust him into an uneasy partnership with his former rival, Abdullah Pasha, for now both effectively acted as satraps for Mehmet Ali's powerful expansionist interests, but that was about to change.

Whatever surface cordiality Emir Bashir had once shown Sheikh Jumblatt was now replaced with with the hostility of a circling predator. Hester sided with Jumblatt, who represented the disaffected Druze abandoned by the Emir's siding with Mehmet Ali, and by his openly declared allegiance to the Maronites, a prosperous and influential section of the population. Jumblatt hoped he could count on Abdullah Pasha's support, and challenged his rival for control of Mount Lebanon and the Bekaa valley. Until then, the communities of Druze, Maronites and Shi'ite Muslims had co-existed fairly peacefully within the territories under the control of the two men, which made up some two-thirds of present-day Lebanon. But those ties now frayed and snapped, to be replaced by sectarian hatred of a deep and abiding kind.

Terrified villagers caught up in the upheaval fled to Hester's fortress at Djoun, in the hope that her influence might save them. She fed many, allowing those who feared punishment or death to stay within her walls.

Open war broke out between the Pasha of Damascus and Abdullah Pasha, and between Emir Bashir and Sheikh Jumblatt. Hester would claim that she took no part in politics on Mount Lebanon, but this was not the case.

Hester's last visit to Emir Bashir ended dreadfully, and was much gossiped about. All of a sudden, she had asked to come and stay at Beit Eddine, rather than in a guest lodge as usual, which suggests that she had a specific plan. That same night, around three in the morning, she was caught rifling through the Emir's desk. Whether he hit her or she fainted is not clear: a servant spread the tale that she was found lying on the floor in her nightgown, and had to be carried back to bed. She was seen leaving Beit Eddine before dawn with her retinue, ashen-faced. She must have concealed a letter in her nightgown, because it survived amongst her papers.[2] It was from Abdullah Pasha, asking the Emir to pledge his support in the event of an invasion ordered by Mehmet Ali. It was the sort of information for which she had risked her life; it was critical to the survival of her friend Jumblatt. This fiasco marked the end of any special relationship with the Emir.

Soon after this, she wrote: 'Acre is mined by the pasha who says he will blow himself up and the town if he can hold out. The perfidy of the Emir Bashir has been great; his head however is now destined for the bowstring.'

As for who the British would back, news on that front from Constantinople and London was frustratingly slow. Hester was willing to have an old friend of hers, Captain Yorke (the future Lord Hardwicke), stay with her, knowing that he had come to make some kind of offer to the Emir. Yorke was given the royal treatment, offered banquets and Turkish baths at Beit Eddine, then interrogated by Hester when he came back to see her.

Yorke wrote rapturous descriptions of the Djoun fortress, and how on arrival he was led through the labyrinth of passages into a small dark room where he saw 'a Bedouin Arab chief, who soon turned out to be Lady Hester'. He said: 'I at once became delighted with her wit, her knowledge, and I must say, her beauty, for she is still one of the finest specimens of a woman I ever saw.' But later, after they had eaten and smoked the 'chibouque', he noticed that 'her mind was wrought to a high pitch of enthusiasm; she talked wildly and was much distressed in mind'. Hester admitted that the sight of him 'brought back to my recollection old times' and she found it hard to concentrate on 'what I was talking about. I was oppressed in body and mind.'

Delayed letters meant that Hester was impatiently expecting Meryon to arrive while he was still in Italy with his new employer. She had latched on to the idea that she should bring up Lucy, his little girl. So keen was she that they come quickly, she had written to Sligo to ask him to stump up the money for the expenses of his journey. She seems to long for a lively little girl to fuss over:

> Set off immediately with your daughter, bringing only some cloth for a handsome blue *benysh* not too dark, and two white turbans and cloth for *sherwals* and a common *jubey*. Your little girl will want nothing but combs, brushes, thimbles and little things not to be got here, like shoes for the house – large, as she will grow, and light, that she could dance in, not black. Also printed cotton or silk handkerchiefs, to tie around the waist in the Oriental way, here to be had with great difficulty . . .
>
> Teach Lucy a little Arabic upon the road, and also to sit with her legs under her, but by degrees. I am prepared to like her, and hope she will turn out quite Oriental with a little French air, dancing, but no Frank grins and jerks.

Hester told Meryon to inform the Duke of Sussex that by the end of the year she hoped to 'do very well'. She was referring to her plan to back Jumblatt's insurrection against Emir Bashir. She had the doctor order almost two hundred pounds' worth of pistols and ammunition to be sent out to her at speed. She had heard that some of the Duke's men would be coming out to her, and advised: 'It would be best now to hurry as much as possible, unless the D[uke] says otherwise.'

She sent more coded dispatches for Meryon, warning him that he might be sent for personally by the Duke of Sussex. Instead he was summoned by the Duke of York and had 'a long conversation with him'. The Duke told Meryon straight out that he had considered Hester's proposals 'but in an evil moment he listened to the vile suggestions of others, and had never had his mind easy from that time'.[3] He seemed contrite and thoughtful, and in that instant, promised Meryon that he would consider what might be done in her favour. But from this exchange it seemed clear that if Hester believed she would have support for her politics in the neighbourhood of Syria, she was mistaken.

In 1822 Meryon met his future wife, Eliza Gardiner, a widow with a young son. Within nine months they were married. Their daughter Eugenia was born soon afterwards, in the same year, 1823. Almost overnight Meryon became a married father-of-two and with the death of his father in 1824, he inherited properties to manage in Rye. Although, with some hesitation, he told Eliza about Lucy, he did not yet mention that he also had a little son tucked away in Paris, nor did he tell Narcisse that he had married.

For all these reasons, Meryon delayed going out to Hester, despite her insistent demands that he come. Money worries pushed him to think seriously about returning. When he sought out James to hold him to his earlier offer, he was startled to discover that both brother and sister appeared to be short of cash. James confided angrily that money seemed to evaporate the moment it got anywhere near Hester, and made it clear that if any more of her bills were to come to him, he would have to refuse to pay them. By his reckoning she owed at least £1,000 to Coutts. James pinned his own financial hopes on property he was due to inherit from Banks. There was just one hitch: Lady Banks, 'who might live one month or ten years', would have to die first. But James surmised that after Lady Banks's death, Hester would 'be well provided for' and should be able to make 'ample provision' herself. James told Meryon that if he decided to go, he would give him a hundred pounds, but he must not expect that Hester would find it easy to pay him in the regular way he might hope for.[4]

James's woes intensified. His beloved Frederica died in 1823 giving birth to their second son. She was not quite twenty-three. The old James died too. He became pious, burying himself in religion, and retreating from life. Frederica's parents, the Mansfields, took him and his son to live with them. The rift with Hester following the mystery Brougham affair meant he did not confide in her.

The Mansfields lived in high splendour at Kenwood, the Earl's seat, then known as Caen Wood, which was set within fifty acres of land, much of which today comprises Hampstead Heath and what was once the water reservoir as well as the swimming ponds. James began to wander the woods and villages of nearby Hampstead and Highgate for most of the night, unable to sleep.

Hester heard of 'poor James' loss' six months later and berated Meryon for not being the one to write first. 'Why do you not talk to me of James's poor little children,' she asked, not realizing that the baby had died too.

William Noel Hill was inadvertently the one to send her the sad news, assuming she knew. His letter was a poignant reminder of a life she had long ago given up, and he seemed to want to salve old hurts. He wrote to her from Genoa, feeling compelled once again to reach out to her: 'You will be surprised to see my old scrawl again, but it is not entirely your fault if you did not see it sooner,' he told her. He revealed that James had warned him it would be better for him not to write, advice he was not willing to accept, but that all this time he had remained 'in terror of not having sufficient command over myself not to write what I thought'.

Hill was still gripped by the memory of her as he had loved her. Now, writing to her at Djoun, he recalled 'the first time I saw you', how radiant she seemed to him at 'Lady Somer's party' long ago. He told her he would soon be returning to London on leave before taking up his post as consul at Naples, and suggested she write to him at his old haunt, 'Warren's Hotel, Regent Street (*you do remember*!!)', he added emphatically. He was still bitter, reminding her that she had promised to come out to *him* in Italy when she left England. Instead she had met Bruce. After that, he told her, he had 'discontinued a correspondence which had become too painful'. He had never been able to properly explain all he felt but he had certainly kept himself informed about her life, as much as he was able. It was as though Hill wanted to shake her into sense:

> Oh, how many happy days does writing to you remind me [of] and I am never to speak and talk to you upon them again!!! I am so out of spirits which I cannot rally that I will not close till tomorrow in the hopes at least that my farewell may be more gay. It is no consolation after all, in speaking of death, to write to those who are dead to the world.[5]

Hester had evidently replied to the letter he sent her with Meryon in 1818. Whatever she had told him about what she considered her own fate and that of the world had evidently not impressed him:

You talk of the world's unkindness more than formerly. You have not been worse used since you left Malta! You therefore overstate its cruelty . . . You cannot complain of the usage of the world when you so treat your friends! It is certainly idle to argue, and when you give me the rhapsody of 'having the fetters of prejudice by the strong arm of reason,' I can only answer that to me your present path seems pointed out much more by the strapping forefinger of insanity. Ask yourself the question whether Mr Pitt (or indeed any person) would approve of your thus quitting the world or your *real* friends, and burying yourself alive (vestal or not.)[6]

He invited her to Italy. 'Why not come and exercise your strong arm *here* – unless it is absolutely palsied except among Turks and Arabs,' he teased. He fervently hoped she would come, he told her.

Hester ignored the heartfelt sentiments of the man who would have married her.* Instead she kept up her intrigues, writing surreptitiously to Sheikh Jumblatt, sending letters through her friend Syt Habŭs. She had begun receiving communiqués from Bartolomeo Pisani, chief adviser to Robert Liston at Constantinople.

It would appear that Hester was doing her best to assure Jumblatt that the British – and the Porte, as well as Abdullah Pasha – would ultimately back him. In the meantime, she gave him a considerable sum of money, borrowed of course.

Jumblatt wrote many letters to her, all in Kufic Arabic, dripping with honorifics and always signed 'Your loving and faithful friend'. They breathe drama, written while Jumblatt was hiding in mountain caves, always courteous and courageous, despite his fear for his life and those of his beloved family. He put his complete trust in her. Back and forth, they discussed Pisani's potential role in interceding on Jumblatt's behalf with the British and the Porte. There are coded messages. She tells him: 'We understand what you said about needing camels, and we have applied for the right

---

* William Noel Hill never married, and died in 1842, the third Baron, Lord Berwick.

papers', which might perhaps be decoded as an urgent request for troops. 'The previous friendship has not been cancelled,' she writes in another, which was a warning that the British had yet to retract their unofficial backing for Emir Bashir. She tried to encourage him. She was doing everything she could to influence both Liston and Abdullah Pasha on his behalf, and to that end, she had even offered the latter advice on building a magnificent garden at Acre.[7]

Hester remained hopeful that Jumblatt would be triumphant, and that in time, a greater gathering to power might still come about. But by early January 1825, the situation looked bad. Many hundreds of 'miserable people' flocked to her fortress to take refuge, and she despaired at the 'prospect of starvation if this business lasts long'.[8]

Emir Bashir routed Jumblatt, catching up with him on the plains around Damascus, where he was surrounded by an escort of two hundred men. Jumblatt might have managed to escape with his life, but instead he chose to trust the assurance he was given that, on the Porte's orders, after his deposition, he, his family and men would be delivered to Abdullah Pasha and spared. Jumblatt surrendered only to be accused of 'sedition and inciting disorder and unrest' and thrown into a Damascus jail. No mercy was shown: he was strangled and then beheaded, his body hacked up and displayed for all of Acre to see, then thrown to the dogs. Jumblatt's wife, who had fled to the Hauran with her young children, was captured. The Emir himself held her terrified little boy in front of her and said to his soldiers: 'Let me see him cut to pieces before my eyes.' After that horror, he had Jumblatt's three young nephews tortured, their eyes burned out and their tongues cut out.

Hester already knew what Emir Bashir had been doing to his victims during this time of war. 'Think of women's breasts squeezed in a vice and chopped off; of men's heads screwed into a tourniquet until their temple-bones were driven in; of eyes put out with red-hot saucers [sic]; men castrated alive and a hundred other barbarities. There never was a more heartless, cruel man.' But his treatment of the Jumblatts filled her with anguish and hatred. She was convinced he intended to come for her too.

Certainly the Emir wanted her out of the way, but he hesitated to kill her. But, just so that she would feel uncomfortable, he sent five hundred of his troops into the villages surrounding her, issuing threats that those who worked for her would 'lose their property and their lives'. Hester was trapped:

My servants can not go out, and the peasants of the villages cannot approach the house. Therefore I am not in a very pleasant situation, being deprived of necessary supplies of food, and what is worse, of water.[9]

Then his soldiers came closer, right up to her fortress walls. 'They killed three men, one between the house and the village, one at the back of my premises, just to let me know what they could do.'

James seems to have methodically prepared his suicide, which occurred on Saturday, 5 March 1825. He was found at around 10 p.m. in one of the outhouses at Kenwood hanging from a beam, suspended by his braces and a long silk scarf. That morning, his manservant disclosed, he had dressed carefully and dismissed him early. The London newspaper reported that he had been due to marry a young woman, who was at Kenwood that same day, but did not name her. He was thirty-nine.

James had methodically burned all of Hester's letters, and ordered that if any were to be found after his death, 'they must be burned unopened'. Many concluded that he simply could not bear the shame of his financial pressures. He had clearly felt unable to confide his problems to his in-laws, but must have at least felt that his own son would be financially secure after his death, knowing that the family loved him. Among the beneficiaries of his will were two former servants from Chevening, one of them Ann Fry.[10]

James's suicide devastated Hester. Meryon sent her the news of the tragedy four days later. She would claim that from the time she heard of his death she never left the perimeter of her hill, an extraordinary fact that appears to be true. She gave up riding and she lost all taste for the outside world. She blamed herself bitterly for not reaching out to him more, and for their rift of recent years, but especially for not writing to console him after hearing of his wife's death, an act that had gone against her natural instinct. She had only heard that news – from Hill – six months after the event, and rationalized to herself that she might reopen a wound that had started to heal. She had begun many letters to him, and held out the hope she would see him before too long. She mourned that perhaps he had never known how much she loved him, and had died thinking her 'a sort of poor mad woman'. Yet James left Hester a future annuity of £1,500, money that would come to her from the Bankses' inheritance after Lady Banks's death (though Lady Banks still seemed in no hurry to die).

Her sister Griselda chose this moment to offer an olive branch, the first letter she had written to Hester since they were both in their early twenties. She sent several more, thinking the first might not have reached her, but Hester did not reply.

The war forced her to take extreme measures, and her money problems worsened. She felt like a 'scare-crow' reduced by 'grief and sickness'. The work required to keep her fortress in order was relentless, time-consuming and expensive. She borrowed more to feed and care for all the 'distressed persons' who came to her, and had even given them most of her clothes 'except for things that are too fine for me to wear under the present circumstances'.

She thought her servants seemed to regard the state of turmoil as an excuse to do anything they pleased; some of them she knew stole supplies and sold them, others she suspected of getting up to more heinous crimes. She had a great deal of difficulty trying to keep them all out of each other's beds; there had already been several pregnancies and, at her insistence, forced marriages. Her financial situation was dire. She confided to Meryon:

> As for my debts, it is not, as you think 25 per cent yearly that I have to pay but 50 and 90; and in one instance I have suffered more loss still. Gold at 28 ½ piastres they counted to me here at 45, which I spent at 28 ½ and am to repay at Beyrout at the rate of 45 – calculate that!

Hester applied to a lodge of Freemasons at Malta for funds. A letter from a 'Hastings' indicates that they did indeed regard themselves as being indebted to her for something, but at that time they were forced 'for the moment' to 'apologetically' refuse her.[11]

By the summer of 1825 gunfire and torchings had swept up the hillsides into the mountain villages. Atrocities, murders and rapes became commonplace. The guns and ammunition that had been intended for Jumblatt were now stockpiled in her store-rooms, and to increase her protection, she took on many of the runaway soldiers who had turned to her, many of them freebooting Albanians, as well as drifting Arab mercenaries. 'Banditti' she called them, 'poor lads, most of them'. In effect, she now had her own ad hoc army at her service.

Towards the end of 1826 a mystery caller identified by Hester only as 'X' came riding up to Djoun to see her. He told her he had been sent by the Duke of Sussex, and had 'an offer and an ultimatum' for her. The Duke 'and an influential committee of Freemasons' were now willing to extricate her from all her financial difficulties. 'X' had come with private papers for her to see, and a confidential passport – a '*par-tout*' – from the Duke of Sussex. He had a request and orders to extract her promise of silence about it. The intimation was that she should expect to have an important 'personage from Europe' live with her in Djoun. Apparently, if she agreed, she would be sent 'a hundred purses' for her current expenses, and the rest would follow, some in jewels that would be sold on her account. She wrote to Meryon: 'If X's story is true, and my debts, amounting to £10,000, or nearly, are to be paid, then I shall go on, making sublime and philosophical discoveries, and employing myself in deep abstract studies, although as my strength is gone, I cannot work day and night as I have done.'

Apparently Hester agreed to what 'X' proposed, for she began to muse on the prospect of 'starting clear'. But she concluded that 'if all that has been told me is a lie, let me be disowned publicly, left to my fate and faith alone, for if I have not a right to what I want, which is in the hands of Messieurs Sharky and Co., I will have nothing. There is nothing else to be done, I shall wait for no more dawdling letters, or fabrication of lies, of which, for these past five years, I have had enough.'

Who was 'X'? What had he offered? Letters which might have revealed some answers were burnt, 'for fear of accidents'. Meryon knew his identity,

as he later communicated with him on Hester's behalf from London.* In a
later letter to Meryon, Hester let slip about 'X' that:

> If he asks what I am to do, say you don't know – that she knows best.
> I fear by and by that everything will be in the newspapers. These sorts
> of men talk before servants to show their importance; all goes to grooms,
> footmen and coachmen.

Whatever was going to be in the newspapers she never mentioned again.
Over the following months, she hinted to Meryon that she intended to
make a journey 'to settle the business'. But shortly afterwards, it is as
though she had learned something else, which either concerned the offer
'X' made, or a proposal of some other kind. She appears to have learned
of some connection to her brother Philip that caused her grave misgivings. She gave specific instructions that if her brother tried to place any
money into her account with Coutts, 'let [him] take it back again . . . you
have no explainations to make, only that I decline it'. Shortly afterwards,
she had a new warning for Meryon that concerned her brother, but she
was careful not to name him. She was frightened: 'I entreat you, keep
away from my family.'

By September 1827 Meryon had set out for Syria, bringing his wife Eliza
and their little girl Eugenia, then four, ignoring Hester's request that he
should bring only Lucy. On their way out the Meryons survived a traumatic capture by Greek pirates, only to be caught up in the wider drama
as the naval forces of England, France and Russia joined together to defeat
the Ottoman fleet in the Bay of Navarino. The battle that made Greek
independence a reality would soon trigger more bloodshed. Ibrahim
Pasha's large Egyptian fleet had been defeated; nevertheless he expected
compensation from the Sultan. Offered Crete, he demanded Syria. In
Cairo, Mehmet Ali and Ibraham Pasha laid plans for war.

The Meryons turned back to Leghorn, spending time in Pisa and Rome

---

* Hester sent Meryon a letter in bastardized English Arabic, which she knew he would understand. Meryon's transcribed version of her letter reads: 'I will not take less than £10,000 for paying
my debts, and £5000 for my income every year; the reason is my affairs must go on'.

while they debated whether to delay or return home. Hester sent them a hundred pounds to help pay their expenses, and they lived for some weeks in limbo. In the end, Eliza prevailed: the Meryons returned to England, to wait until 'circumstances permitted'.

By now in Sidon, in the aftermath of Navarino, the European residents were terrified by the anti-Western atmosphere that had pervaded the country. They were robbed, spat upon and molested, and feared worse. Large numbers of them fled their homes and sought refuge with Hester behind her fortress walls, hoping for safety in numbers. Hester took them all in, fed and housed them as best she could. The crisis lasted many months. Her grand residence took on the appearance of a hostel and a hospital ward, with people bedding down in the passages of her house and in the garden. She wrote:

> I worked like a slave. I have had neither rest, air or exercise for eight months. Constant worry and fatigue with a constant fever which has hurt my eyesight, split my nails, worn away the gums from my teeth, of which however I have not one decayed in my head; but I feared, a fortnight ago, all would come out – not loose, but they were half-bare, although better now; having rubbed them with a root which cooled my mouth. I am a poor creature indeed!

She raged at the uselessness of the consuls, who did nothing to protect their citizens, she said, while she herself had been abandoned by 'the John Bulls of this country', who she surmised were anxious not to offend Emir Bashir. Meanwhile, Hester applied directly for help to the new British Ambassador in Constantinople, her old *bête noire*, Stratford Canning. He sent a warship and the Europeans were duly evacuated. Hester, as usual, stayed on, while Elizabeth let another chance for escape slip through her fingers.

Some time in late 1827 or early 1828 Hester informed Meryon with great urgency that the business with 'X' had reared its head again. She wanted him to set off alone 'with a Dutch passport' and she promised to keep him 'no more than a few months'. But shortly afterwards she added: 'Tell X these few words: "She has ordered me to forbid you evermore to interfere with her affairs, or even to write to her".'

The offers relayed from 'X' then seemed to fizzle out, in the same year as the Duke of York's death. After that, Hester would claim that she had 'no more friends in Europe'.

In May 1828 a 'wild child' who had been imprisoned for most of his childhood turned up in the main square of Nuremberg. The strange enigma of Kaspar Hauser would soon grip Europe. Within a year Hester's brother would circle the sixteen-year-old like a charming predator, then became his legal guardian. Philip Stanhope would become forever linked in the public eye with Kaspar, and devote much of the rest of his life trying to deflect suspicions that he had been involved in his murder.

Rumours began, at first derided but never entirely dispelled, that Kaspar, who had been imprisoned for most of his childhood, was actually the heir to the usurped throne of Baden. It seemed far-fetched and dramatic, but so was everything about Kaspar Hauser.

The most compelling theory suggests that Kaspar may have been the son of the beautiful and coquettish Stéphanie de Beauharnais, related through marriage to Josephine. Napoleon was said to have been so infatuated with Stéphanie that, despite Josephine's objections, he invited her to live with them at the Tuileries and 'adopted' her. In 1806, through Napoleon's efforts, Stéphanie made a notably unhappy marriage to Karl, Grand Duke of Baden, placing her squarely at the heart of the ruling political elite of Europe. She produced five children, among them a healthy son, born in September 1812, whom she intended to call 'Gaspard'. But the baby was said to have died suddenly some weeks after his birth. There were rumours that her son might have been secreted away and a dead child substituted, and dark whispers about Karl's stepmother, the ambitious Duchess of Hochberg, who wanted her own son, Leopold, to succeed.

What becomes clear, after a detailed examination of the story of Kaspar Hauser, is that some secretive consortium did indeed want him silent – or dead. There is every indication that Philip had a hand, not just in Kaspar's murder, but in that of the boy's advocate, the distinguished jurist, Paul Johann Anselm Ritter von Feuerbach, who died just before he was about to reveal his discoveries regarding Kaspar's identity. Hester's brother did not work alone: he received payments from the House of Baden and he lied repeatedly about the facts.[12]

It is intriguing to speculate on the possible motivation for Philip's involvement. One of the words Kaspar uttered in a fever soon after he had come to Nuremberg was 'Erlangen'. This was where, years before, Hester had arranged for Philip to study and where he had made influential friendships. Among them had been Leopold von Hochberg. Leopold's fortunes changed dramatically as the years went on, when one by one, the male descendants of the House of Baden died out. However, a new succession law cleared the way for Leopold's accession, and he certainly stood to lose a great deal if Kaspar were proved to be a genuine heir.

Those who read the facts clearly see that Philip laid his groundwork with Kaspar very methodically, often going to great lengths to create one impression when the truth may have been quite the opposite. He arrived in Nuremberg on 17 October 1829, just a few days before an unknown assailant made a first attempt to murder Kaspar: the boy was wounded in the neck with a butcher's knife, but recovered. Philip's European banker, Merkel of Nuremberg, not only received funds on his behalf from the House of Baden, but also made detailed enquiries about Kaspar, obtaining his picture and the original police report of his discovery. In Nuremberg, Philip made a great show of being merely a wealthy traveller on a grand tour, and affected a complete lack of interest in the local phenomenon of the mysterious 'wild child'.

In 1830 – the same year that Leopold became fourth Grand Duke of Baden – Philip returned to Nuremberg, and began a campaign first to befriend, then adopt, Kaspar, who was then being passed about the homes of various temporary guardians. The dashing English lord seemed like a saviour: he took him out for long rides, bought him a horse, expensive clothes and other gifts. He promised to take him to Chevening, where he would soon meet his new family. Without much difficulty he obtained legal guardianship over the boy. Yet not one of his letters home to his wife and family even mentions Kaspar. Not everyone in Nuremberg was convinced Philip's motives for adoption were benevolent, but for a different reason: he was observed caressing the boy in public in what could only be interpreted as a sexual way.

On Philip's orders, Kaspar was placed in what would become a second prison, the house of a sadistic schoolteacher fifty miles away at Ansbach. Philip left Ansbach on 19 January 1832, and after visiting his bankers, went straight to Mannheim, where Stéphanie de Beauharnais lived. Immediately after Philip's visit, Stéphanie was observed weeping for several days, and he would later confirm that she asked him to bring Kaspar to her. It seems that Hester's brother, with his erudition and apparent charm, managed to convince almost everyone that he had the boy's best interests at heart, and both Stéphanie and Feuerbach trusted him completely. Not long afterwards, Feuerbach wrote to Philip confiding that he had sent a secret letter communicating his discoveries about Kaspar's identity to the Queen Mother of Bavaria (Stéphanie's sister-in-law). As Feuerbach told it (in a long letter to Philip that for many years lay buried and hidden in the Stanhope family papers) the Queen Mother had revealed 'facts . . . which when I think about them, cause shivers to run down my spine . . . and explain the tears and sleepless nights of S[téphanie].' He let slip to Philip that the Queen Mother then sent him a long document, which he knew would place him 'in great danger' if he were to reveal its contents by letter.[13]

Within a matter of days after writing this letter Feuerbach was dead. His son was convinced he had been poisoned with arsenic. Feuerbach had been on his way to Frankfurt, directed there by Philip, who had suggested he meet an intermediary he could trust. This turned out to be Countess Hochberg's lover, Johann von Klüber, whose own son was Leopold's personal secretary. On 29 May 1832, the day Feuerbach died, Philip happened to be in Andermach, only a short distance away. The document in which Feuerbach set such store appears to have been destroyed.[14] In a strange twist, and in obscure circumstances, Klüber then became Kaspar's guardian. Later that same year, on 14 December, Kaspar was lured to the Orangerie in Ansbach by a man who told him he had a message from his mother. This time, the stabbing proved fatal.

Kaspar Hauser's death was announced on 20 December, causing a furore in the nation's newspapers. Philip could hardly have missed seeing it. Nonetheless, he went through a charade of sending a letter to the dead boy, dated 'Vienna, December 16 and 17', but postmarked Munich 23 December, announcing that he expected to come to see him by the end of the following month, and signing himself 'your godfather, who loves you with all his heart, Earl Stanhope'.[15] Philip's behaviour, however, contradicted the apparent spirit of that note. He went into a litigious frenzy, collecting statements and taking depositions from anyone connected with Kaspar, all in an effort to prove the boy a fraud, liar, and falsifier. None of this stopped a Bavarian court from bringing charges of conspiracy to murder against the fourth Earl, proceedings which were later quietly dropped.

Philip went so far as to testify that Kaspar had killed himself, staging his stabbing in an effort to get attention. Above all he tried to assert that Feuerbach had changed his views about the boy, and had been intending, before his death, to unmask him as an impostor, a charge that was diametrically opposed to the truth. Eventually Philip would publish his 'findings' as *Tracts Relating to Kaspar Hauser*. In light of what is known about the facts of the case, this attempt to whitewash the murder and clear his name makes repellent reading.

Might Kaspar have been the unknown 'important personage from Europe' referred to by the mysterious 'X'? Whatever else, Kaspar's fate certainly sheds light on Hester's fear of her brother, demonstrates what he and his circle might have been capable of, and explains why she wanted to keep so well away from him.

In September 1828, after a terrible year of violence and uncertainty, Hester lost her last companion. Both she and Elizabeth had caught 'a kind of fever, which I do not know precisely how to name'. Most of her maid-servants, 'ungrateful sluts', had fled, leaving both Englishwomen gravely ill in their beds. For long stretches of time, only three girls, two of them under the age of twelve, were left to look after them. Hester remembered little of her own illness, except that through her delirium she was aware that her servants were deserting her. Some of them brought strangers with them to loot her property, going so far as to break down a wall in order to remove the larger pieces of furniture. Helpless, too weak to get up, she was aware of people bustling around her, packing up her belongings, stealing clothes and *objets d'art* and whatever else took their fancy.

That she too did not die was due only to the attentions of a local village woman, fetched by the youngest servant, eight-year-old Gayby.

Gayby claimed that on Hester's orders she had given Elizabeth a dose of senna and salt, as well as some of the famous 'black dose', a mixture of senna and laudanum, and three other pills she had found. Hester, usually so precise with her commands, was delirious, and must have confused her. Inadvertently, the child had worsened Elizabeth's already weak condition by triggering terrible stomach cramps and diarrhoea that strained all her organs, especially her heart. The same old woman who found Hester barely alive took Elizabeth to be dead; yet macabrely some hours later warmth returned to her body, and when a local doctor was summoned, he observed that her cheeks were flushed and that 'something kept continually bubbling inside her like boiling water'. Weak, but conscious, Hester gave permission for her to be bled. But when the doctor made an incision in Elizabeth's foot, instead of the expected steady trickle, a torrent spurted out. Elizabeth was forty-two. Hester buried her friend that same Sunday, in the corner of a graveyard within the monastry at Deir-el-Moukhalles. Her gravestone had no inscription, nothing to mark it out as that of a Christian, nor does it still. Hester feared if it did, it would be smashed and the body disinterred by the Emir's men, just to spite her.

Hester could not bear to look at Elizabeth's room, nor sort through her possessions and papers. She had it sealed up and sectioned off the entire passage. Many of the servants would claim it was haunted.

After many delays, Meryon finally brought his family out to Syria, reaching Beirut on 8 December 1830. Lucy remained in England as before, and his step-son John also stayed behind with relatives. Hester had not been much impressed by Meryon's description of his wife Eliza, who vacillated about coming out for more than three years. (Nor can the Meryons have felt encouraged to read her instructions that they should 'dress shabbily' in case word got back to her creditors that 'he might come loaded with money to pay her debts'.)

Meryon had promised he would stay as long as eighteen months or more. Hester put them up in a small cottage, certainly better than Meryon's old mud hovel in Abra, with a garden and 'two black slaves for servants'.

She felt an outflow of affection towards him when they met again and she kissed him affectionately on both cheeks. They had not seen each other for thirteen years. He complimented her on looking extremely well considering what she had been through, and expressed his astonishment at her 'mythical Greek fortress'. Nothing was as it had been before. All her rich furnishings from Cairo and Damascus were gone, and even her cushions and sofa coverings. She had substituted coarse, make-do replacements: cheap planks of wood for tables and chairs made from rush matting.

But when she led Meryon outside, he marvelled as she pointed out her Damask rose bushes; her Quatre Saisons, her Isfahans and Bella Donnas, all miraculous in spring, she promised.

That first night she waved away his weak protests that his wife would by now be worried he had not returned, and made him stay to dinner with her, a pattern she would repeat countless times. Meryon noticed that she had at least seven black African slaves. She appalled him with her story that she had no choice, after her servants abandoned her, but to buy them at market price; she, once a friend to Wilberforce. He was also shocked to see the state of her bedroom; 'hardly better than that of a common peasant', strewn about with writing papers, books, pieces of fabric and Arabic almanacs. Hester's black maid Zezefoon slept on a coarse scrap of cushion behind a length of curtain near her door.

On subsequent visits Hester struck him as being 'more violent in her temper than formerly'. He was taken aback when she boasted that 'nobody could give such a slap in the face, when required, as she could'.[16]

Hester's insomnia was now chronic; she slept a few hours from dawn, then 'seldom rose before four or five in the afternoon'. She had constructed an elaborate, if rather crude-looking system of bellropes, looped through pulleys, a poor imitation of the arrangement that had operated at Chevening.

She asked Meryon to take on the task of unsealing Elizabeth's room and packing up her belongings, and in doing so, he found yet more bills and accounts left unattended in a pile of papers stuffed away in a box.

The doctor soon found that his role was expected to be that of listener. He would sit with Hester for eight or ten hours at a stretch. 'Her brain worked incessantly, and her tongue never knew a moment's repose.' Her conversation was 'like an over-flowing river, it bore down every thing before it', he would say. Even though he was often 'deeply impressed, astonished and highly entertained' by what she told him, he came to dread how interminable these sessions seemed.

He was often struck by how when he tried to record the essence of her conversations, 'even word for word', he could never quite capture 'how well they sounded to the ear when she spoke them'. It was now that he heard a great deal of what he later collated and published as Hester's 'Memoirs'. On the nights he saw Hester, he would have to make his way back to the village in pitch-darkness, often hearing and encountering jackals and wolves and even panthers. It was in all ways an unconventional arrangement, and it is easy to see why Eliza distrusted it.

Eliza's desperate unhappiness and fear of violence made life very difficult for Meryon, and as far as Hester could see, prevented him from carrying out his duties. When he refused to go to Damascus, after Hester's friend Ahmed Bey asked him to tend an imam, who was a close friend of the Pasha of Damascus, Hester was furious. As usual, she had an ulterior motive: Ahmed Bey told her the imam also suffered from 'a complaint of the mouth', which she knew meant he had something urgent to communicate, and she was desperate to know what it was. Within a matter of days she had her answer when a large number of renegade troops passed close by, on their way from Damascus, ready to offer their allegiance to Abdullah Pasha in Acre.

An impasse was reached, with Hester unwilling to let the Meryons go, but Eliza determined that they must. The full brunt of Hester's displeasure was extremely unpleasant to experience, manifested in many acts of churlish pique. Meryon confided to his journal that 'Our situation was now becoming more and more uncomfortable . . . we took long walks every day, talking over our troubles, and contriving how we should free ourselves for we were effectively in prison as though we had been under bars and bolts'. He had not been paid nor yet expected any additional payment.[17] Meryon was forced to ask his brother-in-law for the funds for their return fare. Without her permission to leave, no one in Djoun would even hire out mules and camels to them.

To win his freedom Meryon spent two evenings talking with her until midnight, and she decided to relent. She promised to arrange and pay for a vessel to take them to Cyprus. With this agreed, a truce was declared. Hester accepted Meryon's recommendation of a young Italian doctor, Lunardi, whom he had met at Leghorn, settling his conscience that she would not be long without medical care at hand.

At their last meeting, at Hester's request, as she plied him with tea and fed him cakes, they went over the long list of her creditors. He saw she had given substantial sums to Sheikh Jumblatt's wife, who had gone mad with grief, and his remaining family. There were also amounts given to widows of others assassinated by the Emir, as well as money doled out to any number of needy individuals who had come to her as refugees. She had fallen into borrowing from moneylenders at exorbitant rates of interest. Many of the 'Turks, Christians and Jews' who had offered her loans had presented her papers to sign 'in Arabic, Armenian or Hebrew, which I could not read, and by which I bound myself to pay enormous rates of interest, varying from 25 to 50 per cent', she admitted.[18] He calculated her debts at £14,000, more than £700,000 in contemporary terms.

Once this was done, she fixed her eyes on him, and graciously asked if he would mind placing the list in Elizabeth's room, in the writing desk where she now kept it. When he returned, thinking he would now say his farewell, he found her door bolted and one of the maids waiting outside 'to spare both of us the pain of saying goodbye'.

When he returned to Eliza, he found Hester had sent him great quantities of freshly-baked *mahmoul* cakes and baklava, a beautiful amber-tipped pipe and his favourite tobacco from her own store. In Sidon, when they reached the boat on 7 April they found it already stocked with plentiful provisions on Hester's orders. It was typical of Hester, Meryon mused, that just at the moment when he might have decided to despise her, she was capable of a gesture that made his heart relent.

Among the many things that Hester kept secret from Meryon was the fact that around this time she took an Arab lover from the village of Djoun. He was, by all accounts, a strikingly handsome man, then in his thirties. His name was Almaz. At first she had hired him as her gardener, but soon his own family knew that he was rather more than that.* He would stay with Hester until the end.

Within a year Damascus fell and all Syria was under Egyptian domination, wrested away by Ibrahim Pasha's occupying army and fleet. By the end of November 1831 the infantry and cavalry regiments Hester once so admired in Cairo were swarming up the coast. By early December, they had cordoned off Acre from the sea and commenced intense bombardment. Abdullah Pasha, with his six thousand soldiers, put up a spirited defence, trying to appease Emir Bashir in the hope he would come to his aid, and assuming the Porte would send Turkish forces. He misjudged on both counts. The Ottomans would be forced to cede control of Syria and Palestine.

Throughout the siege of Acre, Muslims, Maronites, Christians and Druze alike were attacked. Gunfire and torchings devastated the mountain villages, and massacres took place. Scores of refugees from what is now southern Lebanon and northern Israel fled to Hester for protection. Some of them, as she graphically put it, 'were literally stripped to the bone', half-naked, 'idiotic from fright', their 'thighs and legs without skin', 'widows and orphans without any resource whatsoever', and some had 'their eyes and noses carried off by a [musket] ball'. By her own account, some seventy-six families arrived, with many women and children, as well as troops from Abdullah Pasha's army, all bringing horrendous stories. 'What sd. I do with so many starving and naked & many in fear of their lives?' she asked herself.

It was the beginning of the apocalyptic nightmare she had been expecting. She was quite literally wading in blood, as both Metta and

---

* I heard the story about Hester's lover from the aunt of my friends, the Stephan sisters – Wafà and Rania – with whom I first went to Djoun, now called Joun, in the early 1990s. They were visiting their family home which they had not seen for more than a decade, owing to the chaos of the civil war. Their aunt Yvette was a fund of stories passed down to her from her father and grandfather, for the history of the Stephan family went back many generations. Among them had been Ayoub al Moussawba, the stone-master who built Hester's house. Yvette confirmed that it was a generally accepted fact in family lore that her great-great-uncle had been Hester's lover. Her own father and grandfather had repeated the story of Almaz's great attachment to her many times. The fact that he remained unmarried for so long was something unheard of in the village, and he married only after Hester's death. She showed me a very early photograph of her great-uncle, a particularly handsome man, though she told me her grandfather had told her he was not as handsome as his father, Almaz.

Loustaunau had once predicted. Her fortress took on the sickly, acidic smell of gunfire and damaged, decayed flesh. The crisis before had seemed dreadful. This was worse. Everywhere she looked, she saw shattered, terrified people, hurt and crying. All had put their hope in her. At one point she estimated she had a thousand people within her walls; she soon lost count. She saw mothers sobbing over children who had been blown apart. She had to make do with what doctors she could find; Mustafa, her reliable bleeder, was put to work as a surgeon. Emergency amputations were performed, wounds cauterized with boiling butter. Many died of their injuries. A common grave was established.

Hester had never felt such helplessness. Much of what she saw was unspeakable, but she took some comfort in saving as many as she could. She used every available resource, and putting her debts out of her mind, borrowed more. '[For] three years my house was like the Tower of Babel, filled as well as the village, with unhappy people from Acre of all nations, but with the blessing of God I got through it all, and saved many doomed to have their heads cut off.'

Mehmet Ali was in a quandary about what to do with his erstwhile friend. She was already suspected of encouraging the Druze to take up arms and drive Ibrahim Pasha's armies back. Certainly many of those who turned to her now were Druze. She even sent her men to give water and food to Druze captives as they were marched through Sidon.

Hester's valiant efforts would go unrecognized, unrewarded, and almost entirely unremarked upon in Britain. She would later justify her actions to the Duke of Wellington, pointing out angrily that the Europeans 'held back in the most extraordinary manner'.

The wretched inhabitants, who expected to find succour from their old friends, found their backs turned upon them, in the dread and awe of Ibrahim Pasha. Therefore these unhappy people had no resource but me, and I did the best I could for them all. Mahomet Ali, Ibrahim Pasha, [Abdullah] Pasha, all set upon me at once, in order to make me give up certain persons, who immediately would have lost their heads . . . I fought them all round, single-handed . . . Can you as a soldier blame me for what I have done?[19]

Beirut fell, Sidon fell, each city like a bead on a string for the new Egyptian overlord. Ibrahim Pasha wanted to take Hester's fortress too, but he, like Emir Bashir, decided against it. The villagers heard that the soldiers from both armies who camped in the nearby Chouf mountains were afraid that she might set *djinns* on them. But they tried to cut off her access to water by blocking off several nearby springs, unaware that she had a secret spring within her hillside. She no longer went outside the inner walls of her fortress. The siege of Acre, the last city to fall, ended on 27 May 1832 after more than five months, just as her roses were at their most beautiful.

Tales of the dramatic siege and of Hester's role as protectress stirred the visiting French poet Alphonse de Lamartine, who made a pilgrimage to see her in September 1832 when life under the new regime was outwardly more settled. He had travelled out to the Holy Land and Syria with his English wife and their daughter, to 'behold her, one of the wonders of Syria'.

She received him in semi-darkness, with candles flickering behind her, dressed dramatically in a long white robe and turban. (A number of Hester's guests reported that they would be served wine in solitude, and expected to dine alone. After a long wait, they would be ushered into her presence, sometimes in a half-darkened room, sometimes in the garden, always at dusk.) Although he visited her several times over the space of a week, Lamartine never realized that she was continuing to shelter several hundred refugees. That she chose to keep them out of obvious view, and not to tell him, suggests she was careful about giving out such information. Many of those under her protection still feared for their lives.

Lamartine's detailed account of his 'interview' with Hester, whom he called 'this modern magician, this Circe of the Desert', would be eagerly devoured by readers on both sides of the Channel when his *Voyage en Orient* was published in 1835. She would be shocked when she finally saw it, especially because he published the account of Lascaris's dragoman Fathallah Sâyigh, whom she considered 'a lying rascal', as an appendix. She said about his book that 'one half is invented, the other half incorrect; some of it made me angry, some of it made me laugh very heartily for it showed how comically travellers interpret to their advantage what they wish to believe'. After this, she refused entry to all but the most exceptional strangers, vowing that 'no traveller hereafter shall betray or forge my conversation'.

Yet Lamartine's account certainly captured the public imagination, with its depiction of her discourse by flickering candles that was almost 'too elevated for human understanding'. She herself was credited with the sort of eternal beauty 'that years cannot alter'. By now Hester had a reputation for making predictions of uncanny accuracy. She asked him whether he wanted to know what the future held for him, and with a shudder he declined. When, several months later, his young daughter Julia died of tuberculosis, he wondered afterwards whether she had seen it coming.

> The prophetess announced to me that we were on the eve of a stupen-
> dous convulsion which would destroy the recognized value of all
> property upon the earth; and declaring that those only who should
> be in the East at the time of the great change could hope for great-
> ness in the new life that was at hand, she advised me, whilst there
> was yet still time, to dispose of my property in poor, frail England,
> and to gain a station in Asia.

So wrote Alexander Kinglake, describing his meeting with Hester in 1835. His account would be published in his travel memoir, *Eothen*, a book that became an instant classic. She was then almost sixty. His mother had given him an awestruck account of the young Hester, whom she had known while she was at her grandmother's at Burton Pynsent, in her wild phase.

It was true that Hester rarely saw many English any more. She favoured good-natured captains, but other visitors bored her with their tedious vulgarity. At other times, she knew the memories certain visitors would reawaken would be too painful for her. But she made an exception for Kinglake and sent her men to summon him after receiving his letter. He was greatly impressed when 'a couple of horsemen covered with mud suddenly dashed into the *locanda* in which I was staying, bearing them-selves as ostentatiously as though they were carrying a cartel from the devil to the archangel Michael'.

Kinglake's account of his Djoun visit would propel the 'Lady Prophetess' into the realm of popular mythology, as a Scheherazade whose fascinating conversation could transport the listener to another world. He gave a description to rival Lamartine's, relating how he too had been ushered in to see her as darkness fell, and how she had risen from her seat 'very formally' and remained standing 'perfectly still and motionless' until he sat down. 'Her face was of the most astonishing whiteness; she wore a very large turban, made seemingly of pale Cashmere shawls . . . her dress was a mass of white linen, loosely folding . . . an ecclesiastical sort of affair.' Black slave-girls were beckoned, coffee served and pipes lit. They talked for 'hours and hours' of coming chaos, revolution and rebirth.

But he thought her 'a good, business-like, practical prophetess'. He noted how fiercely proud, and rather vain, she was. He had been told that in youth, she had been a true beauty, 'and that any notion of a resemblance betwixt her and the great Chatham must be fanciful', but as he looked at her now, she certainly reminded him of Copley's portrait of the dying statesman. Despite what was said of her, he saw nothing about 'this wondrous white woman' that suggested she had lost her mind. He was in awe.

Kinglake wondered whether her 'longing for the East' was something shared by certain other 'proud people goaded by sorrow'. They talked of Islam, and 'the Twelve', and Hester informed him that the 'Hidden Imam' or Mahdi would shortly reveal himself, implying that she would play a role. When he asked her about a story he had heard of a mysterious Arab tribe now being gathered together 'towards the rising of the sun by the finger of Providence', she turned her full attention on him.

Only when she was convinced that he had sufficient reverence and experience of such subjects did she allow him a glimpse of her mysterious spiritual world. She had been initiated into many wonders, she told him, but still 'trusted alone to the stars for her sublime knowledge' and spent her nights 'communing with these heavenly teachers'. He listened enthralled when the subject turned to what she referred to as 'the common and everyday phenomena produced by magic art':

She spoke as if she would make me understand that all sorcerous spells were completely at her command, but that the exercise of such powers would be derogatory to her high rank within the heavenly kingdom. She said that the spell in which the face of an absent person is thrown upon a mirror was within the the the reach of the humblest and most contemptible magicians, but that the practise of such arts was unholy as well as vulgar.

In his memoir Kinglake repeated what he had heard said about Hester, that in her pursuit of 'spiritual power' she had dared 'to boast some mystic union with the very God of very God!' He too heard the stories that she would intone spells and incantations to summon *djinns* and was herself possessed by them. He found himself wavering, wanting to believe that she truly had developed such powers. He chose to think that she was 'not an unhesitating follower of her own systems'. He concluded with absolute certainty that she was many things, but not mad.

There were moments in the middle of this dramatic conversation in which Hester exhibited flashes of her talents as 'a capital mimic'. When she descended to worldly chat, he thought 'she was the sort of woman that you sometimes see in London drawing rooms – cool, decisive in manner, unsparing of enemies, full of audacious fun'.

Kinglake had listened to her telling of his own fortune, but inwardly smiled at her 'bad shot' when she predicted that after leaving her he would go to Egypt, but return to Syria. His plans were firmly set: he was to visit the Pyramids, then take a ship from Alexandria for Greece. But as it turned out, 'the unbelieved Cassandra was right after all' for while he was in Egypt, plague broke out, and he was forced to change his route, and back to Syria he came.

In 1836 Hester welcomed the Duchess of Plaisance and her grown-up daughter Elizabeth to Djoun. The Duchess, Sophie de Marbois-Lebrun, was an American, born in Philadelphia, where her father had served as French consul-general. She had married one of Napoleon's closest cronies, Charles-François Lebrun, whom he appointed Arch-Treasurer. Sophie, clearly a woman of means, had gone on to lead a colourful life on her own after separating from Lebrun in 1811. An ardent supporter of Greek independence, she had plunged into political life in Athens, making it her business to establish funding for schools.

As far as Hester was concerned, Sophie seemed to answer the description of the woman in Metta's prophecy. With evident excitement, Hester informed Meryon, who had by now settled in Nice, that 'a woman of high rank and good fortune . . . has announced her intention of passing the rest of her life with me, so much has she been struck with my situation and conduct'. She told him that 'Madame de Feriat' (which seems to have been an invented name) was preparing to move to Syria and share her mountain, and was 'now selling her large, landed estate'. Meanwhile, she added that 'the beautiful boy has also written' so that she waited 'until destiny marks the period of our meeting'. Who this boy was remains a mystery.

But the Duchess of Plaisance's adventure in Syria ended disastrously when her daughter Elizabeth died suddenly with symptoms indicating tuberculosis, just like Lamartine's daughter. Quite how long they had stayed with Hester it is difficult to ascertain (Meryon later heard gossip that the women were seen dressed in 'white trowsers [and] white peaked hats' like Druze *akals*, whirling in the garden).[20] Grief-stricken, Sophie returned with her daughter's body to Greece.

Perhaps Hester had already acquired the same illness. By 1836 she was complaining of horrendous symptoms, reporting graphically that over a single week she had vomited 'blood enough times to kill a horse', but ascribed this to 'anxiety, agitation and fatigue along with the violent passions I sometimes put myself in'.

Sometimes she barely noticed 'blood running out of my mouth', she told Meryon, almost proudly. The symptoms lessened, even disappeared, the more she had herself bled; she assured him that 'an English medical man' had recently examined her, and 'said he never saw such a constitution in his life'.

# 21

## The Mahdi's Bride

Word had been spreading in Christian circles that Christ's second coming was imminent, that he would arrive in flames at Jerusalem's Holy Mount in time to usher in blessed annihilation. Hester had already met and clashed with the American missionary Joseph Wolff, who preached that the Lord was about to 'come in clouds of heaven and stand upon the Mount of Olives in AD 1847'. She termed Wolff, and missionaries in general, 'paid speculating wanderers', and scornfully singled out Wolff for 'abandoning' his Jewishness, 'a religion rich in itself, though defective . . . to embrace the shadow of one, I mean the Christian religion'. She intended some day 'to write a great book against Christianity', or so Meryon claimed she told him.

Hester was not impressed to hear that a fiery millennialist spinster, Harriet Livermore, had arrived in the Holy Land, determined to be there when these great events took place. Then forty-nine, this daughter of a Congressman from New Hampshire had addressed Congress. A portrait shows Livermore in plain Quaker dress, with a white encompassing bonnet and large staring eyes looking out from beneath heavy brows, her lips grimly pursed. She proclaimed the Advent gospel, and its Doomsday prediction, asserted by William Miller: 21 October 1844 was the world's date with destiny.

Livermore later told a certain Reverend Abel C. Thomas of her visit that year to see Hester at Djoun. Hester never refers to her at all, which either means she never met her, or that if she did, she found her too contemptible to mention.[1] Hester had exiled old Loustaunau for the same

371

reasons she would have reviled Livermore; for boring her to death with her version of the End, for her one-dimensional understanding of 'the Turk', whose demise the New Hampshire spinster believed was nigh, inaugurating a time when Jesus would return and rule for a thousand years.

Yet Hester's own version of the coming Apocalypse seems to have been just as literal, if profoundly different. She too believed the countdown had already begun. She expected a 'Counsel of Sovereigns' would preside over mankind, and 'execute judgement on the wicked'. In the past when Meryon asked what being she expected to appear she scoffed:

> I suppose if the Messiah were to appear according to yr notions he must come with a string of angels behind him out of a hole in the clouds. But what I mean by a Messiah is a person endowed in a peculiar manner by God who will come and set things to rights.

She was otherwise tight-lipped on the subject although Meryon described her referring freely to the Messiah and the Mahdi (which she sometimes pronounced 'Murdah' to scare her maids). Meryon himself remained woefully unclear as to which she was intended to assist in their quest. He knew she 'did not allude to a Christian Messiah'. She would talk of 'Hamzy, the sort of Messiah of the Druze, who is expected to return in another form'.

She wrote to Meryon that 'If an Alexander appeared in the world, who gained for himself a little of the Great, who was so very much above all men and whose luck was so constant in everything he undertook . . . if he were to appear, I would then come out of my Tub'.

Whoever the Messiah – or the Mahdi – might be and whenever he appeared, Hester wanted to be ready. If Babylon was about to fall, she intended to be Jerusalem's bride, riding together through the dark into the smoke and flames.

With the publication of Lamartine's book, Hester acquired a significant cult following. Fame brought adulation from unexpected quarters. A Cornish wine-merchant turned would-be Messiah, John Nichols Thom, loudly proclaimed his infatuation with Hester around this time, claiming that he had gone on a pilgrimage to see her but had been cruelly rejected. There is no indication he ever left Britain.

\*　\*　\*

'I hope I shall not claim in vain the assistance of an old friend, at the moment I most require one I can depend upon to settle the business of my debts, &c. now made public.'[2] With this unusually humble plea, Hester turned to the one person she felt she could rely on to untangle her horrendously perplexing 'pecuniary affairs'. Once more, she summoned Meryon. To all appearances, these were less dangerous times. Since Egypt's invasion, many Europeans were of the opinion that civic order had greatly increased.

Again, disregarding Hester's express request, Eliza refused to let him go alone. Both John and Eugenia were brought along, prepared to be as mulish as their mother. A governess, Mademoiselle Longchamps from Nice, was hired, and so was an Italian woman from Leghorn, who Meryon thought might do for Hester as a housekeeper, 'Signora L'. Eliza was only mollified by Meryon's promise that he intended to write an account of his own association and adventures with Hester, which was bound to create great interest and sell well.

Still, when the Meryons arrived, the icy antagonism Hester felt towards Eliza and her offspring showed no sign of thawing. While she was prepared 'to shew civility' to 'all who belong to [him]' she needed Meryon, and him alone. For their own sake she suggested he settle them in Beirut, while he attended to her business. Eventually Mar Elias, despite its bad state of repair, was settled upon as a suitable temporary refuge. Old Loustaunau was still there, 'sinking into imbecility', and after Metta's recent death, his widow and son had gone to live with him, but they all graciously made room for the arrivals. Looking askance at fissured walls, Eliza was nonetheless glad of the company, odd as it was.

This time, Meryon observed that Hester's establishment at Djoun was far less threadbare than it had been on his last visit. He counted some thirty-five employees and servants in her household.

An unimagined macabre farce made the Meryons' stay at Mar Elias intolerable, however. 'Signora L' arrived shortly after they did, exhibiting symptoms of brain fever. The Meryons watched open-mouthed as she disported herself – almost stark naked – 'to the great scandal and consternation' of all who saw her. The following morning, she got a pair of sewing scissors and cut all her hair off 'close to the roots'. Within days she was delirious, like a woman possessed by an evil *djinn*: raving, frothing at the mouth, refusing food, tearing at her dress and her bedsheets, dancing and striking obscene poses.

When Hester was alerted, she immediately sent her chief blood-letting specialist, Mustafa, to do his work. She also sent packets of her own medicine. Meryon, when he saw them, went pale, no doubt thinking of Elizabeth. He created a makeshift straitjacket and pinioned his hapless patient to her bed. 'Signora L' died two weeks after she had arrived. Hester paid for her Catholic funeral. For the rest of their visit, Eliza and the children stayed in Beirut.

The public exposure of her debts had been brewing for several years. One of Hester's most irate creditors, an Arab by the name of Homsy (to whom she owed 5,250 Spanish dollars), had finally given up pelting her with reminders. He had rounded up other aggrieved petitioners and was shrewdly advised to go directly to none other than Mehmet Ali, who sent on his complaint to the British Consul-General in Syria, Colonel Patrick Campbell, Barker's replacement.

At first Campbell, who had no wish to hound 'Her Ladyship', harrumphed that nothing could be done. But Homsy was not about to drop his case. Campbell could not fault his logic, when he renewed his claim in 1837, complaining that when British merchants brought cases against Turks, 'the most ready attention was paid to them'. Therefore, he argued, 'British subjects should be equally obliged to pay their just debts to the natives of the country'. This time, Campbell wrote to Lord Palmerston, telling him of 'the extreme embarrassment in which I am placed by the unfortunate conduct of Lady Hester Stanhope, and the prejudice which might arise in consequence of it to the interests of Her Majesty's subjects'.

Palmerston, fresh in his role as Secretary of State for Foreign Affairs, took an uncompromising attitude. Perhaps he felt an obscure wish to punish Hester, whose entanglement with his once-close friend, Michael Bruce, he had disapproved of. She had no choice: she must pay her debts. If she refused, her pension would be cut off. Until now, as a result of Coutts's entreaties, Hester had been required to sign a quarterly 'proof of life' statement, and have it duly certified, a formality that for some years her friend, Henri Guys, the French consul at Beirut, had presided over.

Although he admitted to feeling like an executioner, Campbell followed his orders. He duly informed Hester that as 'H.M.'s Agent for Egypt and Syria', it was his duty to alert her that all the consuls of Syria, including Guys, were under orders they must no longer co-sign this document. Therefore, from now on, no matter what bills she signed against her pension, he informed her, '[it] would not be paid at home'. In other words, under Queen Victoria's government, Hester's very existence would, through this peculiar legal loophole, become a point of debate.

Hester's angry creditors ranged from well-known moneylenders to grocers' shops in Sidon. Many of the debts Meryon had looked over on his previous visit had remained unpaid. As he made fresh calculations, he discovered the worst horror was the '5,000 per cent interest' she had agreed to pay an Armenian moneylender for six months on an amount of 24,000 piastres.[3] Her pension had evaporated after paying bonds to support the debts, with the little left over used 'to pay my servants and tradepeople and to put a little provision in my house'. Matters were made worse by the fact that since old Coutts's death, she was forced by the bank to draw her pension at Constantinople at nightmarish rates of exchange.

Hester would often bitterly complain that she herself was the victim, and that the money with which she might have paid her debts was owed to her by 'that fiend' Abdullah Pasha, who was now languishing by the Bosphorus.[*]

Homsy's petition was bound up with another matter Ibrahim Pasha was determined to enforce that is bound to have added weight to Mehmet Ali's own insistence that the matter be dealt with. In Ibrahim Pasha's eyes, Hester's crimes were clear. She was accused of illegally harbouring

---

[*] Hester was hardly the first foreigner to accumulate heavy debts while in Syria. According to John Barker (now retired and tending his roses and silkworms at Suwediyah) Rzewuski borrowed heavily from almost all of the European consuls, and racked up extravagant sums with local merchants. Nothing was settled by the time he left Syria, and on his return to Europe, 'the Consuls and Jew bankers' were forced to take legal action, even threatening his mother, who also refused to pay. 'They never recovered a penny of the amount they had paid.' Nor was she unique among her old friends. On his death, the Duke of York's debts had been the talk of London; and in Caen, her old friend Beau Brummell had fallen catastrophically into poverty, and would shortly be forcibly removed from running up bills at his last home at the Hotel d'Angleterre to a lunatic asylum.

a large number of citizens, as many as 'seventy-six Arab families', some for as long as three years. As far as he was concerned she was 'detaining' them, preventing these individuals from carrying out their obligations to their new overlords, paying their taxes and presenting themselves for conscription.

Ibrahim Pasha was hungry for men to stock his Egyptian armies, not only in Syria but also in that great burial ground, the Hijaz. Each city, town and district in Syria was assigned a quota, and that number of men had to be rounded up by his soldiers, by whatever means. Meryon wrote eyewitness reports of seeing fathers 'imprisoned and bastinadoed' to reveal their son's whereabouts, a practice that was then extended to neighbours and acquaintances of fleeing conscripts.

Hester's heart had been moved by the plight of mothers and sisters pleading for their sons and husbands not to be taken. (There was one young man whom she admitted to the doctor that she could not bear to have around her – 'he was too handsome!' – and to his mother she had given 500 piastres in the hope he could be bribed out of harm's way.)[4] Some runaway conscripts she hid away in her fortress's inner enclosures. She was also well aware of the young men hiding in the caves around Djoun, and sent them food and provisions.

One of her visitors around this time who dared ask whether she might consider leaving all her troubles behind and return to England described how 'her eyes flashed fire' at the thought. She had spent half her life 'constantly engaged in stirring scenes' and what would he have her do now, she mocked. 'Knit or sew like an Englishwoman?'

If Meryon needed any reminding how quickly his own life was passing by, it came in a letter from Rye. His daughter Lucy, whose birth had coincided with the beginning of his employment with Hester, had married that November. She was now a grown woman of twenty-six; her new husband William Gilbert was a forty-year-old 'gentlemanly man' who had some land in Wiltshire.

Hester had taken the decision not to go quietly. She was incensed to learn that in the House of Commons, questions had been asked about why she had been given such a generous pension in the first place. What most appalled her, however, was that she felt she had been given no warning of the cessation of her pension, nor any opportunity to explain the nature of her debts. She was adamant that her creditors were demanding far more than they were rightfully owed, and that in some cases, she had been deceived into paying 'exorbitant interest'.

She wanted a public enquiry into her debts 'and for what I have contracted them', confident that 'the good I have done in the cause of humanity' would stand up to scrutiny. On 12 February 1838 she wrote to Queen Victoria:

> Your Majesty must allow me to say, that few things are more disgraceful and inimical to Royalty than giving commands without examining all their different bearings, and to cast without reason an aspersion on the integrity of any branch of a family who has faithfully served their country and the House of Hanover.
>
> As no inquiries have been made of me what circumstances induced me to incur the debts alluded to by Y.M.'s Secretary of State for Foreign Affairs, I deem it unnecessary to enter into any details or explanations on the subject. But I shall not allow the pension given by your Royal grandfather to be stopped by force. I shall resign it for the payment of my debts, and with it the name of an English subject and the slavery at present annexed to it. And as Y.M. has given publicity to this business, by Y.M.'s orders to consular agents, I surely cannot be blamed for following your Y.M.'s example.

That same day, she also wrote an extraordinary, passionate letter to the Duke of Wellington to offer him a full account of her conduct during Ibrahim Pasha's siege of Acre, and of her debts on behalf of those who fled to her for assistance. She pointed out to him that Abdullah Pasha, who had absconded with her money, was now living in Constantinople, and that no one appeared to be of a mind to hold *him* to account.

Should Wellington wonder why she had not asked her own family for help, she explained that '[her] brother, Lord S' had 'shocked' her so profoundly in the past by his 'cold-blooded' behaviour she had resolved to have nothing whatsoever to do with him. This may have had an un-desired effect: Wellington was friendly to her brother's family; in London, the fourth earl was a respected, distinguished figure, active in parliament.

She informed him that she had asked Sir Francis Burdett to act on her behalf, and that as things stood, she believed that she was due money from an inheritance which should at a stroke wipe out most of her debts (an amount that to another correspondent she estimated at some '£7,000 to £8,000'). 'I am not a swindler and will not appear like one' she told him.[5]

She wrote letters to the Speakers at both Houses of Parliament. She told Sir Edward Sugden, the Speaker of the House of Lords, that as a young woman 'there was nothing I feared so much as plague, shipwreck and debts; it has been my fate to suffer from them all'.

Palmerston sent her a perfunctory note that merely acknowledged receipt of her letter to the Queen and ignored her points.[6] Witheringly, Hester replied, 'If your diplomatic dispatches are as obscure as the one which now lies before me, it is no wonder that England should cease to have that proud preponderance in her foreign relations, which she once could boast of.'

It was his crime, she told him, to have 'taken the liberty of using Her Majesty's name, and alienating from her and her country, a subject who, the great and small must acknowledge (however painful it must be to some) has raised the English name in the East higher than anyone has yet done, and this without having spent one farthing of public money'.

If nothing could be 'definitely settled respecting my affairs' by the time the next packet ship brought news from England, then she intended to act on the threat she now made:

I shall break up my household and build up the entrance gate to my premises, and there remaining, as if I were in a tomb, till my character has been made justice to, and a public acknowledgement put in the papers, signed and sealed by those who have aspersed me. There is no trifling with those who have Pitt blood in their veins, nor expecting that their spirit would ever yield to the impertinent interference of Consular authority.

In her room, Hester burned her travel documents, watching as the flame consumed her name. 'I have thrown their pension in their face,' she would shortly announce, 'I consider myself no longer as an English subject.'[7]

## 22
## The Last Dance

Hester had not quite succumbed to despair, but she was close. For this reason she almost refused her next gentleman caller, Prince Hermann von Pückler-Muskau. A few years younger than herself, Pückler-Muskau at first gave every appearance of being the sort of puffed-up European fop she never wished to see. But he managed to coax and flatter her:

Like you my lady, I look for our future salvation in the East, where nations still nearer to God and to nature can alone, one day purify the rotten civilization of decrepit Europe . . . where we are menaced by a new kind of barbarism. Like you, madam, I believe that astrology is not an empty science, but a lost one. Like you, I am an aristocrat by birth and in principle . . . I love to sleep by day and be stirring by night.

There the comparisons must stop, he told her, for he had heard no one could resemble her. He might be old, he said, but his heart still felt passionately about these things, and he wanted to talk with her alone.

A coquettish dance ensued, with Hester resisting being pinned down, even to one meeting. 'My object was, if possible, not only to be endured, but wished for,' he wrote; and when her response was at first not quite as enthusiastic as he hoped, he sent a cool reply, 'implying I had more important missions to make than she was aware of'. He observed that 'It was rather comical to carry out Goethe's axiom, "Provoke and beguile", so successively with a sexagenarian dame'.

Meryon played go-between. Hester was willing to relent. She decided she liked the sound of Pückler-Muskau, a former cavalry officer who had travelled widely in Europe, the Magreb and Northern Africa. She was lonely and longed for someone cultivated who could make her laugh. She agreed he could stay for a week on the condition that he must agree to meet her every night at midnight. 'Hah, this is as it should be in the land of one thousand and one nights,' Pückler-Muskau told Meryon, 'it [will] suit my nocturnal habits . . . I await my first midnight rendezvous with real impatience.'

This was Hester's last performance as Scheherazade. On Easter Sunday, 15 April 1838, Prince Pückler-Muskau was admitted to her fortress. He came to see her for eight successive nights, and they talked from midnight until dawn. 'I must truly say I never felt a moment's fatigue or ennui,' he later marvelled, 'and after each of them, I felt more and more attracted to this most remarkable woman, who combined with an iron character, such child-like belief in the marvellous, with such profound knowledge of men and the world, such touching traits of naivete as are generally met with only in a young girl.' He thought that 'no one could be more natural or more real'.

Pückler-Muskau was a fellow horticultural enthusiast. His *Notes on Landscape Gardening* would become an instant classic in Germany. One night, 'when the moon shone nearly as brightly as the sun', Hester led him into her private garden; 'a whole world of roses, of all sizes and colours and all in full bloom, shone resplendent in the magic illumination of the full moon,' he wrote, and described burying his face in one 'as in a purple cushion'. From where they stood together, ahead of them was 'the most beautiful view over the billowy mountains and wide stretch of sea beyond'.

Of the Bedouin sheikhs she told him about, in her retelling of her desert exploits, he noticed she seemed to give particular importance to the man who became Muhanna al Fadil's son-in-law, Dayr, and she showed him a letter he had written her, which for years she had kept in a gold-embroidered cover. It was as though she was hinting at a secret, although she had no intention of revealing it.

Dayr, the Lion of the Desert, to Hester, the Star of the Morning, sends greeting, with love and service. Those who . . . obey the sabre of Dayr, hold the Great Desert in the hollow of their hand, even as the ring encircles the finger. Warriors without number, horses, camels, powder and shot, what is required . . . all is ready. You need only to send your orders.

Your true friend, Dayr

'Was he your lover?' Pückler-Muskau asked her. Hester's answer was ambiguous. She smiled, and shook her head. 'The Arabs have never looked upon me in the light of either a man or of a woman, but as *un être à part*,' was her reply.

Her days of 'ambitions' and 'grand projects' were over, she told him. As to her views on the subjects Pückler-Muskau was so keen to discuss – 'the opinions and customs of the Arabs, the different religious sects of the Levant, the mysterious creed of the Druze, the folk-lore, the mythology and the history of these various races' – Hester shook her head irritably.

She had devoted years to studying these subjects, she said, and each could fill a book; she had no wish for any 'half-comprehended utterances' of hers to end up adding to another 'false and superficial' traveller's tale. She told him that if he wished, he could use her name 'at the Dervishes monastery in Tripoli' but as for 'the Ansaries, the Ismaelites . . . and all the sects on the mountains between Tripoli and Latakia' he should know that he would 'get nothing out of them'. It was better they not speak of such matters. She admitted that despite her 'long practise and experience' much of what she quested after required 'greater knowledge and higher qualities than have fallen to my lot'.

The greater mysteries 'remain unattainable to me', she told him, 'although [being] initiated, I can discern many hidden things'. Only once in her life had she ever considered herself to be in the presence of a divine one, a great prophet or holy man, a keeper of 'this great secret', she said.[1] She did not elaborate.

She preferred to tell him fables and stories, amazing him with the fluidity of her narration, and her retentive memory; she cast his horoscope, giving him his compatible animals, plants and minerals – and advised him which medicines would suit him. Just as they were parting, she told him what seemed to him a very odd story about an enormous two-headed serpent, and where exactly he might expect to find it lying in wait, with geographical descriptions of certain rivers and caves. Only later did he realize she was giving him an explicit warning about Ibrahim Pasha's army, which had now splintered into two large factions, one camped near Damascus, the other near Antioch.

The Druze insurrection that began that year was gathering strength, and an unlikely alliance would soon be struck with the Bedouin, united by common hatred of their enemies. Ibrahim Pasha's armies began to be severely dented. Hester heard reports that more than ten thousand of his men were killed. The Druze began to attack Maronite Christians, against whom they had nurtured so much resentment under the occupation. Many suffered the trademark punishment, their right hand cut off at the wrist.

Hester was kept closely informed by her spies. Meryon noticed a Druze woman who came and went from Djoun and he guessed Hester had trained a female spy. Ever since the Egyptians had arrived 'like a plague of locusts', as she put it, Meryon observed that she had 'encouraged in every way the hostile disposition of the Druze'.[2]

Meryon knew that in Beirut, unable to speak Arabic, his family were oblivious to the warning signs, but he was now fearful for their safety. The insurgency's strength had outstripped all predictions: a full-scale civil war looked likely. Much to the astonishment of all, Ibrahim Pasha had been forced back, and by the end of summer his continued grip on the country was by no means looking certain. War of much greater magnitude was coming, Hester knew it.

It was time for her to make final amends where she could. That summer, she ordered Meryon to leave, and knowing he would go through Malta, she wrote to Elizabeth's sister, Mrs David. It is clear that she wanted her to have the five hundred pounds she had always intended to leave Elizabeth. She said, wryly, that she was but 'a child in the affairs of commerce' having obviously inherited 'the family indifference to money', but the amount she had set aside for Elizabeth in England by now should have accumulated a good deal of interest; Meryon would tell her the details. But she tried to be reassuring; she was quite well, she said. 'I have had no return of spitting blood, or rather, vomiting blood.'

Only those she felt she had no need to impress, who themselves came by stealth, were now admitted, among them one who was her house guest, the travelling scholar Dr Loewe, apparently sent out to Syria by the Duke of Sussex. But Hester seemed to have disengaged from her world of intrigue.

She spent much of her time writing to her friend Henri Guys, who had managed to raise enough cash to keep her in food and pay her servants for the next few months. In this last stage of her life Guys was her closest friend. She regarded him as a fellow philosopher and enthu- siast – he was engaged in compiling a ground-breaking book on the Druze – but also someone she could share her thoughts with, even her plants. He too was an avid gardener and their packets to each other usually contained seeds or cuttings. He was being transferred to Aleppo, and she told him she was 'wretched at [his] departure'. He was, she told him, her *true* friend, 'dearer to me than my own'.

To him she confided her bitter thoughts about her brother. There were those who were astonished at his cruel treatment of her, and had offered to do what they could for her at a distance. '*You know every-thing*,' she told him. She had heard that Philip Stanhope and his wife had managed to secure some kind of possession over the two proper- ties that had been willed to her. 'They wait for my death, I fancy, to dispose of one, and then to produce the other.'[3] All the same, she believed her legacy would come to her. 'I shall be rich enough, but I wish it were now.'

She found herself thinking more and more about her long-lost cousin Camelford. All the money in the world had not saved him from his own pride, but he certainly went to his end willingly, and so would she. She wrote to Sir Francis Burdett, telling him that she did not begrudge him for failing to get to the bottom of her inheritance tangles, comparing herself to 'a lion in the desert, caught in the huntsman's net' who was in need of 'a little mouse . . . to gnaw the master knot, and burst the noose' so that the lion might 'come out stronger than ever'.

I am now building up every avenue to my premises and there shall wait
with patience, immured within the walls, til it pleases God to send me
a little mouse, and whoever presumes to force my retirement, by scaling
the walls or anything of the like, will be received by me as Lord Camelford
would have received them.[4]

To Meryon it was clear she was bent on self-immolation. Her vision
had been thwarted, now all that was left was the dimming of the light. 'We
were now without money in the house, the last two thousand piastres
having been spent,' he noted. Seven thousand piastres were due for payment
of wages, and everyone in 'the bazaars, the baths and the barbers' of Sidon
and Beirut knew that 'her income had been stopped by the Queen.'

Yet, Meryon saw 'no disposition was manifested by her to curtail a
single expense. There were still thirty-five, or thirty-four servants.' He
could see she was shadowed by melancholy. He was disturbed by the way
Djoun's skeletal, unloved cats had begun to migrate up the hill and disport
themselves in her courtyard, as though they sensed an opportunity. 'I
shall not die in my bed,' she told the doctor, 'or I had rather not; my
brothers did not and I have always had the feeling my end would be in
blood – that does not frighten me in the least.'

She urged him to go. She had nothing to offer him. Besides, she
wanted him to arrange for the publication of her letters – to Queen
Victoria, Wellington and Palmerston – in *The Times*, so that public
opinion might sway in her favour, and shame the government into
retracting their decision.

On 6 August 1838 Meryon went to see her for the last time, knowing
she had asked Ayoub al Moussawba, the stone mason who had built her
fortress, to come and wall up her gateway. Stones and material were piled
up around the entrance; one small opening, just large enough for a mule
to pass through laden with water, would be the only link to the outside
world.

Meryon took her hand and kissed it. He gave her two thousand piastres, which she promised to repay, and he undertook to send a message
for Lunardi to return to her. As he rode down the hill, he caught sight
of Zezefoon, Hester's black slave girl, watching him leave.

\*   \*   \*

Hester received encouraging news from her friend Lord Hardwicke, who felt confident that the government would be unable to stop her pension if she returned.* He gave her his detailed calculations as to how her financial woes could be resolved, estimating her debts were some '£8,000 or £10,000' which might be paid 'were you in England, as the value of your property', given that her pension and annuity could be sold for much as £20,000, he estimated.† But to achieve this, she would have to return to England, to be 'seen and known'. In the present state of affairs, 'with yourself in Syria, it will fetch nothing,' he warned.[5]

> In my opinion, nothing can be done unless you come home. Your pension will, I understand, be paid up . . . It would be folly to sell your annuity and pension for less than it is worth . . . I assure you that I see no way out of your difficulties . . . without your presence in England.**

Meryon had been true to his word. Her letters to all the leading protagonists in the dispute were published in *The Times*. An appeal had been mounted on her behalf, headed by a one-time admirer, General Sir William Napier. She was 'no crack-brained lady', he indignantly assured the readers of *The Times*. 'To more than woman's quickness of perception, intuitive judgement and fortitude, she adds more than man's sagacity, intrepidity, and daring. Her influence is vast with the Arab tribes and with all those who have suffered from Ibrahim Pasha's army, or who sigh over the tottering condition of the Turkish empire.' She 'more than any other person' was capable of securing for England 'the friendship of nations whose goodwill must be vitally essential to our interests' when 'we have to contend with Russia for the independence of the Porte'.[6]

---

* A Ministerial print was republished in *The Times* on 6 December 1838 offering a somewhat lame iteration that 'there never was any intention on the part of the Government to deprive her Ladyship of her pension'.

† Hester had, it would appear, managed to reduce her earlier debts by £6,000. There is no evidence to explain where this money came from.

** After her death, lawyers at Freshfields in London concluded that in fact, if Hester's status as a resident of Syria was taken into due consideration, all matters concerning probate would have to be conducted according to 'Mohammedan law', which according to at least one lawyer, 'gave no preference to judgements on bad debts or bonds'.

This tribute reached Hester in Djoun, and deeply touched her. She wrote Napier a graceful letter of thanks, enquiring after all his 'dear, kind, good' family. When it came to herself, she had reached a philosophical truce. 'There is my crime, to be independent,' she said. She considered herself a mere nothing, she said, 'before men I have met with in the East' – but still 'a giant before Lord Palmerston and his squad'.[7]

She felt more optimistic, despite the fearful state of the country. Still, she was 'well walled-in'. She wrote to Guys in Aleppo, telling him that she saw no one any more. 'I have shut myself up in prison until my affairs are arranged, and if they come to disturb my tomb, it may be that they will not retrace their footsteps.'[8] That month, in February 1839, a hyena found its way into her garden and her gardener bludgeoned it to death; she thought it had been frightened so much by the wild dogs on the outside 'that it scaled the wall'.

On 5 June 1839 she wrote a short, elegant note to Guys thanking him for news he had forwarded her. She now had a reliable French agent in Beirut, who would be able to carry out her business for her away from the eyes of the consuls, she told him. The following day she replied to Lord Hardwicke, thanking him for all his 'kind-hearted' trouble on her account. 'What you say about coming to England sounds very reasonable, but I cannot, will never, go there, but in *chains* . . . When I have quite made up my mind about what I shall do, I shall let you know.' She had no wish to see what was left of her family; she had been enraged to hear that her 'impudent relations' had been trying to get Coutts to release everything held in her name. She could not bring herself to mention her brother by name. 'I believe in my duty, the duty of every one of *every* religion; I have no reproaches to make of myself, but that I went rather too far . . . but such is my nature.' That same day she gave her last instructions.

Her dreams were becoming more intense, filled with people she had not seen since what she now called '*mes beaux jours*'. It was odd, in the early hours of a hot June morning, to dream of cold and snow, of being young again.

Then there she was in her garden in Djoun; her body suddenly weightless, her arms outstretched, and spinning, as though the divine trance had taken hold of her at last. Then she was gone, and all that remained was what she had seen from her window, the rays of first light, and the floating amnesia of the sea.

# Epilogue

Almaz would say that it was he who dressed her 'in her blue robe with gold buttons' as her female servants were too frightened to touch her. Against her wishes, the missionary had given her the detested Christian burial, but he said the prayers in Arabic as she had requested. She wanted nothing on her grave; no plaque, no inscription.

She had scribbled a last codicil to her will, granting Almaz, her faithful gardener and, it would appear, her last secret companion, the contents of her house, and the right to live there with her remaining animals, until his own death. In the tangle of her debts, this last bequest of hers was ignored.

After protracted negotiations, a petition was filed with the London firm Freshfields by a consortium of some seventeen disgruntled creditors. Philip, Earl Stanhope, was kept closely informed. Her sister Griselda was summoned from Bagshot, Surrey, to swear an affidavit. The case dragged on until 1844. An initial disbursement was made after the sale of her effects which came to £2,000, and the majority of her debts were paid over time out of her estate.[1]

Many obituary notices appeared. The *Morning Post* in London paid tribute to her as 'the modern Zenobia' and noted that in Syria and Arabia she had been 'looked upon as the future deliverer of Asia, and especially the Holy Land'. Her fame 'was diffused from Mount Lebanon, with its settled dwellers, to the farthest tribes in the sands of Arabia'.

\*   \*   \*

'Were you going to write a book? You had better not, you will make sad mistakes . . . you had better not be a Man of two faces.' Hester's words pursued Meryon beyond the grave.

She left written instructions that all of her papers – except some selected correspondence – be burnt, so that not a scrap of her writing should remain after her death. She worried about any of her most confidential – and personally revealing – letters falling into anyone else's hands. 'I expect that you will give me your word of honour that you have burnt every writing of mine that you have in your possession,' she wrote to Meryon in 1829. But if he had burned her letters it scarcely mattered, because he had made copies of them. On his return to England, and after her death, in the welter of eulogies trumpeted in *The Times*, Meryon battled with a sense of guilt for leaving her and betraying her command.

He had returned with his family to Nice, with one object in mind, to extricate himself from his own dire financial difficulties. In a rented apartment near the Promenade des Anglais, Meryon cannibalized his journals and Hester's letters, eagerly plundering raw material, swiftly working up a great, sprawling opus. It would ultimately become six volumes detailing the adventures of his erstwhile employer. He would claim to Lord Stanhope, who tried to stop its publication, that he had written his books 'in compliance with Lady Hester's wishes . . . It was her legacy to me'. This was a startling claim, which he insisted was true.

It is not clear what Hester herself would have thought of this rear-guard action. Meryon deliberately waited until after her death even to venture such a remark, let alone produce his version of her life. Would she have given her consent to a man whom she did not consider to be her equal socially or intellectually? Three months before she died, she told Meryon: 'Some day I shall write a manifesto, which will be superb, and open people's eyes in all directions.' But Hester, who wrote constantly, kept a sporadic journal and compiled papers obsessively, ordered almost everything she had written to be burned before her death.

Meryon's motivations were three-fold: he hoped to write a best-seller that would in some way recompense him for enduring so many years of service to someone who provoked love, fear and exasperation in equal measures. His books would also bear witness to his own adventures. But he also regarded his narrative as an act of loyalty, to rescue her reputation and 'free' her 'as the purest diamond from stain' from the 'ridiculous reports that were spread about her . . . either malicious or misinformed, and not to be deterred from her noble, though somewhat Quixotic enterprises, by ridicule or abuse'.[2] He wrote, he claimed, as 'a gentleman'. Yet successive biographers perpetuated the myth of the 'mad' Hester, revelling in the many Meryon-related anecdotes; the rages, the tantrums, the bells rung at all hours, the crockery hurled at walls. The fact that Meryon scribbled down a version of what he remembered her saying, sometimes hours and sometimes years after the event, offered ample opportunity for embellishment.

We should know more about Hester from Meryon's accounts of her, yet oddly, reading them, his renditions of her seem strangely hollow: her inner life, her deepest thoughts are missing. She was in every way Meryon's muse, and yet he found himself utterly unable to convey the essence of her. That is found instead in her own voice, her own letters.

The Meryons were able to return to London, and settled in Normanton Cottage at North End, Fulham, and into what the doctor's relatives in Rye thought was 'a very Bohemian life'. Half-heartedly, the celebrated author resumed his medical practice. Lucy died, aged just thirty-four, of childbirth complications. Her husband emigrated to Australia with their three daughters.

Charles Meryon, the doctor's artist son, travelled further as a seaman than ever his father had dreamed, as far as the obscure little French settlement of Akaroa on the Banks Peninsula (named after Sir Joseph Banks) in New Zealand. From the moment he joined the French navy as a young teenager, he never saw his father again. His etchings of Maori tribesmen and of Pacific landscapes and fauna would cause excitement, but it was the mastery and 'inner sorrow' of his Parisian scenes that would make the name of Meryon famous. Victor Hugo, Baudelaire and Van Gogh all marvelled at his talent, but it was matched by intense melancholy and poverty. He was committed to an asylum at the age of thirty-six, dying there in 1868.

Meryon outlived Eliza by almost twelve years, and died at Normanton Cottage on 11 September 1877 aged ninety-four. In 1898 his heirs sold his journals and his copies of Hester's letters to Lord Stanhope's daughter, the Duchess of Cleveland, for fifty pounds. A considerable number of those letters, as well as those about her, were quietly disposed of, and offending sections of Meryon's journals were heavily censored or excised. The gaping holes remain tantalizingly suggestive.

Michael Bruce went on to become an MP for Ilchester in 1830. In 1831 his friend Lord Palmerston offered him a lucrative post as Commissioner for Great Britain to arbitrate disputes arising in Brazil and Argentina. But the friendship foundered as soon as Palmerston's behaviour over Hester's pension was made public. 'I once knew [Palmerston] I would say intimately, but circumstances occurred which produced a coolness between us,' he would say.

His life was scarred by the tragedy of the deaths of both his daughters in early childhood, but his son Michael would grow up to become a general. Soon after his wife's death Bruce decided to fulful his life's dream of going to China, and made preparations. 'I have been vegetating for many years in a state of moral and intellectual stagnation; I want to embark on some undertaking which will produce excitement,' he wrote to a young woman. He thought the 'religious and political revolution' in China was 'about to affect the present and future destinies of the human race'. He never got there, but died in 1861, his head on his pillow, after an afternoon playing with his little grandchildren in Bognor Regis.*

After his four-month stint in Newgate gaol, Sligo married his own Hester – Hester Catherine de Burgh – early in the spring of 1816. In 1834 he was made the first Governor of Jamaica. By the time he left two years later, his efforts to assist the cause of emancipation had won him wide popularity amongst the colony's former slaves and he was hailed by the Jamaicans as 'The Emancipator'. Jamaica's first Free Village was named

---

* In 1944, Bruce's great-grandson, Ian Bruce, would discover among his papers a great many letters that hint at a life very much involved in the footnotes of history. Among his correspondents (after Napoleon's death) were General Lallemand and General Foy. After his death, among Bruce's papers were found several chapters of Napoleon's own manuscript of his Egyptian campaign, as well as private documents to General Bertrand concerning Napoleon's imprisonment on St Helena, and the former Emperor's original letter of abdication signed at Fontainebleau. A great many private papers and letters also point to Bruce's active involvement with the cause of Greek independence between 1824 and 1826.

Sligoville in his honour. He died in 1845, having fathered fourteen children, one of whom died in infancy.

In the same year as Hester's death, Emir Bashir was forced to flee Syria when the Ottomans reasserted control. Another member of the Shihab family, becoming Emir Bashir III, would preside over Mount Lebanon. In 1841 a horrendous massacre of Maronite Christians by Druze took place at Deir-el-Kamar. The fleeing survivors were slaughtered by the Ottoman army and the conflagration triggered a full-scale civil war. In 1860 Napoleon III sent seven thousand troops into the territory, supporting the Maronites against the British-backed Druze, a conflict resolved only when the Congress of Europe intervened. A year later, the 'Mountain' of Lebanon was declared an autonomous province within the Ottoman Empire, sowing the seeds for the Greater Lebanon under the French Mandate, and ultimately the independent Lebanese Republic.

Twenty years after Hester's death, Lord Palmerston, then Prime Minister, would declare of the proposed Suez Canal, which French investors had begun work on in 1859, that it was a ridiculous project, merely a 'device for French interference in the East'. He could hardly have been more wrong. His failure of imagination would have come as no surprise to Hester.

In August 1988, as the Lebanese civil war intensified, the Foreign and Commonwealth Office (FCO) in Whitehall received a telex from Beirut concerning 'the earthly remains of Lady Hester Stanhope. The Red Cross had been contacted, then the British Embassy. A skull and human bones had been found in the hills around Sidon'. Given that the region had been the scene of intense fighting for almost a decade, such a discovery hardly seemed unusual, but in this case, the remains were almost a hundred and fifty years old. It was said they belonged to a famous Englishwoman still well remembered in these parts. With them was her 'ram's head walking stick'.

There was some confusion about how they had been found: Druze militiamen claimed that when they searched the hills around Djoun, they came across a gravesite, already opened and desecrated. They blamed

Shi'ite Amal militia, probably looking for treasure. The Red Cross were wary of any financial transactions, while the FCO advised that it might not be desirable to 'get into the position of bargaining for Lady Hester's bones'. There was also the awkward business of trying to identify the remains: some of the bones were clearly male, assumed to be those belonging to Loustaunau. But rumours spread, later repeated by villagers in Joun, that there were also bones that appeared to belong to an unknown young female. Neither skull was found.

The Stanhope family had been informed. Some debate ensued about whether whatever was left of Hester should be returned to the chapel at her childhood home, Chevening. The fact that there appeared to be 'other bones buried in the same grave' was an unexpected complication. The decision was made that she should stay in Joun. It was, after all, where she had chosen to be.

In the end, no fee changed hands. Her remains were loaded onto the back of a truck, to be shuttled through checkpoints of rival militia all the way up the country. Even as heavy fighting continued in the Chouf mountains, the decision was made to re-inter Hester in the garden of the British Embassy's summer residence at Abey, overlooking Beirut.

On 23 June 2004, Hester's ashes were finally scattered across her garden in Joun. The residence at Abey had been sold; once again, a decision had to be reached about what to do with her remains. This time all parties determined it must be permanent. An Anglican service was held for her, presided over by Lord William Stanhope, one of her distant descendants, the British Ambassador James Watt, the Mayor of Joun, Roger Jawish, and Father Freijat from Deir-el-Moukhalles. The Stanhope crest and the British and Lebanese national flags were raised in her honour.

That night in Beirut a dinner was held at which she was the posthumous guest of honour. The direct descendant of Hester's friend Sheikh Jumblatt, Walid Jumblatt, and his wife Nora, came; glasses were raised, and promises pledged – not for the first time – that it should become an annual event.

No doubt Hester herself would never have guessed how long her shadow would be. Perhaps it was inevitable that one way or another, trickle-down rumours of the macabre and the fantastic would prove unshakeable. In Joun, talk still turns to 'the Sytt'. Salam Chami, now in his late sixties, recalled his elders talking about her as though she were still alive. His grandfather told him there was a saying about her when she first came to Djoun: 'You can have dinner with El Sytt, and even sleep with her, but do not stay in her house. When a man goes to be with her, it will not be long before he will not wake up.' In her own country, she would be cast so persistently as a remote and reckless risk-taker who came to a sticky end, dismissed so often as 'poor, mad Lady Hester' when compared with women adventurers who followed, and caricatured so glibly as a prototype English eccentric. Damned for being an icon of liberation, and for daring to be a woman apart, her life blazed, spluttered and smouldered itself out. Yet perhaps her friend Sir Francis Burdett was right when he predicted that she would rise again 'Phoenix-like' once the smoke and ash cleared. Maybe now that the hidden material surrounding her life has resurfaced, her aspirations and bravery can be recognized, alongside the heavy price she paid to lead her life in her own way. If much of her striving was, in the end, futile, her vision was broad, her effort unstinting, and her resolve extraordinary

No doubt Hester would relish the thought that her impetuous, laughing presence still hovers over the corridors and dining rooms of Walmer and 10 Downing Street, as well as over her former home of Djoun, amongst the men and women whose ancestors knew her, feared her, and loved her.

# *Bibliography*

### Archives

Centre for Kentish Studies, Maidstone, Special Collection, Stanhope Family Papers

Bodleian Library, Oxford, Department of Special Collections and Western Manuscripts, Bruce Family Papers

British Library, Manuscript Collection and Oriental and India Office Collections

Wellcome Library for the History and Understanding of Medicine

Public Record Office

Joseph Banks Research Project, Natural History Museum

British Museum

Victoria and Albert Museum, National Art Library, Forster Collection

Colindale Library

Dorset County Record Office

Foreign and Commonwealth Office

Cumbria Record Office, Carlisle Headquarters

Chevening Library

Belmore Papers, Private Collection, Ireland

Meryon Papers, Private Collection, Meryon Family

Beinecke Rare Book and Manuscript Library, Yale University, Marquis of Sligo Letters

Sterling Memorial Library, Yale University, Manuscripts and Archives, Sir Joseph Banks Papers

Archives Nationales de Paris
American University of Beirut Library

*Books and Journals*

Ali Bey el Abbassi [Domingo Badia y Leblich], *Travels of Ali Bey in Morocco, Triploi, Cyprus, Egypt, Arabia, Syria and Turkey between the years 1803 and 1807*, 2 vols, Longman, London, 1816

Abu-Izzeddin, Nejla M., *The Druzes, A New Study of Their History, Faith and Society*, E. J. Brill, Netherlands, 1993

Allen, Charles, *God's Terrorists: The Wahhabi Cult and the Hidden Roots of Modern Jihad*, Little, Brown, London, 2006

Al-Sayyid Marsot, Afaf Lufti, *Women and Men in Late Eighteenth Century Egypt*, University of Texas Press, Texas, 1995

Asmar, Maria Theresa, *Memoirs of a Babylonian Princess*, Henry Colburn, London, 1844

Auriant, *La Vie du Chevalier Théodore Lascaris*, Gallimard, Paris, 1940

Barker, John, *Syria and Egypt under the last five sultans of Turkey*, ed. Edward B. Barker, 2 vols, Samuel Tinsley, London, 1876

Bentham, Jeremy, *Memoirs*, ed. John Bowring, William Tait, Edinburgh, 1842

Berjaud, Leo, *Boutin: agent secret de Napoléon 1er et précurseur de l'Algérie Française*, Frédéric Chambriand, Paris, 1950

Bessborough, Earl of, and Aspinall, A., eds., *Lady Bessborough and Her Family Circle*, John Murray, London, 1842

Betts, Robert Brenton, *The Druze*, Yale University Press, New Haven, Conn., 1988

Black, Jeremy, *Pitt the Elder: The Great Commoner*, Sutton Publishing, London, 1992

Boigne, Comtesse de, *Memoirs*, Heinemann, London, 1907

Bounni, Dr Adnan, *Palmyra*, Damascus, 2000

Browning, Iain, *Palmyra*, Chatto & Windus, London, 1979

Brownrigg, Lady Beatrice, *The Life and Letters of Sir John Moore*, Blackwell, Oxford, 1923

Bruce, Ian, *Lavallette Bruce, His Adventures and Intrigues before and after Waterloo*, Hamish Hamilton, London, 1953

Bruce, Ian, *The Nun of Lebanon: The Love Affair of Lady Hester Stanhope and Michael Bruce*, Collins, London, 1951

Buckingham, J. Silk, *Travels among the Arab Tribes inhabiting the Countries East of Syria and Palestine*, London, 1825

Burckhardt, J. L., *Notes on the Bedouins and Wahhabys*, 2 vols, London, 1830

Chapman, Caroline, in collaboration with Jane Dormer, *Elizabeth and Georgiana: The Two Loves of the Duke of Devonshire*, John Murray, London, 2002

Chelhod, Joseph, 'Un nouvel éclairage sur la mission et la morte d'Ali Bey', *Studia Islamica*, no. 80, 1994

Cleveland, Duchess of, *The Life and Letters of Lady Hester Stanhope*, John Murray, London, 1914

Colley, Linda, *Britons: Forging the Nation 1707–1837*, Pimlico, London, 2003

Collins, Roger, *Charles Meryon: A Life*, Garton and Co., Wiltshire, 1999

Coote, Stephen, *Napoleon and the Hundred Days*, Simon and Schuster, London, 2004

Cronin, Vincent, *Napoleon*, HarperCollins, London, 1994

Day, Roger, *The Life of Sir John Moore*, Leo Cooper, Barnsley, 2001

Dedopulos, Tim, *The Brotherhood: Inside the Secret World of the Freemasons*, Carlton Press, London, 2006

Denon, Dominique Vivant, *Voyage dans la Basse et la Haute Egypte pendant les campagnes du Général Bonaparte en 1798 et 1799*, 2 vols, London, 1807

Douglass, Paul, *Lady Caroline Lamb*, Palgrave Macmillan, New York, 2004

Driault, Edouard, *La Formation de l'Empire de Mohammed Aly, de l'Arabie au Soudan 1814–1823 : Correspondance des Consuls de France en Egypt*, Institut Français d'Archéologie du Caire pour la Société Royale de Géographie d'Egypte, Cairo, 1925

Drury, Nevill, *The Watkins Dictionary of Magic*, Watkins, London, 2005

*The Love Letters of William Pitt*, First Lord Chatham, edited by Ethel Ashton Edwards, Chapman and Hall, London, 1926

Esdaile, Charles, *The Peninsular War*, Allen Lane, London, 2002

Firmin Didot, Ambroise, *Notes d'un Voyage fait dans le Levant en 1816 et 1817*, Imprimerie de Firmin Didot, Paris, 1826.

Foreman, Amanda, *Georgiana, Duchess of Devonshire*, HarperCollins, London, 1999

Fraser, Antonia, *The Warrior Queens: Boadicea's Chariot*, Phoenix Press, London, 1988

Fraser, Flora, *The Unruly Queen: The Life of Queen Caroline*, John Murray, London, 1996

Fullerton, Susannah, *Jane Austen and Crime*, Jane Austen Society of Australia, 2004

Gleeson, Janet, *An Aristocratic Affair: The Life of Georgiana's Sister, Harriet Spencer, Countess of Bessborough*, Bantam Press, London, 2006

Gontant, Duchess de, *Memoirs*, translated by J. W. Davis, London, 1894

Hague, William, *William Pitt the Younger*, HarperCollins, London, 2004

Hamel, Frank, *Lady Hester Lucy Stanhope*, Cassell, London, 1913

Hancock, Graham, and Bauval, Robert, *Talisman: Sacred Cities, Secret Faith*, Penguin, London, 2004

Headlam, Cuthbert, ed., *The Letters of Lady Harriot Eliot 1766–1786*, T & A Constable, Edinburgh, 1914

Héneiné, Alice, *Voyageurs d'Orient*, Editions Dar Lahad Khater, Beirut, 1983

Herold, J. Christopher, *Bonaparte in Egypt*, Hamish Hamilton, London, 1963

Hibbert, Christopher, *The French Revolution*, Allen Lane, London, 1980

——*Napoleon: His Wives and Women*, HarperCollins, London, 2003

——*Nelson: A Personal History*, Viking, London, 1994

——*Wellington: A Personal History*, HarperCollins, London, 1997

Hilton, Boyd, *A Mad, Bad and Dangerous People? England 1783–1846*, Clarendon Press, Oxford, 2006

Hitti, Philip K., *History of the Arabs*, Palgrave Macmillan, London, 2002

Holmes, Richard, *Wellington, the Iron Duke*, HarperCollins, London, 2003

Hopkirk, Peter, *The Great Game: On Secret Service in High Asia*, John Murray, London, 2006

Horne, Alistair, *The Age of Napoleon*, Random House, New York, 2004

Hourani, Albert, *A History of the Arab Peoples*, Faber, London, 2005

Irwin, Robert, *For Lust of Knowing: The Orientalists and their Enemies*, Allen Lane, London, 2006

Jesse, Captain, *The Life of Beau Brummell*, London, 1932

Keegan, John, *Intelligence in War: Knowledge of the Enemy from Napoleon to Al-Qaeda*, Pimlico, London, 2004

Kelly, Ian, *Beau Brummell*, Hodder & Stoughton, London, 2005

Kinglake, Alexander, *Eothen, or Traces of Travel*, London, 1844

Kubler, George, A., *The Era of Charles Mahon, Third Earl of Stanhope, Stereotyper, 1750–1825*, New York, 1938

Lamartine, Alphonse Marie, *Souvenirs, Impressions et Pensées Pendant un Voyage en Orient*, Paris, 1833

Lancaster, John, *The Rwala Bedouin Today*, Cambridge University Press, Cambridge, 1981

Lawrence, T. E., *Crusader Castles*, London, 1936

Lever, Sir Tresham, *The House of Pitt*, London, 1947

Leveson Gower, Lord Granville, *Private Correpondence 1781 to 1821*, ed. Castalia, Countess Granville, 2 vols, John Murray, London, 1916

Lewis, Bernard, *The Assassins: A Radical Sect in Islam*, Weidenfeld & Nicolson, 2001

Lewis, Norman, British *Journal of Middle Eastern Studies*, Vol. 22, 1995

Lewis, Norman, *Nomads and Settlers in Syria and Jordan 1800–1980*, Cambridge University Press, Cambridge, 1987

MacCarthy, Fiona, *Byron: Life and Legend*, John Murray, London, 2002

McCarthy, Justin, *The Ottoman Turks*, Longman, London, 1997

McIntyre, Ian, *Joshua Reynolds: The Life and Times of the First President of the Royal Academy*, Penguin, London, 2004

Madden, R. R., *Travels in Turkey, Egypt, Nubia and Palestine*, 1829

Mansel, Philip, *Constantinople: City of the World's Desire*, Penguin, London, 1995

Mansfield, Peter, *A History of the Middle East*, Penguin, London, 2003

Marcellus, Comte de, *Souvenirs de l'Orient*, Paris, 1839

Masson, Jeffrey Moussaieff, *Lost Prince: The Unsolved Mystery of Kaspar Hauser*, The Free Press, New York, 1996

Melbourne, Lady, *Byron's Corbeau Blanc: The Life and Letters of Lady Melbourne*, Rice University Press, 1997

Meryon, Charles Lewis, *Memoirs of Lady Hester Stanhope As Related by*

*Herself in Conversations With Her Physician; Comprising Her Opinions and Anecdotes of Some Of The Most Remarkable Persons Of Her Time*, 3 vols, Henry Colburn, London, 1845

Meryon, Charles Lewis, *Travels of Lady Hester Stanhope, Forming the Completion of Her Memoirs Narrated by Her Physician*, 3 vols, Henry Colburn, London, 1846

Meyer, Frédéric, *Vincent-Yves Boutin, Colonel d'Empire*, Éditions France-Empire, Paris, 1991

Miranda, General Francisco, *Archivo del General Miranda, Negociaciones y Diversos, 1809–1810 Tomo XXIII*, Editorial Lex, Havana, 1950

——*Fragments from an XVIIIth Century Diary: The Travels and Adventures of Don Francisco de Miranda, 1771–1789*, compiled and translated by Jordan Herbert Stabler, Caracas, 1931

Montorgueil, Georges, 'Le Colonel du génie Boutin et la conquîte de l'Algérie', *Revue du Génie*, Paris, 1930

Montorgueil, Georges, *Lady Stanhope et le colonel Boutin*, Mercure de France, Paris, 1924

Moore, Wendy, *The Knife Man*, Transworld Publishers, London, 2005

Murray, Venetia, *High Society in the Regency Period 1788–1830*, Penguin, London, 1998

Napier, Sir W., *The Life and Opinions of General Sir Charles James Napier*, London, 1857

Newman, Aubrey, *The Stanhopes of Chevening*, Macmillan, London, 1969

Newton, Michael, *Savage Girls and Wild Boys: A History of Feral Children*, Faber, London, 2002

Paule, Henry-Bordeaux, *Lady Stanhope en Orient, La Circe du Désert*, Librarie Plon, Paris, 1924

Perrier, Ferdinand, *La Syrie sous le gouvernement de Mehmet Ali jusqu'en 1840*, Paris, 1842

Pocock, Tom, *Stopping Napoleon: War and Intrigue in the Mediterranean*, John Murray, London, 2004

Pocock, Tom, *The Terror before Trafalgar: Nelson, Napoleon and the Secret War*, John Murray, London, 2002

Pocock, Tom, *A Thirst for Glory: The Life of Admiral Sir Sidney Smith*, Aurum, London, 1996

Picard, Lisa, *Dr Johnson's London 1740–1770*, Phoenix Press, London, 2001

Porter, Roy, *English Society in the Eighteenth Century*, Penguin, London, 1990

Porter, Roy, *Flesh in the Age of Reason: How the Enlightenment Transformed the Way We See Our Bodies and Souls*, Penguin, London, 2004

Price, Rev. Thomas, *Literary Remains*, Wales, 1854

Pückler-Muskau, Prince Hermann von, *Die Rückkehr, Vom verfasser der Briefe eines verstorbenen*, Berlin, 1846–48

Racine, Karen, *Francisco de Miranda: A Transatlantic Life in the Age of Revolution*, Scholarly Resources, Delaware, 2003

Robertson, William Spence, *The Life of Miranda*, University of North Carolina Press, 1929

Rodger, N. A. M, *The Wooden World: An Anatomy of the Georgian Navy*, HarperCollins, London, 1988

Rosebery, Lord, *Pitt*, Macmillan and Co., London and New York, 1895

Roussier, Paul, 'Les derniers projets et le dernier voyage de Domingo Badia', *Revue Africaine*, 1930

Rudé, George, *Paris and London in the Eighteenth Century*, Collins, London, 1979

Ruthven, Malise, *Islam in the World*, Penguin, London, 2000

Rzewuski, Count Waclav Seweryn, *Impressions d'Orient et d'Arabie: Un cavalier Polonais chez les Bédouins, 1817–1819*, text established by Bernadette Lizet with Françoise Aubaile-Sallenave, Piotr Daszkiewicz and Anne-Elizabeth Wolfe from the manuscript preserved in the National Library of Poland, Librairie Jose Corti/Muséum National d'Histoire Naturelle, 2002

Salibi, Kamal, *A House of Many Mansions: The History of Lebanon Reconsidered*, I. B. Tauris, London, 2003

Sâyigh, Fathallah, *Le désert et la gloire*, translated and annotated by Joseph Chelhod, Gallimard, Paris, 1991

Sebba, Anne, *The Exiled Collector: William Bankes and the Making of an English Country House*, John Murray, London, 2004

Sim, Katharine, *Desert Traveller*, Phoenix Press, London, 2000

Smith, G. Barnett, *Women of Renown: Nineteenth-Century Studies*, W. H. Allen & Co., London, 1893

Stanhope, Ghita, and Gooch, G. P., *The Life of Charles, Third Earl Stanhope*, Longmans, London, 1914.

Stanhope, Philip Henry, 5th Earl, *Life of the Right Honourable William Pitt*, London, 1861

——*The Stanhope Miscellanies*, London, 1863

Strachey, Lytton, *Books and Characters, French and English*, Chatto & Windus, London, 1924

Strathern, Paul, *Napoleon in Egypt: The Greatest Glory*, Jonathan Cape, London, 2007

Thomson, W. M., *The Land and the Book*, Nelson, London, 1859

Tillyard, Stella, *Aristocrats*, Chatto & Windus, London, 1994

Tolstoy, Nikolai, *The Half-Mad Lord*, Jonathan Cape, London, 1978

Tomalin, Claire, *Jane Austen: A Life*, Penguin, London, 2000

Trench, Richard, *Arabian Travellers*, Macmillan, London, 1986

Urban, Mark, *The Man Who Broke Napoleon's Codes*, Faber, London, 2001

*Your Most Dutyfull Servant*, edited by Marian Mills, Kent Country Arts and Libraries, Hurst Village Publishing, 1992

Warburton, Eliot, *The Crescent and the Cross*, London, 1845

Watkins, Susan, *Jane Austen in Style*, Thames and Hudson, London, 1990

Watney, John, *Travels in Araby of Lady Hester Stanhope*, Gordon Cremonesi, London, 1975

Zamoyski, Adam, *Holy Madness: Romantics, Patriots and Revolutionaries*, Weidenfeld & Nicolson, London, 1999

# *Notes*

I hope the reader will recognize that I frequently refer to what is modern-day Lebanon as Syria, as it was in Hester's time. The reference to Mount Lebanon remains the same today as it was then, although Djoun, as it was in Hester's day, is now Joun.

## Abbreviations

| | |
|---|---|
| BL | British Library |
| Bod. | Bodleian Library, Oxford University |
| Col. | Colindale Library |
| Kent | Centre for Kentish Studies, Maidstone |
| PRO | Public Record Office |
| Banks | Joseph Banks Research Project, Natural History Museum |
| DRO | Dorset County Record Office |
| FCO | Foreign and Commonwealth Office. |
| CRO | Cumbria Record Office |
| Beinecke | Beinecke Rare Book and Manuscipt Library, Yale University |
| Sterling | Sterling Memorial Library, Manuscripts and Archives, Yale University |

## Prologue

1 The full account given by Thomson can be found in his book, *The Land and the Book*, W. M. Thomson. Also quoted in full by Eliot Warburton, *The Crescent and the Cross* (Henry Colburn, London, 1845), Vol II, pp. 94–5.
2 Warburton, op. cit.
3 Ibid.

4 Moore also wrote an account to Philip, Earl Stanhope, in a letter dated 26 June 1839. Duchess of Cleveland, *The Life and Letters of Lady Hester Stanhope* (John Murray, London, 1914), pp. 427–9.

5 Ibid.

6 Ibid.

## Chapter 1: Beginnings

1 See Countess Stanhope's letter to her steward John Brampton on his wife's inability to breast-feed, Geneva, 7 January 1771; Marian Mills (ed.), *Your Most Dutyfull Servant* (Kent Country Arts and Libraries, Hurst Village Publishing, 1992), p. 71.

2 Countess Grizel Stanhope to Lady Chatham, 14 March 1776, Kent, U1590 S5.

3 Seventeen years after his death, in an attempt to clear the Pitt name, the former Governor's own defensive rebuttal asserting complete innocence in the matter was published posthumously by his grandson, William Pitt the Elder, in the *Daily Post* on 3 November 1743.

4 Old Sarum, near Salisbury, was the most famous of the so-called 'rotten boroughs' when in the nineteenth century it continued to return two Members of Parliament while ceasing to have any voters at all.

5 A fish market thrived at nearby Chepsted, which today is Chipstead, which means trading place.

6 Lord Rosebery, *Pitt* (Macmillan and Co., London, 1895), p. 3.

7 Kent, U1590, Thomas Cholmondeley of Vale Royal to Lady Stanhope, 8 October 1774.

8 Fifth Earl Stanhope, *Life of the Right Honourable William Pitt* (London, 1861). William Pitt to Lady Chatham, 11 February 1779, Vol 1, p. 28.

9 Kent, U1590, Countess Stanhope to Lady Chatham, 20 December 1780.

10 Ibid.

11 *The Letters of Lady Harriot Eliot* (Constable, Edinburgh, 1914). Lady Harriot Pitt to Lady Chatham, 29 May 1780.

12 Ibid.

13 Earl Stanhope, op. cit., William Pitt to Lord Mahon, 3 November 1783, Vol I, p. 132.

14 Sterling, Sir Joseph Banks Papers, Lord Mahon to Joseph Banks.

15 Louisa Stanhope had given birth to a second boy in 1784 who died while he was being delivered. It was common medical practice at that time, if the mother's life was judged to be in danger, for the attending doctor

to crush the baby's skull before it could emerge. It was brutal, but often the only way to safeguard the survival of the mother. Few doctors dared to risk performing a Caesarean; that would be left to the next generation.

16 Charles Stanhope, *Observations on Mr Pitt's plan for the Reduction of the National Debt* (T. Cadell, London, 1786).

17 Duchess of Cleveland, *The Life and Letters of Lady Hester Stanhope*, p. 8.

18 Ghita Stanhope, G. P. Gooch, *The Life of Charles, Third Earl Stanhope*, p. 236.

## Chapter 2: The Minority of One

1 Meryon, *Memoirs of Lady Hester Stanhope* (Henry Colburn, London, 1845), pp. 9–10.

2 Ghita Stanhope, op. cit., p. 238.

3 Freemasons were also put under increased surveillance, deemed to be politically volatile, a point significant to note because Stanhope was a very active Freemason. From 1799, Pitt's Unlawful Societies Act banned any meetings of groups which required members to take an oath or obligation, which included Freemasonry. All members were henceforth required to submit the details of their age, profession and address to their local Clerk of the Peace.

4 Ghita Stanhope, op. cit., Captain John Leard to Lord Stanhope, 21 February 1797.

5 Meryon, *Memoirs*, op. cit., Vol II, p. 60.

6 *Memoirs of the Duchess de Gontant*, translated by J. W. Davis (London, 1894), Vol I, pp. 128–9.

7 *Memoirs of the Comtesse de Boigne* (Heinemann, London, 1907), Vol I, p. 137.

8 Meryon, *Memoirs*, Vol II, pp. 52–3.

9 *Memoirs of the Comtesse de Boigne*, Vol I, p. 137.

10 Meryon, *Memoirs*, Vol II, p. 16. Sir Sidney Smith paid a tribute to her beauty when she first came out. 'You entered the room in your pale shirt, exciting our admiration . . .'

11 Cleveland, op. cit., p. 2.

12 Nikolai Tolstoy, *The Half-Mad Lord* (Jonathan Cape, London, 1978), pp. 88–9. In his biography of Lord Camelford, he makes this intriguing conjecture, presenting compelling evidence that there was unlikely to be another reason why Camelford would attack his close friend, a man he

had invited to travel with him aboard the *Charon*, the ship he was preparing to command at Sir Sidney Smith's request, to Constantinople.

13  Ibid., HLS to T. J. Jackson, 27 May 1802, p. 120.

14  HLS to Evelyn St Clare, undated, Kent, UI590 C253/1–10.

15  Kent, TR 2322/10, Chevening Registers from 1561–1812, p. 132. Records taken from the archives of the village church at Chevening show that on 20 July 1800, a 'naturel d. of Ann Fry, "Mary Ann" was baptised', the birth recorded as 29 June. 'Naturel' meant, in this case, the child of an unwed mother.

16  Meryon, *Memoirs*, Vol II.

17  PRO 30/70/6, HLS to Lady Chatham, 1800.

18  Many years later, HLS wrote to H. W. Wynne from Syria, at one point musing disparagingly about the sort of gardens her Grenville relatives preferred: the 'dullness and grandeur of S[towe] and the confined missified [*sic*] beauties of D[ropmore]'. But then she writes, 'as for B[oconnoc] it was made for its later owner, and for a *great mind*'. This recollection, long after Camelford's death, suggests she once saw the beautiful estate of Boconnoc for herself; it certainly betrays her admiration for its creator.

19  It would also affront their high Tory Temple relatives, who only managed to boot out Tooke, 'the Jacobin Shuttlecock', by passing an act prohibiting clergymen from being MPs.

20  Alexander Kinglake, *Eothen* (London, 1844).

21  Cleveland, op. cit., HLS to T. J. Jackson, 3 February 1802, pp. 31–2.

22  Ibid., 18 October 1801, pp. 29–30.

23  Tolstoy, op. cit., p. 132. Tolstoy cites dossiers found in the Archives Nationales, Paris: F7 6307, dossier BP 6386 and 6402; F7 6334, dossier BP 7501; F7 6339, dossier BP 7155; Addn. MS 59493, pp. 150–77.

## Chapter 3: The Company of Men

1  Cleveland, op. cit., HLS to T. J. Jackson, 19 November 1803, pp. 52–3.

2  Frank Hamel, *Lady Hester Lucy Stanhope* (Cassell, London, 1913), p. 41.

3  Meryon, *Memoirs*, Vol II, p. 67.

4  Ibid., p. 78.

5  Aubrey Newman, *The Stanhopes of Chevening*, (Macmillan, London, 1969), Lord Mahon (the future fourth Earl Stanhope) to Lord Carrington, 12 October 1803. See also Kent, UI590.

6  Lord Granville Leveson Gower, *Private Correspondence 1781–1821*, ed.

Castalia, Countess Granville (John Murray, London, 1917). Lady Bessborough to GLG, September or October 1804, Vol I, p. 462.

7   PRO 30/29/6/2, HLS to GLG, 'Friday, 10 o'clock'.

8   Granville Leveson Gower, op. cit., Lady B to GLG, September or October 1804, Vol I, p. 462.

9   Ibid., Vol I, p. 466.

10  Kent, U1590 S6/5/5. In his entry for Feb 1815, Charles Meryon wrote: 'Lady H told me that on Lord G's departure, she resolved to kill herself and swallowed laudanum with that intention.'

11  Ibid.

12  PRO/30/29/6/2 f. 48, HLS to GLG, 29 December 1804.

13  Ibid.

14  Ibid. In this letter, Hester tells Granville that after she had recovered, Pitt 'appeared less surprised than affected at the violence of emotions he saw was not of my power to command. He . . . tormented me with remarks, questions and allusions & the advice he gave me . . . was that now you were gone, to forget you, hard as it may first appear, however improbable.'

15  Granville Leveson Gower, op. cit., Lady B to GLG, 5 March 1805, Vol II, p. 36.

16  Ibid., Lady B to GLG, 7 June 1805, Vol II, p. 76.

17  Ibid., Lady B to GLG, 28 June 1805, Vol II, p. 89.

18  Ibid., Lady Stafford to GLG, 28 December 1804, Vol I, p. 504.

19  Ibid., Lady B to GLG, 26 August 1805, Vol II, p. 108.

20  Ibid., Lady B to GLG, 6 December, 1805, Vol II, p. 144.

21  Kent, U1590 C253/5, George Canning to HLS, 1805.

22  Ibid.

23  Col. *Lady's Magazine*, 1806, Vol XXXVII, p. 30

24  Cleveland, op. cit., p. 69.

## Chapter 4: A Summoning of Strength

1   Meryon MSS, Kent, U1590 S5/2, HLS to CM undated.

2   Granville Leveson Gower, op. cit., Lady B to GLG, undated, October 1805, Vol II, p. 221.

3   Kent, U1590 C253/4, Moore to HLS, 16 October 1808.

4   Ibid.

5   Cleveland, op. cit., p. 82.

6   Ibid.

STAR OF THE MORNING

7  Kent, U1590/C253/8.

8  *Archivo del General Miranda, Negociaciones y Diversos, 1809–1810, Tomo XXIII* (Editorial Lex, La Habana, 1950), Vol 60, 29 April 1809.

9  Ibid.

10 William Spence Robertson, *The Life of Miranda* (University of North Carolina Press, 1929), Vol II, p. 64.

11 Ibid., p. 203.

12 The paintings were left in the care of a Mrs Price of Strand House, in Builth Wells, and were passed down in the same family for several generations.

13 The current owners of the Glan Irfon farmhouse, the Davies, say that they heard this story from the previous owner, who lived there more than fifty years ago, and surprised them by suddenly asking out of the blue: 'Is the orange blossom tree still thriving?' That former owner, now very elderly, said she had always heard a story that when Lady Hester 'split up with her boyfriend' she came to Wales and planted the tree.

14 Kent, U1590 S6/2. Meryon's diary from 1809 confirms the presence of General Miranda that evening.

15 The same hotel where Lord Nelson stayed before embarking on HMS *Warrior*. The hotel no longer exists; it was destroyed by German bombs in 1940.

16 *Archivo del General Miranda*, Vol 60, p. 320.

17 Ibid., pp. 321–2.

18 Ibid., pp. 320–21.

19 Ibid., p. 322.

20 Ibid., p. 323.

21 PRO 30/29/6/2, HLS to GLG, undated.


**Chapter 5: Love and Escape**

1  Kent, U1590 S6/2, CM to his family, 23 March 1810.

2  Meryon, *Memoirs*, Vol II, p. 217.

3  PRO, CO 158/23/85756.

4  Bod., Bruce MSS, MS. Eng. d. 2834-35.

5  Kent, U1590 S6/2, CM to his family, 14 July 1810.

6  Ibid., Journal, 8 June 1810.

7  Ibid.

8  Beinecke, OSB MSS 74, Marquess of Sligo Letters 1810. Box 1, The Levantine Correpondence of Howe Peter Browne, Second Marquess of

Sligo, August–December 1810 (Arthur Freeman, Rare Books and Manuscripts, 2001), Athens, 15 September 1810, to his mother.

9  Ibid.

10  Fiona MacCarthy, *Byron, Life and Legend* (John Murray, London, 2002), p. 131.

## Chapter 6: A Bolt-hole on the Bosphorus

1  Constantinople, 14 November 1810, to his mother.

2  Bod., Bruce MSS, MS. Eng. d. 2835–45.

3  Ibid.

4  Ibid.

5  Ibid.

6  Ibid.

7  Ibid. Anonymous letter, sent to Crauford Bruce, postmarked Dover, received August 1810.

8  Bod., Bruce MSS, MS Eng. d. p. 2835–45.

9  Ibid.

10  Susannah Fullerton, *Jane Austen and Crime* (Jane Austen Society of Australia, 2004), p. 77.

11  Jane Austen, *Pride and Prejudice*, chapter 28.

12  Susan Watkins, *Jane Austen in Style* (Thames and Hudson, London, 1990), p. 76.

13  *Byron's Corbeau Blanc*, The Life and Letters of Lady Melbourne (Rice University Press, 1997), Lady Melbourne to Lady Caroline Lamb, 13 April 1810, Melbourne, p. 107.

14  Bod., Bruce MSS, MS. Eng. d. 2834–45.

15  Ibid. HLS to CB, 12 December 1810, pp. 79–80.

16  Ibid.

17  Ibid. Meryon also relates an earlier similar incident, in Patras, when they visited the elderly Bey of Corinth.

18  Joseph Banks Research Project, Natural History Museum, HLS to Sir Joseph Banks, 2 May 1812, Damietta, D.T.C. 18, pp. 160–61.

19  Bod., Bruce MSS, MS. Eng. d. 2835–7.

20  Ibid., CB to MB, 7 April 1811.

21  Ibid., JS to MB, undated.

22  Ibid., MB to JS, 24 December 1810.

23  Ibid.

24  Ibid., MS. Eng. c. 5751, fols. 38–9. William Bankes to MB, 20 May 1811.

25 Beinecke, OSB MSS 74, Sligo to his mother, 28 December 1810.

26 Cleveland, op. cit., HLS to Stratford Canning, Brusa, undated, probably March 1811, p. 100.

27 Only one drawing seems to have survived, which Hester sent to Crauford Bruce in a letter from Therapia. All of Hester's other sketches are presumed to have been lost in the shipwreck off Rhodes later that year. See Bod., MS. Eng. c. 5759, fols. 173–4.

28 Bod., Bruce MSS, MS. Eng. d. 2834–45, HLS to Crauford Bruce, 17 February 1811.

29 Ibid.

30 Ibid.

31 Cleveland, op. cit., HLS to Stratford Canning, undated, probably June 1811, p. 109.

32 Ibid.

33 Meryon, *The Travels of Lady Hester Stanhope* (Henry Colburn, London, 1846), Vol I, pp. 69–70.

34 Cleveland, op. cit., HLS to General Oakes, Brusa, 2 June 1811, p. 111. (The Duchess of Cleveland has mistakenly categorized this as a letter to Stratford Canning.)

35 Bod., Bruce MSS, MS. Eng. d. 2834–2845, MB to CB, Brusa, 28 March 1811.

36 Ibid.

## Chapter 7: Indecision

1 Bod., Bruce MSS, MS. Eng. d. 2834–2845, MB to CB, Brusa, 28 March 1811.

2 Cleveland, op. cit., Henry Williams Wynne to his mother, Constantinople, 4 October 1811, pp. 112–13.

3 Ibid., Bebec, 14 November 1811, p. 119.

4 Ibid., HLS to Mr Murray, 2 January 1812, p. 117.

5 Dressing like a Turk was hardly new, although it was the equivalent of the haute couture of its day, and therefore the preserve of the wealthy. The fashion went back to the late sixteenth century, when one of the most flamboyant figures on the London scene was Sir Robert Shirley, notable for his extensive sojourns in Persia and his Circassian wife, Teresia. Together they set the trend for posing in oriental dress; their portraits by Anthony Van Dyck gaze down from the gallery hall at Petworth House with an air of worldly defiance. Men had worn turbans (usually sloppily-tied, eccentric-looking creations) and Turkish caps as long as there was a fashion

for wigs, as an informal way of covering up their shaved or bald heads. In 1666, Samuel Pepys had been impressed by the playwright Sir Robert Howard's 'undress' of Turkish turban and embroidered robe. In the 1750s, the Swiss artist Jean-Etienne Liotard fuelled the flames of 'Turcomania' with his serenely exotic depictions of harem life and his portraits of society ladies like the Countess Mary of Coventry dressed as one of the Sultan's captive beauties. At the French court, masked balls frequently had a Turkish theme, while Louis XV's duelling mistresses, Madame de Pompadour and Madame Barry, staged a 'Sultana' war, both commissioning the fashionable painter Van Loo and each trying to upstage the other's portrait.

6   Ian Bruce, *The Nun of Lebanon* (London, 1951), HLS to MB, 'From the old Spot', 5 March 1816, pp. 376–7.

7   Ibid., HLS to MB, Haifa, 22 March 1815, pp. 335–6.

8   Cleveland, op. cit., HLS to Stratford Canning, undated, 1812, pp. 130–33.

9   Banks, D.T.C. 18, p. 160A, HLS to Sir Joseph Banks, March 1812.

10  Meryon MSS, Kent, U1590 S6/1.

11  Bruce, *The Nun of Lebanon*, HLS to MB, 7 September 1814, pp. 299–301.

12  Banks, D.T.C. 18–20, HLS to Sir Joseph Banks, Damietta, 2 May 1812, pp. 160–61.

13  Cleveland, op. cit., HLS to Stratford Canning, October 1812, pp. 132–3.


**Chapter 8: Friendships**

1   During the 1990s, the American Research Centre in Egypt, in collaboration with the Egyptian Supreme Council of Antiquities, restored Nafissa al-Bayda's *sabil-kuttab* and *wekala* façade as the first of a series of conservation projects in historic Cairo. A permanent exhibition is now on display.

2   J. Christopher Herold, *Bonaparte in Egypt* (Hamish Hamilton, London, 1963), p. 232.

3   Meryon, *Travels*, Vol II, p. 161.

4   Bruce, *The Nun of Lebanon*, HLS to Crauford Bruce, p. 139. 'I am so well disguised by my dress & have so adopted Turkish manners as to be able to enter a Mosck during prayers & depart again unabused, I take off my shoes and go up the fountain as they do put on an air of solemnity & respect & attract no attention whatever.'

5   Frédéric Meyer, *Vincent-Yves Boutin, Colonel d'Empire* (Éditions France-Empire, Paris, 1991).

6   Archives Nationales de Paris, T. XXI, *Correspondance de Napoléon*, pp.

448–50. See also Leo Berjaud, *Précurseur de l'Algérie Francaise* (Paris, 1950), p. 173. This quotes a letter from Napoleon about Boutin's mission in Egypt and Syria.

7  Berjaud, op. cit., p. 178.
8  Ibid., p. 175.
9  Bruce, *The Nun of Lebanon*, Madame Ney to MB, 6 April 1816, p. 396.
10  Ibid., MB to CB, Cairo, 20 April 1814, p. 132–3.
11  Private Collection, Meryon family, CM to his sister, 30 September 1812.
12  Bruce, *The Nun of Lebanon*, HLS to CB, 'On board my boat upon the Nile', 2 May 1812, pp. 133–41.
13  Ibid., MB to Crauford Bruce, Cairo, 20 April 1812, pp. 132–3.
14  Ibid., HLS to CB, 'On board my boat upon the Nile,' 2 May 1812, pp. 133–41.
15  Ibid., HLS to CB, Damascus, 23 September 1812, pp. 149–54.
16  Dominique Vivant Denon, *Voyage dans la Basse et la Haute Egypte pendant les campagnes du Général Bonaparte en 1798 et 1799,* 2 Vols (London, 1807).
17  Kent, U1590 C248A. Extract from HLS's journal through Syria.
18  It was Süleyman the Magnificent who restored Jerusalem's Dome of the Rock in the sixteenth century. The glittering alloy that shines like burnished gold was added more recently in the twentieth century.
19  Jaffa Gate was then known as Bethlehem Gate.
20  Kent, U1590 S6/2.
21  Ibid.
22  Cleveland, op. cit., HLS to unnamed correspondent, undated, p. 126.
23  The earliest source of this kind of accusation seems to have originated with an account by the Spanish Jew, Benjamin of Tudela, who travelled close to the Druze kingdom in the twelfth century, at the time of the Crusaders.
24  Bod., Bruce MSS, MS. Eng. d. 2835–36, HLS to CB, 24 August 1812.

**Chapter 9: Under the Minaret**

1  Banks, D.T.C. 19, HLS to Sir Joseph Banks, Damietta, dated 2 May 1812. In this letter, HLS told Banks that she was already being called 'Queen of the East or Zenobia'.
2  Charles Allen, *God's Terrorists* (Little, Brown, London, 2006), p. 64.
3  Cleveland, op. cit., p. 138.
4  Ibid., pp. 137–8.

5  Kent, U1590 S6/1, HLS to General Oakes.

6  Bod., Bruce MSS, MS. Eng. d. 2835–36, HLS to CB, 23 September 1812.


## Chapter 10: The Desert Queen

1  Some sources, including Meryon, indicate that Lady Hester went into the desert with Lascaris and his wife, Mariam. They are mistaken. In a letter to Monsieur Henri Guys, the French consul in Beirut, written towards the end of her life, Hester is clear about having 'made an excursion into the desert with Lascaris alone, keeping the doctor and the married servants, on one pretext or another, from accompanying me'. See also Kent, U1590 S6/1/3.

2  Fathallah Sàyigh, *Le désert et la gloire* (translated and annotated by Joseph Chelhod, Gallimard, Paris, 1991), p. 205.

3  Bod., Bruce MSS, MS. Eng. d. 2835–36, HLS to CB, Hamah, 27 January 1813.

4  Cleveland, op. cit., HLS to Wynne, Hamah, 15 January 1813, p. 149.

5  John Barker, *Syria and Egypt under the last five sultans of Turkey*, edited by Edward B. Barker (Samuel Tinsley, London, 1876), 2 Vols. Hester relayed this anecdote to John Barker, who in turn told his son Edward.

6  Sàyigh, op. cit., p. 94.

7  Ibid.

8  Bod., Bruce MSS, MS. Eng. d. 2835-36, HLS to CB, Hamah, 27 January 1813.

9  Ibid.

10  Ibid., MB to Oakes, Hamah, 19 March 1813.

11  Ibid., HLS to CB, Latakia, 5 October 1813.

12  Ibid.

13  This was how Hester described this moment to Alexander Kinglake many years later; he wrote it up as part of his chapter on her in *Eothen*.

14  Cleveland, op. cit., HLS to Oakes, pp. 154–9.

15  Georges Montorgueil, 'Le Colonel du génie Boutin et la conquête de l'Algérie (*Revue du Génie*, Paris, 1930), HLS to Vincent Boutin, undated, 1814.

16  Berjaud, op. cit., Major Misset to M. Aziz, 25 March 1813, pp. 186–7.

17  Bod., Bruce MSS, MS Eng. c. 5766, MB to General Oakes, Hamah, 13 March 1813.

18  Bod., Ibid., MS. Eng. c. 5759. Fragment found in Michael Bruce's papers after his death.

## Chapter 11: Separation and Despair

1   Bod., Bruce MSS, MS. Eng. c. 5747–5759. Latakia, 14 July 1813.
2   Meryon, *Travels*, Vol II, p. 250.
3   Banks, D.T.C. 19, HLS to Joseph Banks, The Convent of Mar Elias, 1 July 1814, pp. 30–35.
4   Meryon, *Travels*, Vol II, p. 243
5   Banks, D.T.C. 19, HLS to Sir Joseph Banks, Latakia, 7 July 1813.
6   Bod., Bruce MSS, MS. Eng. c. 5744–59. Hester speaks of her intentions to travel to these places, and to South America.
7   Meryon, *Travels*, Vol III, p. 92.
8   Bod., MS. Eng. c. 5744–59, HLS to CB, Latakia, 5 October 1813.
9   Ibid.
10  Ibid., HLS to MB, Acre, 11 March 1815.
11  Beaudin was a French Mameluke whom Bruce acquired on his last trip to Aleppo. Hester nicknamed him 'Boudin' or 'Pudding'. Beaudin was to return from Aleppo with Hester's commissions, while Giorgio was to travel with Bruce as far as Constantinople, and possibly go to Vienna if she did not send for him sooner. Hester noted that Giorgio could scarcely contain his excitement at the prospect of visiting grand European cities.
12  Hamel, op. cit., Meryon to Miss Williams, Latakia, pp.169.
13  Bod., Bruce MSS, MS. Eng. d. 2835–36, HLS to MB, 18 October 1813.
14  Ibid.
15  Ibid.
16  Ibid., HLS to MB, Latakia, 8 November 1813.
17  Ibid.
18  Ibid., HLS to MB, Sidon, 6 April 1814.
19  Stanley Poole Lane, *Life of Stratford Canning* (Longmans, Green & Co., London, 1888), Vol I, HLS to Stratford Canning, p. 121.
20  Bod., Bruce MSS, MS. Eng. d. 2835–36, HLS to MB, Abra, 28 February 1814.
21  Ibid., MS. Eng. c. 5759, John Barker to Sir Sidney Smith, 14 August 1814.
22  Meryon, *Travels*, Vol II, pp. 294–5.
23  Ibid., Vol II, p. 316.

## Chapter 12: 'The Queen Orders Her Minister'

1   Hamel, op. cit., HLS to Maalem Aziz, Mar Elias, 4 February 1814, p. 179.
2   Bruce, *The Nun of Lebanon*, HLS to MB, The Convent of Abra, 28 February 1814, pp. 245–8.
3   Ibid., MB to HLS, Constantinople, 4 January 1814, pp. 231–5.

4 Ibid.

5 Ibid., MB to HLS, Constantinople, 20 January 1814, pp. 237–8.

6 Ibid.

7 Théophanie Escalon may have been from a Huguenot family; records at Buca Cemetery in Constantinople show that several members of the Escalon family were buried there.

8 Montorgueil, op. cit. Colonel Vincent-Yves Boutin's last official dispatch was sent from Cairo, dated 14 December 1813.

9 Berjaud, op. cit., HLS to Boutin, undated, April 1814, pp. 205–7.

10 Ibid.

11 Ibid.

12 Ibid., HLS to Boutin, undated, pp. 207–8.

13 These would have been the French victories at Champaubert, Montmirail, Champ-Thierry, Vauchamps and Montereau against the Russians, Prussians, Westphalians and Austrians, between 10 and 18 February 1814 – before the spectacular events of April resulted in Napoleon's abdication on 11 April.

14 Some twenty years later, as he prepared his papers for publication, Meryon passed judgement on this period in Hester's life. 'Her position was difficult and delicate. Had she visited these distant lands, in which she travelled and sojourned, with only myself, her doctor, as the companion of her journeys, she might have compromised her reputation no less than in accepting the services of a man of fortune.' He never explained this sentence. Afterwards, he took a thick red pen and slashed across this sentence, with a word that crops up frequently throughout the pages of his blue, lined journals: 'Omitted'.

15 Twenty-seven letters from Hester to Colonel Vincent-Yves Boutin were found in his belongings after his death and returned to his brother, Joseph. They were published in Georges Montorgueil's *Lady Stanhope et le colonel Boutin* (Mercure de France, Paris, 1924).

16 Meryon, *Travels*. Meryon estimated this figure, adding that an average of eleven people were dying each day in Sidon, but that no plague cases were reported after 24 June 1814.

17 The so-called 'serpent's stone' was bezoar, a calcareous concretion allegedly created, in this case, by the saliva of writhing snakes, said to be formed in the intestine or the brain. Other bezoar stones, extracted from the stomach or bladder of various reptiles, birds and mammals, containing concentrated ammonia or superphosphate, were equally legendary. Pliny

had written of such stones, reputed to have antidotal power, drawing on references he found recorded about the stone from India. Banks had certainly heard of such stones, for bezoar is documented in Albertus Seba's *Cabinet of Natural Curiosities*, published in the eighteenth century, but he may not have inspected one himself.

18  Banks, D.T.C. 19, HLS to Sir Joseph Banks, Mar Elias, 18 May 1814.
19  Ibid.
20  Ibid., HLS to Sir Joseph Banks, 1 July 1814.
21  Ibid.
22  Berjaud, op. cit., HLS to Boutin, undated, April 1814, pp. 207–8.
23  Ibid., p. 209.
24  Ibid.
25  Ibid., HLS to Boutin, 23 May 1814, p. 210.
26  JSTOR, Norman Lewis, Vol 22, 1995, pp. 161–3. Barker mentions Smith as the recipient of the 'Lascaris papers' in a letter, dated 29 September 1814. See Bod., MS. Eng. c. 5759, fol. 167.
27  Bod., Bruce MSS, MS. Eng. c. 5759. HLS to John Barker, 12 August 1814.
28  Ibid., HLS to Barker, Mar Elias, 8 June 1814.

## Chapter 13: A Chained-up Tigress

1  Bod., Bruce MSS, MS. Eng. c. 5744–59, June 1814.
2  Ibid.
3  Ibid., MS. Eng. c. 5759, CB to James Stanhope, Upper Grosvenor Street, 29 April 1814.
4  Bod., Bruce MSS, MS., Eng 5744–59.
5  Ibid., MS. Eng. c. 5744–5759, HLS to CB, 25 June 1814.
6  Ibid.
7  Ibid., MS. Eng. c. 5755–57.
8  Ibid., MS. Eng. c. 5759, HLS to Barker, 24 August 1814.
9  Barker, op. cit., HLS to John Barker, 7 February 1815, pp. 224–5.
10  Hamel, op. cit., p. 188. Manuscripts cited as in Frank Hamel's private collection.
11  Ibid. Hester would tell Meryon that she always allowed herself the possibility of suicide.
12  Bod., Bruce MSS, MS. Eng. c. 5744–59, HLS to MB, 29 August 1814.
13  Ibid., HLS to MB, 'From my tent', 7 September 1814.
14  Hamel, op. cit. From a letter dictated by HLS to Meryon for Beaudin, Meshmushy, 5 August 1814, pp. 188–9.

15  Berjaud., op. cit., HLS to Boutin, 23 August 1814, p. 213–15.

16  Ibid., 24 August 1814.

17  Ibid.

18  Jeremy Bentham, *Memoirs*, edited by John Bowring (William Tait, Edinburgh, 1842), pp. 468–88.

19  Bod., Bruce MSS, MS. Eng. c. 5744–5758–9, HLS to MB, 6 August 1814.

## Chapter 14: 'I Will Be No Man's Agent'

1  Berjaud, op. cit., HLS to Boutin, 16 October 1814, p. 215–16.

2  Meryon, *Travels*, Vol III, p. 25.

3  Ibid., Vol III, p. 59.

4  Bruce, *The Nun of Lebanon*, HLS to MB, Tripoli, 11 January 1815, pp. 317–19.

5  Between them, the various members of the Guys family had a monopoly as French consuls in the early nineteenth century in Syria: Henri Guys – who became a great friend of Hester's – in Sidon; Charles-Edmond Guys in Tripoli and Constantin Guys in Aleppo. Hester gave Mustafa Berber's horse to her friend Selim.

6  Meryon, *Memoirs*, Vol II, p. 136.

7  Meryon, *Travels*, Vol III, pp. 61–2.

8  Ibid., p. 12.

9  Kent, UI590 S6/5/5.

10  Ibid.

11  Barker, op. cit., HLS to John Barker, pp. 220–21.

12  Kent, U1590 C242, HLS to Sir Sidney Smith.

13  Both Hester and Meryon refer to Dervish Mustafa Aga as the Capugi Bachi, and in some cases as the Zaym.

14  Meryon, *Travels*, Vol III, p. 94.

15  Barker, op. cit., pp. 237–8.

16  Bod., Bruce MSS, MS. Eng. c. 5744–5759, HLS to MB, Acre, 11 March 1815.

17  Bod., Bruce MSS, MS. Eng. c. 5758–9, HLS to General Richard Grenville, begun April 1814, sent 23 June 1814.

18  Meryon, *Travels*, Vol III, p. 140.

19  Ibid., HLS to John Barker, 3 May 1815.

20  Ibid., HLS to MB, 24 June 1815.

21  Tom Pocock, *The Terror before Trafalgar* (John Murray, London, 2002), pp. 227–8.

## Chapter 15: The Broken Statue

1 Banks, D.T.C. 19, HLS to Joseph Fox, Acre, 7 May 1815, pp. 149–53.

2 The following year, in 1816, Lancaster broke off his association with Fox and the other trustees of the Royal Lancasterian Society to found his own school in Tooting. This time he went bankrupt and was forced to serve time in prison for failure to pay his debts. He emigrated to the United States, and founded a school in Baltimore, but once again was beset with money difficulties, a pattern he repeated first in Venezuela, then in Canada.

3 Banks, D.T.C. 19, HLS to Joseph Fox, Acre, 7 May 1815, pp. 149–53.

4 Ibid.

5 Ibid.

6 Banks, D.T.C. 19, HLS to Joseph Banks, 24 June 1815.

7 Kent, U1590 C473/29, HLS to Mrs La Riviere, undated.

8 Ibid.

9 CRO, D/LONS/Li/2/52.

10 Meryon admitted to confusion, but took her name to be Trungore Rashyelo and Elias was in fact Elias Jegurgos, possibly a relative of the King, Tecla Georgis.

11 Hester reminded Lord Valentia that the couple were 'persons of note' and that he had written of the family and their connection to Ras Walda Sellassie, the King of Tigray, in his *Travels*. Perhaps he could send them some tokens of friendship, she suggested, 'some books bound like prayer books, with a few Crosses and Jesus Christs and Virgin Marys upon them, with blank sheets, and about the size of a very thick duodecimo, would be a very acceptable present'. Evidently, she wanted to encourage her 'very amiable, clever' guests to record their adventures.

12 Bruce, *The Nun of Lebanon*, HLS to MB, undated, 1817, p. 389.

13 Comte Waclav Seweryn Rzewuski, *Impressions d'Orient et d'Arabie* (José Corti/ Museum National d'Histoire Naturelle, Paris, 2002), p. 190. Rzewuski refers to Boutin as 'Bodin'.

14 Alice Héneiné, *Voyageurs d'Orient* (Editions Dar Lahad Khater, Beirut, 1983). Charles-Edmond Guys to Talleyrand, 25 October 1815, Vol I, p. 123. See also Archives Nationales de Paris, Série Affaires Etrangères, Correspondance Consulaire, R.16.

15 Bruce, *The Nun of Lebanon*, HLS to MB, undated, 1817, p. 389.

16 Berjaud, op. cit., p. 226.

17 Bruce, *The Nun of Lebanon*, HLS to MB, undated, 1817, p. 388.

## Chapter 16: Revenge

1 British Museum, MSS 27620, Burckhardt to Renouard, undated.

2 A complete inventory of Boutin's effects, some acknowledged to have been submitted by Hester, was prepared by Constantin Guys, and sent to Joseph Boutin.

3 Banks, D.T.C. 19–20, HLS to Sir Joseph Banks, Mount Lebanon, 19 November 1815.

4 Ibid.

5 Ibid.

6 Cleveland, op. cit., p. 210.

7 Captain Jesse, *The Life of Beau Brummell*, (London, 1932).

8 Kent, U1590 C234.

9 Bruce, *The Nun of Lebanon*, HLS to James Stanhope, 15 April 1816, pp. 382–3.

10 Earl of Bessborough and A. Aspinall, *Lady Bessborough and her family circle* (John Murray, London, 1842), The Duke of Wellington to Lady Caroline Lamb, 19 April 1816, p. 257.

11 Bruce, *The Nun of Lebanon*, HLS to MB, 5 March 1816, pp. 376–7.

12 Berjaud, op. cit., HLS to Joseph Boutin, 4 December 1817, Mar Elias, pp. 230–32.

13 DRO, James Silk Buckingham to Burckhardt, c/o Henry Salt, Cairo, 1816.

14 DRO, HLS to William Bankes, 14 May 1816.

15 Katharine Sim, *Desert Traveller* (Phoenix Press, London, 2000), p. 402.

16 Cleveland, op. cit., pp. 188–93.

17 Ibid.

18 Kent, U1590 C247 – 1 and 2, HLS to unknown correspondent in French, probably Henri Guys, 18 May 1816.

## Chapter 17: 'I Am Done With All Respectability'

1 Barker, op. cit., pp. 278–9.

2 Ian Bruce, *Lavallette Bruce* (Hamish Hamilton, London, 1953), Théophanie Escalon to MB, 9 October 1814, p. 73.

3 Terence de Vere White, *Lost Correspondence, The letters of Peter, Marquess of Sligo, to Lord Lowther* (Twentieth Century, 1958) p. 233.

4 Shortly after she heard of the Allied victory early in 1814, Hester had written to tell Bruce that 'the extraordinary events upon the Continent which I never expected have completely put out of the question' her former plan. 'You know I told you never to mention the idea, neither to *him* or

anyone else,' she said. She seems to be alluding to some kind of adjustment to her original 'Napoleon plan'.

If Bruce went to Elba, he was secretive for a reason. There has never been any entirely satisfactory explanation as to why copies of certain confidential letters were found in Bruce's possession when he was arrested. One, unsigned, postmarked Vienna, referred to 'the theories that Bonaparte would be extracted from the Island of Elba' and continued 'I beg of you to think about this seriously, does not the tranquillity of the world deserve some attention?' Copies of two other letters, made in his own handwriting, were also later found in Bruce's possession. Both were written on 23 April 1814, signed by Fouché. One of them was a cover letter to Talleyrand, the other to Napoleon himself, and advocates making an escape, '. . . from this island, the sea, the wind, and a felucca can carry you quickly to any of the countries that are most liable to disturbances, emergencies and revolutions'. In this letter, Fouché advised Napoleon to take refuge in 'the United States of America . . . where you could begin your existence anew, among a new people who would admire your genius without fearing it.' To the Allies, at the same time, Fouché's language was far less polite: the 'ogre' should be removed, he advised.

5  If anyone was going to attempt what Hester had in mind, she told him, it should be her cousin, Lord Ebrington. The mission Hester believed Ebrington suited for was apparently the one she had once coveted herself, to penetrate Napoleon's defences and discern his plans. Like Bruce, he was in Paris, and Hester was aware that they saw each other regularly, although she was not impressed with Bruce's favourable impression of Ebrington's mistress, the courtesan Harriette Wilson – 'the Beast lady', she called her.

6  Bruce, *Lavallette Bruce*, MB to CB, 10 July 1815, pp. 121–2.

7  Among those who wrote to Bruce at this time was one of Napoleon's former mistresses, Josephine Grassini, who asked to see him urgently about a specific undisclosed matter. See Bod., Bruce MSS, MS. Eng. 5753.

8  Meryon, *Travels*, Nasir al Fadil to HLS, undated, 1816, Vol III, pp. 349–50.

9  Edouard Driault, *La Formation de l'Empire de Mohammed Aly, de l'Arabie au Soudan 1814-1823* (Cairo, 1927), Roussel to the Duc de Richelieu, Alexandria, 1 December 1816.

10  Ibid., Roussel to the Duc de Richelieu, Alexandria, 23 April 1817.

11  Héneiné, op. cit., Roussel to the Duc de Richelieu, 22 July 1817, p. 101.

## Chapter 18: Mr Kocub's Spy

1 Bruce, *The Nun of Lebanon*, pp. 222–4.
2 Ibid.
3 Kent, U1590 C246/2.
4 Bruce, *The Nun of Lebanon*, HLS to MB, undated, pp. 387–92.
5 Meryon, *Memoirs*, Vol II, p. 287.
6 Barker, op. cit., HLS to Barker, p. 235.
7 Kent, U1590 C253/1–10.
8 Ibid.
9 Kent, U1590 C253/2, Elizabeth Williams to CM, Castle of Jebba, October 1817.
10 Kent, U1590 S/6/5 1–7.
11 Ibid.
12 Ibid.
13 Kent, UI590 S6/2/7.
14 Kent, U1590 C253/1–10, CM to HLS, 23 June 1818 and 30 July 1818.
15 Ibid., 17 October 1817.
16 Kent, U1590 S6/5/1, HLS to Meryon, undated, 1817.
17 Kent, U1590 S6/1/1, CM to HLS, No.19, London, 16 April 1818.
18 Vincent Cronin, *Napoleon* (HarperCollins, London, 1994), p. 424.
19 Kent, U1590 S6/3.
20 Pocock, op. cit., pp. 226–7.
21 Kent, U1590 C253/1–10, HLS to CM, 21 February 1818.
22 Ibid.
23 Archives Nationales de Paris, Série Affaires Etrangères, Section Outre-Mer, Afrique III 8 B, Ali Bey el Abbassi to Regnault, 16 August 1818.
24 Sterling, op. cit., SML MS58, Ali Bey el Abbassi to Sir Joseph Banks, Paris, 5 April 1814.
25 Ibid., also Héneiné, op. cit., Vol II, p. 113.
26 Regnault to Comte Molé, 10 October 1818, Arch. Nat. Section Outre-Mer, Afrique III 8 B
27 Ibid.
28 Rzewuski, op. cit., pp. 132–3.
29 Joseph Chelhod, 'Un nouvel éclairage sur la mission et la morte d'Ali Bey', *Studia Islamica*, No. 80, pp. 165–8.
30 Rzewuski, op. cit., p. 137.
31 Paul Strathern, *Napoleon in Egypt* (Jonathan Cape, 2007), p. 427.
32 Transcript of letter HLS to CM, UI590 S6/1-UI590 S 6/8.

33  Meryon, *Memoirs*, Vol I, pp. 9–10.

34  Kent, UI590 S6/7.

35  Meryon refers specifically to Hester's possession of this book in his journal. This edition with its commentary by David Kimhi was published by Joshua Solomon Soncino in 1486. A copy can be seen in the Rare Book and Special Collections Division in the Library of Congress. Meryon (who misspelled Kimhi as 'King' and referred to the book as 'Levi on the Prophets') noted in 1818 that this book had been 'sent to her at her request – the word of a learned Jew to prove that the saviour had not yet come'. The book she had bore signs of the Papal censor and was mutilated in parts, which infuriated Hester.

36  Kent, U1590 S6//5/5.

37  Cleveland, op cit., pp. 213–16.

38  Rzewuski, op. cit., pp. 141–9.

39  Ibid.

40  Ibid.

41  Ibid.

42  Ibid.

43  Al-Uzza, 'the Mightiest One' or 'the Strong', was a pre-Islamic Arabian fertility goddess connected to Mecca, one of three known as the 'daughters of God'. The debate about whether Uzza had been at one time endorsed as a temporary intercessor with Allah lies at the heart of the infamous *Satanic Verses* controversy. Also see Philip K. Hitti, *History of the Arabs* (Palgrave Macmillan, London, 2002), p. 99.

44  Kent, U1590 S6/2.

45  When he returned to Europe, Rzewuski would publish an 800-page work, *On Oriental Horses and Those Descended from Eastern Breeds*. In it he says that despite all his wanderings, he came across the most beautiful horses he had ever seen in stables of certain individuals, including Emir Bashir and Sheikh Jumblatt, in the area of Mount Lebanon.

46  Meryon, *Memoirs*, Vol I, pp. 197–8.

47  Kent, UI590 S6/2/7.

48  Kent, UI590 S6/2.

49  Kent, UI590 S6/2, HLS to Meryon, 12 March 1819.

50  Meryon, *Memoirs*, Vol II, p. 121.

51  Kent, U1590 S/6.

52  Ibid., May 1819.

53  Writing in 1862, Meryon considered that this might be 'possibly the first

recorded demonstration of an early phantasmagoria device outside of America at this time'.

## Chapter 19: The Sun At Midnight

1   Meryon private journal, private collection, Meryon family.
2   Pocock, op. cit., p. 233.
3   Kent, U1590 725/16, Sir Sidney Smith to HLS, Paris, 13 January 1820.
4   Ibid.
5   Archives Nationales de Paris, ETR. COR, CON, R. 27, letter from Monsieur Martin, French consul at Sidon, 3 January 1820.
6   Ibid.
7   By 11 December 1819, Jean Baptiste appears to already have established himself in Hester's affections; she cites him, as well as his father, as a potential beneficiary in a codicil to her will, notarized on that day in Sidon. This document is curious, for it points to the relationship beginning earlier than is assumed.
8   Ferdinand Perrier, *La Syrie sous le gouvernement de Mehmet Ali jusqu'en 1840* (Paris, 1842).
9   Ibid.
10  Comte de Marcellus, *Souvenirs de l'Orient* (Paris, 1839). See also Héneiné, op. cit., Vol II, pp. 112–13.
11  Paul Roussier, 'Les derniers projets et le dernier voyage de Domingo Badia' (*Revue Africaine* 1930), M. Keraudren to the Minister of the Marine, 29 May 1821, p. 367.
12  Kent, U1590 C247/2, HLS to Monsieur Le Doux, Consul of Rhodes, 2 October 1820.
13  Kent, U1590 S6/1/2, CM to HLS, 2 February 1820.
14  Ibid., HLS to CM, 12 October 1820.
15  Pocock, op. cit., pp. 226–7.
16  Barker, op. cit., p. 296.
17  Meryon, *Memoirs*, Vol I, pp. 142–3.
18  Barker, op. cit., HLS to Barker, 11 February 1817, pp. 270–71.
19  Meryon, *Memoirs*, Vol I, p. 145.
20  Ibid., Vol I, p. 146.
21  Meryon, *Memoirs*, Vol II, p. 264.
22  Ibid., pp. 260–61.
23  Meryon, *Memoirs*, Vol I, pp. 275–6.

## Chapter 20: Djoun

1 Meryon's private journal, private collection, Meryon family.
2 Tewfic al-Shami, the interim mayor of Djoun (1945–1949) and its resident pharmacist, wrote a memoir to preserve stories passed down from his grandparents and great-grandparents. He also noted that he was given this letter in 1936 by the Sheikh of Djoun, Daoud Metri Moussawba, and was therefore able to confirm its contents. The letter asked for 'military help to stand against the campaign led by Ibrahim Pasha against Constantinople, which would pass from Egypt through Arab lands'. Private collection, Stephan family.
3 Kent, U1590 S61/5, CM to HLS, 159 Regent Street, 22 February 1824.
4 Ibid., Colonel James Stanhope to CM, 5 November 1822.
5 Kent, U1590 C235/4, William Noel Hill to HLS, 8 March 1823.
6 Ibid.
7 Kent, U1590 C246A/10, C246A11, C246A13, C24614. Letters between HLS and Sheikh Bashir Jumblatt in Arabic and French, previously untranslated.
8 Kent, UI590, HLS to Captain Yorke, 8 January 1825.
9 Meryon, *Travels,* HLS to John Webb, 30 May 1827, Vol III, pp. 50–54.
10 Kent, U1590 S6, CM to HLS, 9 March 1825.
11 Kent, U1590 C236–246, Hastings to HLS, 1825.
12 A great deal of unpublished material lies in the Stanhope archives, including drawings by Kaspar Hauser. See Kent, U1590.
13 Feuerbach to Earl Stanhope, 12 May 1832, Johannes Mayer, *Philip Henry Lord Stanhope* (1988), pp. 416–17, letter also at Kent.
14 Jeffrey Moussaieff Masson, *Lost Prince: The Unsolved Mystery of Kaspar Hauser* (New York, The Free Press, 1996), p. 33.
15 Jeffrey Moussaieff Masson, op. cit., p.23.
16 Meryon, *Memoirs,* Vol I, p. 97.
17 Kent, U1590 S6, CM to HLS, 19 May 1830.
18 Meryon, *Memoirs,* Vol I, p. 341.
19 Cleveland, op. cit., HLS to the Duke of Wellington, 12 February 1828, pp. 350–52.
20 Meryon, *Travels,* Vol III.

## Chapter 21: The Mahdi's Bride

1 The story of the alleged quarrel found its way back to the parlours of New Hampshire, and inspired the poet John Greenleaf Whittier, a

family friend of the Livermores, to write his somewhat less than flattering ode, *Snowbound*, in which Livermore is described as 'A not unfeared, half-welcome guest', a blend of 'the vixen and the devotee'. Hester is characterized in his 'Dedication' to the poem as 'a woman . . . fantastic and mentally strained':

> Or startling on her desert throne
> The crazy Queen of Lebanon
> With claims fantastic as her own . . .

2 Meryon, *Memoirs*, HLS to CM, 21 August 1836, Vol I, pp. 240–46.
3 Meryon, *Memoirs*, Vol, I, p. 354. 'List of Lady Hester Stanhope's Debts'.
4 Ibid., p. 120.
5 Cleveland, op. cit., HLS to Duke of Wellington, 12 February 1838, pp. 350–53.
6 Ibid., Lord Palmerston to HLS, 25 April 1838, pp. 399–400.
7 Kent, U1590, HLS to Mrs David, 7 August 1838.

## Chapter 22: The Last Dance
1 Cleveland, op. cit., pp. 363–87.
2 Meryon, *Memoirs*, Vol III, p. 76.
3 Kent, U1590, HLS to Henri Guys, 8 September 1838.
4 Cleveland, op. cit., HLS to Sir Francis Burdett, 20 July 1838, pp. 404–5.
5 Ibid., Lord Hardwicke to HLS, 18 March 1839, pp. 423–5.
6 *The Life of General Sir William Napier*, edited by H. A. Bruce (London, 1864), Vol I, p. 529.
7 Hamel, op. cit., p. 304. HLS to General Sir William Napier, 11 February 1839.
8 Kent, U1590, HLS to Henri Guys, 8 September 1838.

## Epilogue
1 Hamel, op. cit., pp. 320–23. The Probate Act to Lady Hester's Will. See also Kent, U1590 C235/2–5. Freshfields, the London firm appointed by the fourth Earl Stanhope to handle the matter, compelled the foreign debtors to prove their claims, and established a case that some of the debts were 'founded in usury'.
2 Meryon, *Memoirs*, Vol I, pp. x–xi.

## *Acknowledgements*

A great many people have provided help with this book, in many different ways, ranging from information and documentation, to hospitality, time and expertise.

In Lebanon, my chief acknowledgement, along with grateful thanks for help and friendship, must go to the Stephan family, who brought me to Joun for the first time. Rania Stephan first told me about Hester Stanhope, planting the seed of an obsession that would take some years to germinate.

On several memorable occasions, Rania and her sister, Wafâ Tarnowska, took me with them to visit their family in Joun, as well as in Beirut and Beit Meri, and many of their elderly relatives shared their memories for this book. It was the Stephan sisters' aunt Yvette who told me, on the first night of my research trip to Lebanon, that Hester had an Arab lover. Such moments are more remarkable, when researching a biography, for being so unexpected, and it was the first of a great many things I would discover that had never been uncovered by previous biographers. Rania and Wafâ's family, especially Yvette and the late Nabih Stephan, looked after me while I was in Lebanon, and also allowed me to see private papers and contemporary accounts in Arabic which gave concrete details I would have otherwise missed.

Wafâ's presence on the road with me, to Damascus and Palmyra, and in seeking out traces of Hester throughout Lebanon, was invaluable, and her indefatigable energy and humour as interpreter made these travels great fun as well as tremendously productive. Her translations from the

Arabic for this book, specifically of Sheikh Bashir Jumblatt's letters, brought much new material to light.

Roger and Dolly Jawish discussed Hester with me over many meetings and several dinners, and made several explorations of her fortress. Thanks also to Fadi Nachef, and to Hneineh El Chami, Celine El Chami and Fadi El Chami for their insights. I was glad of the presence of Bassan, a gentle, bespectacled man who drove me around Lebanon (despite having lost his left leg to a landmine) and who proved a fund of knowledge on plants growing in the ruins of Hester's garden. He managed to find a still-flowering rose bush near what had been her grave, which gave me an inexpressible sensation to see.

At the Deir-el-Moukhalles monastery, thanks to Fathers Freijat, Raymond Obteh and Paul Sleiman. In Mouktara, Walid and Nora Jumblatt were gracious as hosts and with information, and I was grateful for Walid's suggestion that I speak to his former college teacher, Professor Abbas Abou Saleh, about Druze history and theology, and to Colonel Charif Fayad of the PSP, who knew a great deal about events concerning Joun during the civil war. In Abra, I was lucky to meet Farid Sleiman, who told me much local history as well as the stories his own family carried down with them about the time when Hester and Dr Meryon lived there. In Machmouche, thanks to Dr Maurice Elias Helar and Abou Toni Samra and his family.

In Beirut, Ambassadors Richard Kinchen and James Watts were both unfailingly helpful, and I was especially glad of the chance to see Hester's former grave at Abey, and to discuss the posthumous complications Hester had caused the Foreign Office. I am indebted to David Hirst for serendipitous advice and introductions; to Fayza el Khazen, and to Guy Abela for allowing me to spend time in his wonderful library and stumble across many volumes in French I may have otherwise missed, and for sending me a photograph of the whimsical portrait made of Hester in her old age by the son of one of his forebears, Joseph Abela, then British consul at Sidon.

In Britain, at Chevening, Colonel Richard Brook gave a great deal of his time and took me on a tour throughout all the main rooms, kitchen and servants' quarters, patiently waiting as I tried to examine everything, which helped me greatly in gaining a vivid picture of how life must have been in Hester's time. I was served coffee from a silver service that Hester once used at Montagu Square, and given her ram's head walking stick to hold, the one that she had clutched as she died. From the ridge of the hill, I was able to admire the view through Lucy Pitt's famous 'Keyhole'. In the magnificent library, Dr Michael Wilson was generous with his expertise. I am grateful to the Chevening Estate for copies of otherwise unobtainable Stanhope family diaries and for providing images of private portraits.

At Walmer Castle, Rowena Shepherd, with the English Heritage Trust, kindly interrupted her maternity leave to walk me through a very clear reconstruction of exactly how rooms and gardens would have looked during the time Pitt and Hester lived there. Virginia Hinze provided me with detailed notes on the changes Hester made to the gardens.

In Builth Wells, Gwen and Colin Davies helped me find Glan Irfon, and the Davies family offered what information they could about the farm during Hester's time. Hugh D. Richards sent me his book on Elizabeth Williams, whose unmarked grave I sought out in Joun.

Thanks to the Hon. William Stanhope and also to the Hon. Serena Stanhope, Viscountess Linley, for their interest in this book. Also to Lord Altamont, the Marquess of Sligo, who made available a portrait of his ancestor for this book, and to Lady Altamont.

The Meryon family were enormously kind, entrusting me with never-before published letters and diaries and inviting me to many teas and lunches while we discussed their ancestor's adventures. I was riveted to read through the many, often poignant letters sent by Rusty Arran Smith from Australia. These letters, which could form a book on their own, brought to life many of Meryon's private dilemmas, and I regretted having to leave them out of this work, which had already grown too long. Special thanks must go to Corinne and Keith Bennett, and to the late Peter Meryon and his wife Daphne, who told me the astonishing fact that by their marriage, the Meryons and the Stanhopes came close to meeting: Daphne's grandfather being related to the sixth Countess Stanhope, Evelyn Henrietta. Also thanks to Joy Harris and David William Meryon Easton.

At the Centre for Kentish Studies, Stuart Bligh and Helen Orme were welcoming. I owe an especial debt of gratitude to palaeographer Elizabeth

Finn, whose careful deciphering eye helped me to come to grips with impossible-looking handwriting and double-hatched letters that otherwise might have driven me to despair. Her professionalism and humour made an otherwise daunting task immense fun.

At the Bodleian Library, Oxford, Colin Harris and Paul Cartwright helped me find my way through the relevant archives. At the Natural History Museum, London, Neil A. Chambers of the Banks Archive Project offered the unexpected boon of copies of Hester's unpublished letters to Sir Joseph Banks. At Miranda House in London, Gloria Carnevale allowed me a free run of General Francisco de Miranda's diaries and archive material, thus saving me a trip to Caracas. Peter Marson, family archivist to the Earl of Belmore at Castle Coole, generously shared his research and sent much useful material. Colin Wilson and James Scarff at the Foreign and Commonwealth Records and Historical Department, as well as Judy Nokes, efficiently helped me track down unpublished letters that uncovered the story of what happened to Hester's mortal remains. Dr Ian Brown at the Dorset Records Office offered friendly assistance.

Elsewhere, a number of libraries and archives were consulted. Thanks to the staff at Yale University's Beinecke Rare Book and Manuscript Library and the Sterling Memorial Library, and to the Archive Nationale de Paris and Musée de l'Armée. I am grateful to Nicholas Dunne-Lynch for his discoveries on my behalf at the Château de Vincennes, and to Corporal-Chef Yamamoto. Thanks, at the American University of Beirut, to Elie Choueiry and Nawal Namany, and at Istanbul Library in Sultanhamet, to Neslihan Yalav. From the Indiana University of Pennsylvania, Professor Michael W. Vella offered information about Harriet Livermore, as did Richard E. Winslow III, at the Portsmouth City Museum and Records Service. My aunt-by-marriage, Jean Friedman, served as my scout and guide to Portsmouth and enlisted the help of Ursula Wright at the Portsmouth Athenaeum, while I was trying to establish whether Hester actually met the 'firebrand' from New Hampshire. While straying into more research territory than I later found this story required, I was assisted by the Whittier Museum at Amesbury, Massachusetts, and shown the desk at which John Greenleaf Whittier wrote *Snowbound*, introducing a generation of Americans to Hester as 'the crazy Queen of Lebanon'. Thanks to the United Grand Lodge of England for making me an honorary reader of the Library of Freemasonry.

In translating Count Rzewuski's memoirs, I was ably assisted by Andrew Tarnowski, without whom I may not have stumbled across the important, if only fleeting, role he played in Hester's life.

To my family, especially to Louise Longdin, Ian Eagles and Howard Ellis, a thousand thanks for their helpful suggestions reading through drafts of this book, also to Fran Parkin; all were always prepared to discuss matters pertaining to Hester.

I am profoundly grateful for the advice and support of my agent, Bill Hamilton, and without his enthusiasm, this book would not exist. I am indebted to Michael Fishwick, who commissioned it, for his early guidance. Thanks also to Michael Carlisle for his efforts on my behalf. At HarperCollins, great thanks to my editor Annabel Wright, for her unfailingly insightful advice and good humour, to George Miller for his incisive skill, and to Richard Betts's error-seeking eyes in the final edit. Also to Alice Massey and Sophie Goulden.

I am grateful to Lesley Downer for her suggestions and advice at every stage, Tom Gettler for encouragement in the beginning, Betsy Blair, for providing a writing oasis in Belsize Park, and Alison Sloga for help in finding wonderful images. Sarah Pickles offered unexpected insights, and Sylwia Gopowicz's help with literally holding the baby was invaluable.

My greatest thanks are reserved for Michael, my beloved husband, who saw many evenings sacrificed while I was working on this and weathered interminable discussions at the most perplexing stages of my research when I was trying to decipher the complicated puzzle of Hester's Napoleonic-era machinations. His good-humoured patience never failed, even when my office was almost knee-deep in books and papers and when I returned from Istanbul and Damascus with substantial portions of my advance spent on Turkish carpets. Finally, I would like to mention the unique influence of my son, Nathaniel, who came with me to Palmyra *in utero*, and soon provided the best possible distraction throughout the writing of this book.

August 2007

# Index

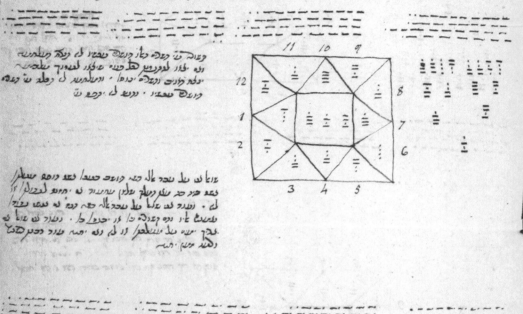

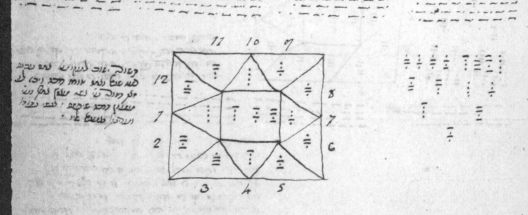